You.

9

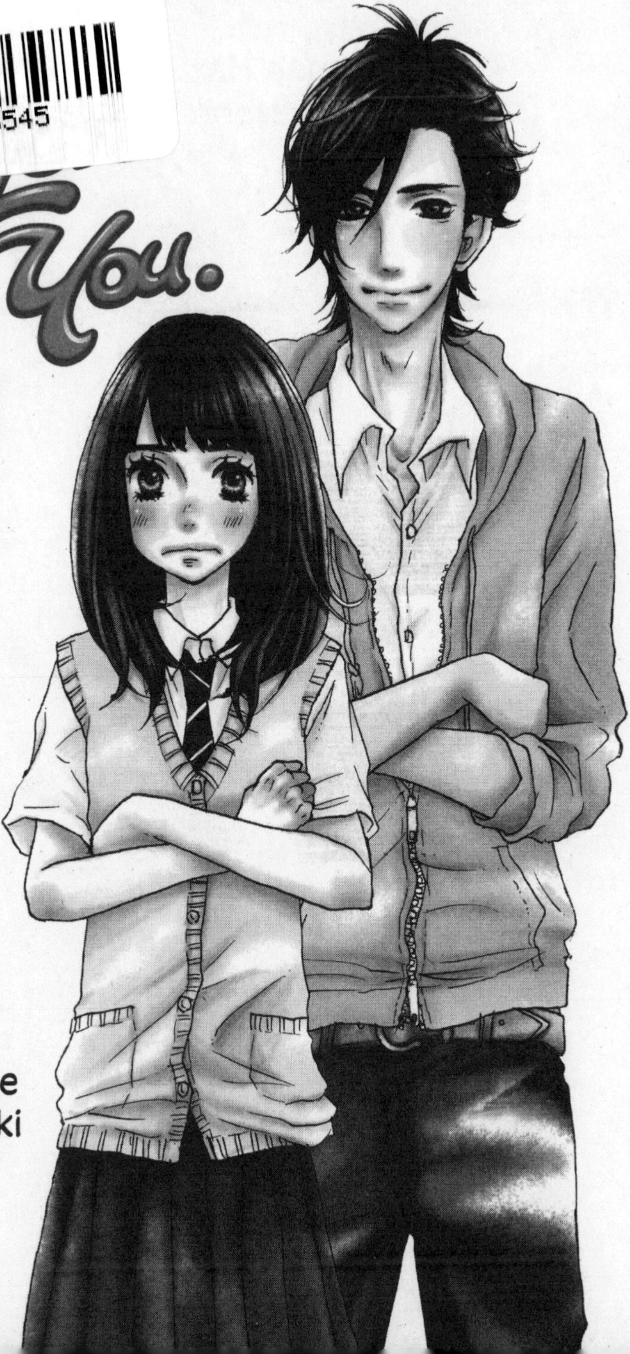

by
Kanae
Hazuki

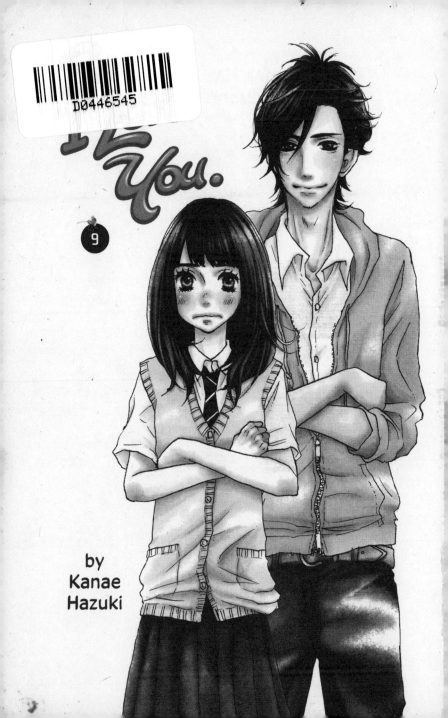

Kanae Hazuki
presents

Chapter 33

Chapter 34

Chapter 35

Chapter 36

CHARACTERS

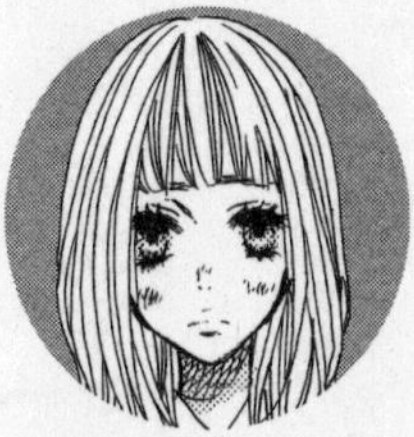

Mei Tachibana

A girl who hasn't had a single friend, let alone a boyfriend, in sixteen years, and has lived her life trusting no one. She finds herself attracted to Yamato, who, for some reason, just won't leave her alone, and they start dating.

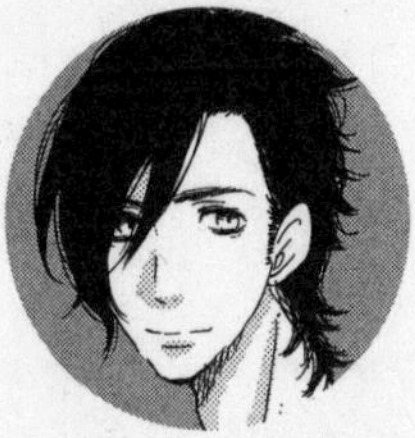

Yamato Kurosawa

The most popular boy at Mei's school. He has the love of many girls, yet for some reason, he is obsessed with Mei, the brooding weirdo girl from another class.

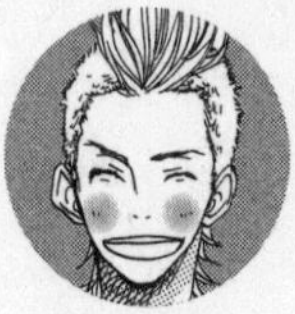

Kai

Yamato's classmate from middle school who had been the victim of bullying. For his own reasons, he started high school a year late. He likes Mei and told her so, but...?

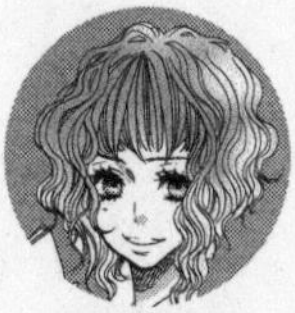

Megumi

An amateur model who has her sights set on Yamato. She transferred to his school and got him a modeling job, and the two gradually grew closer. She was plotting to pull Mei and Yamato apart, but...?

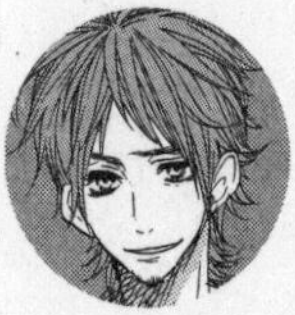

Daichi

Yamato's brother and a hairstylist. He helped Mei out for the fireworks show and the beauty contest. Due to his very high standards, it is not uncommon for him to butt heads with his clients.

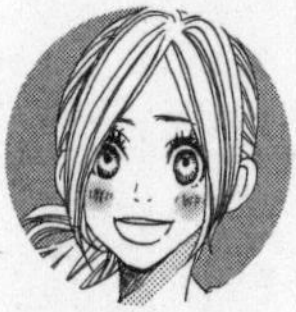

Asami

A girl who treats Mei as a real friend. She had a thing for Yamato, but now she is dating his friend Nakanishi. She and Mei were put in different classes in their second year of high school.

STORY

Mei Tachibana spent sixteen years without a single friend or boyfriend, but then, for some reason, Yamato Kurosawa, the most popular boy in school, took a liking to her. Mei is drawn in by Yamato's kindness and sincerity, and they start dating. About a year later, Mei and Yamato enter the school festival's contest to choose the school idols. In an effort to win the grand prize, Mei tries for the first time in her life to improve her looks, but the award goes to Yamato and Megumi, the girl who is trying to steal him for herself. The pair has won a date together, and Mei confesses to Yamato that she is anxious about this development, but...?!

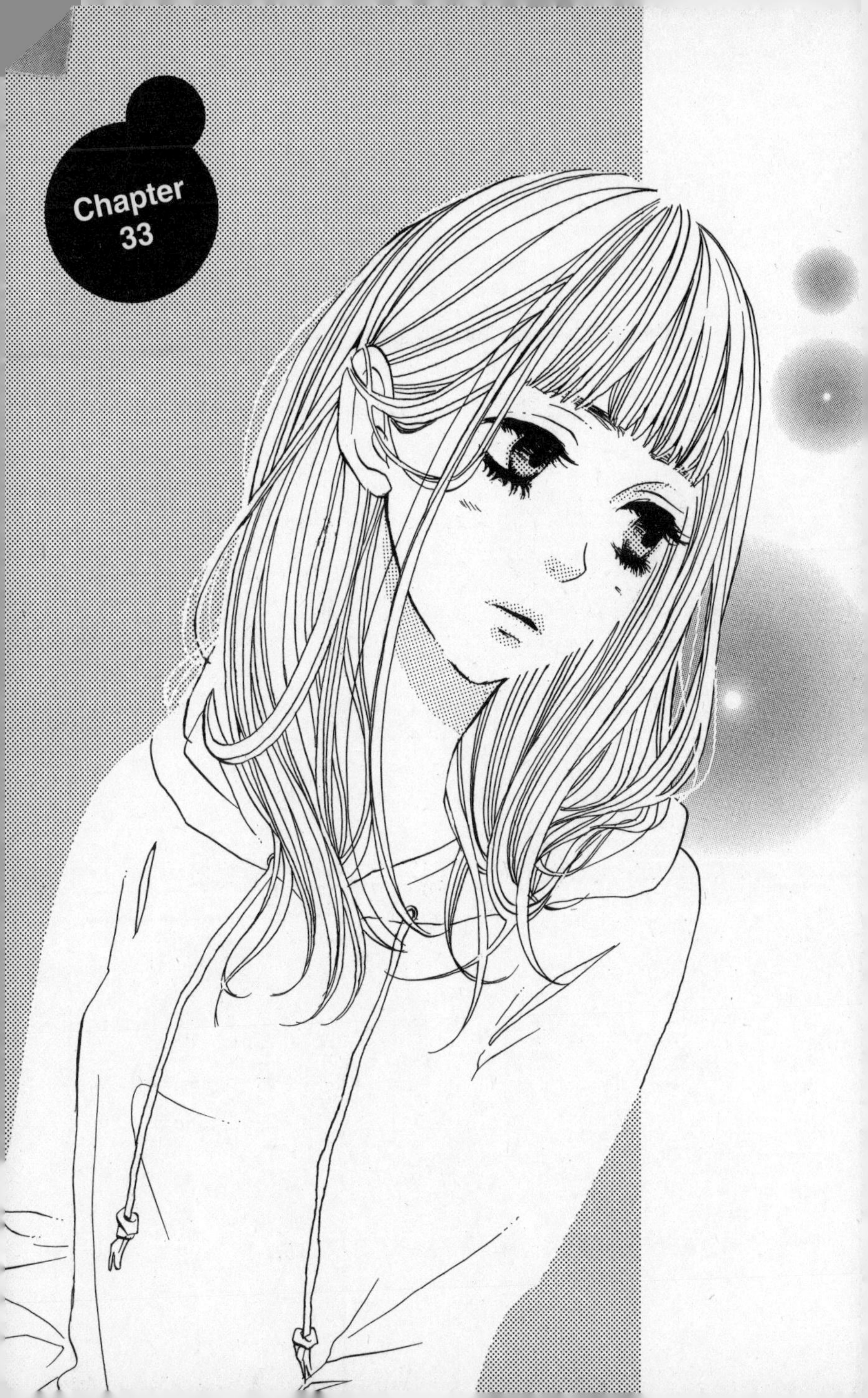
Chapter
33

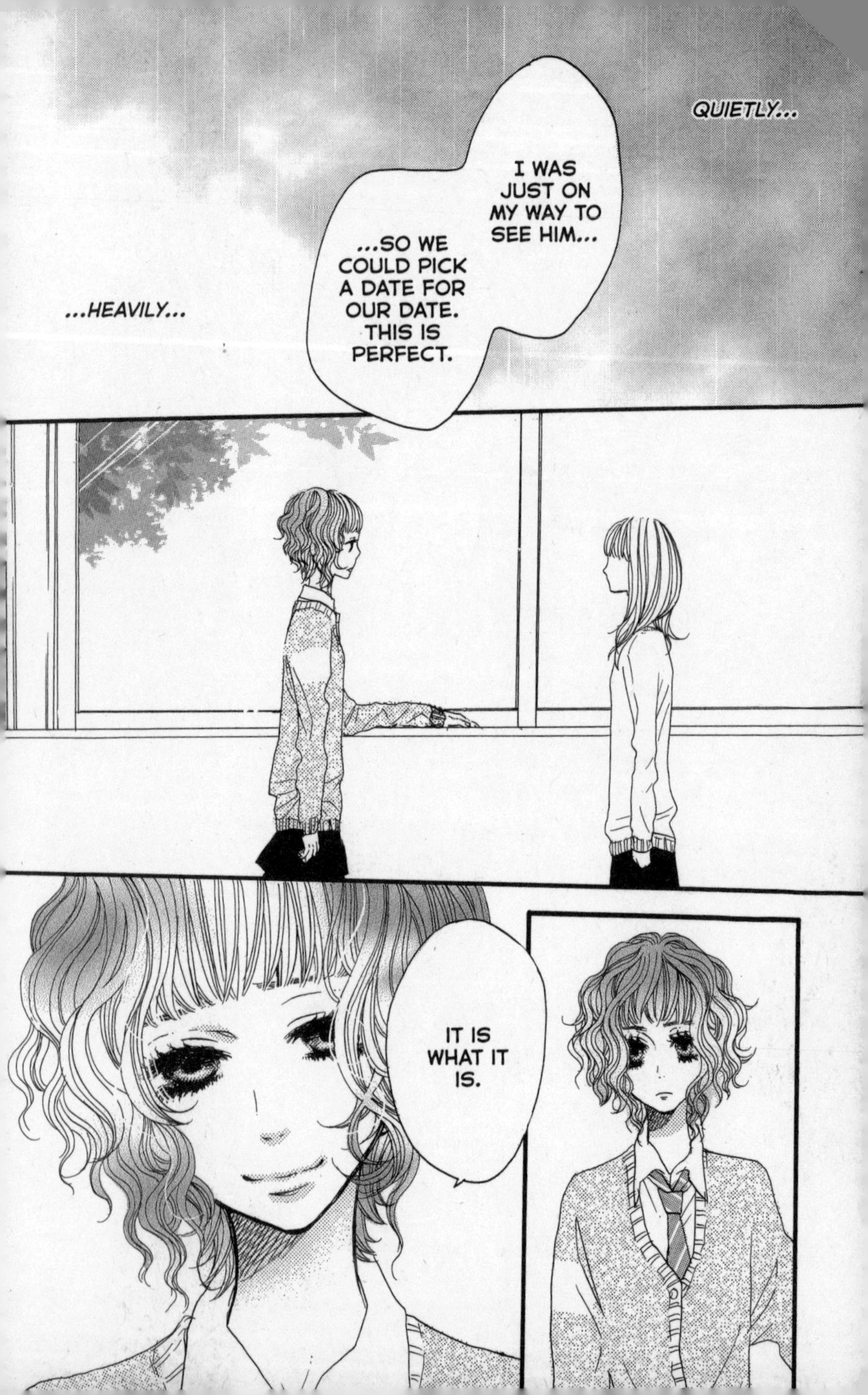
QUIETLY...
I WAS JUST ON MY WAY TO SEE HIM...
...SO WE COULD PICK A DATE FOR OUR DATE. THIS IS PERFECT.
...HEAVILY...
IT IS WHAT IT IS.

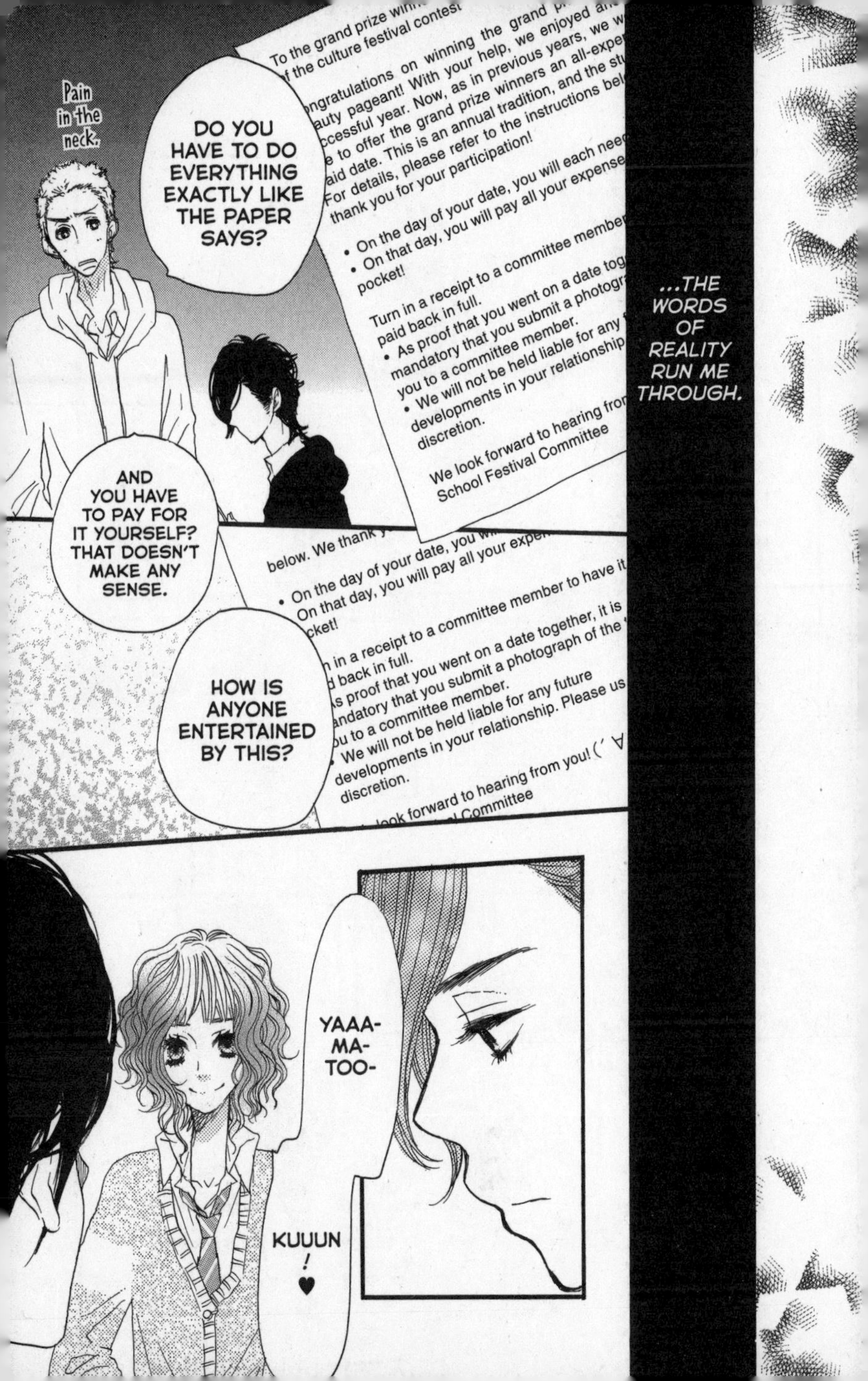
...THE WORDS OF REALITY RUN ME THROUGH.
To the grand prize win
of the culture festival contest
ongratulations on winning the grand p
auty pageant! With your help, we enjoyed a
ccessful year. Now, as in previous years, we w
e to offer the grand prize winners an all-expe
aid date. This is an annual tradition, and the stu
For details, please refer to the instructions bel
thank you for your participation!
• On the day of your date, you will each nee
• On that day, you will pay all your expense
pocket!
Turn in a receipt to a committee member
paid back in full.
• As proof that you went on a date tog
mandatory that you submit a photogr
you to a committee member.
• We will not be held liable for any
developments in your relationship
discretion.
We look forward to hearing fro
School Festival Committee
Pain in the neck.
DO YOU HAVE TO DO EVERYTHING EXACTLY LIKE THE PAPER SAYS?
AND YOU HAVE TO PAY FOR IT YOURSELF? THAT DOESN'T MAKE ANY SENSE.
below. We thank y
• On the day of your date, you wi
On that day, you will pay all your exp
cket!
in a receipt to a committee member to have it
d back in full.
s proof that you went on a date together, it is
andatory that you submit a photograph of the
u to a committee member.
• We will not be held liable for any future
developments in your relationship. Please us
discretion.
look forward to hearing from you!
Committee
HOW IS ANYONE ENTERTAINED BY THIS?
YAAA-MA-TOO-
KUUUN! ♥

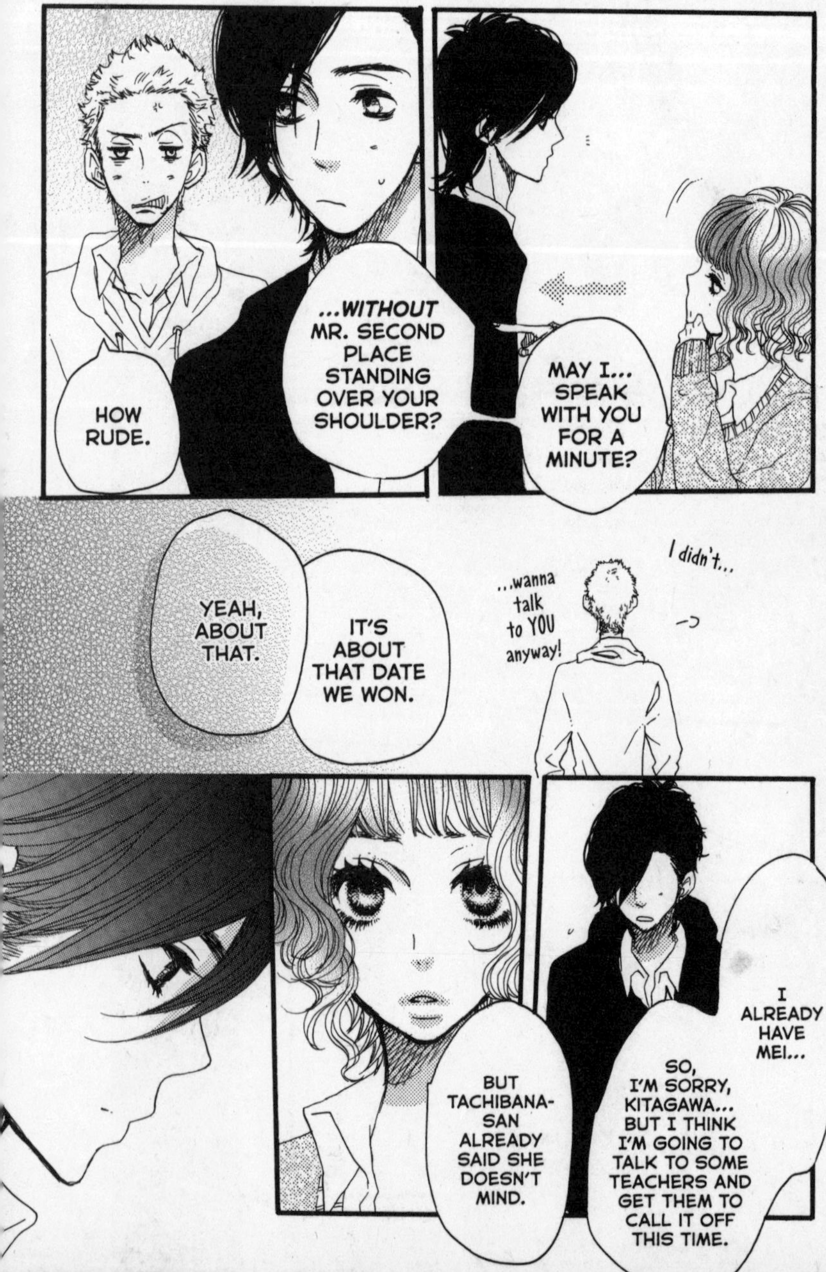
MAY I... SPEAK WITH YOU FOR A MINUTE?
...WITHOUT MR. SECOND PLACE STANDING OVER YOUR SHOULDER?
HOW RUDE.
I didn't...
...wanna talk to YOU anyway!
IT'S ABOUT THAT DATE WE WON.
YEAH, ABOUT THAT.
I ALREADY HAVE MEI...
SO, I'M SORRY, KITAGAWA... BUT I THINK I'M GOING TO TALK TO SOME TEACHERS AND GET THEM TO CALL IT OFF THIS TIME.
BUT TACHIBANA-SAN ALREADY SAID SHE DOESN'T MIND.

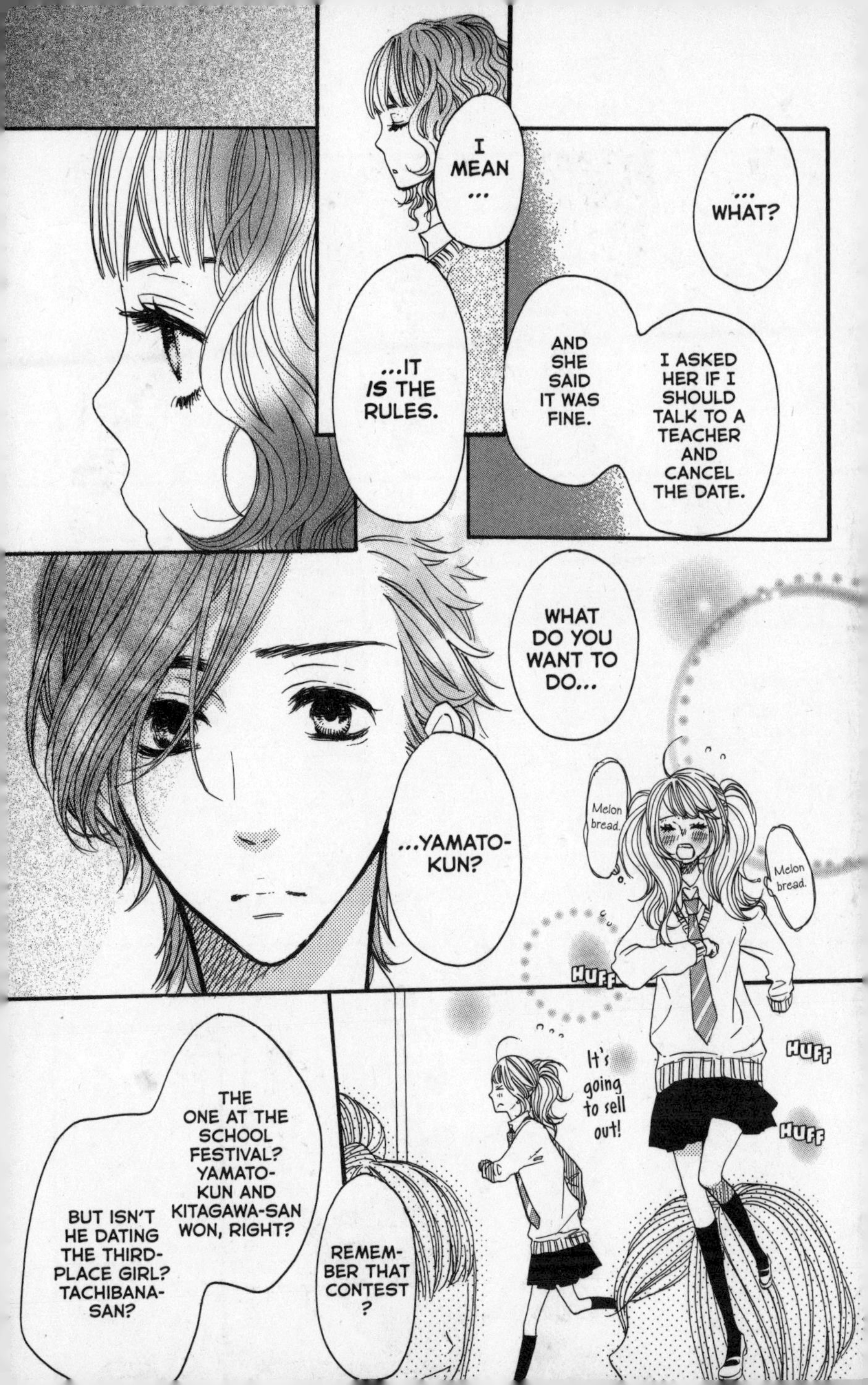
I MEAN...
...WHAT?
I ASKED HER IF I SHOULD TALK TO A TEACHER AND CANCEL THE DATE.
AND SHE SAID IT WAS FINE.
...IT *IS* THE RULES.
WHAT DO YOU WANT TO DO...
...YAMATO-KUN?
Melon bread.
Melon bread.
HUFF
HUFF
HUFF
It's going to sell out!
REMEMBER THAT CONTEST?
THE ONE AT THE SCHOOL FESTIVAL? YAMATO-KUN AND KITAGAWA-SAN WON, RIGHT?
BUT ISN'T HE DATING THE THIRD-PLACE GIRL? TACHIBANA-SAN?

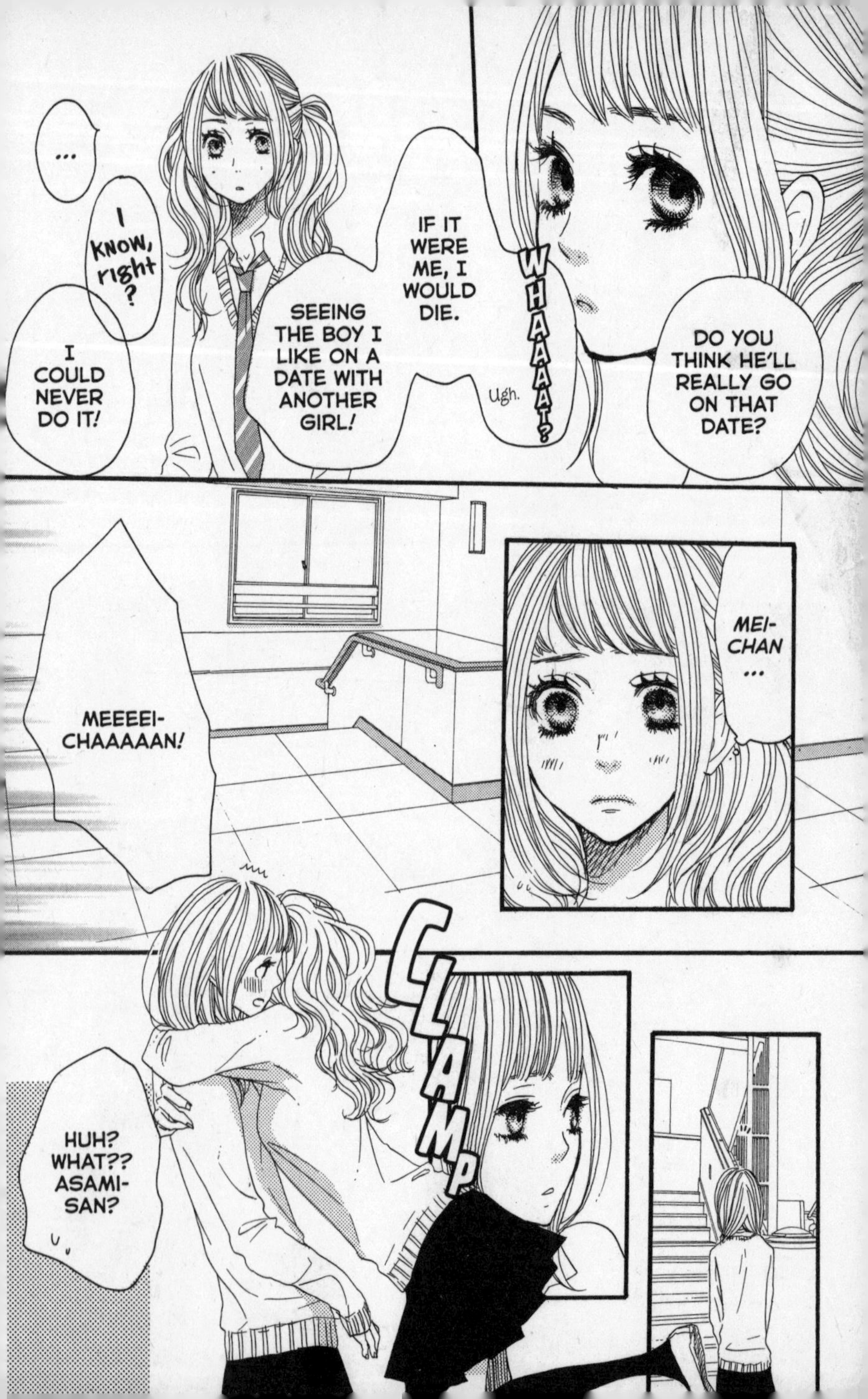
DO YOU THINK HE'LL REALLY GO ON THAT DATE?
WHAAAAT?
Ugh.
IF IT WERE ME, I WOULD DIE.
SEEING THE BOY I LIKE ON A DATE WITH ANOTHER GIRL!
...
I KNOW, RIGHT?
I COULD NEVER DO IT!
MEI-CHAN...
MEEEEI-CHAAAAAN!
CLAMP
HUH? WHAT?? ASAMI-SAN?

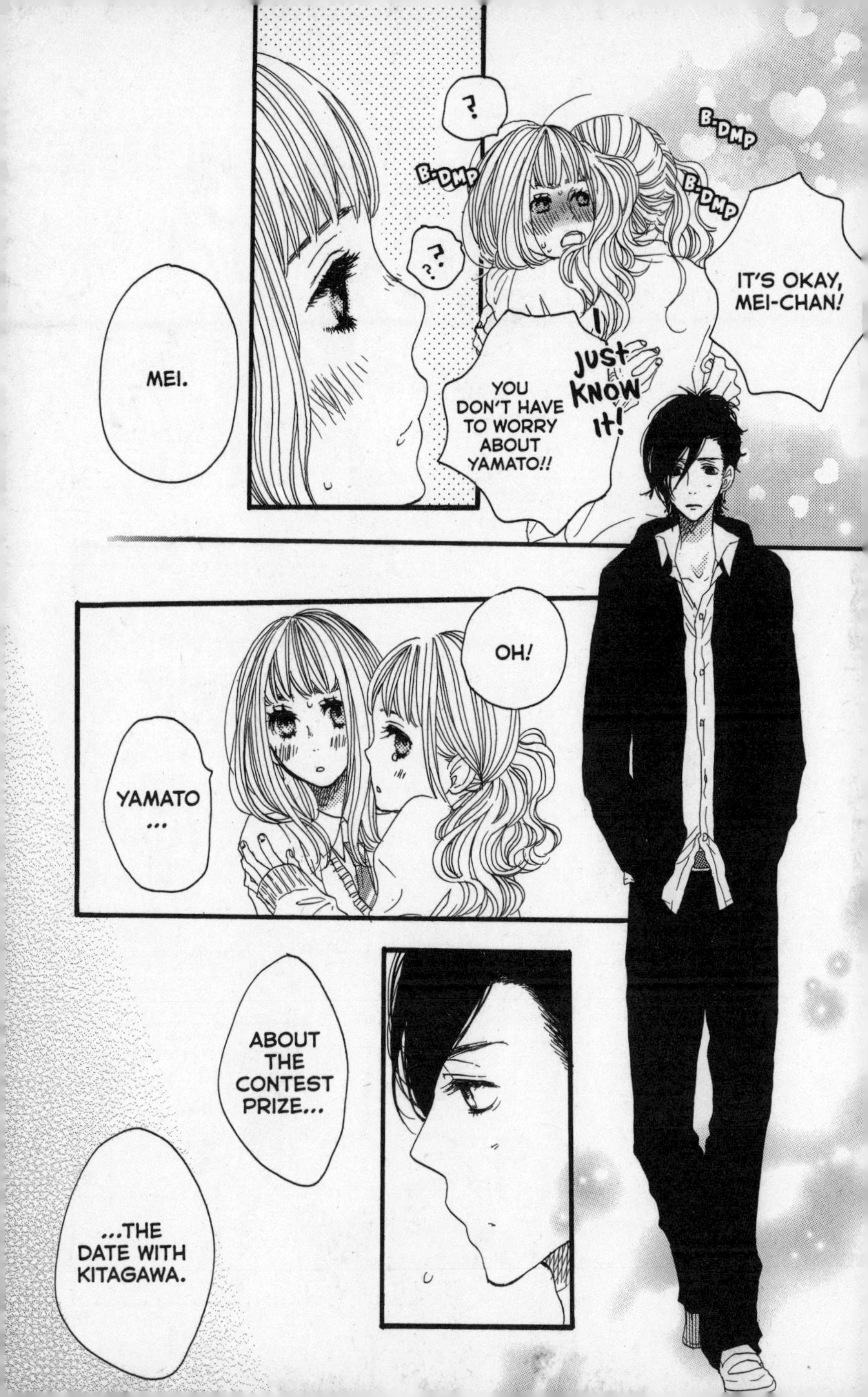

B-DMP
B-DMP
IT'S OKAY, MEI-CHAN!
B-DMP
YOU DON'T HAVE TO WORRY ABOUT YAMATO!!
I JUST KNOW IT!
?
? ?
MEI.
OH!
YAMATO ...
ABOUT THE CONTEST PRIZE...
...THE DATE WITH KITAGAWA.

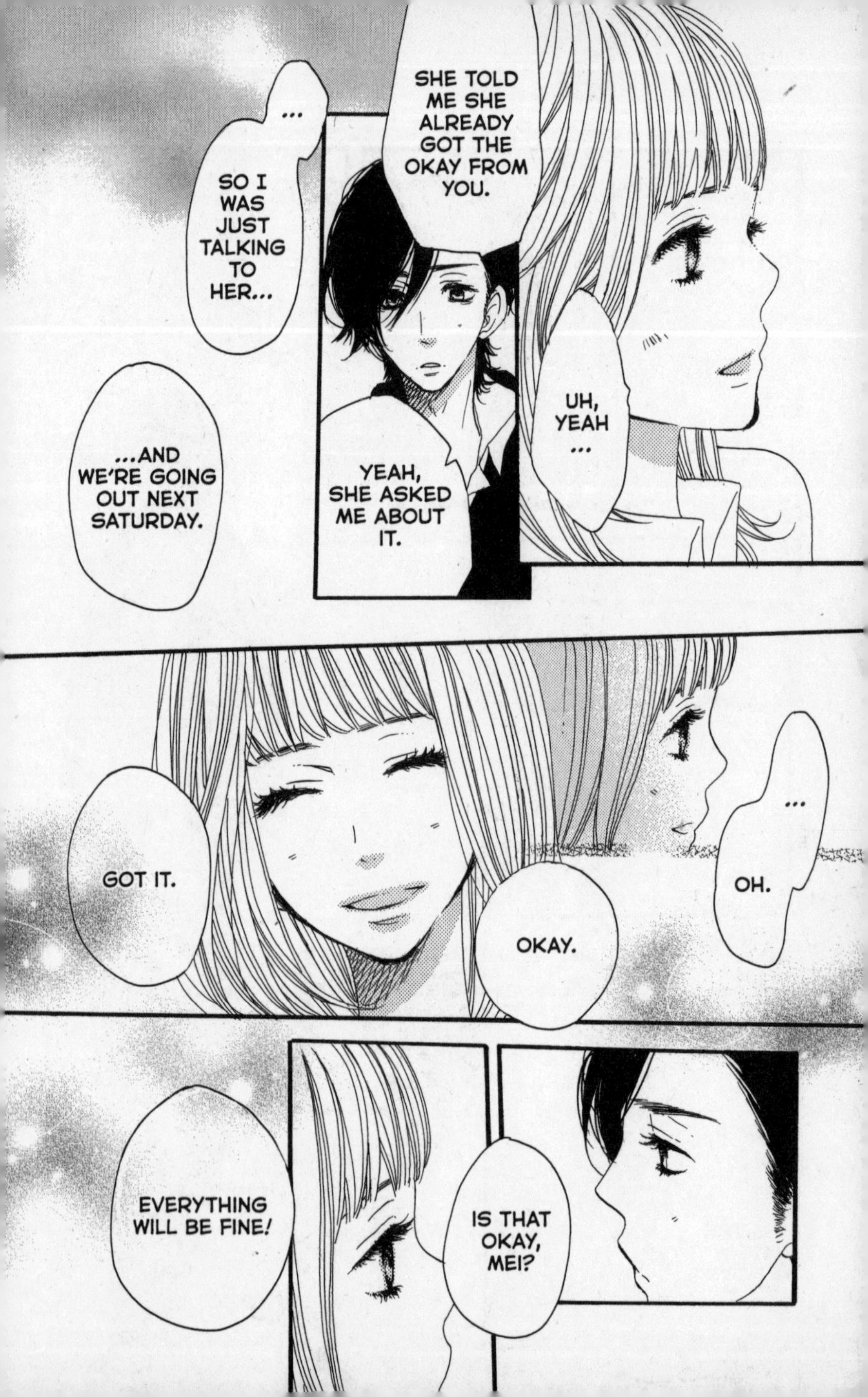
SHE TOLD ME SHE ALREADY GOT THE OKAY FROM YOU.
UH, YEAH ...
YEAH, SHE ASKED ME ABOUT IT.
...
SO I WAS JUST TALKING TO HER...
...AND WE'RE GOING OUT NEXT SATURDAY.
...
OH.
OKAY.
GOT IT.
IS THAT OKAY, MEI?
EVERYTHING WILL BE FINE!

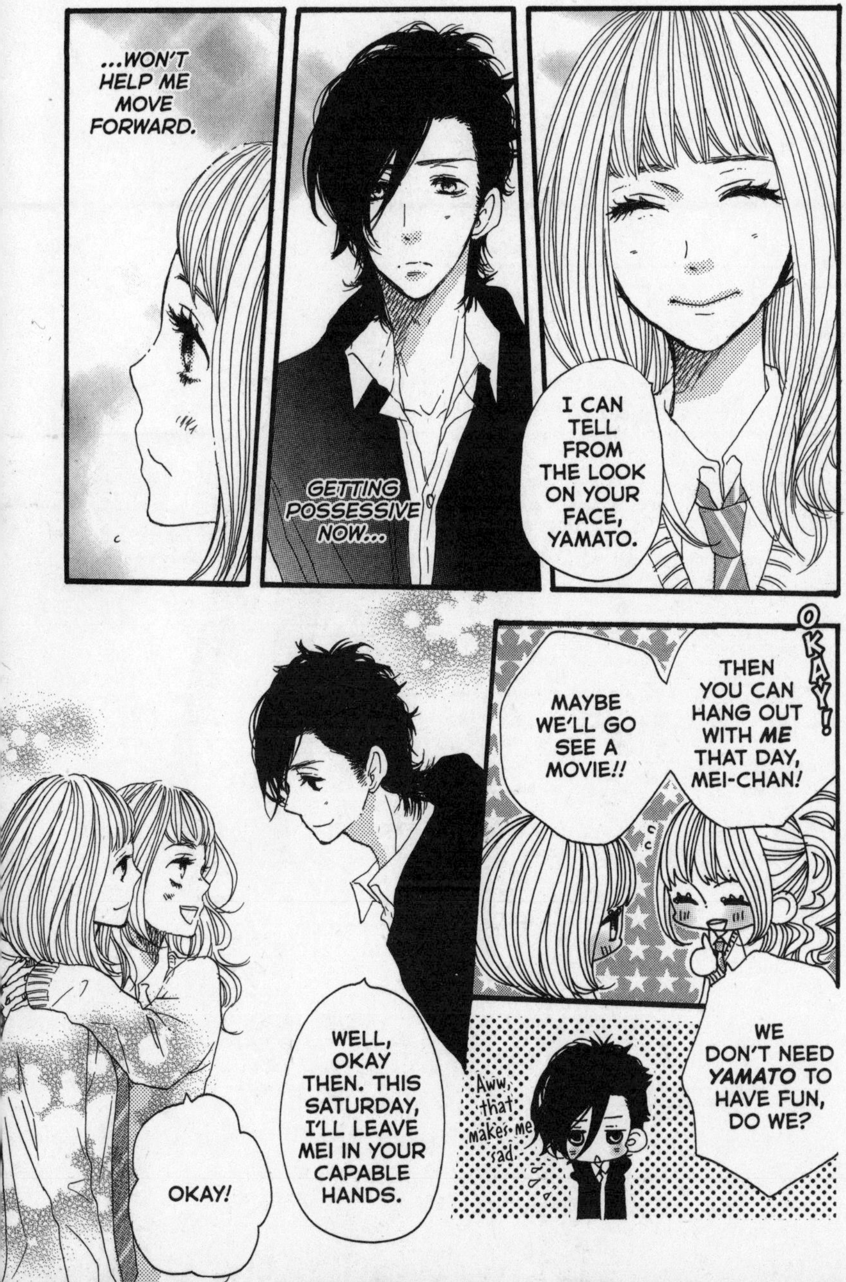
I CAN TELL FROM THE LOOK ON YOUR FACE, YAMATO.
GETTING POSSESSIVE NOW...
...WON'T HELP ME MOVE FORWARD.
OKAY!
THEN YOU CAN HANG OUT WITH *ME* THAT DAY, MEI-CHAN!
MAYBE WE'LL GO SEE A MOVIE!!
WE DON'T NEED *YAMATO* TO HAVE FUN, DO WE?
Aww, that makes me sad.
WELL, OKAY THEN. THIS SATURDAY, I'LL LEAVE MEI IN YOUR CAPABLE HANDS.
OKAY!

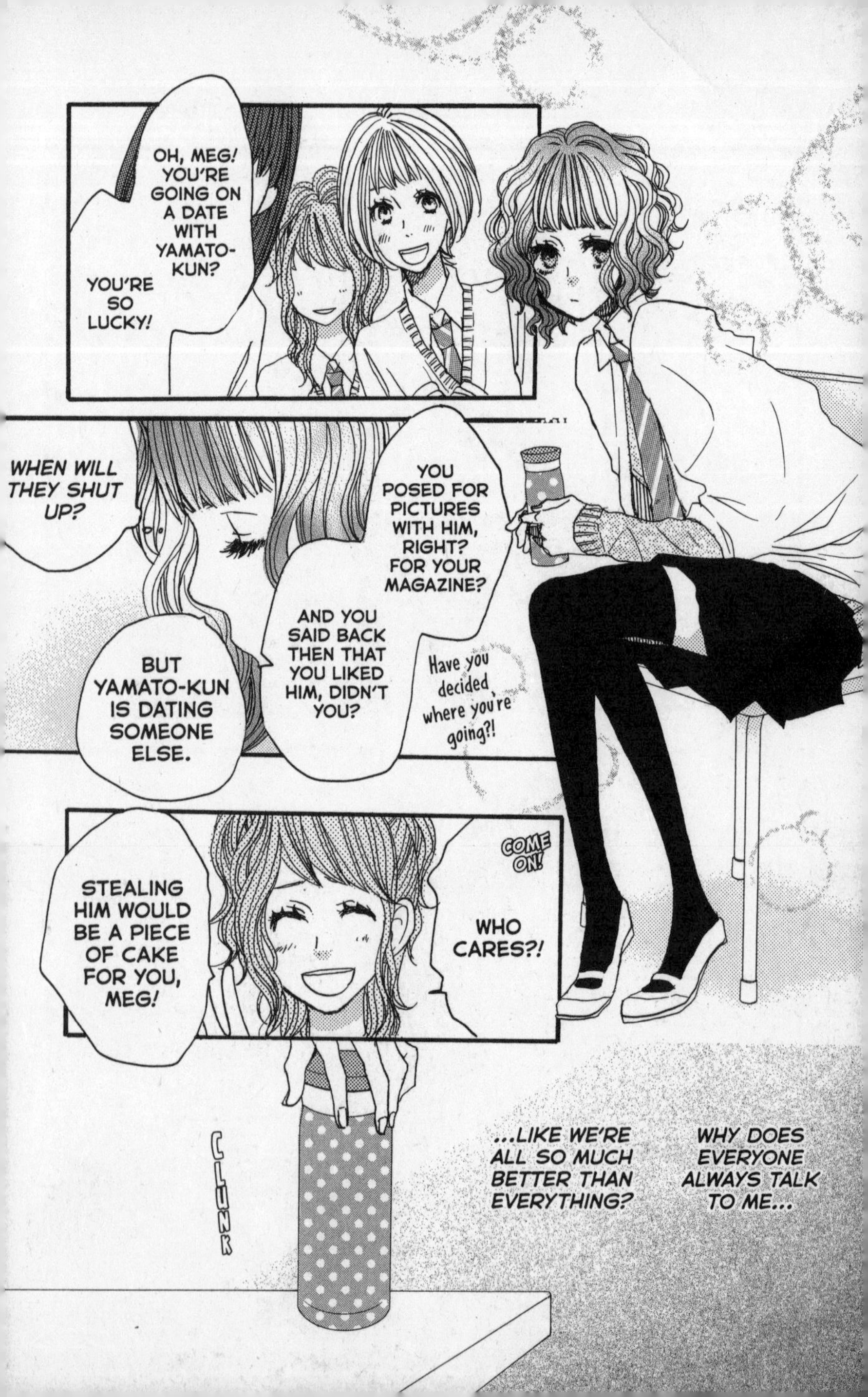
OH, MEG! YOU'RE GOING ON A DATE WITH YAMATO-KUN?
YOU'RE SO LUCKY!
YOU POSED FOR PICTURES WITH HIM, RIGHT? FOR YOUR MAGAZINE?
AND YOU SAID BACK THEN THAT YOU LIKED HIM, DIDN'T YOU?
Have you decided where you're going?!
WHEN WILL THEY SHUT UP?
BUT YAMATO-KUN IS DATING SOMEONE ELSE.
COME ON!
WHO CARES?!
STEALING HIM WOULD BE A PIECE OF CAKE FOR YOU, MEG!
WHY DOES EVERYONE ALWAYS TALK TO ME...
...LIKE WE'RE ALL SO MUCH BETTER THAN EVERYTHING?
CLUNK

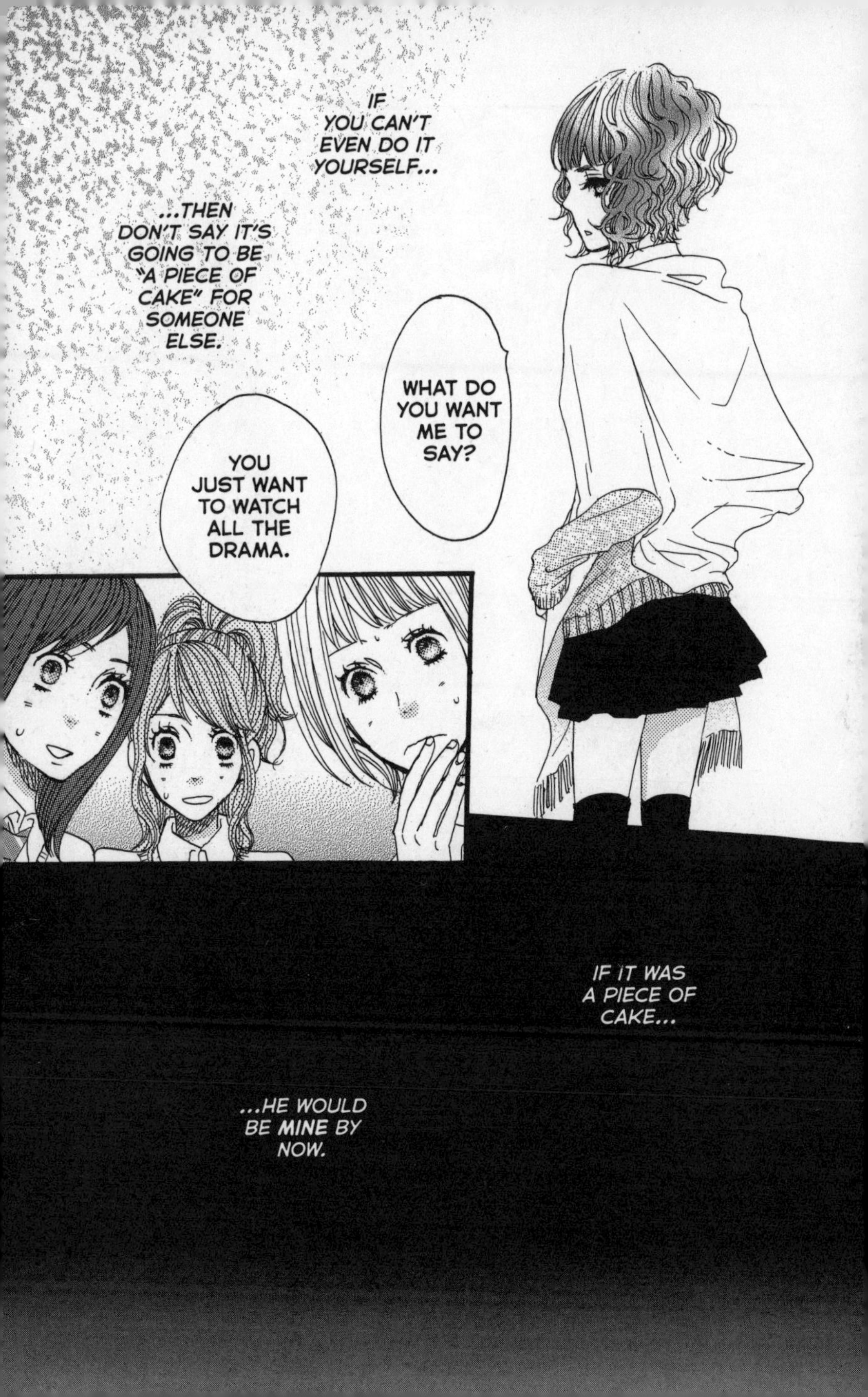
IF YOU CAN'T EVEN DO IT YOURSELF...
...THEN DON'T SAY IT'S GOING TO BE "A PIECE OF CAKE" FOR SOMEONE ELSE.
WHAT DO YOU WANT ME TO SAY?
YOU JUST WANT TO WATCH ALL THE DRAMA.
IF IT WAS A PIECE OF CAKE...
...HE WOULD BE MINE BY NOW.

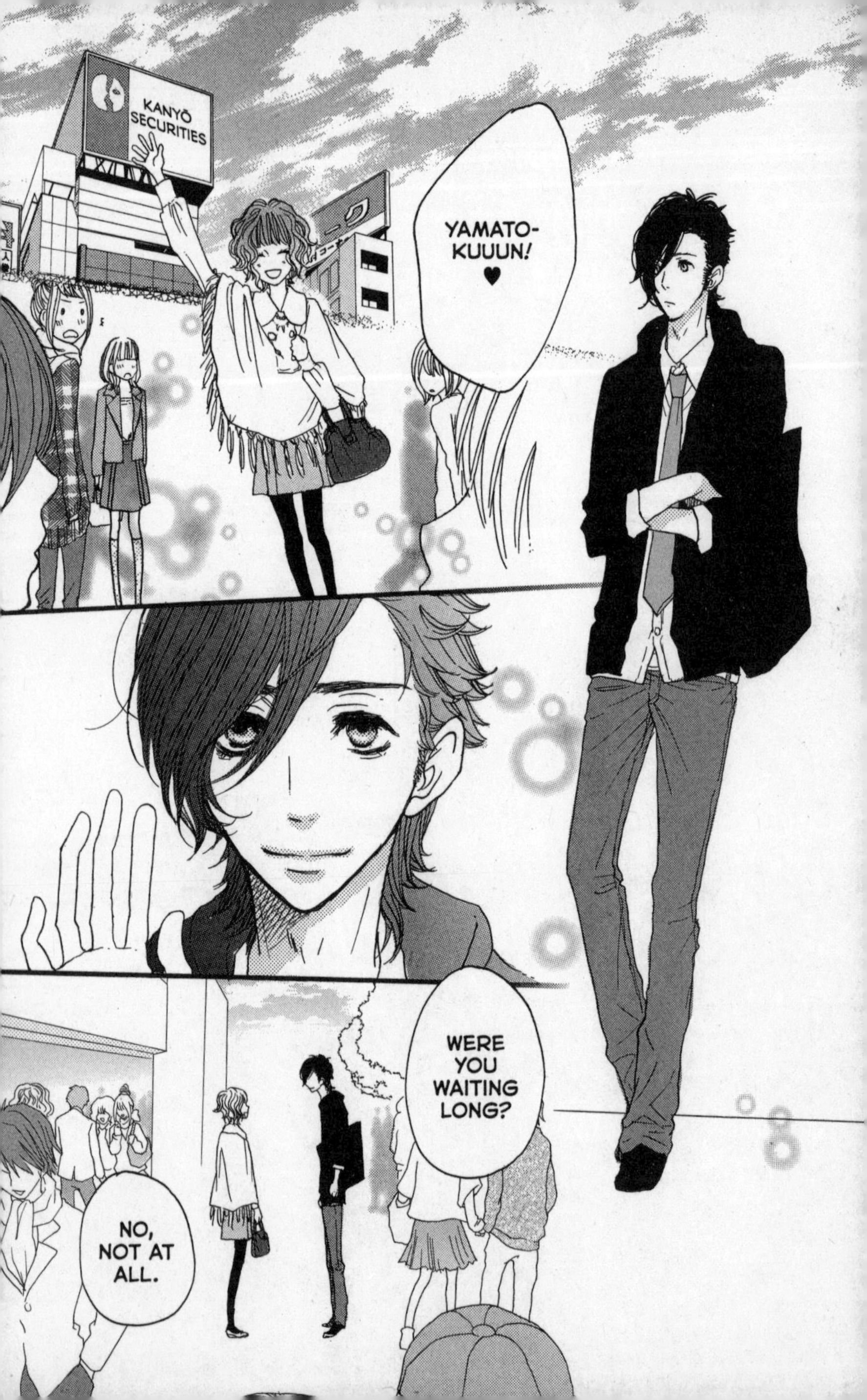
YAMATO-KUUUN! ♥
KANYŌ SECURITIES
WERE YOU WAITING LONG?
NO, NOT AT ALL.

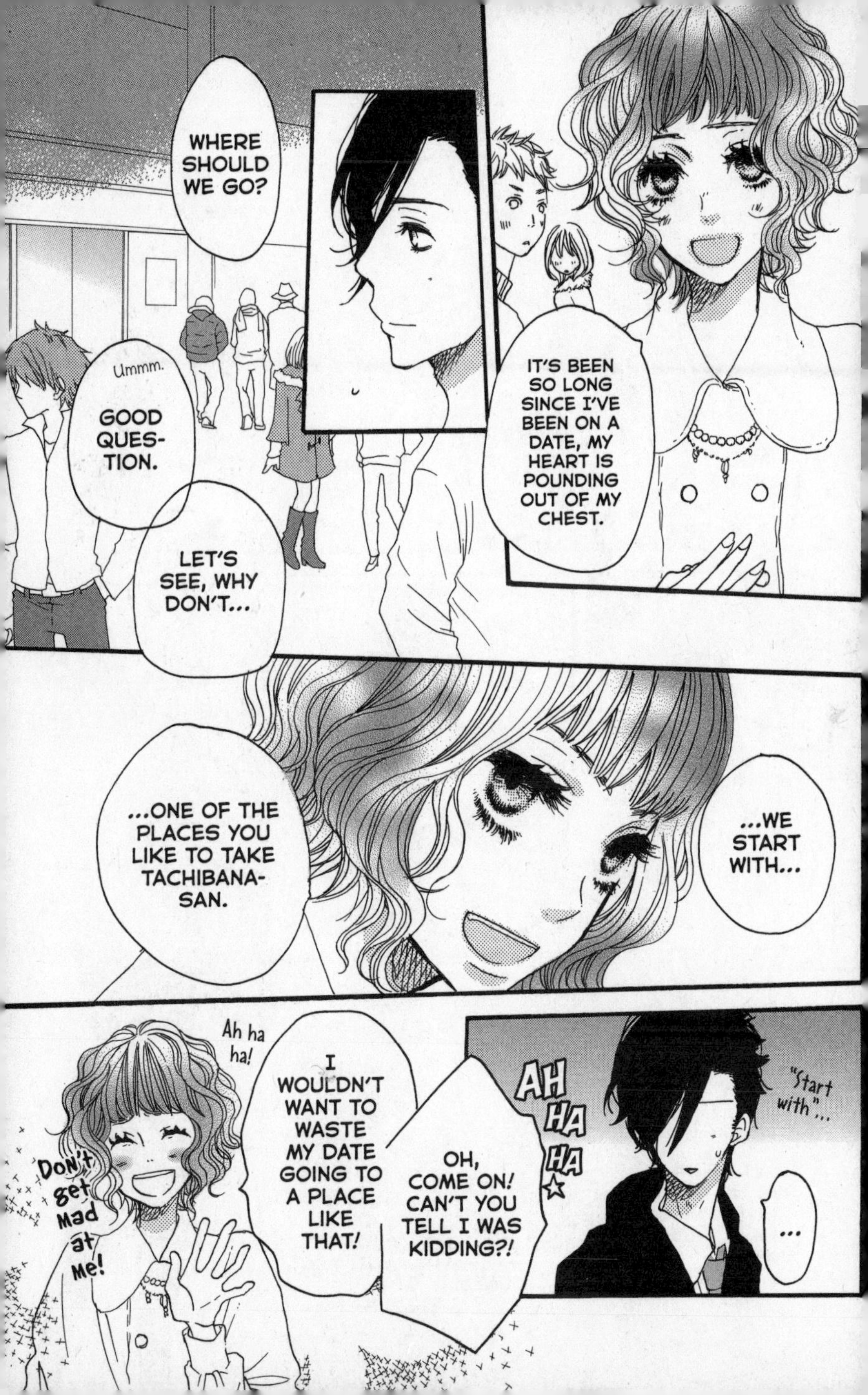
IT'S BEEN SO LONG SINCE I'VE BEEN ON A DATE, MY HEART IS POUNDING OUT OF MY CHEST.
WHERE SHOULD WE GO?
Ummm.
GOOD QUES-TION.
LET'S SEE, WHY DON'T...
...WE START WITH...
...ONE OF THE PLACES YOU LIKE TO TAKE TACHIBANA-SAN.
"Start with"...
...
AH HA HA☆
OH, COME ON! CAN'T YOU TELL I WAS KIDDING?!
I WOULDN'T WANT TO WASTE MY DATE GOING TO A PLACE LIKE THAT!
Ah ha ha!
Don't get Mad at Me!

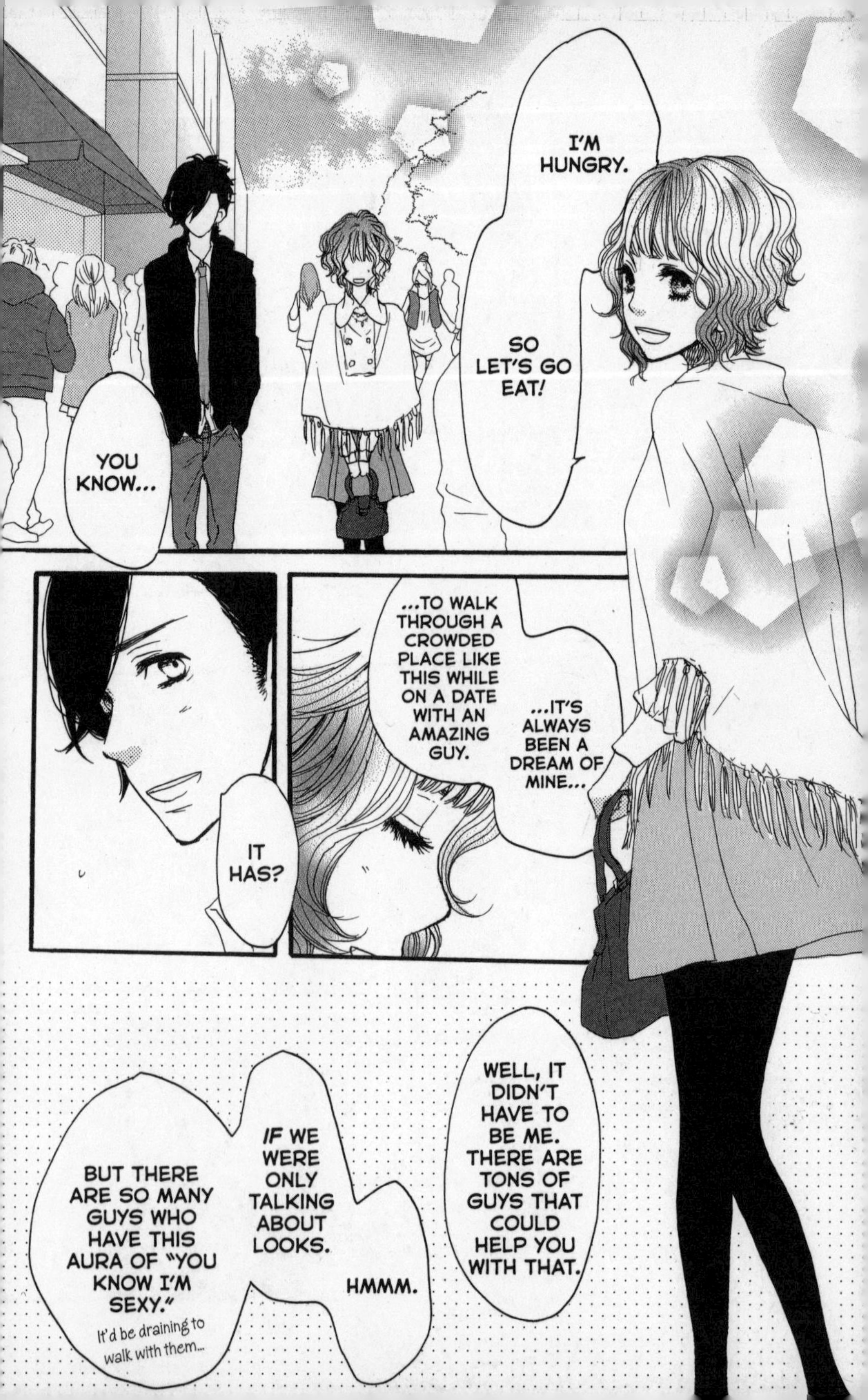
I'M HUNGRY.
SO LET'S GO EAT!
YOU KNOW...
...TO WALK THROUGH A CROWDED PLACE LIKE THIS WHILE ON A DATE WITH AN AMAZING GUY.
...IT'S ALWAYS BEEN A DREAM OF MINE...
IT HAS?
WELL, IT DIDN'T HAVE TO BE ME. THERE ARE TONS OF GUYS THAT COULD HELP YOU WITH THAT.
HMMM.
IF WE WERE ONLY TALKING ABOUT LOOKS.
BUT THERE ARE SO MANY GUYS WHO HAVE THIS AURA OF "YOU KNOW I'M SEXY."
It'd be draining to walk with them...

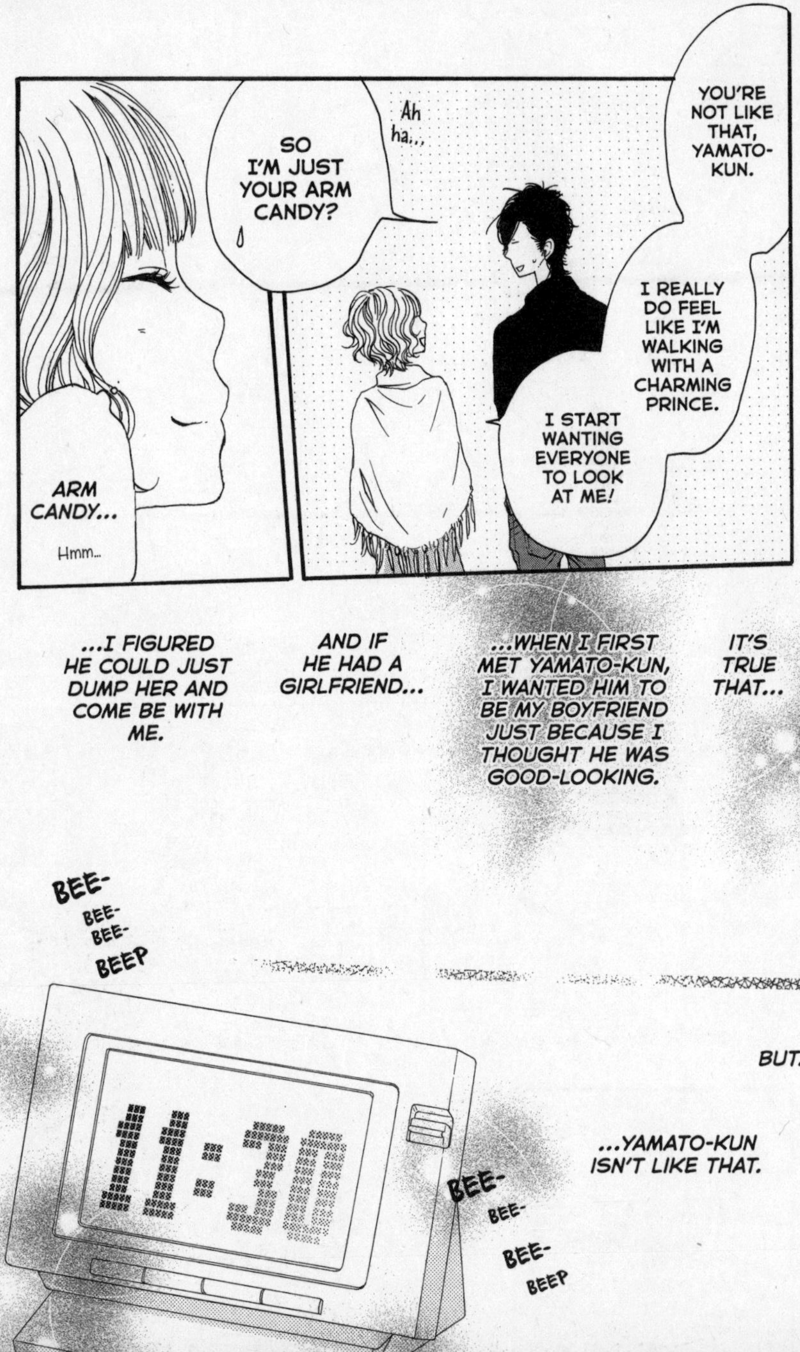
YOU'RE NOT LIKE THAT, YAMATO-KUN.
I REALLY DO FEEL LIKE I'M WALKING WITH A CHARMING PRINCE.
I START WANTING EVERYONE TO LOOK AT ME!
Ah ha...
SO I'M JUST YOUR ARM CANDY?
ARM CANDY...
Hmm...
IT'S TRUE THAT...
...WHEN I FIRST MET YAMATO-KUN, I WANTED HIM TO BE MY BOYFRIEND JUST BECAUSE I THOUGHT HE WAS GOOD-LOOKING.
AND IF HE HAD A GIRLFRIEND...
...I FIGURED HE COULD JUST DUMP HER AND COME BE WITH ME.
BUT...
...YAMATO-KUN ISN'T LIKE THAT.
BEE- BEE- BEE- BEEP
11:30
BEE- BEE- BEE- BEEP

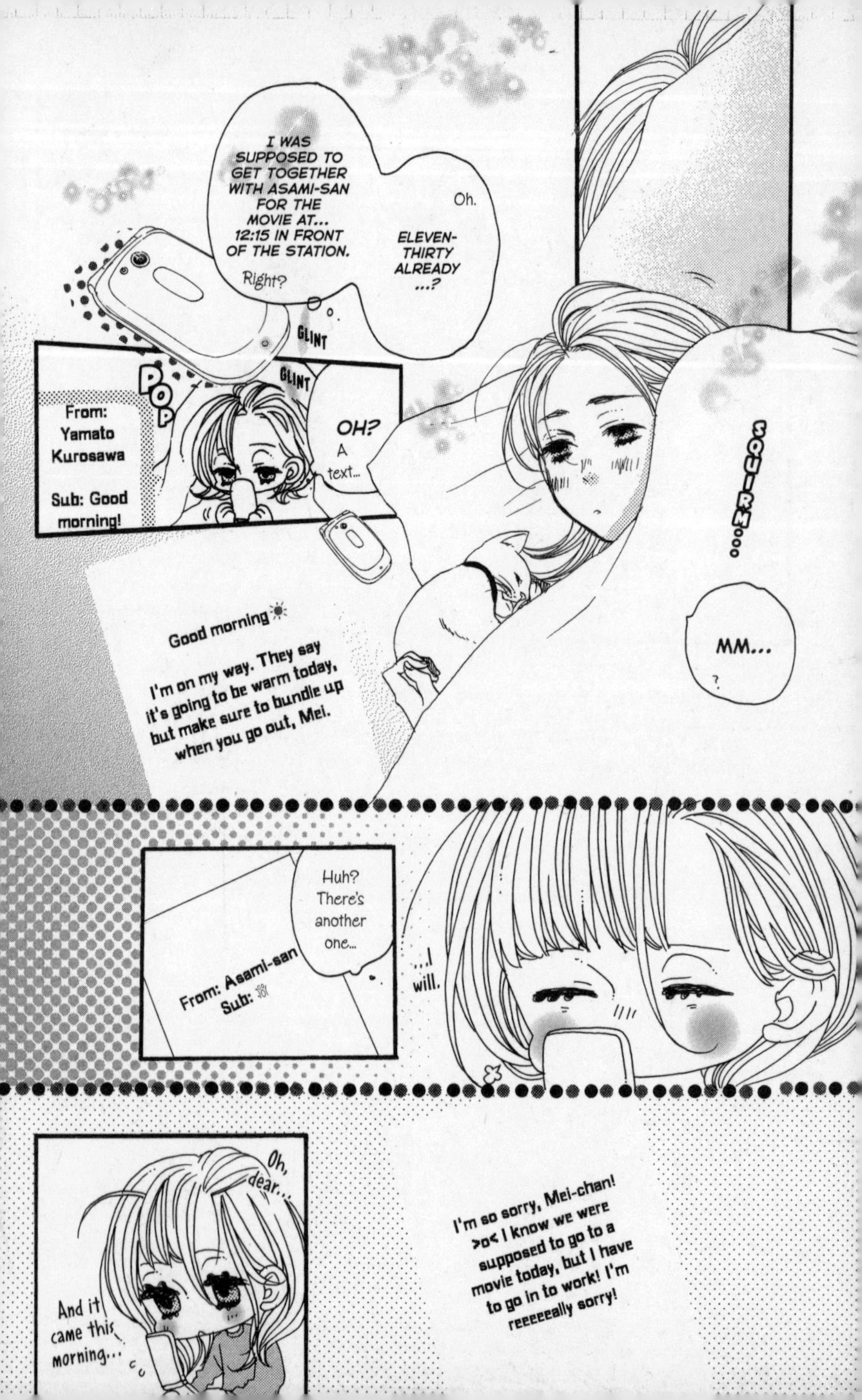
SQUIRM...
MM...
?
GLINT
GLINT
OH? A text...
POP
From: Yamato Kurosawa
Sub: Good morning!
Good morning
I'm on my way. They say it's going to be warm today, but make sure to bundle up when you go out, Mei.
Oh.
ELEVEN-THIRTY ALREADY...?
I WAS SUPPOSED TO GET TOGETHER WITH ASAMI-SAN FOR THE MOVIE AT... 12:15 IN FRONT OF THE STATION.
Right?
...I will.
Huh? There's another one...
From: Asami-san
Sub:
I'm so sorry, Mei-chan! >o< I know we were supposed to go to a movie today, but I have to go in to work! I'm reeeeeally sorry!
Oh, dear...
And it came this morning...

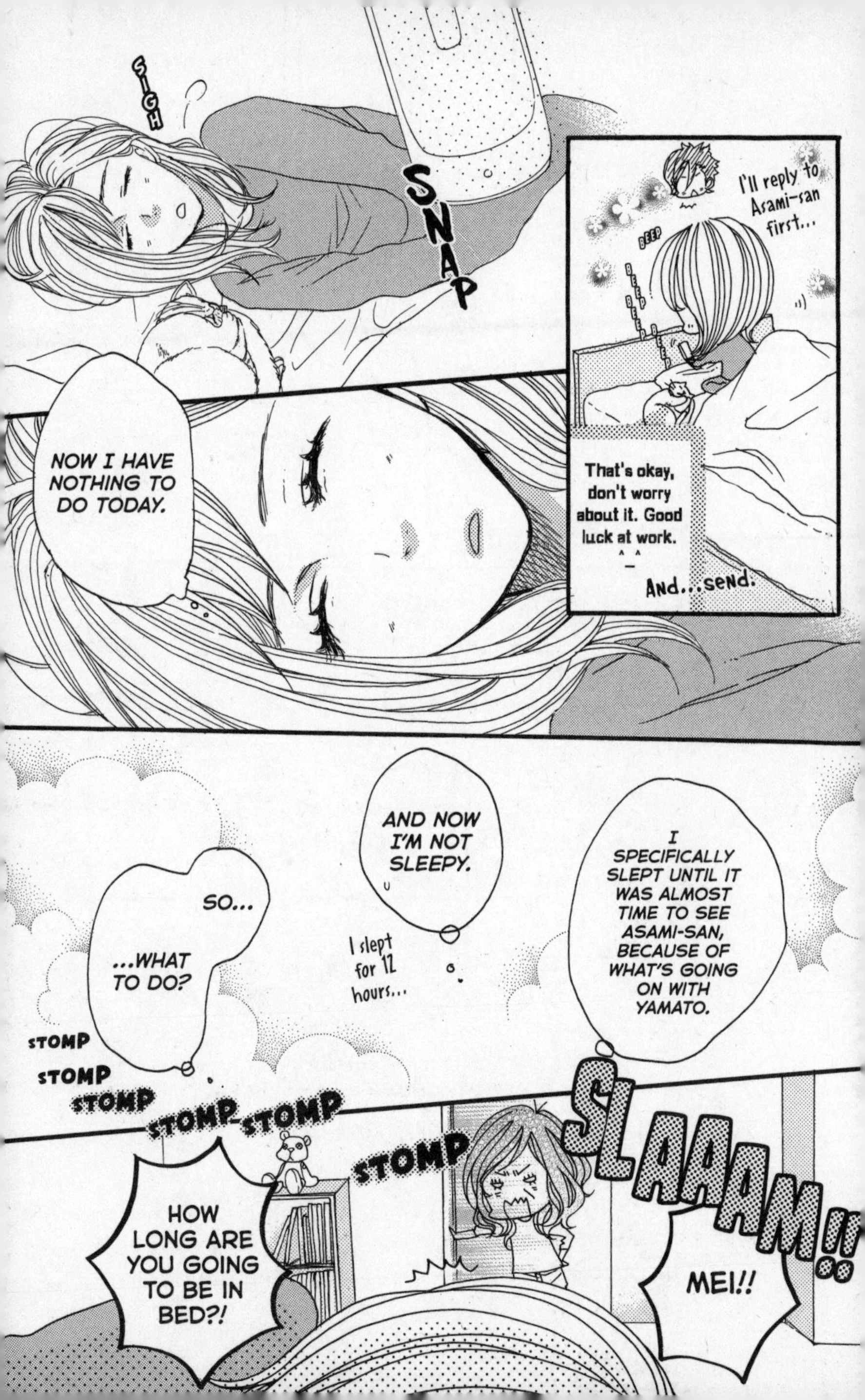

I'll reply to Asami-san first...
BEEP
BEEP BEEP BEEP BEEP
That's okay, don't worry about it. Good luck at work. ^_^
And...send.
SIGH
SNAP
NOW I HAVE NOTHING TO DO TODAY.
I SPECIFICALLY SLEPT UNTIL IT WAS ALMOST TIME TO SEE ASAMI-SAN, BECAUSE OF WHAT'S GOING ON WITH YAMATO.
AND NOW I'M NOT SLEEPY.
I slept for 12 hours...
SO...
...WHAT TO DO?
STOMP
STOMP
STOMP
STOMP STOMP
STOMP
SLAAAM!!
MEI!!
HOW LONG ARE YOU GOING TO BE IN BED?!

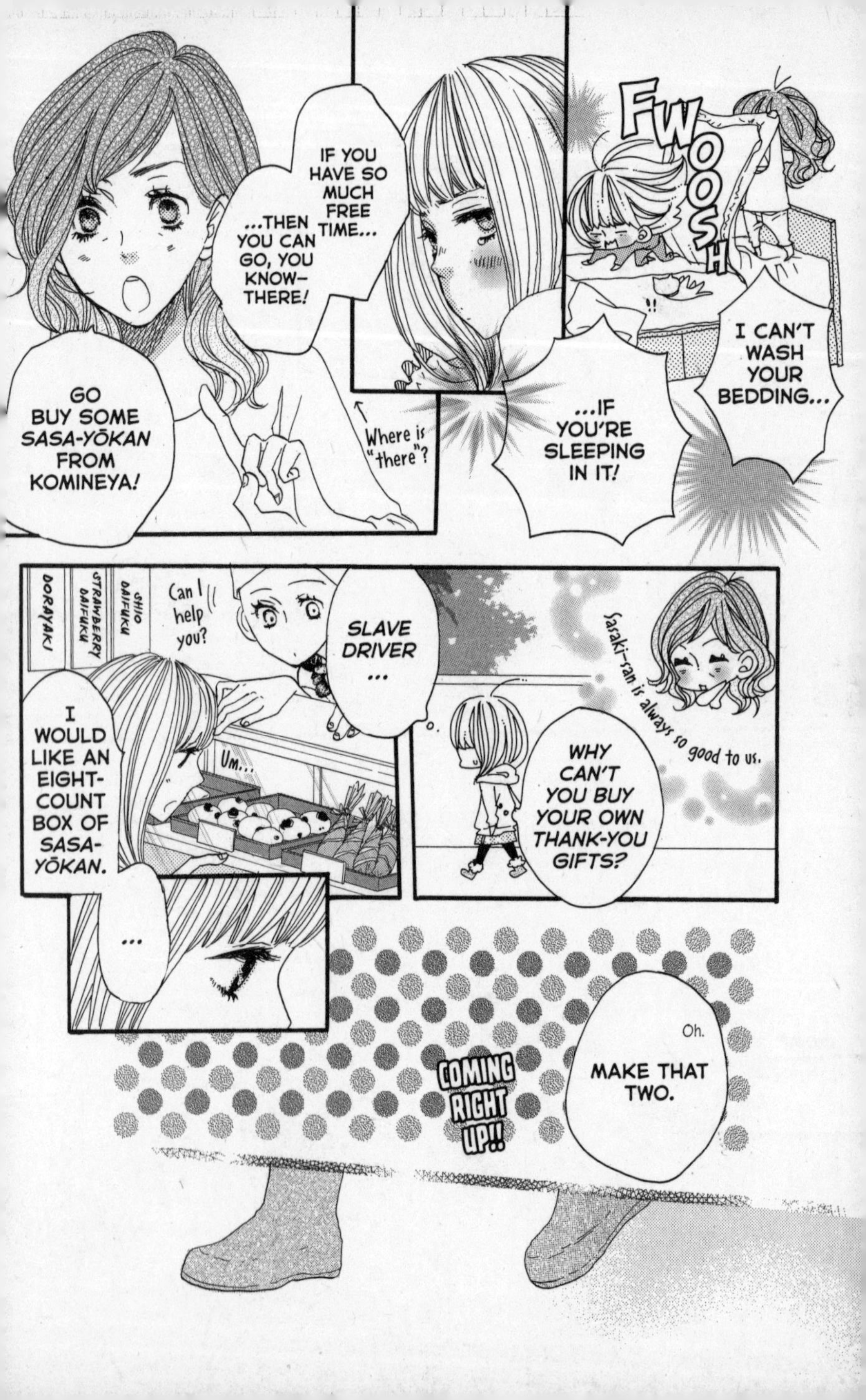
FWOOSH
!!
I CAN'T WASH YOUR BEDDING...
...IF YOU'RE SLEEPING IN IT!
IF YOU HAVE SO MUCH FREE TIME...
...THEN YOU CAN GO, YOU KNOW— THERE!
Where is "there"?
GO BUY SOME SASA-YŌKAN FROM KOMINEYA!
Sasaki-san is always so good to us.
WHY CAN'T YOU BUY YOUR OWN THANK-YOU GIFTS?
SLAVE DRIVER ...
Can I help you?
SHIO DAIFUKU
STRAWBERRY DAIFUKU
DORAYAKI
Um...
I WOULD LIKE AN EIGHT-COUNT BOX OF SASA-YŌKAN.
...
Oh.
MAKE THAT TWO.
COMING RIGHT UP!!

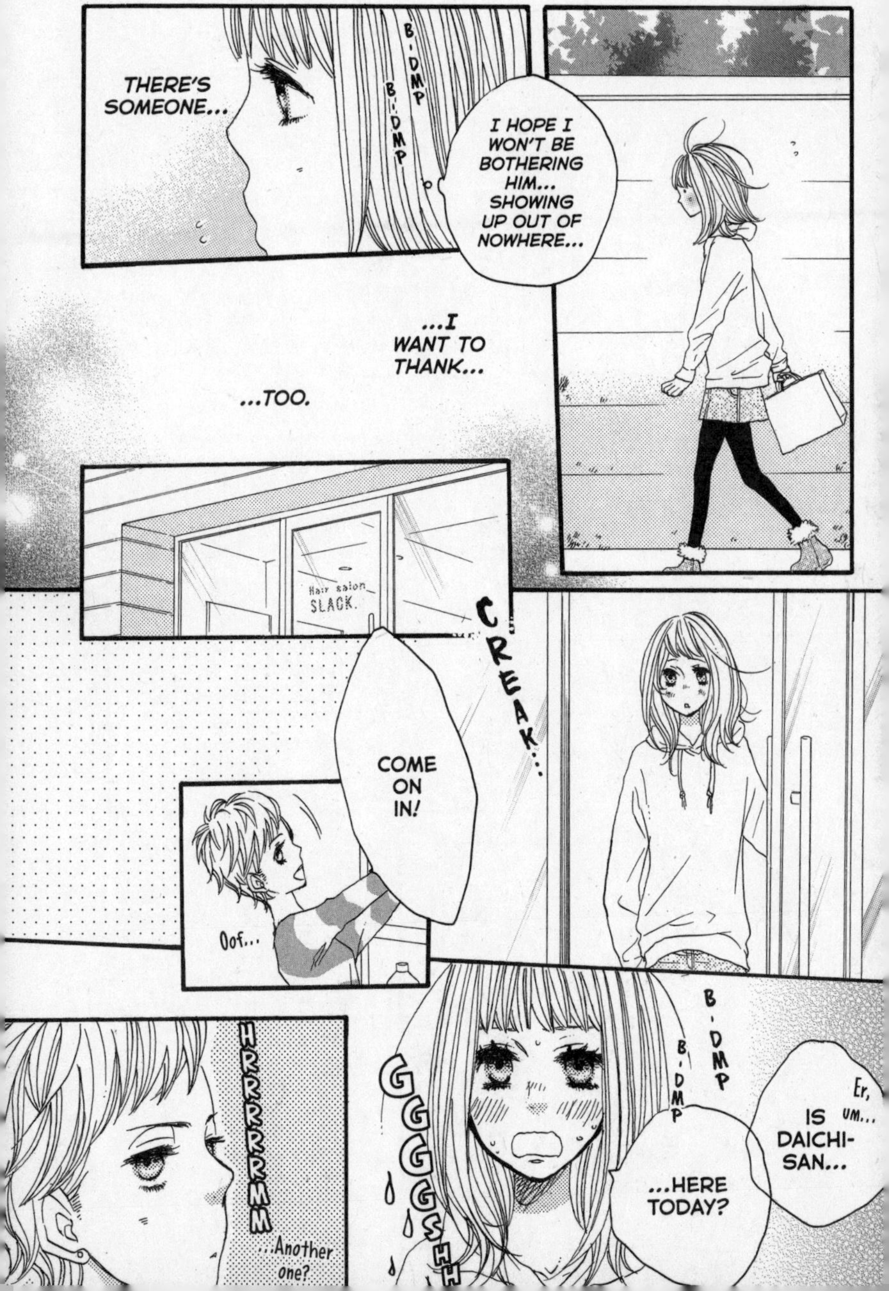
I HOPE I WON'T BE BOTHERING HIM... SHOWING UP OUT OF NOWHERE...
B-DMP
B-DMP
THERE'S SOMEONE...
...I WANT TO THANK...
...TOO.
Hair salon
SLACK.
CREAK...
COME ON IN!
Oof...
Er, UM...
IS DAICHI-SAN...
...HERE TODAY?
B-DMP
B-DMP
GGGGSHH
HRRRRRMM
...Another one?

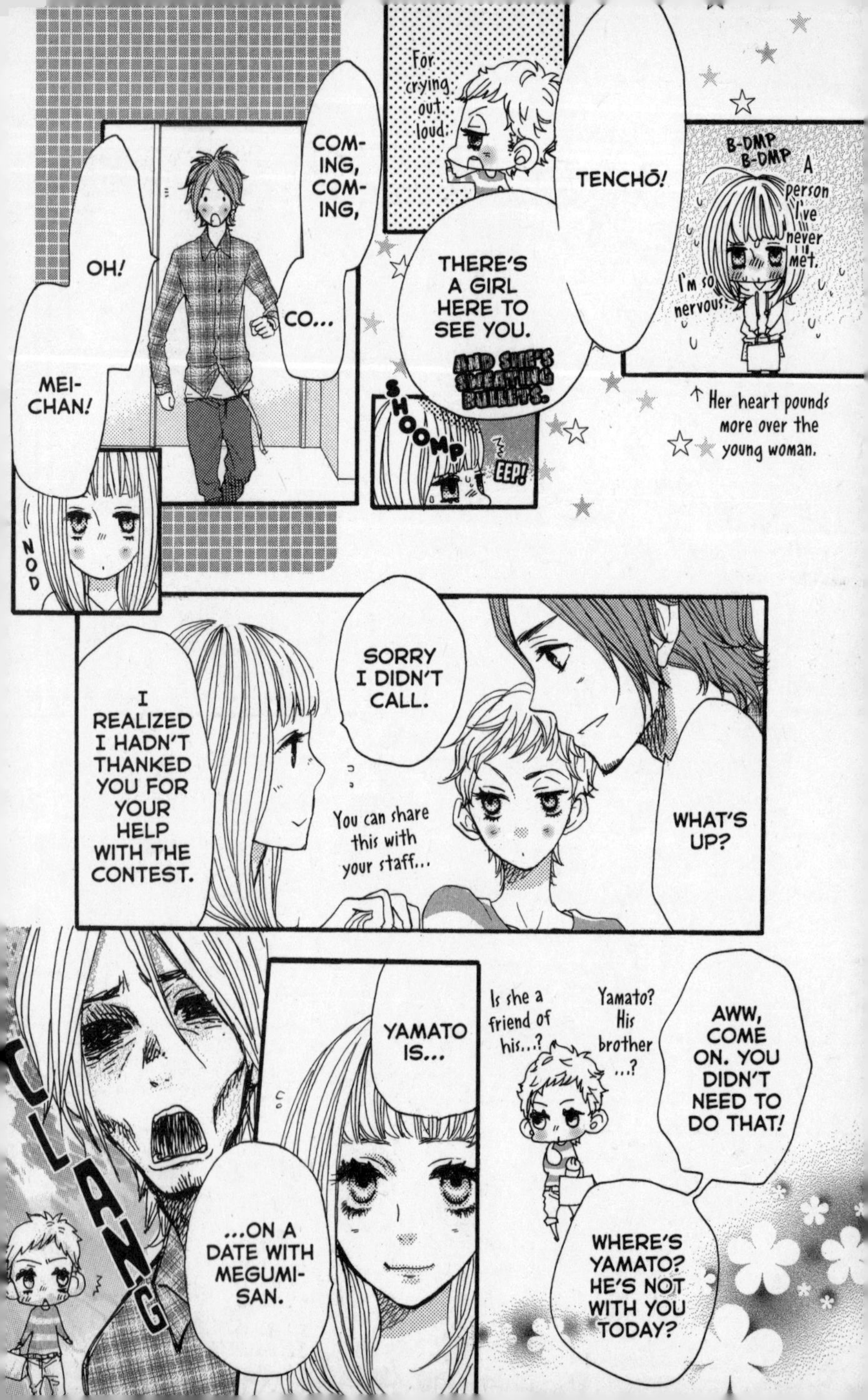
B-DMP
B-DMP
A person I've never met.
I'm so nervous.
↑ Her heart pounds more over the young woman.
TENCHŌ!
For crying out loud.
THERE'S A GIRL HERE TO SEE YOU.
AND SHE'S SWEATING BULLETS.
SHOOMP
EEP!
COMING, COMING,
CO...
OH!
MEI-CHAN!
NOD
WHAT'S UP?
SORRY I DIDN'T CALL.
You can share this with your staff...
I REALIZED I HADN'T THANKED YOU FOR YOUR HELP WITH THE CONTEST.
AWW, COME ON. YOU DIDN'T NEED TO DO THAT!
WHERE'S YAMATO? HE'S NOT WITH YOU TODAY?
Yamato? His brother ...?
Is she a friend of his...?
YAMATO IS...
...ON A DATE WITH MEGUMI-SAN.
CLANG

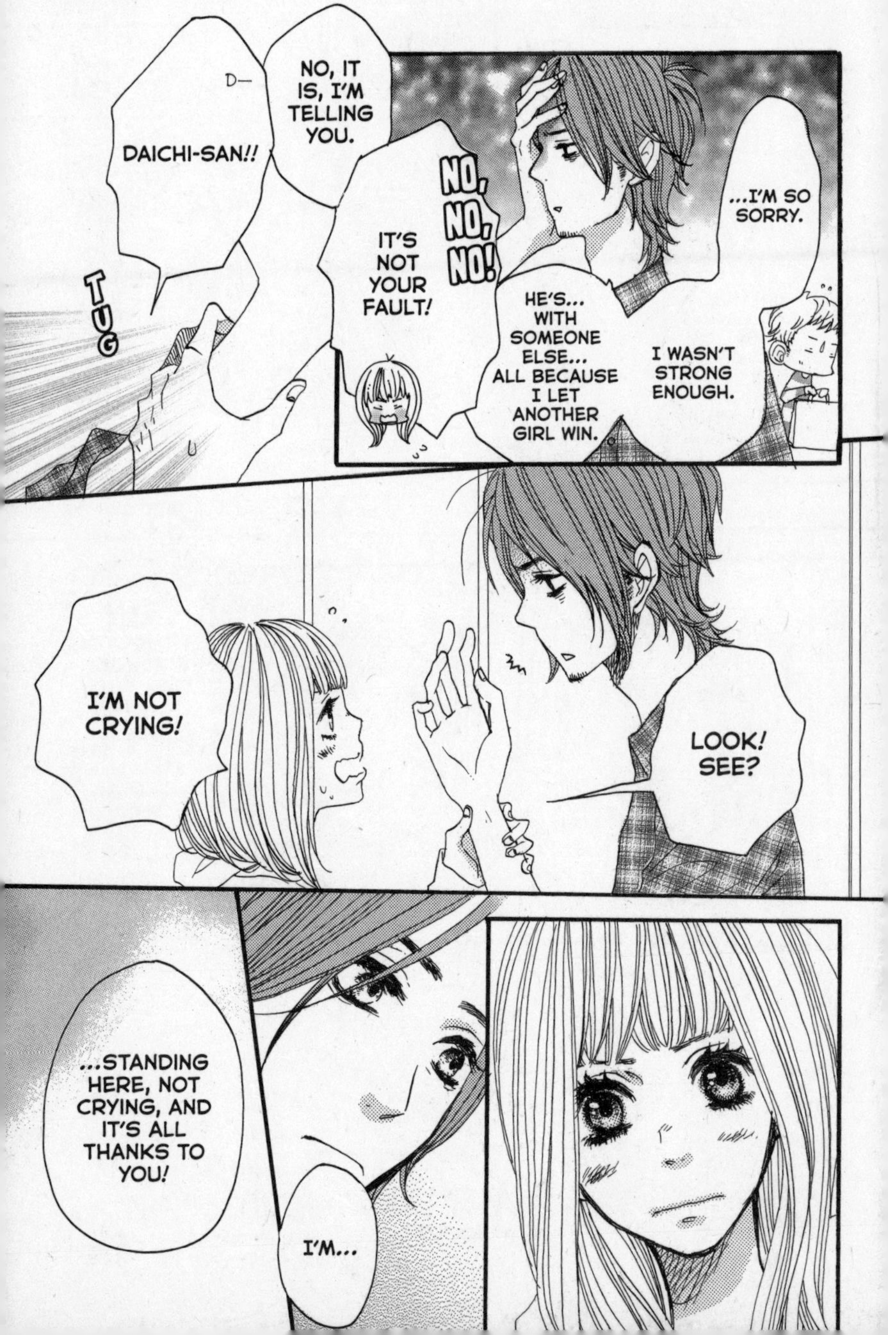
...I'M SO SORRY.
I WASN'T STRONG ENOUGH.
HE'S... WITH SOMEONE ELSE... ALL BECAUSE I LET ANOTHER GIRL WIN.
NO, NO, NO!
IT'S NOT YOUR FAULT!
NO, IT IS, I'M TELLING YOU.
D— DAICHI-SAN!!
TUG
LOOK! SEE?
I'M NOT CRYING!
I'M...
...STANDING HERE, NOT CRYING, AND IT'S ALL THANKS TO YOU!

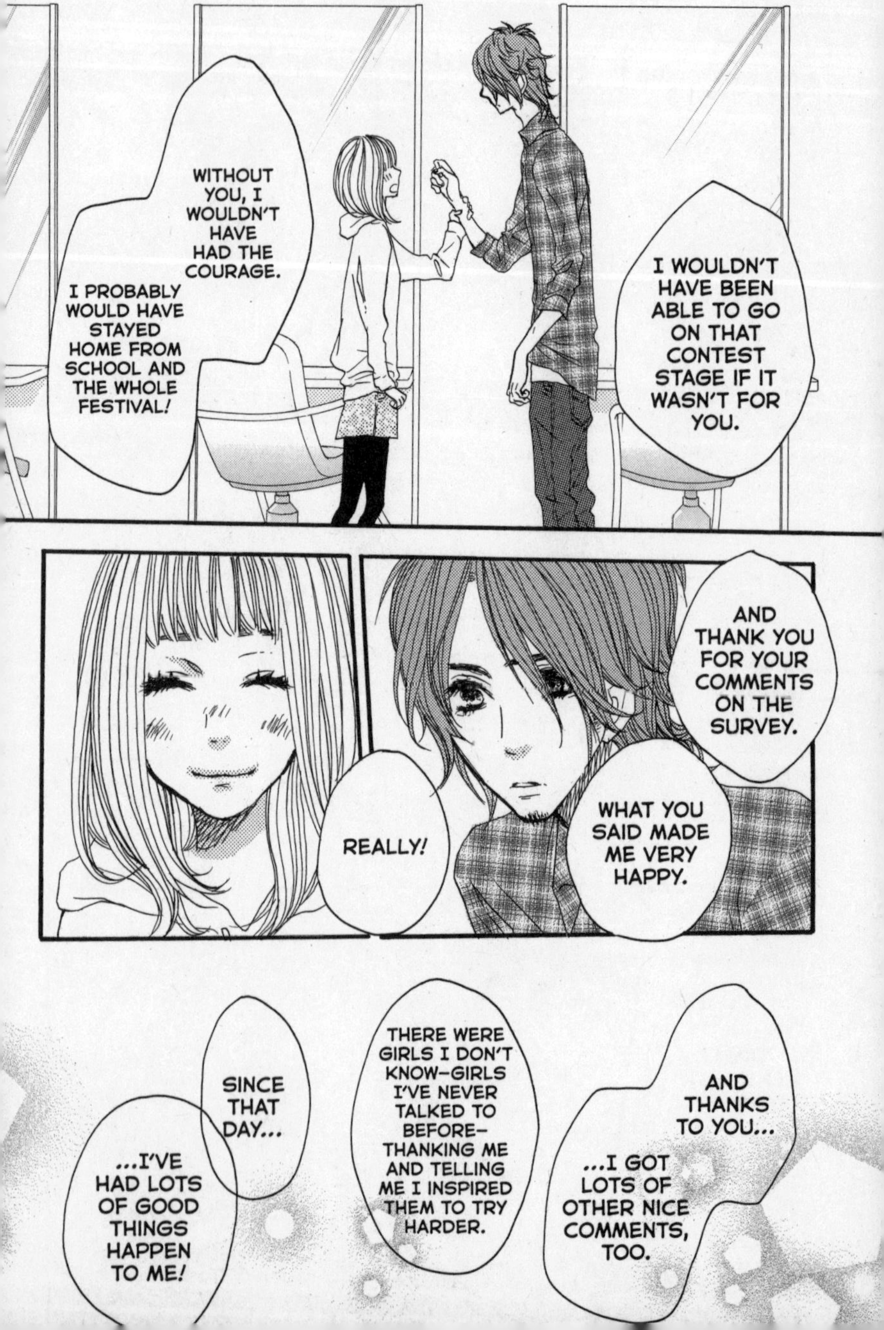
I WOULDN'T HAVE BEEN ABLE TO GO ON THAT CONTEST STAGE IF IT WASN'T FOR YOU.
WITHOUT YOU, I WOULDN'T HAVE HAD THE COURAGE.
I PROBABLY WOULD HAVE STAYED HOME FROM SCHOOL AND THE WHOLE FESTIVAL!
AND THANK YOU FOR YOUR COMMENTS ON THE SURVEY.
WHAT YOU SAID MADE ME VERY HAPPY.
REALLY!
AND THANKS TO YOU...
...I GOT LOTS OF OTHER NICE COMMENTS, TOO.
THERE WERE GIRLS I DON'T KNOW—GIRLS I'VE NEVER TALKED TO BEFORE—THANKING ME AND TELLING ME I INSPIRED THEM TO TRY HARDER.
SINCE THAT DAY...
...I'VE HAD LOTS OF GOOD THINGS HAPPEN TO ME!

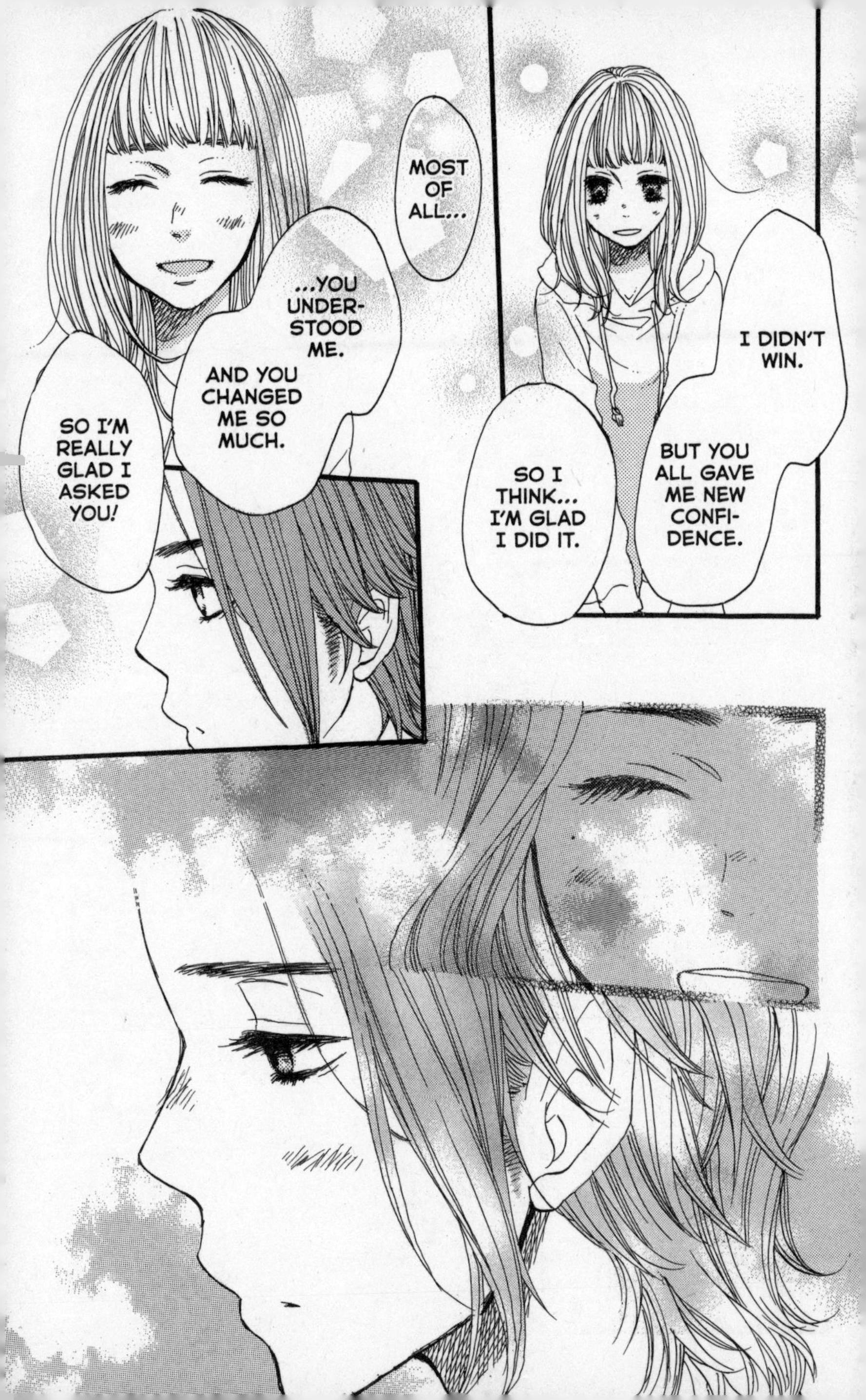
I DIDN'T WIN.
BUT YOU ALL GAVE ME NEW CONFIDENCE.
SO I THINK... I'M GLAD I DID IT.
MOST OF ALL...
...YOU UNDERSTOOD ME.
AND YOU CHANGED ME SO MUCH.
SO I'M REALLY GLAD I ASKED YOU!

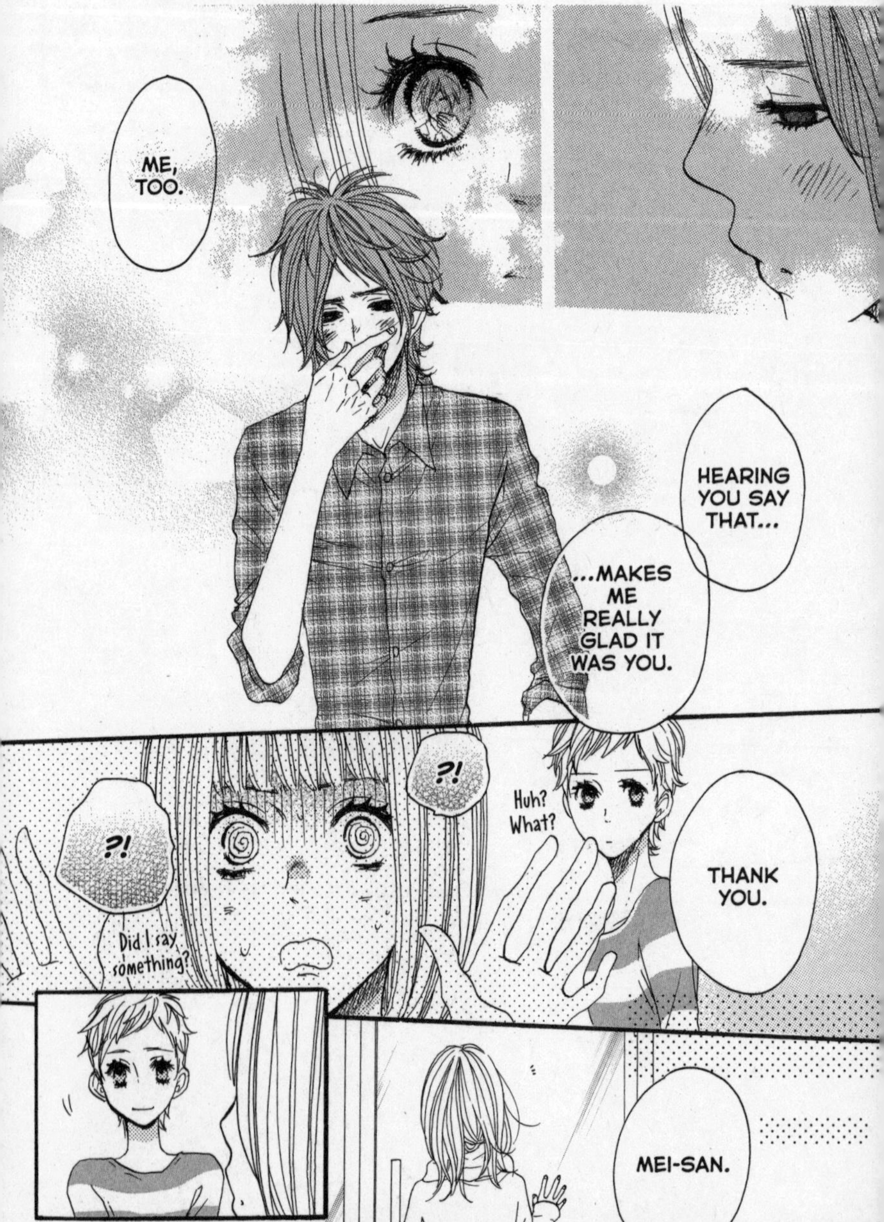
ME, TOO.
HEARING YOU SAY THAT...
...MAKES ME REALLY GLAD IT WAS YOU.
THANK YOU.
Huh? What?
?!
?!
Did I say something?
MEI-SAN.

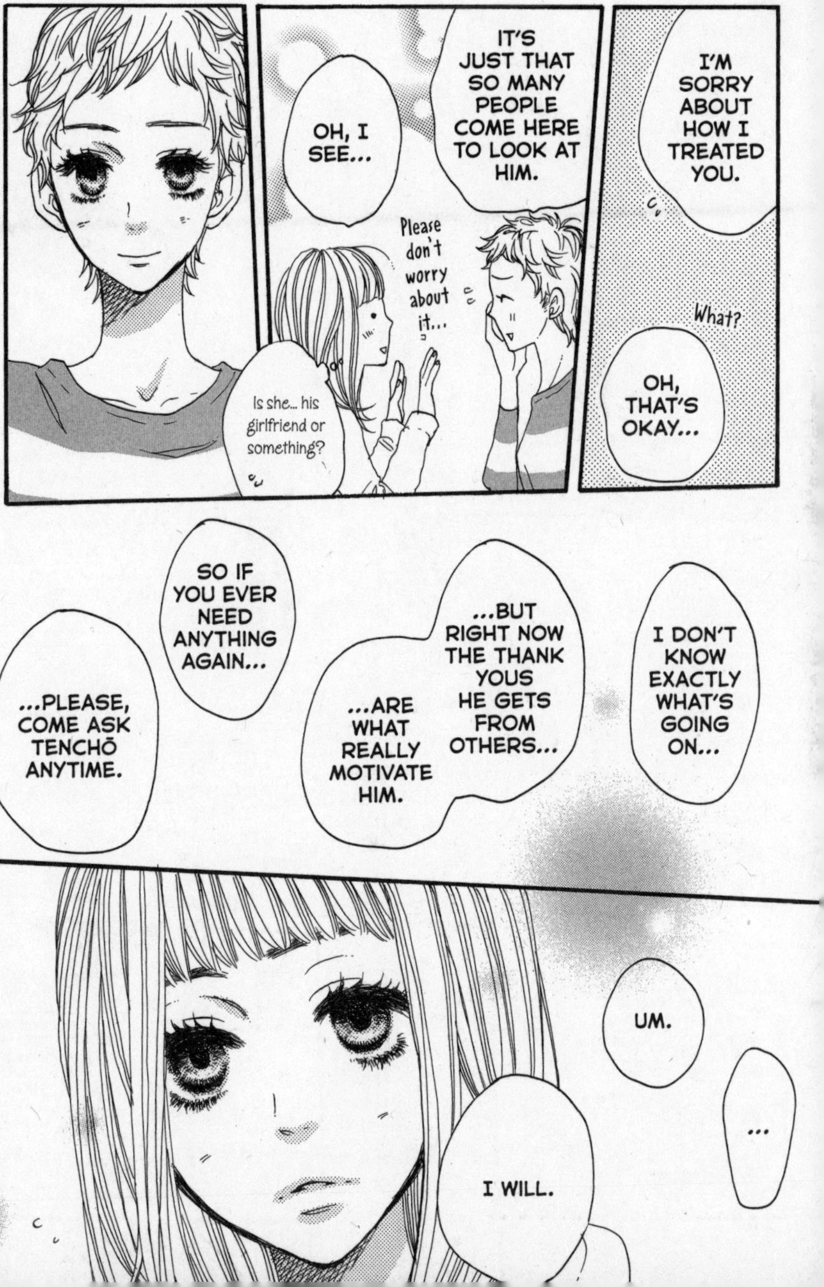
I'M SORRY ABOUT HOW I TREATED YOU.
What?
OH, THAT'S OKAY...
IT'S JUST THAT SO MANY PEOPLE COME HERE TO LOOK AT HIM.
OH, I SEE...
Please don't worry about it...
Is she... his girlfriend or something?
I DON'T KNOW EXACTLY WHAT'S GOING ON...
...BUT RIGHT NOW THE THANK YOUS HE GETS FROM OTHERS...
...ARE WHAT REALLY MOTIVATE HIM.
SO IF YOU EVER NEED ANYTHING AGAIN...
...PLEASE, COME ASK TENCHŌ ANYTIME.
UM.
...
I WILL.

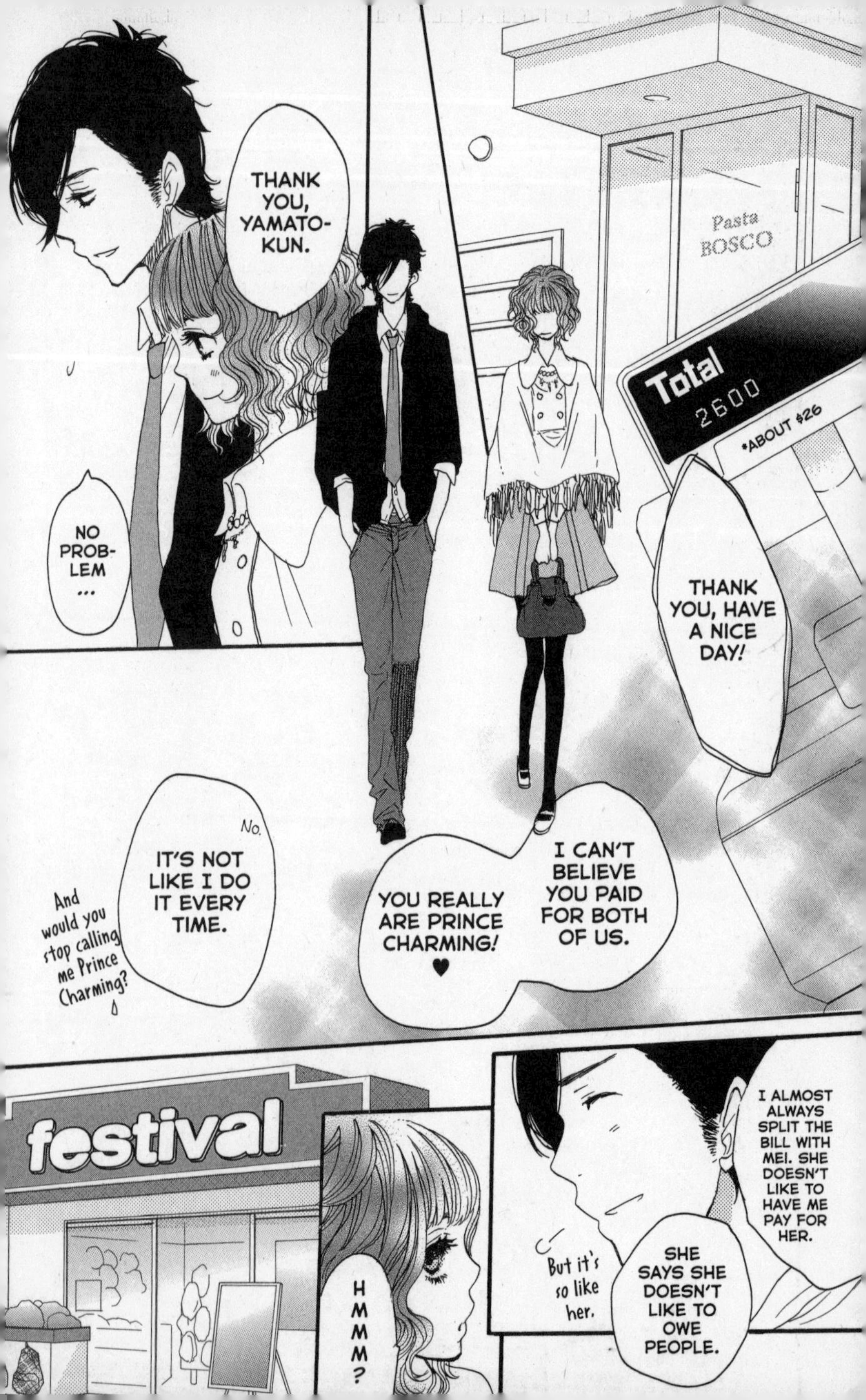
Pasta BOSCO
Total 2600
*ABOUT $26
THANK YOU, HAVE A NICE DAY!
THANK YOU, YAMATO-KUN.
NO PROBLEM...
I CAN'T BELIEVE YOU PAID FOR BOTH OF US.
YOU REALLY ARE PRINCE CHARMING! ♥
No.
IT'S NOT LIKE I DO IT EVERY TIME.
And would you stop calling me Prince Charming?
I ALMOST ALWAYS SPLIT THE BILL WITH MEI. SHE DOESN'T LIKE TO HAVE ME PAY FOR HER.
SHE SAYS SHE DOESN'T LIKE TO OWE PEOPLE.
But it's so like her.
HMMM?
festival

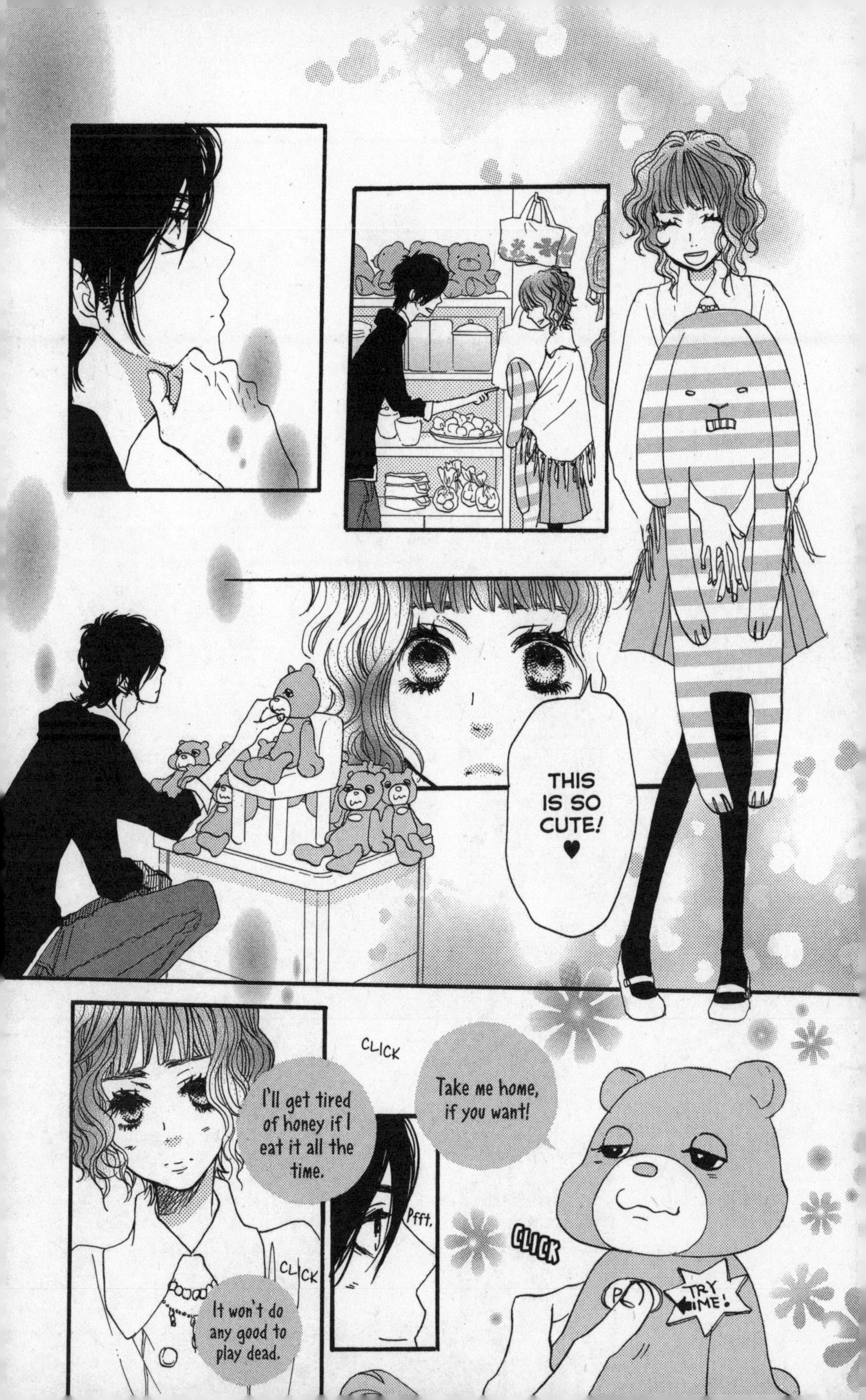
THIS IS SO CUTE! ♥
CLICK
Take me home, if you want!
CLICK
TRY ME!
Pfft.
I'll get tired of honey if I eat it all the time.
CLICK
It won't do any good to play dead.

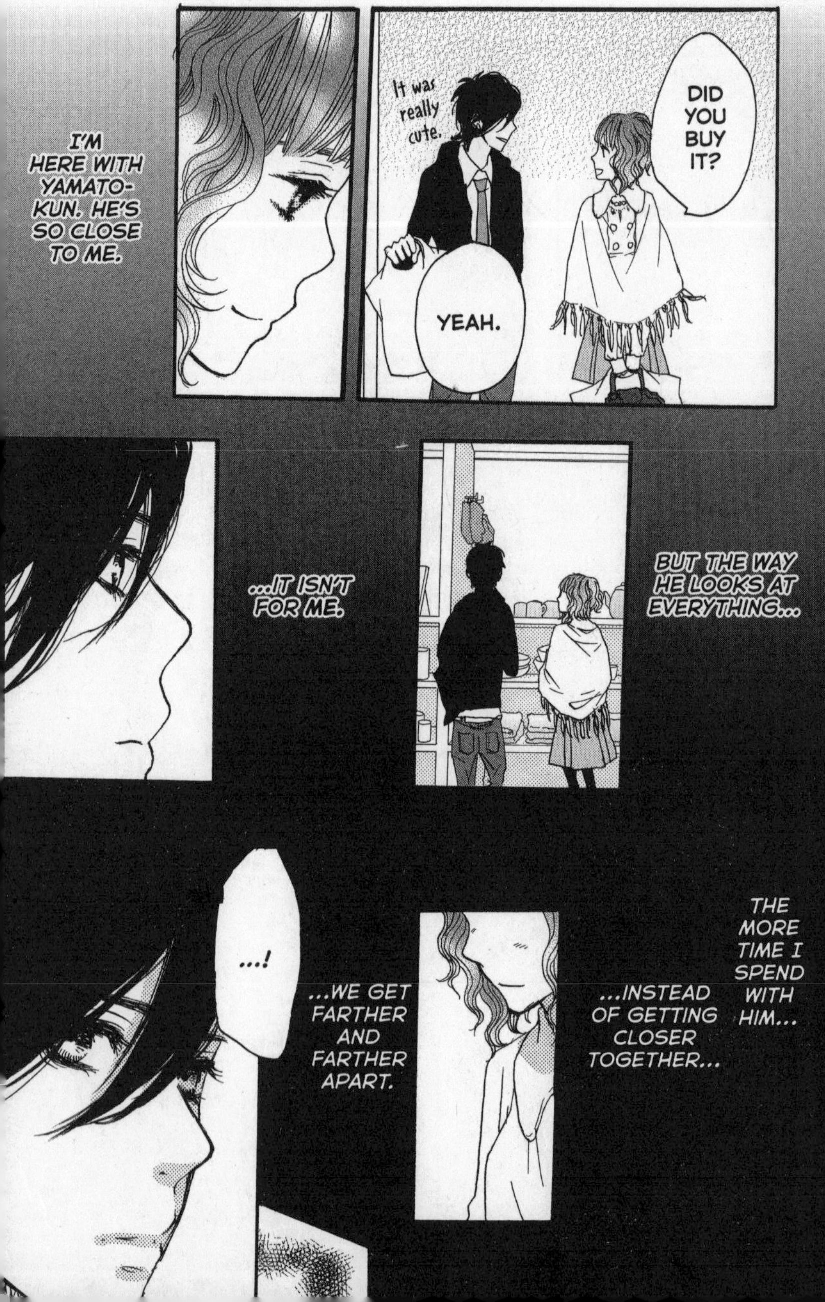
DID YOU BUY IT?
It was really cute.
YEAH.
I'M HERE WITH YAMATO-KUN. HE'S SO CLOSE TO ME.
BUT THE WAY HE LOOKS AT EVERYTHING...
...IT ISN'T FOR ME.
THE MORE TIME I SPEND WITH HIM...
...INSTEAD OF GETTING CLOSER TOGETHER...
...WE GET FARTHER AND FARTHER APART.
...!

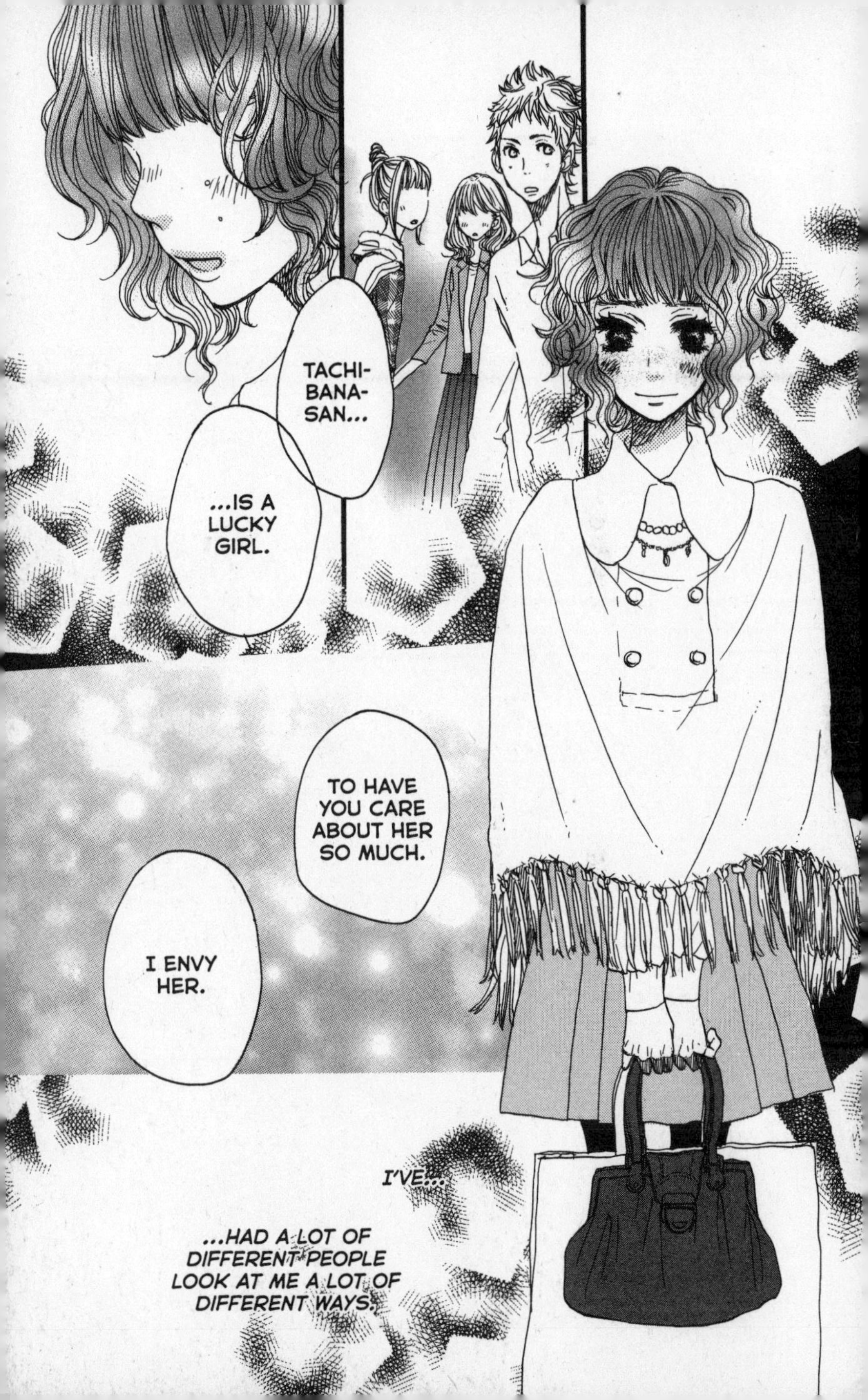
TACHI-BANA-SAN...
...IS A LUCKY GIRL.
TO HAVE YOU CARE ABOUT HER SO MUCH.
I ENVY HER.
I'VE...
...HAD A LOT OF DIFFERENT PEOPLE LOOK AT ME A LOT OF DIFFERENT WAYS.

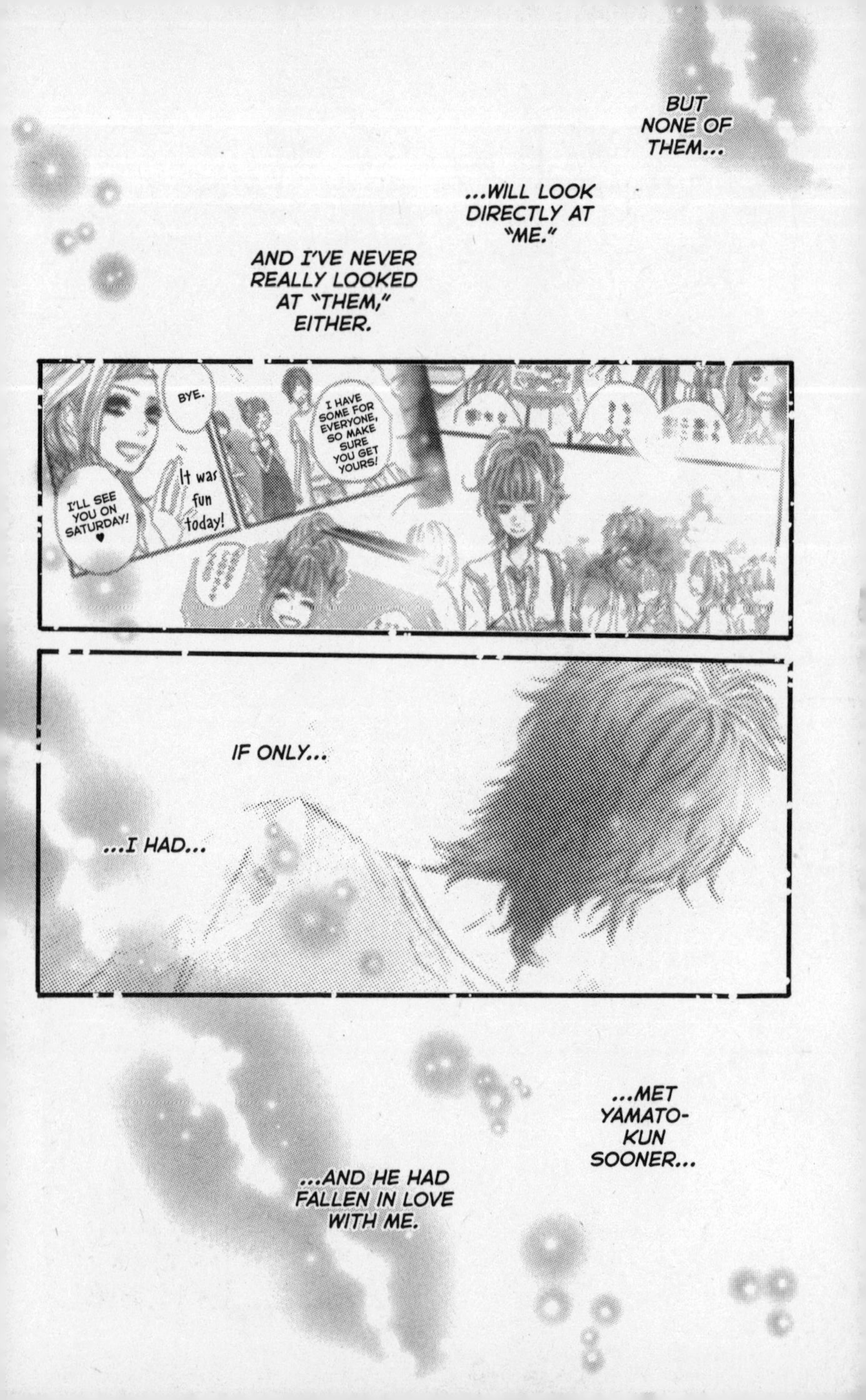
BUT NONE OF THEM...
...WILL LOOK DIRECTLY AT "ME."
AND I'VE NEVER REALLY LOOKED AT "THEM," EITHER.
I HAVE SOME FOR EVERYONE, SO MAKE SURE YOU GET YOURS!
BYE.
It was fun today!
I'LL SEE YOU ON SATURDAY! ♥
IF ONLY...
...I HAD...
...MET YAMATO-KUN SOONER...
...AND HE HAD FALLEN IN LOVE WITH ME.

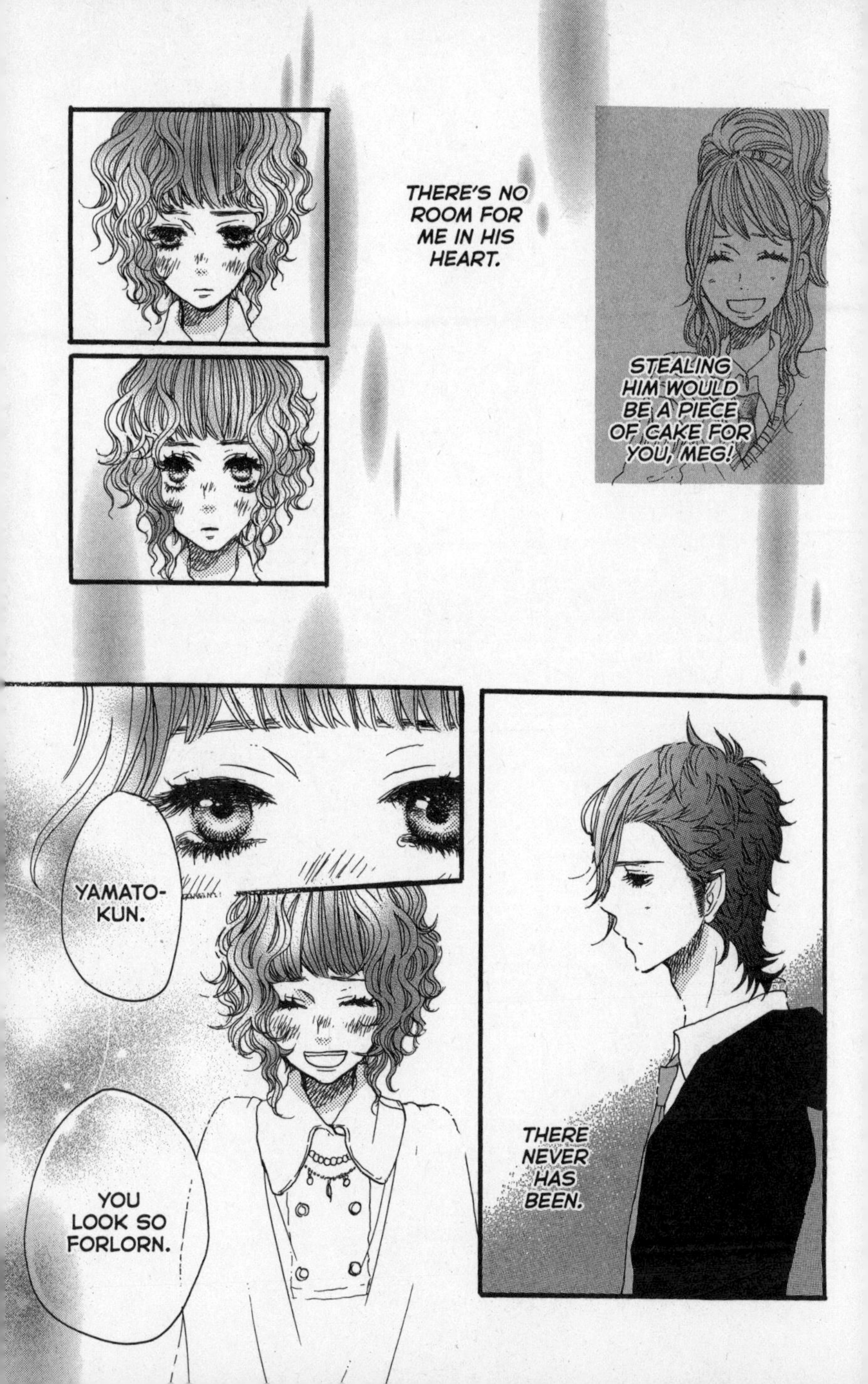
STEALING HIM WOULD BE A PIECE OF CAKE FOR YOU, MEG!
THERE'S NO ROOM FOR ME IN HIS HEART.
THERE NEVER HAS BEEN.
YAMATO-KUN.
YOU LOOK SO FORLORN.

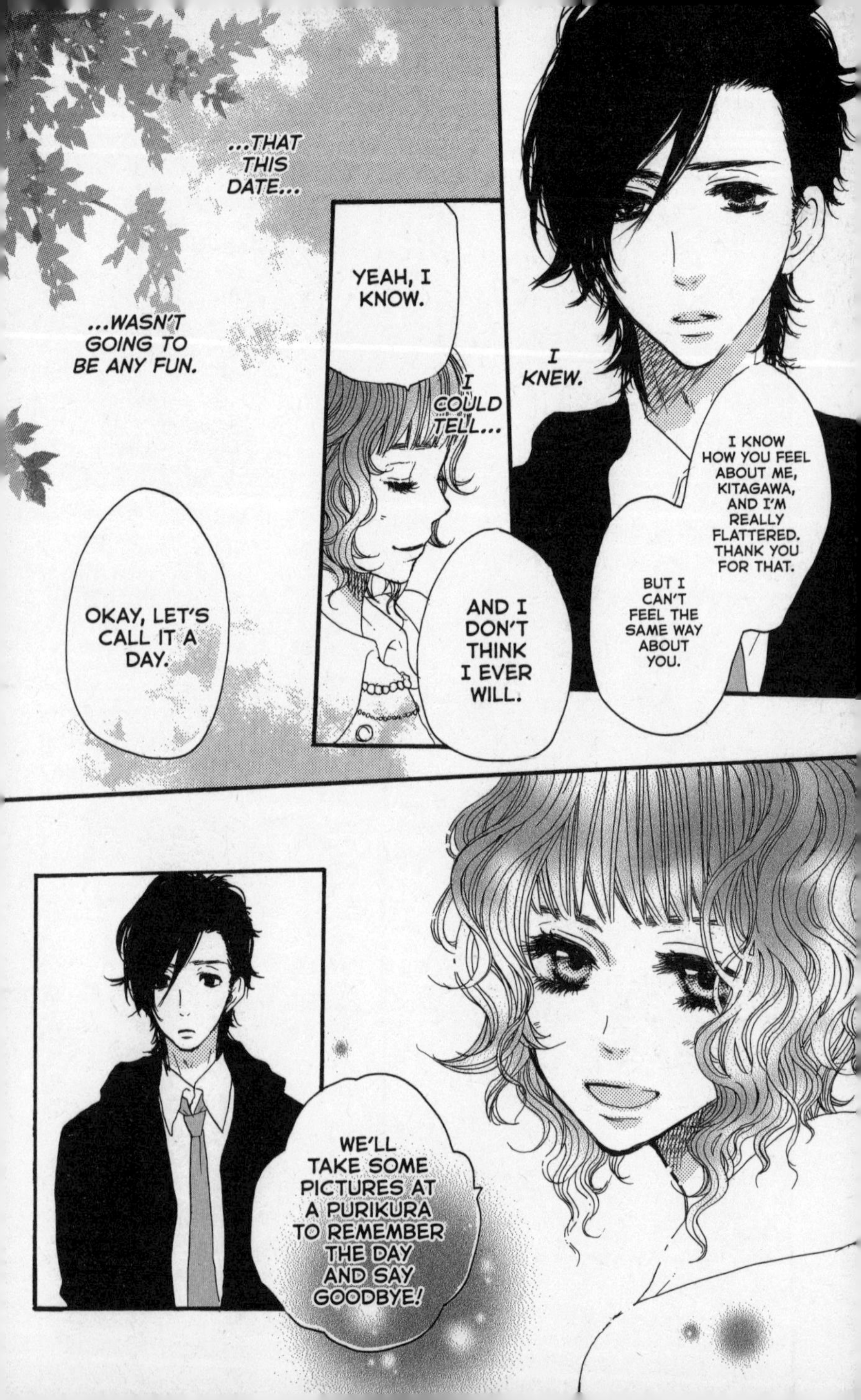
I KNOW HOW YOU FEEL ABOUT ME, KITAGAWA, AND I'M REALLY FLATTERED. THANK YOU FOR THAT.
BUT I CAN'T FEEL THE SAME WAY ABOUT YOU.
AND I DON'T THINK I EVER WILL.
I KNEW.
YEAH, I KNOW.
I COULD TELL...
...THAT THIS DATE...
...WASN'T GOING TO BE ANY FUN.
OKAY, LET'S CALL IT A DAY.
WE'LL TAKE SOME PICTURES AT A PURIKURA TO REMEMBER THE DAY AND SAY GOODBYE!

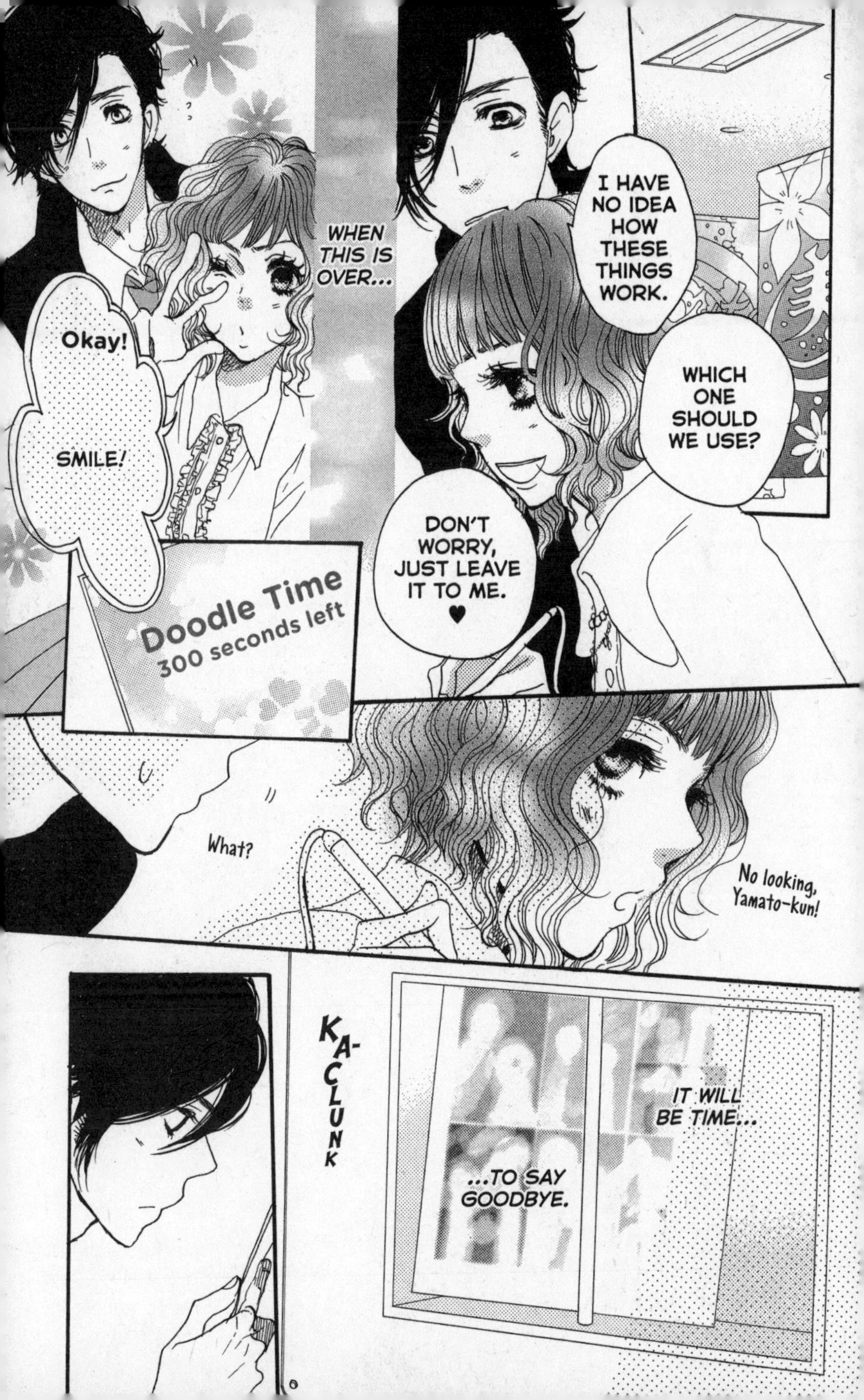

I HAVE NO IDEA HOW THESE THINGS WORK.
WHICH ONE SHOULD WE USE?
DON'T WORRY, JUST LEAVE IT TO ME. ♥
WHEN THIS IS OVER...
Okay!
SMILE!
Doodle Time
300 seconds left
No looking, Yamato-kun!
What?
IT WILL BE TIME...
...TO SAY GOODBYE.
KA-CLUNK

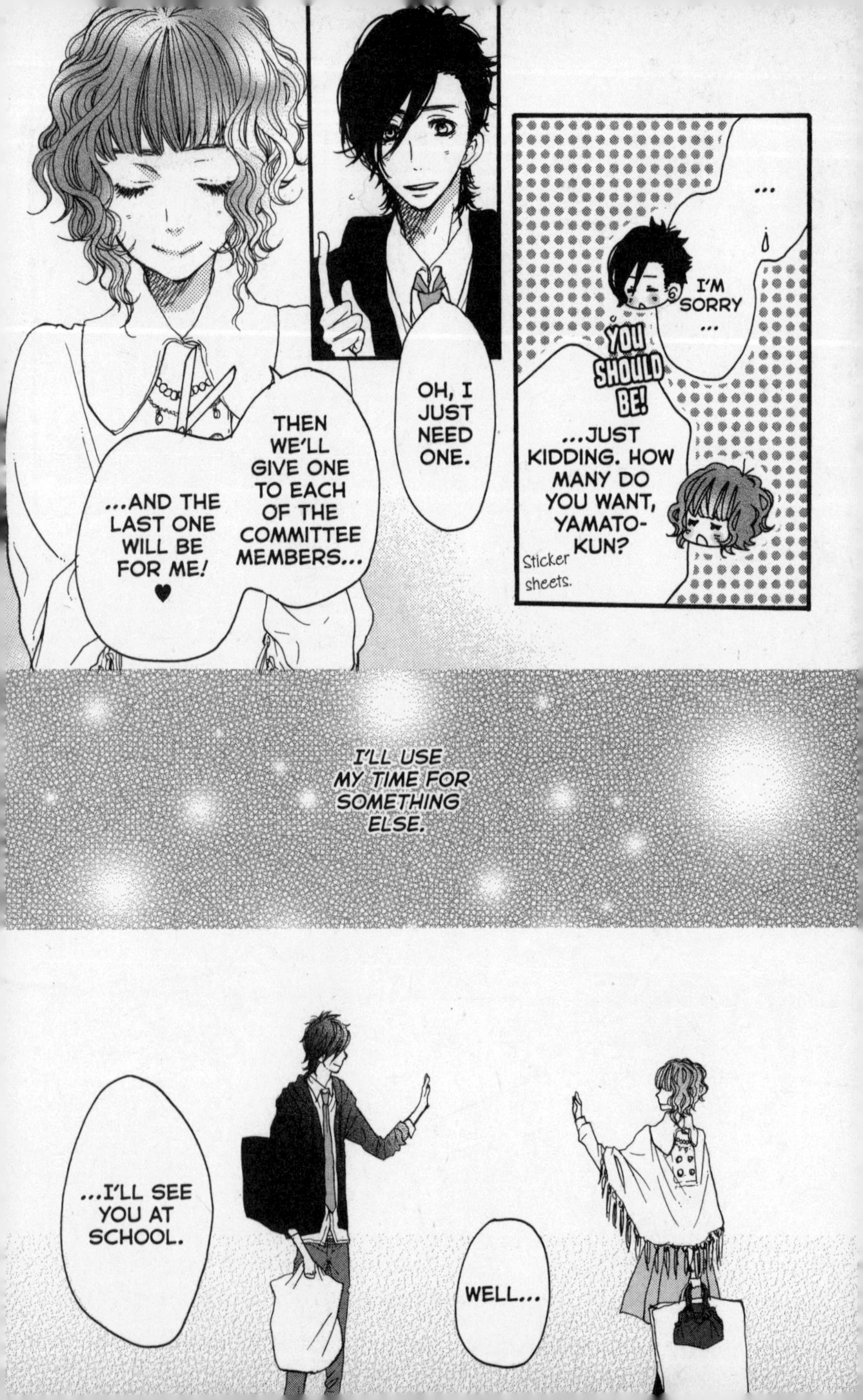
...
I'M SORRY...
YOU SHOULD BE!
...JUST KIDDING. HOW MANY DO YOU WANT, YAMATO-KUN?
Sticker sheets.
OH, I JUST NEED ONE.
THEN WE'LL GIVE ONE TO EACH OF THE COMMITTEE MEMBERS...
...AND THE LAST ONE WILL BE FOR ME! ♥
I'LL USE MY TIME FOR SOMETHING ELSE.
WELL...
...I'LL SEE YOU AT SCHOOL.

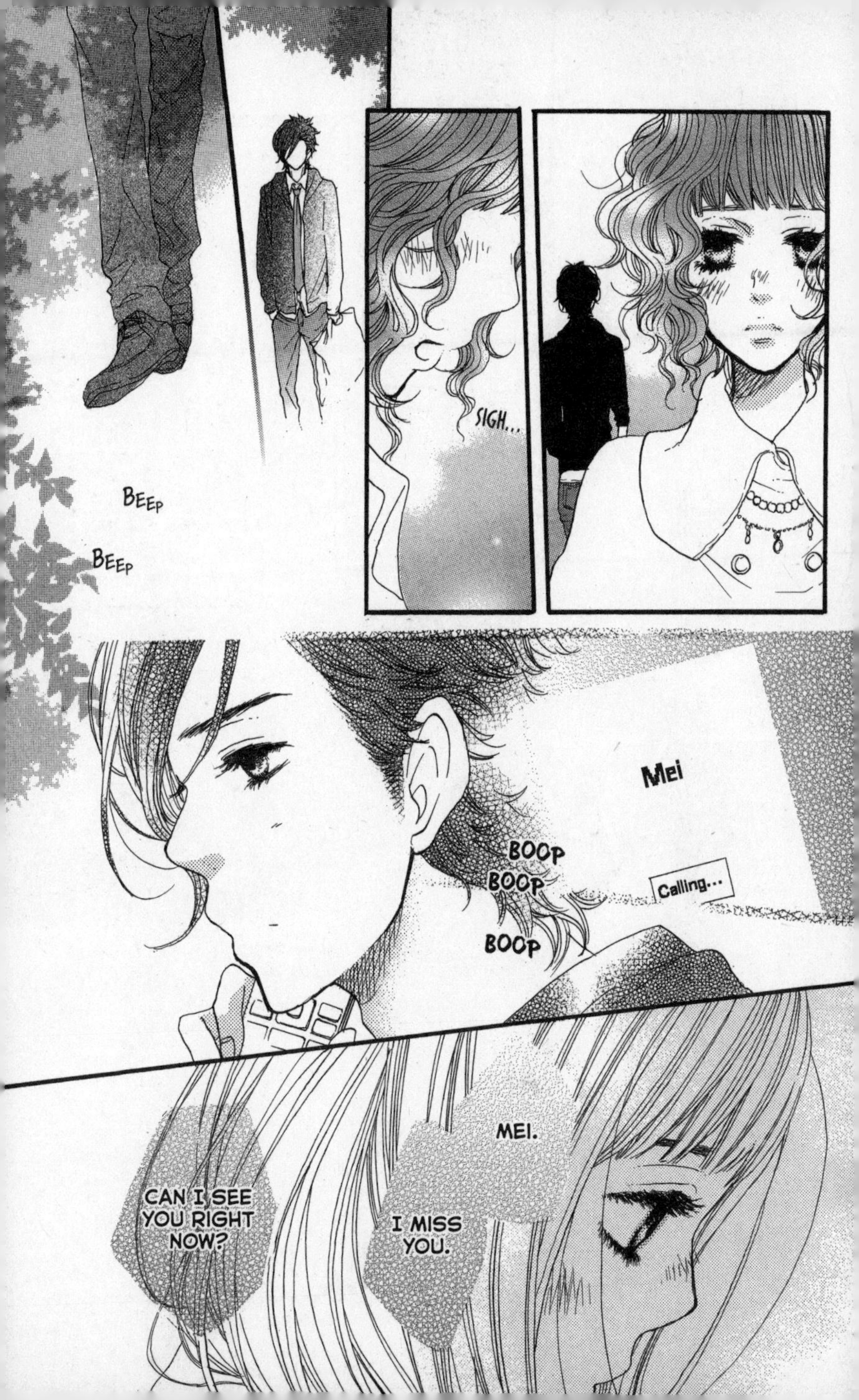
SIGH...
BEEP
BEEP
Mei
Calling...
BOOP
BOOP
BOOP
MEI.
I MISS YOU.
CAN I SEE YOU RIGHT NOW?

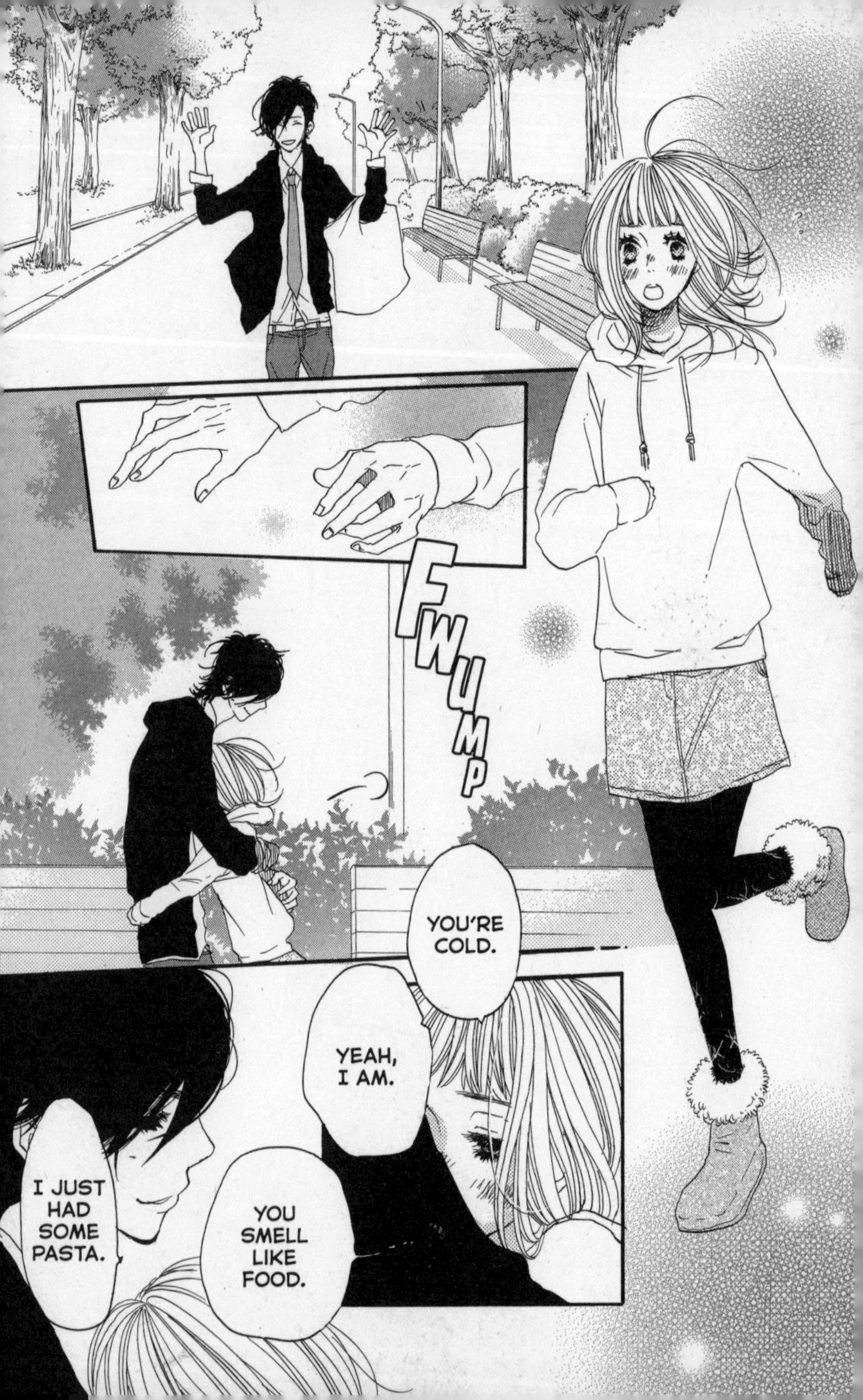
FWUMP
YOU'RE COLD.
YEAH, I AM.
YOU SMELL LIKE FOOD.
I JUST HAD SOME PASTA.

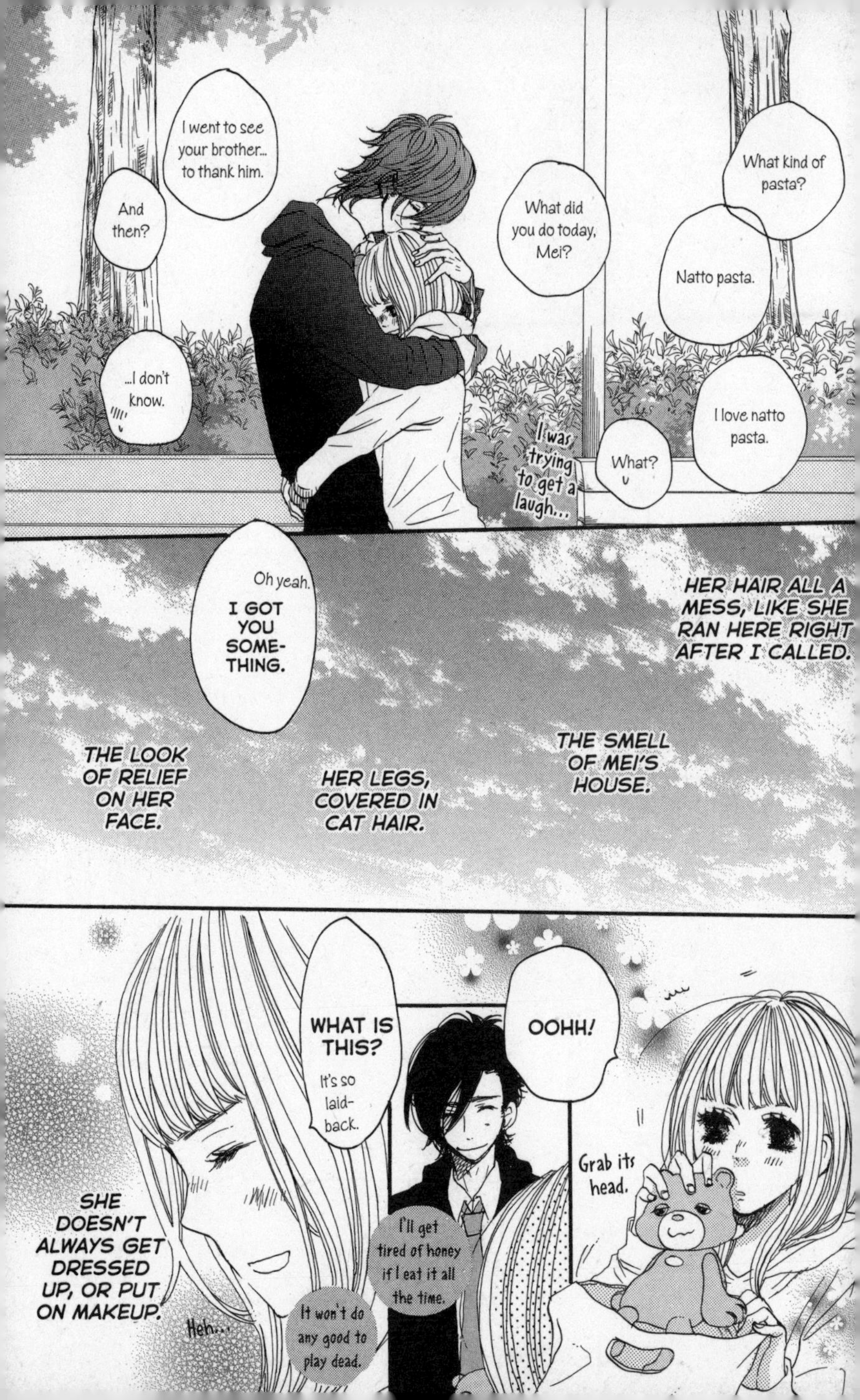
What kind of pasta?
Natto pasta.
I love natto pasta.
What?
I was trying to get a laugh...
What did you do today, Mei?
I went to see your brother... to thank him.
And then?
...I don't know.
HER HAIR ALL A MESS, LIKE SHE RAN HERE RIGHT AFTER I CALLED.
Oh yeah.
I GOT YOU SOMETHING.
THE SMELL OF MEI'S HOUSE.
HER LEGS, COVERED IN CAT HAIR.
THE LOOK OF RELIEF ON HER FACE.
OOHH!
Grab its head.
WHAT IS THIS?
It's so laid-back.
I'll get tired of honey if I eat it all the time.
It won't do any good to play dead.
SHE DOESN'T ALWAYS GET DRESSED UP, OR PUT ON MAKEUP.
Heh...

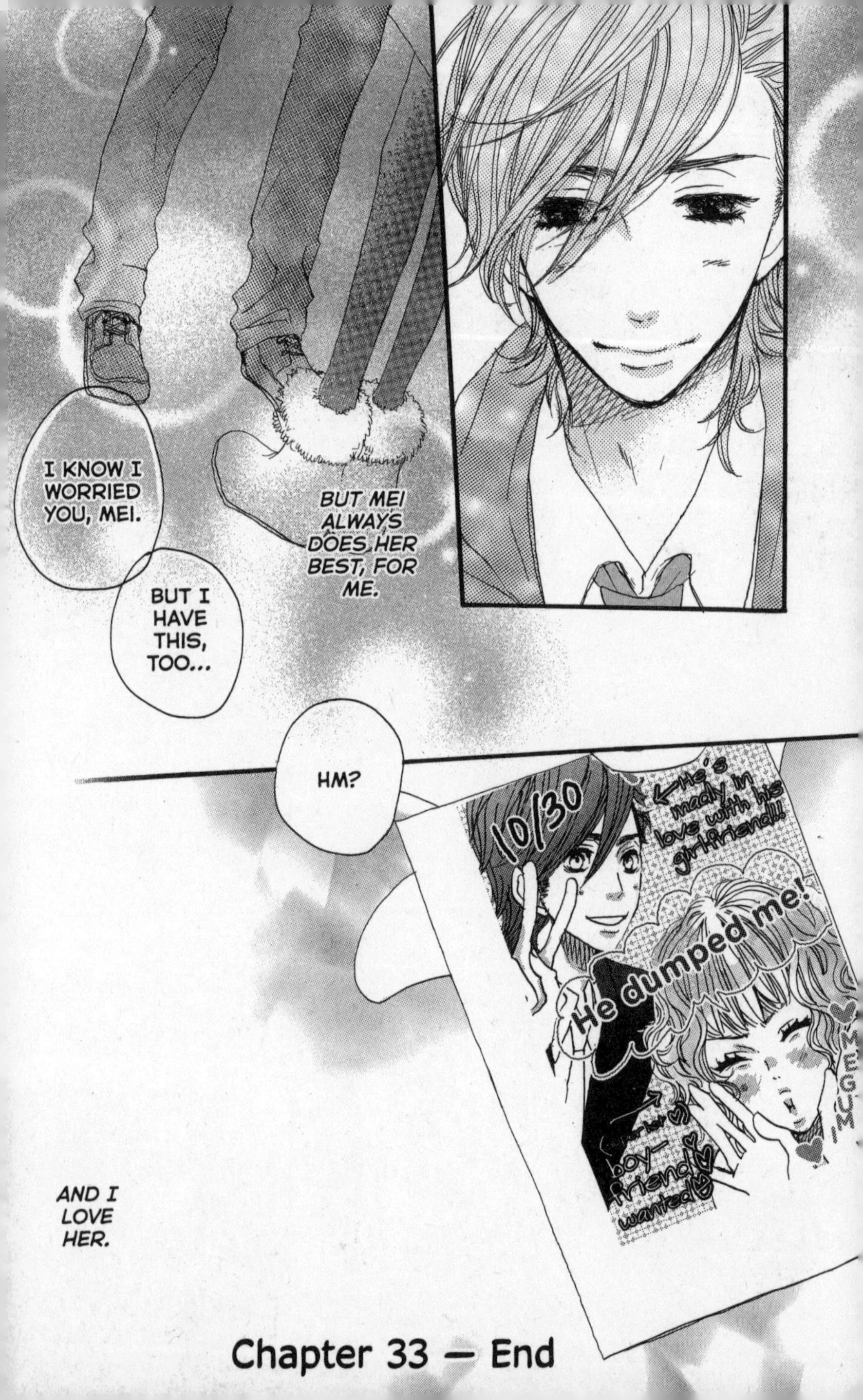
I KNOW I WORRIED YOU, MEI.
BUT MEI ALWAYS DOES HER BEST, FOR ME.
BUT I HAVE THIS, TOO...
HM?
10/30
←He's madly in love with his girlfriend!!!
He dumped me!
MEGUMI
boyfriend wanted
AND I LOVE HER.

Chapter 33 — End

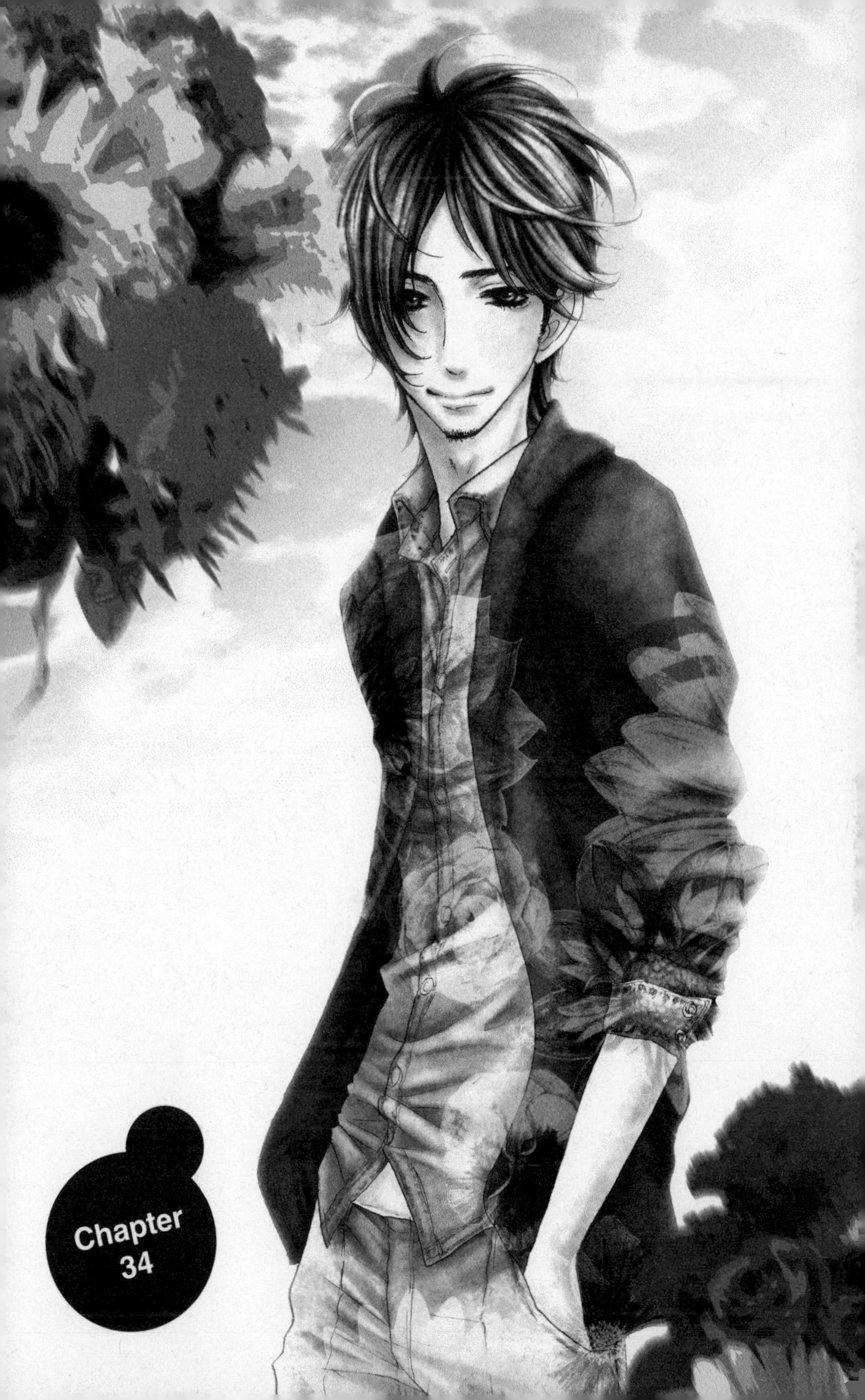
Chapter
34

can't say I LOVE YOU.

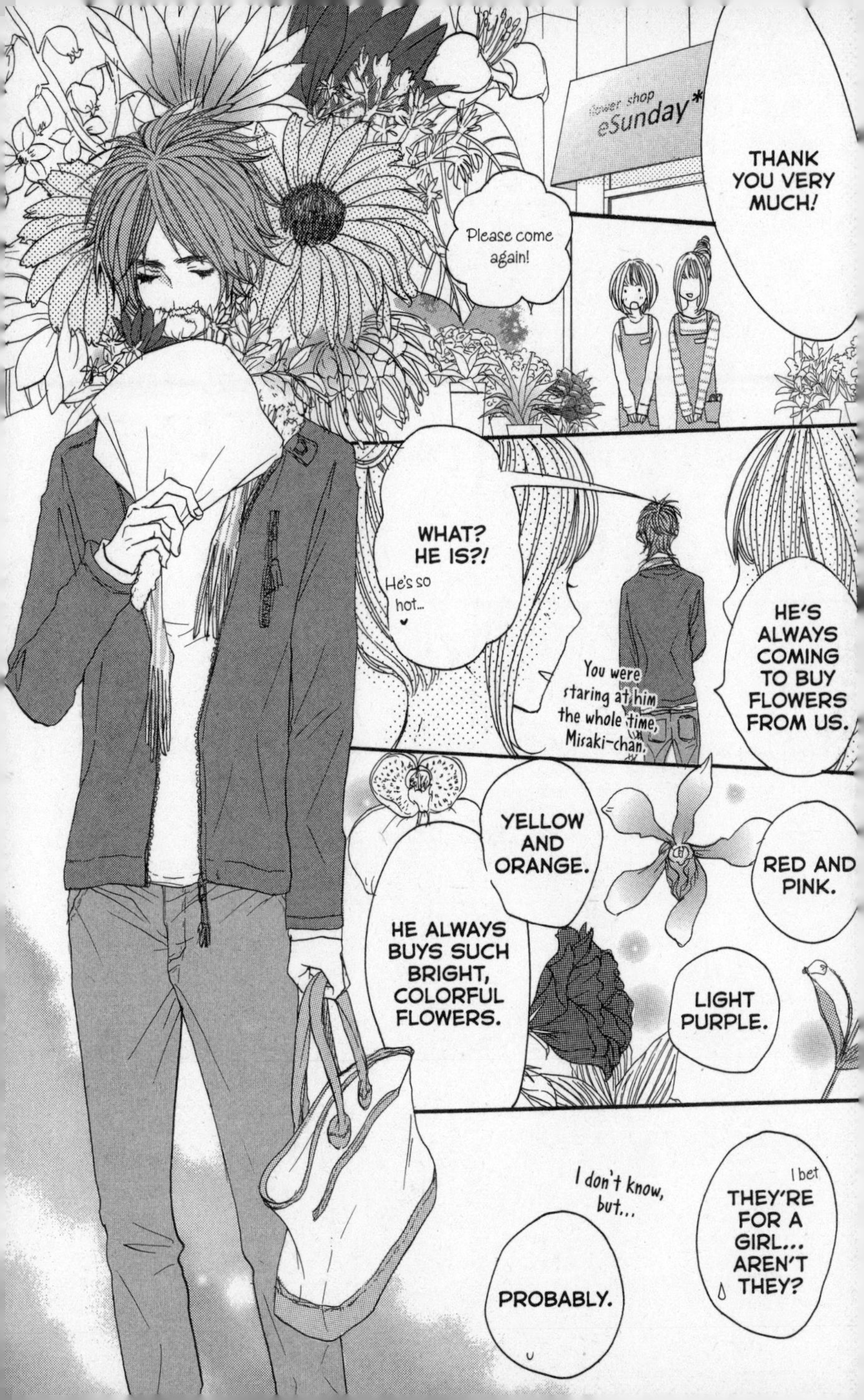
flower shop
eSunday*
THANK YOU VERY MUCH!
Please come again!
HE'S ALWAYS COMING TO BUY FLOWERS FROM US.
You were staring at him the whole time, Misaki-chan.
WHAT? HE IS?!
He's so hot...
RED AND PINK.
YELLOW AND ORANGE.
LIGHT PURPLE.
HE ALWAYS BUYS SUCH BRIGHT, COLORFUL FLOWERS.
I bet THEY'RE FOR A GIRL... AREN'T THEY?
I don't know, but...
PROBABLY.

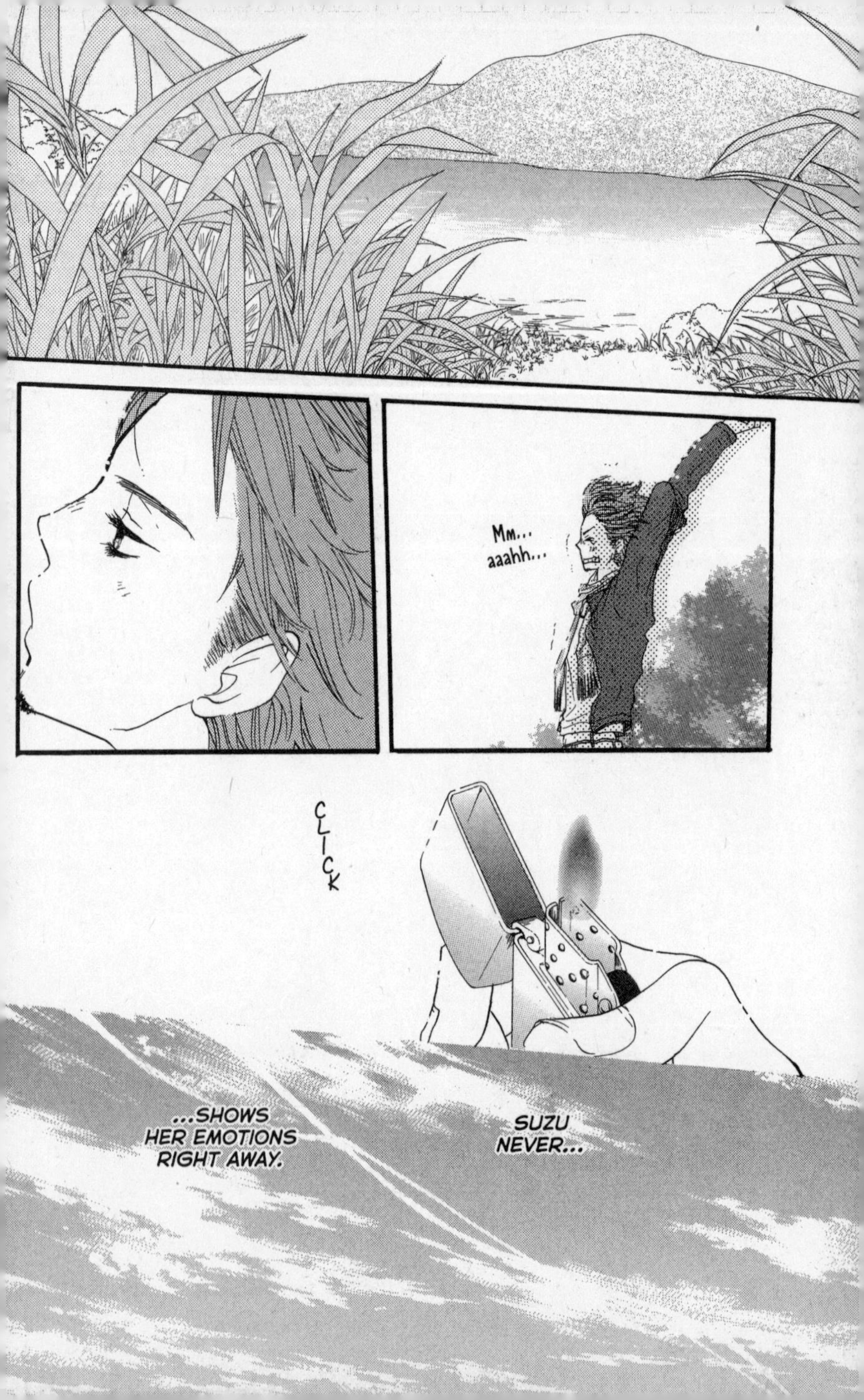
Mm... aaahh...
CLICK
SUZU NEVER...
...SHOWS HER EMOTIONS RIGHT AWAY.

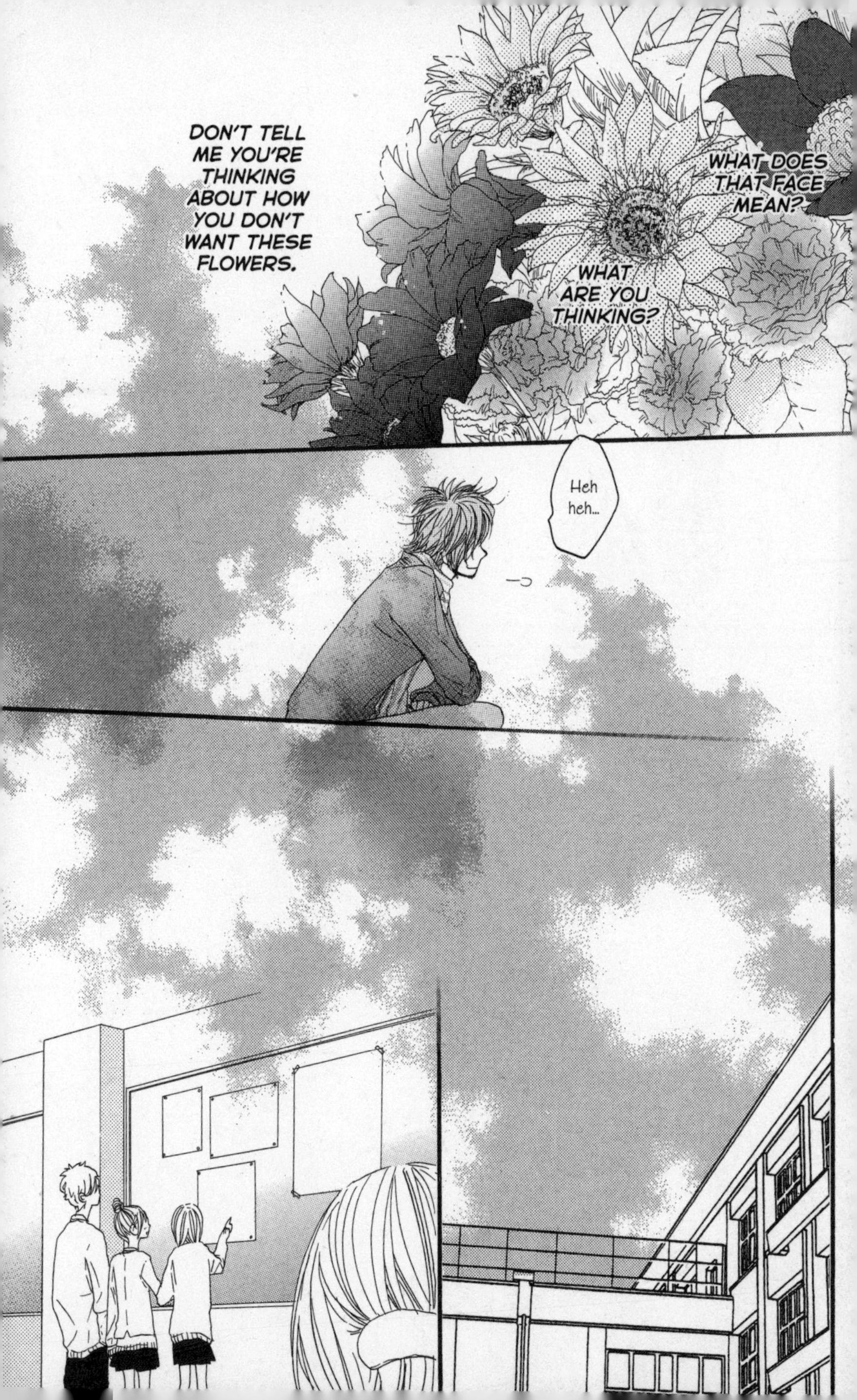
WHAT DOES THAT FACE MEAN?
WHAT ARE YOU THINKING?
DON'T TELL ME YOU'RE THINKING ABOUT HOW YOU DON'T WANT THESE FLOWERS.
Heh heh...

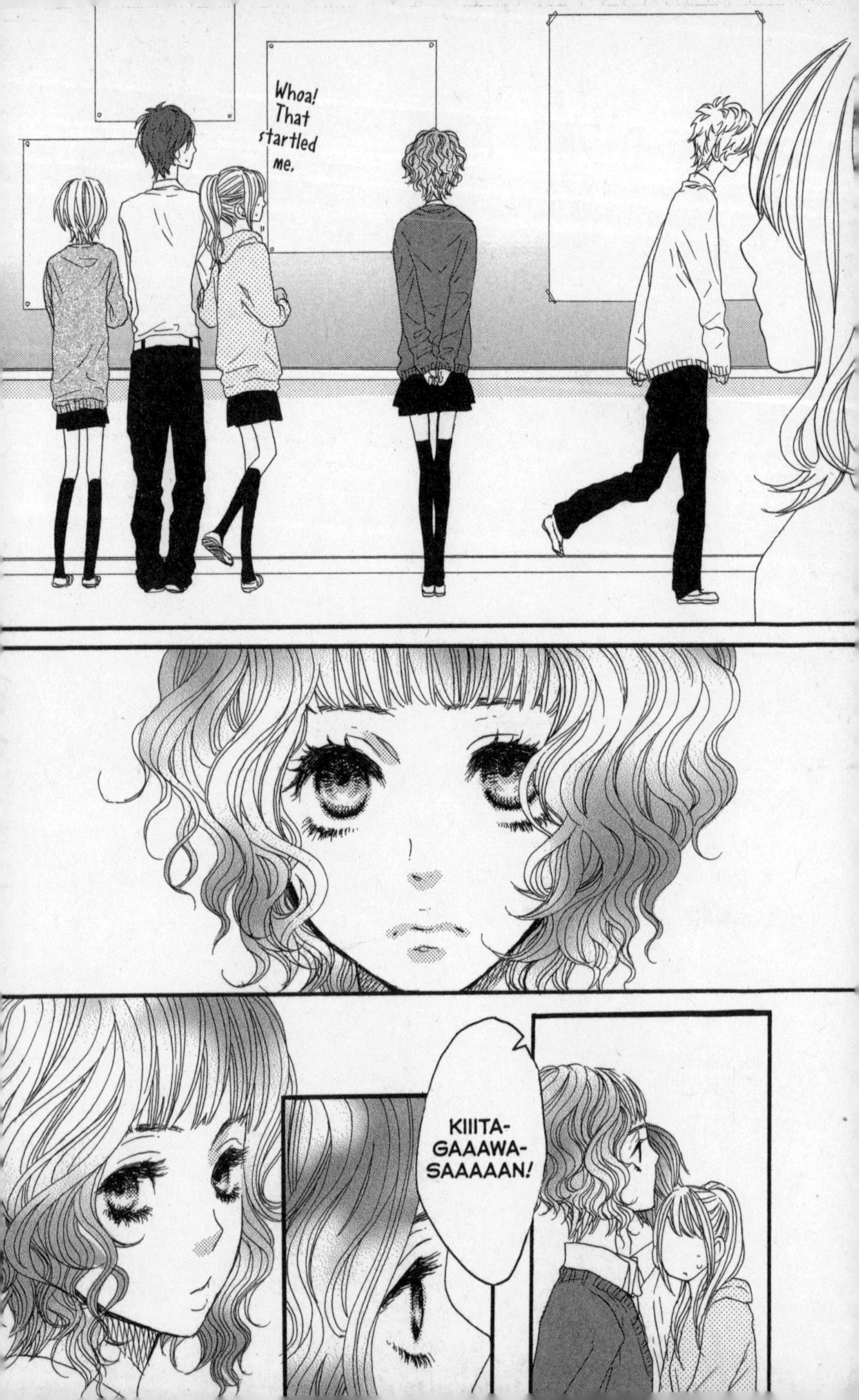
Whoa! That startled me.
KIIITA-GAAAWA-SAAAAAN!

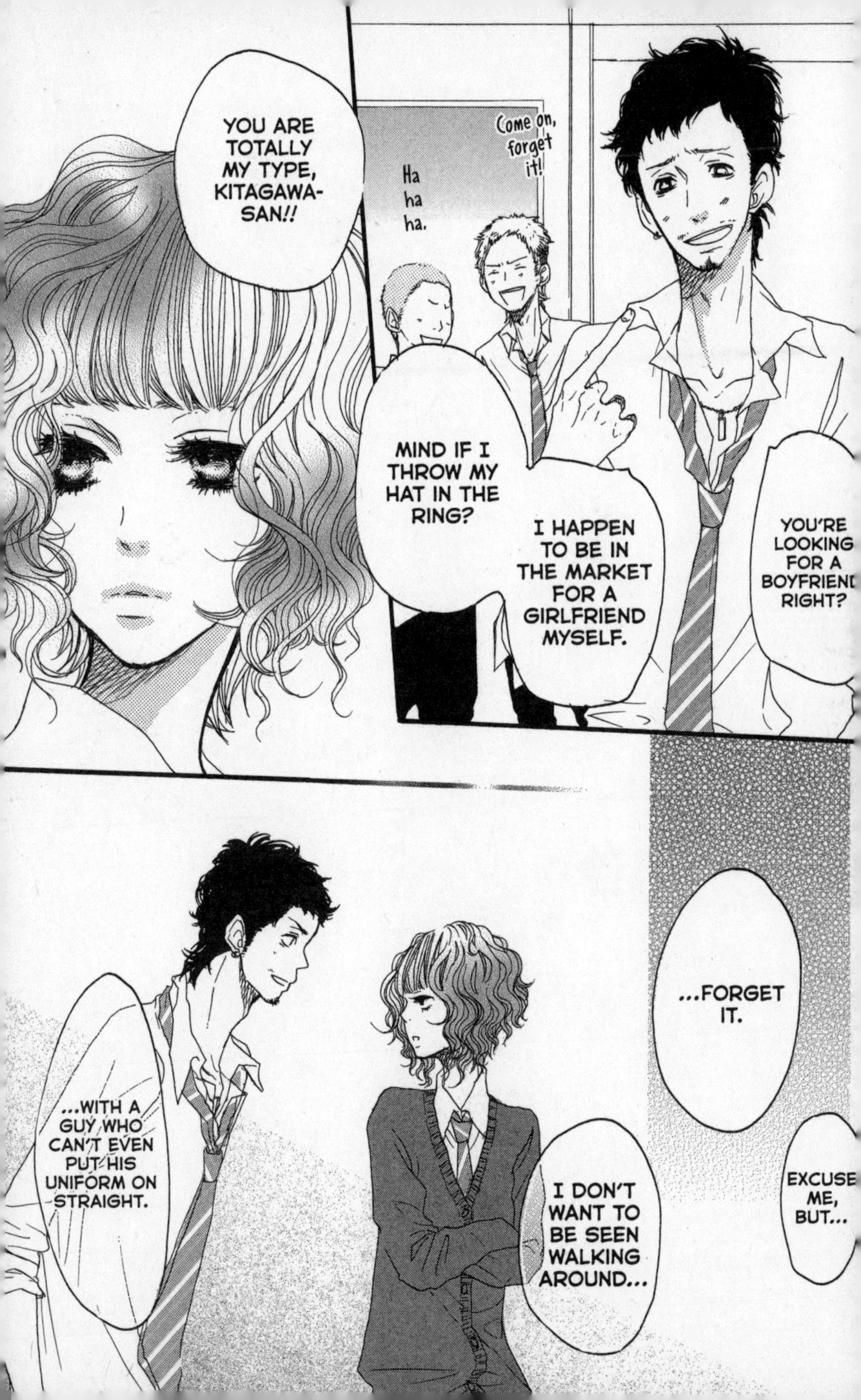
Come on, forget it!
Ha ha ha.
YOU'RE LOOKING FOR A BOYFRIEND RIGHT?
I HAPPEN TO BE IN THE MARKET FOR A GIRLFRIEND MYSELF.
MIND IF I THROW MY HAT IN THE RING?
YOU ARE TOTALLY MY TYPE, KITAGAWA-SAN!!
...FORGET IT.
EXCUSE ME, BUT...
I DON'T WANT TO BE SEEN WALKING AROUND...
...WITH A GUY WHO CAN'T EVEN PUT HIS UNIFORM ON STRAIGHT.

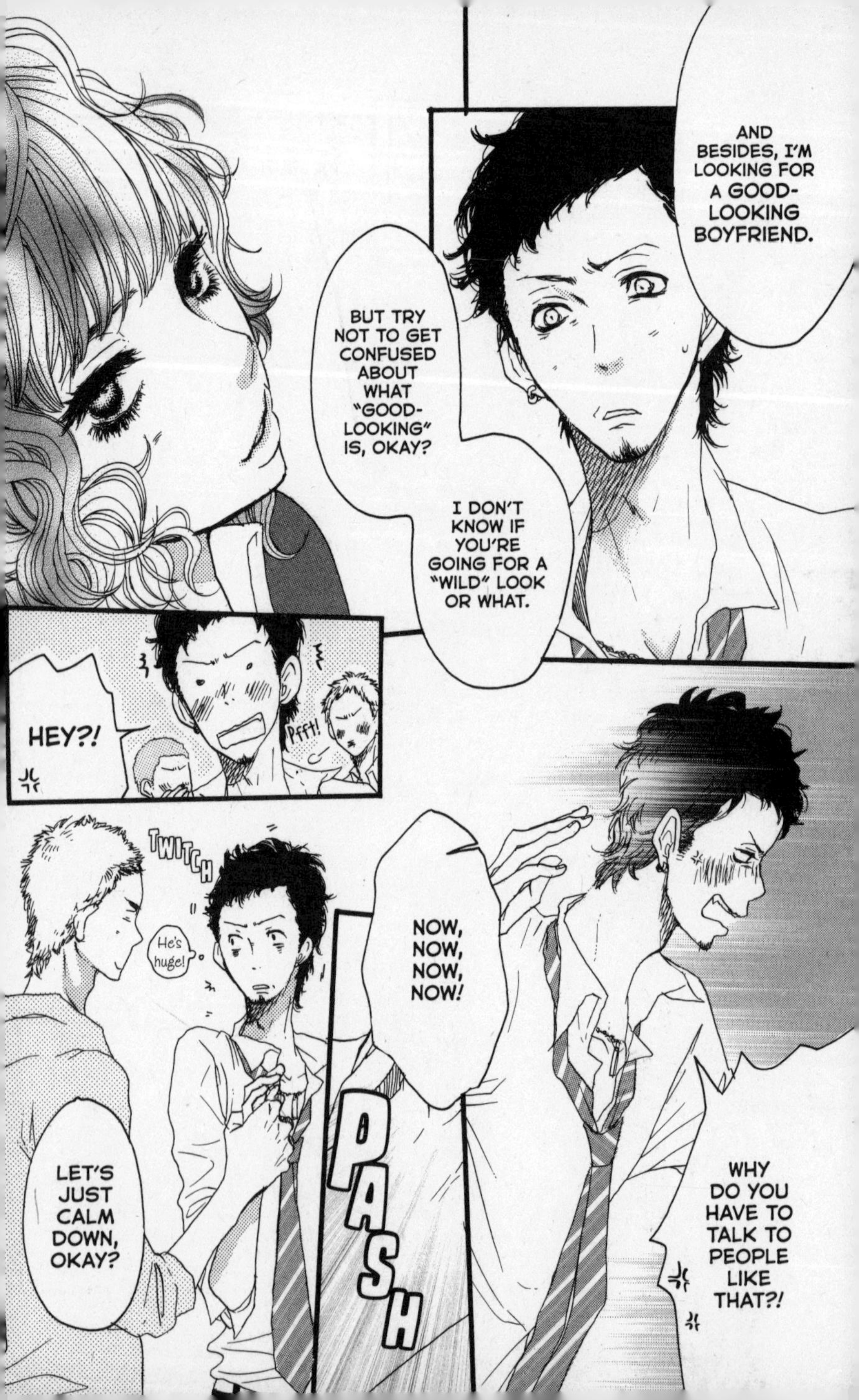
AND BESIDES, I'M LOOKING FOR A GOOD-LOOKING BOYFRIEND.
BUT TRY NOT TO GET CONFUSED ABOUT WHAT "GOOD-LOOKING" IS, OKAY?
I DON'T KNOW IF YOU'RE GOING FOR A "WILD" LOOK OR WHAT.
Pfft!
HEY?!
WHY DO YOU HAVE TO TALK TO PEOPLE LIKE THAT?!
NOW, NOW, NOW, NOW!
PASH
TWITCH
He's huge!
LET'S JUST CALM DOWN, OKAY?

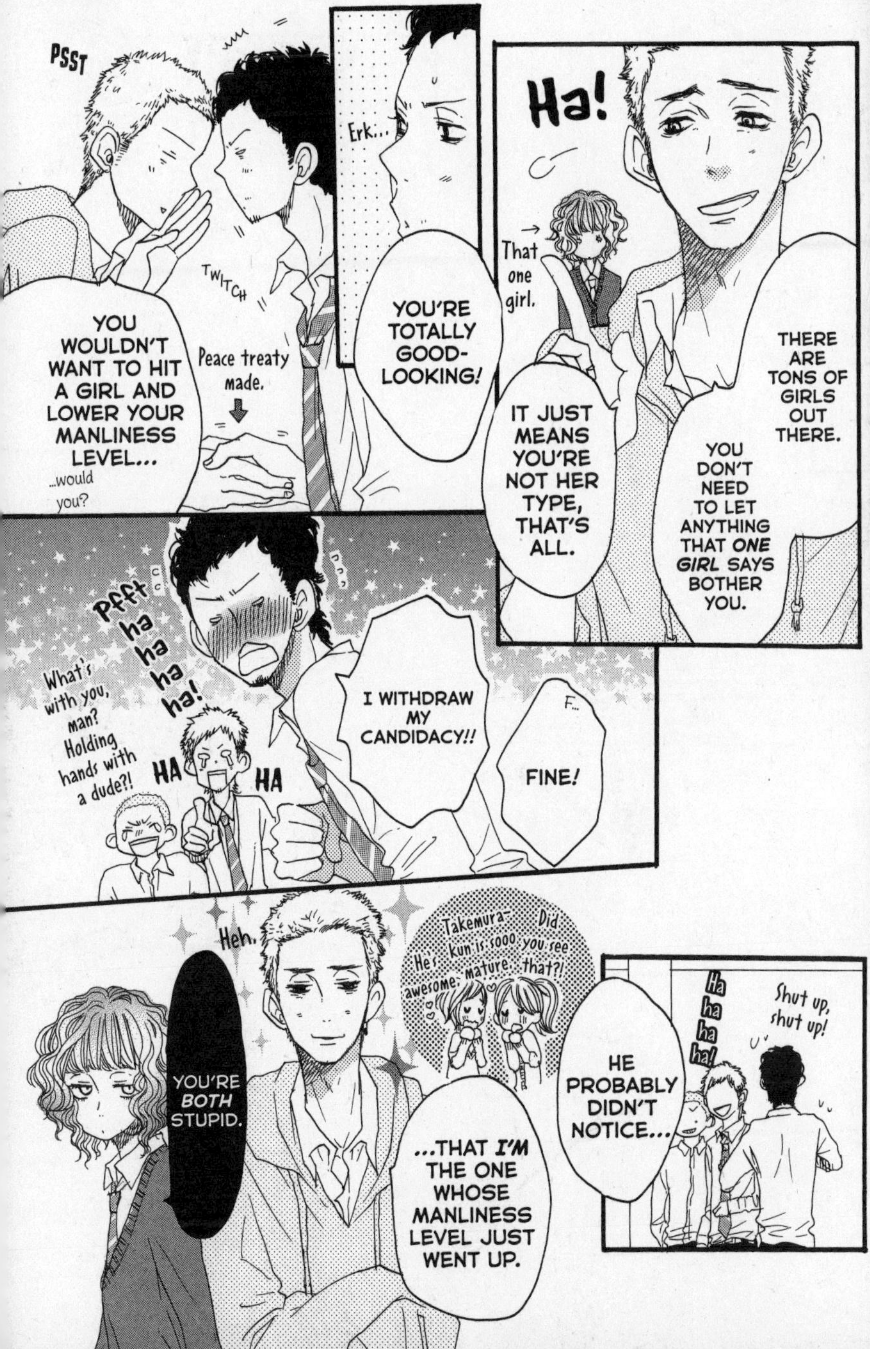
Ha!
That one girl.
THERE ARE TONS OF GIRLS OUT THERE.
YOU DON'T NEED TO LET ANYTHING THAT *ONE GIRL* SAYS BOTHER YOU.
IT JUST MEANS YOU'RE NOT HER TYPE, THAT'S ALL.
Erk...
YOU'RE TOTALLY GOOD-LOOKING!
PSST
YOU WOULDN'T WANT TO HIT A GIRL AND LOWER YOUR MANLINESS LEVEL...
...would you?
TWITCH
Peace treaty made.
F...
FINE!
I WITHDRAW MY CANDIDACY!!
Pfft ha ha ha ha!
What's with you, man? Holding hands with a dude?!
HA
HA
Shut up, shut up!
Ha ha ha ha!
HE PROBABLY DIDN'T NOTICE...
...THAT *I'M* THE ONE WHOSE MANLINESS LEVEL JUST WENT UP.
Heh.
Did you see that?!
Takemura-kun is sooo mature
He's awesome
YOU'RE *BOTH* STUPID.

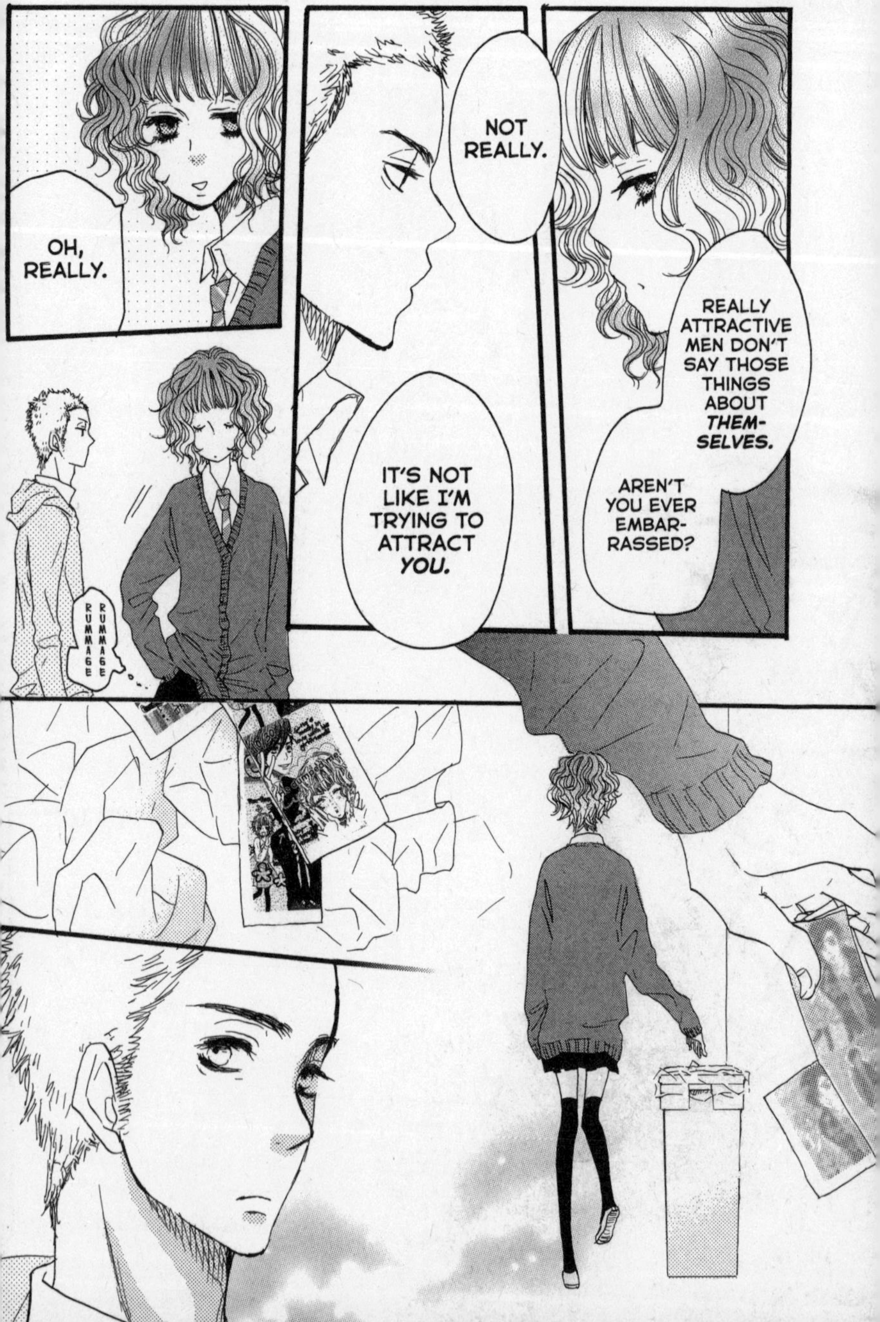
REALLY ATTRACTIVE MEN DON'T SAY THOSE THINGS ABOUT *THEMSELVES.*
AREN'T YOU EVER EMBARRASSED?
NOT REALLY.
IT'S NOT LIKE I'M TRYING TO ATTRACT *YOU.*
OH, REALLY.
RUMMAGE RUMMAGE

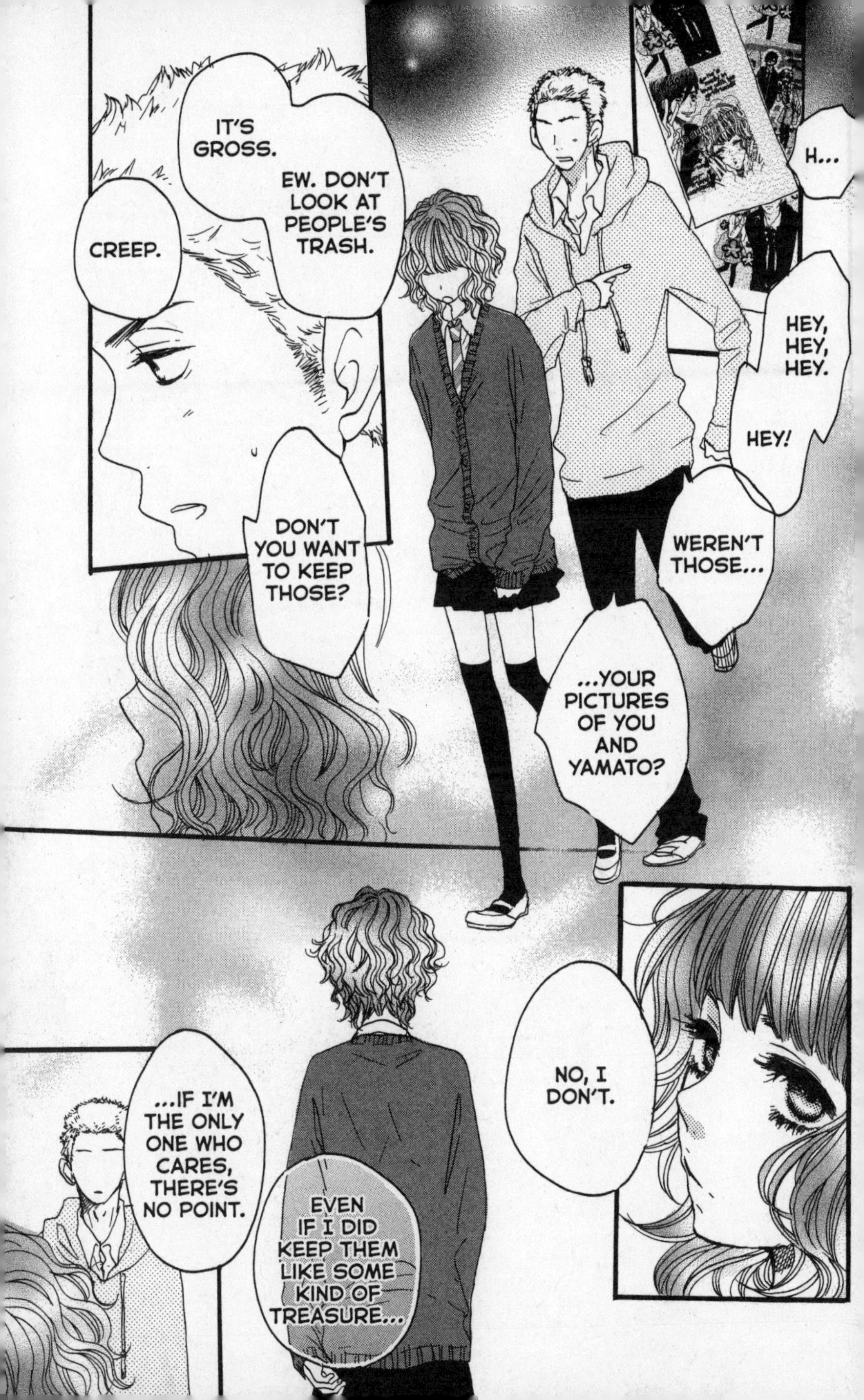
H...
HEY, HEY, HEY.
HEY!
WEREN'T THOSE...
...YOUR PICTURES OF YOU AND YAMATO?
DON'T YOU WANT TO KEEP THOSE?
IT'S GROSS.
EW. DON'T LOOK AT PEOPLE'S TRASH.
CREEP.
NO, I DON'T.
EVEN IF I DID KEEP THEM LIKE SOME KIND OF TREASURE...
...IF I'M THE ONLY ONE WHO CARES, THERE'S NO POINT.

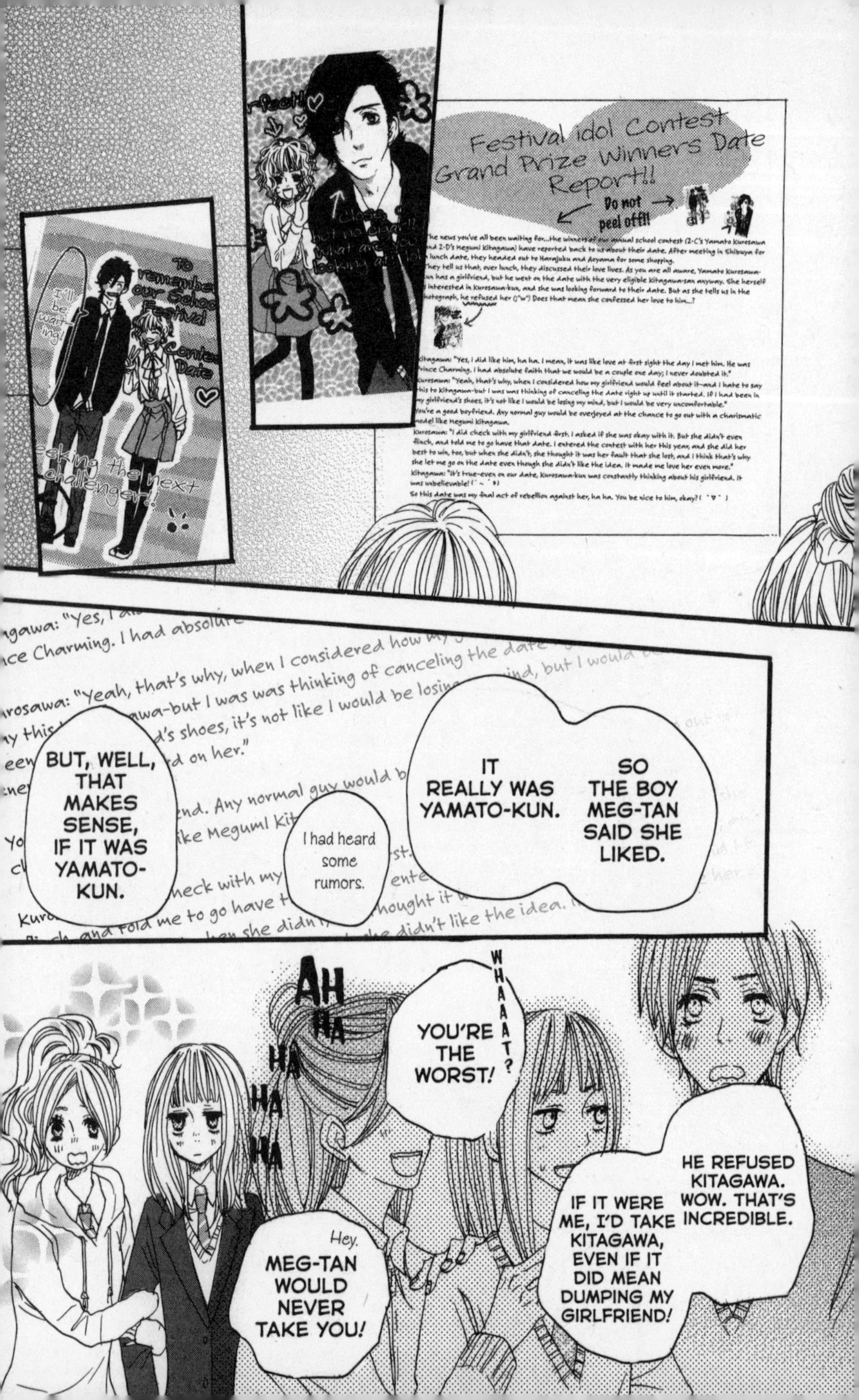
Festival idol Contest Grand Prize Winners Date Report!!
Do not peel off!!
he news you've all been waiting for...the winners of our annual school contest (2-C's Yamato Kurosawa nd 2-D's Megumi Kitagawa) have reported back to us about their date. After meeting in Shibuya for lunch date, they headed out to Harajuku and Aoyama for some shopping.
hey tell us that, over lunch, they discussed their love lives. As you are all aware, Yamato Kurosawa-un has a girlfriend, but he went on the date with the very eligible Kitagawa-san anyway. She herself interested in Kurosawa-kun, and she was looking forward to their date. But as she tells us in the hotograph, he refused her (;^w^) Does that mean she confessed her love to him...?
itagawa: "Yes, I did like him, ha ha. I mean, it was like love at first sight the day I met him. He was rince Charming. I had absolute faith that we would be a couple one day; I never doubted it."
urosawa: "Yeah, that's why, when I considered how my girlfriend would feel about it—and I hate to say his to Kitagawa—but I was was thinking of canceling the date right up until it started. If I had been in y girlfriend's shoes, it's not like I would be losing my mind, but I would be very uncomfortable."
ou're a good boyfriend. Any normal guy would be overjoyed at the chance to go out with a charismatic odel like Megumi Kitagawa.
Kurosawa: "I did check with my girlfriend first. I asked if she was okay with it. But she didn't even flinch, and told me to go have that date. I entered the contest with her this year, and she did her best to win, too, but when she didn't, she thought it was her fault that she lost, and I think that's why she let me go on the date even though she didn't like the idea. It made me love her even more."
Kitagawa: "It's true—even on our date, Kurosawa-kun was constantly thinking about his girlfriend. It was unbelievable!
So this date was my final act of rebellion against her, ha ha. You be nice to him, okay?
To remember our School Festival Contest Date
I'll be waiting!
eeking the next challenger!!
SO THE BOY MEG-TAN SAID SHE LIKED.
IT REALLY WAS YAMATO-KUN.
I had heard some rumors.
BUT, WELL, THAT MAKES SENSE, IF IT WAS YAMATO-KUN.
HE REFUSED KITAGAWA. WOW. THAT'S INCREDIBLE.
IF IT WERE ME, I'D TAKE KITAGAWA, EVEN IF IT DID MEAN DUMPING MY GIRLFRIEND!
WHAAAT?
YOU'RE THE WORST!
AH HA HA HA HA
Hey.
MEG-TAN WOULD NEVER TAKE YOU!

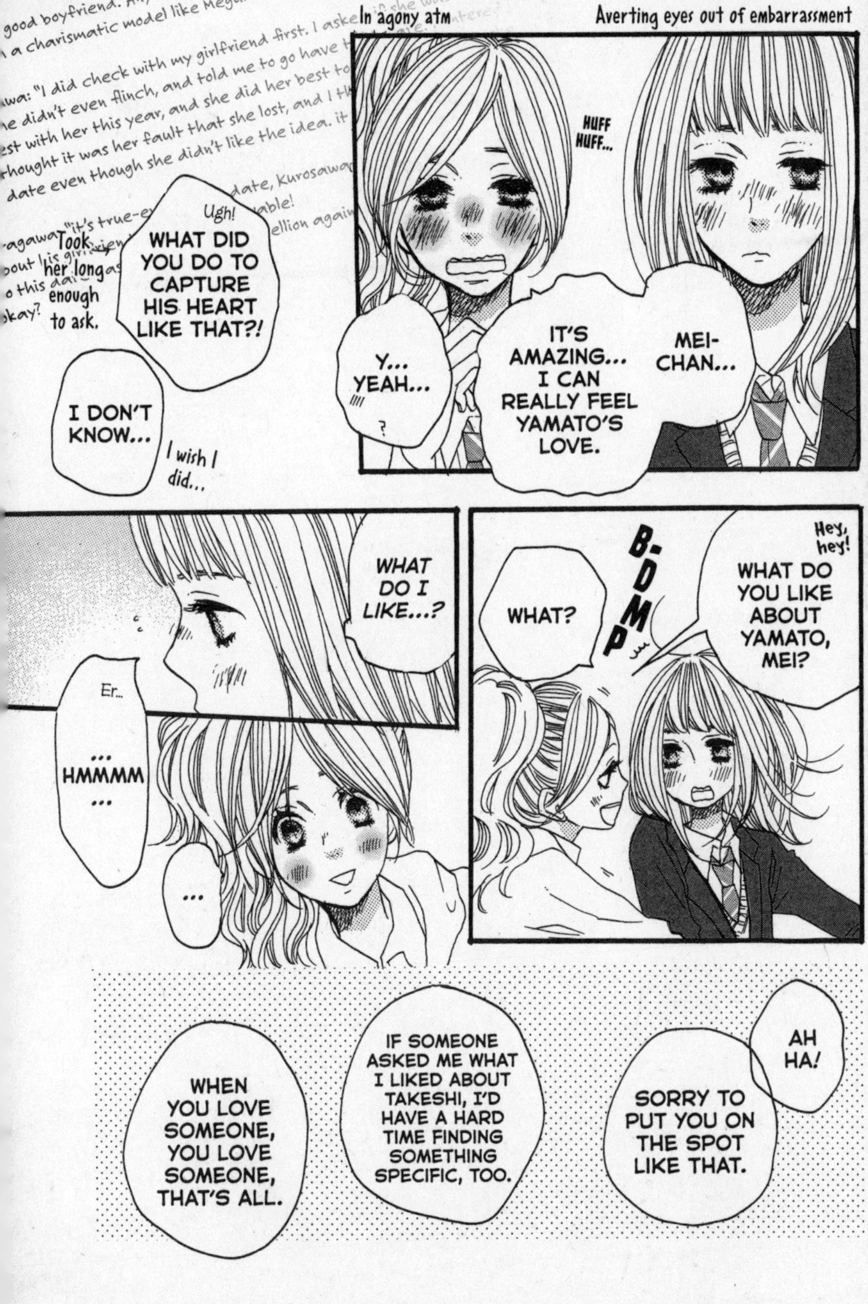
Averting eyes out of embarrassment
In agony atm
MEI-CHAN...
IT'S AMAZING... I CAN REALLY FEEL YAMATO'S LOVE.
HUFF HUFF...
Y... YEAH...
Ugh!
WHAT DID YOU DO TO CAPTURE HIS HEART LIKE THAT?!
Took her long enough to ask.
I DON'T KNOW...
I wish I did...
Hey, hey!
WHAT DO YOU LIKE ABOUT YAMATO, MEI?
B-DMP
WHAT?
WHAT DO I LIKE...?
Er...
... HMMMM ...
...
AH HA!
SORRY TO PUT YOU ON THE SPOT LIKE THAT.
IF SOMEONE ASKED ME WHAT I LIKED ABOUT TAKESHI, I'D HAVE A HARD TIME FINDING SOMETHING SPECIFIC, TOO.
WHEN YOU LOVE SOMEONE, YOU LOVE SOMEONE, THAT'S ALL.

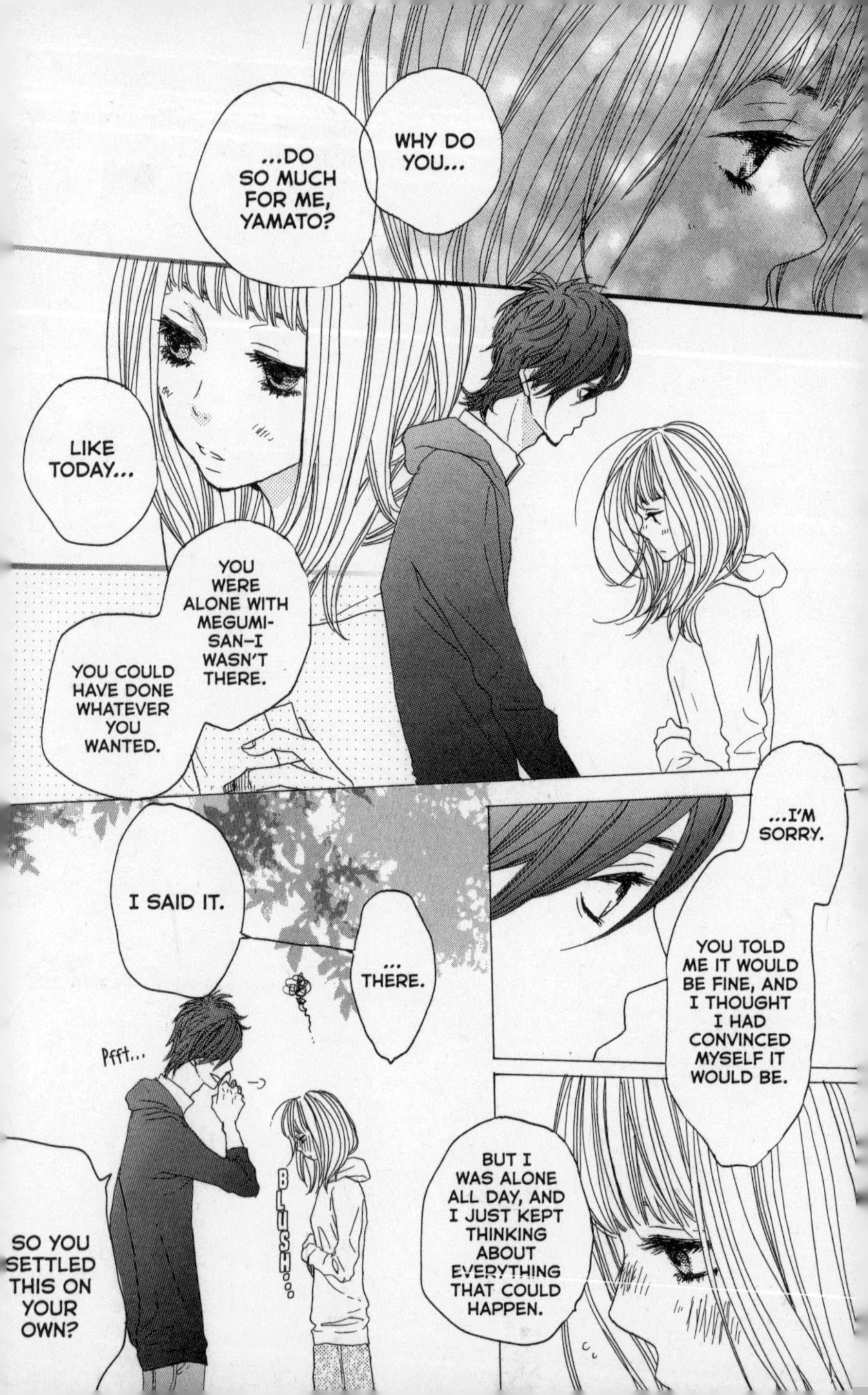
WHY DO YOU...
...DO SO MUCH FOR ME, YAMATO?
LIKE TODAY...
YOU WERE ALONE WITH MEGUMI-SAN—I WASN'T THERE.
YOU COULD HAVE DONE WHATEVER YOU WANTED.
...I'M SORRY.
YOU TOLD ME IT WOULD BE FINE, AND I THOUGHT I HAD CONVINCED MYSELF IT WOULD BE.
BUT I WAS ALONE ALL DAY, AND I JUST KEPT THINKING ABOUT EVERYTHING THAT COULD HAPPEN.
I SAID IT.
... THERE.
Pfft...
BLUSH...
SO YOU SETTLED THIS ON YOUR OWN?

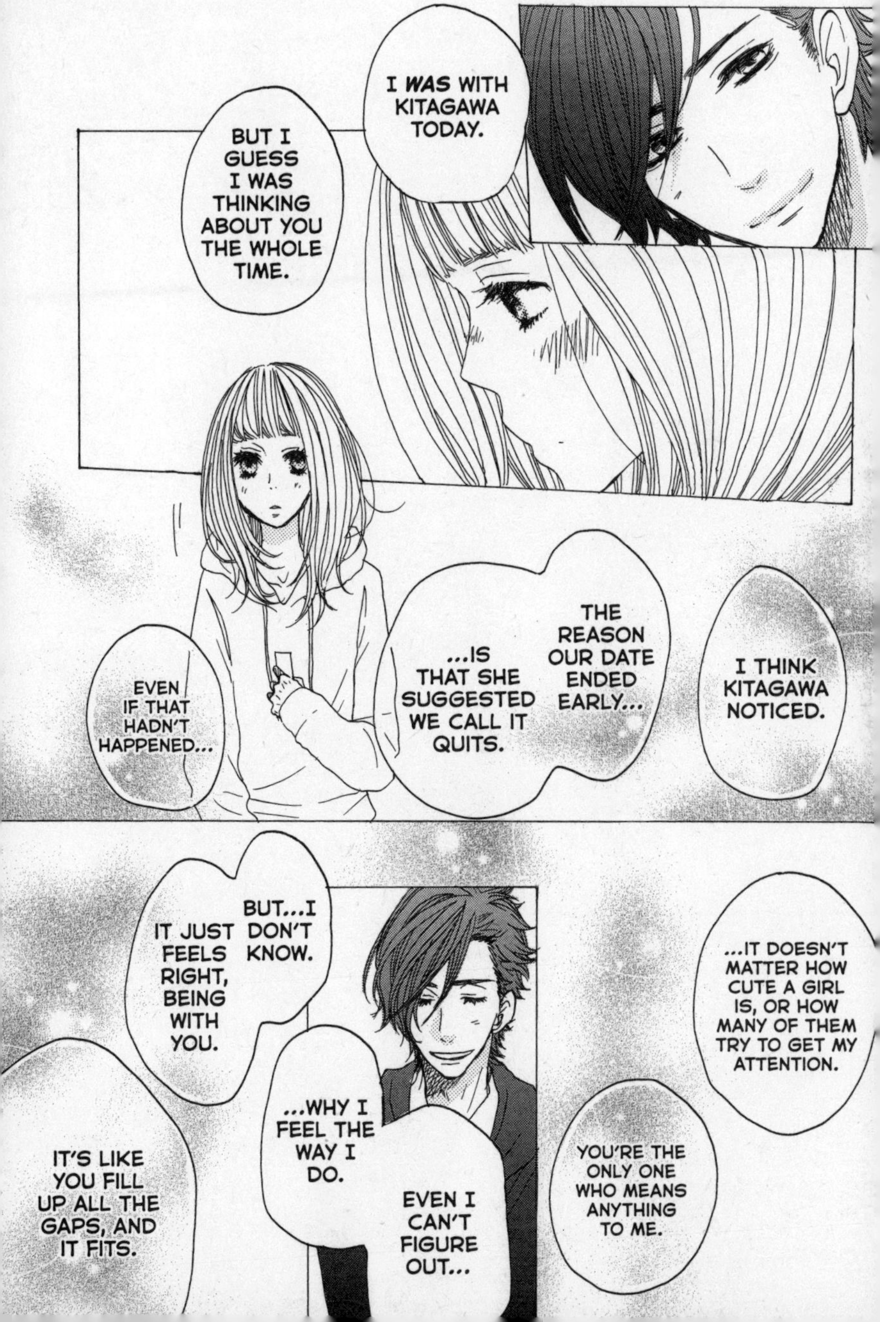
I *WAS* WITH KITAGAWA TODAY.
BUT I GUESS I WAS THINKING ABOUT YOU THE WHOLE TIME.
I THINK KITAGAWA NOTICED.
THE REASON OUR DATE ENDED EARLY...
...IS THAT SHE SUGGESTED WE CALL IT QUITS.
EVEN IF THAT HADN'T HAPPENED...
...IT DOESN'T MATTER HOW CUTE A GIRL IS, OR HOW MANY OF THEM TRY TO GET MY ATTENTION.
YOU'RE THE ONLY ONE WHO MEANS ANYTHING TO ME.
BUT...I DON'T KNOW.
IT JUST FEELS RIGHT, BEING WITH YOU.
EVEN I CAN'T FIGURE OUT...
...WHY I FEEL THE WAY I DO.
IT'S LIKE YOU FILL UP ALL THE GAPS, AND IT FITS.

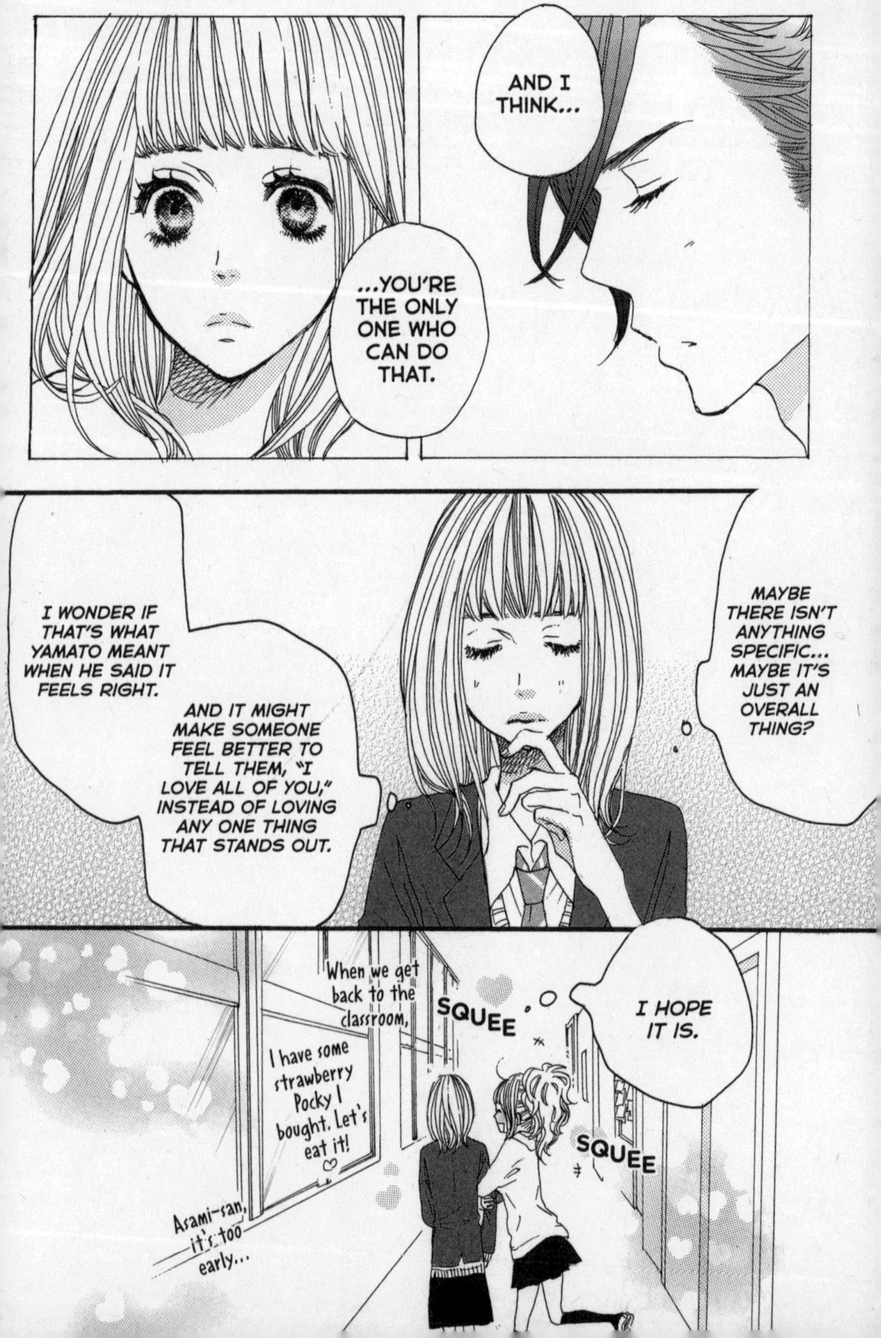
AND I THINK...
...YOU'RE THE ONLY ONE WHO CAN DO THAT.
MAYBE THERE ISN'T ANYTHING SPECIFIC... MAYBE IT'S JUST AN OVERALL THING?
I WONDER IF THAT'S WHAT YAMATO MEANT WHEN HE SAID IT FEELS RIGHT.
AND IT MIGHT MAKE SOMEONE FEEL BETTER TO TELL THEM, "I LOVE ALL OF YOU," INSTEAD OF LOVING ANY ONE THING THAT STANDS OUT.
I HOPE IT IS.
SQUEE
SQUEE
When we get back to the classroom,
I have some strawberry Pocky I bought. Let's eat it!
Asami-san, it's too early...

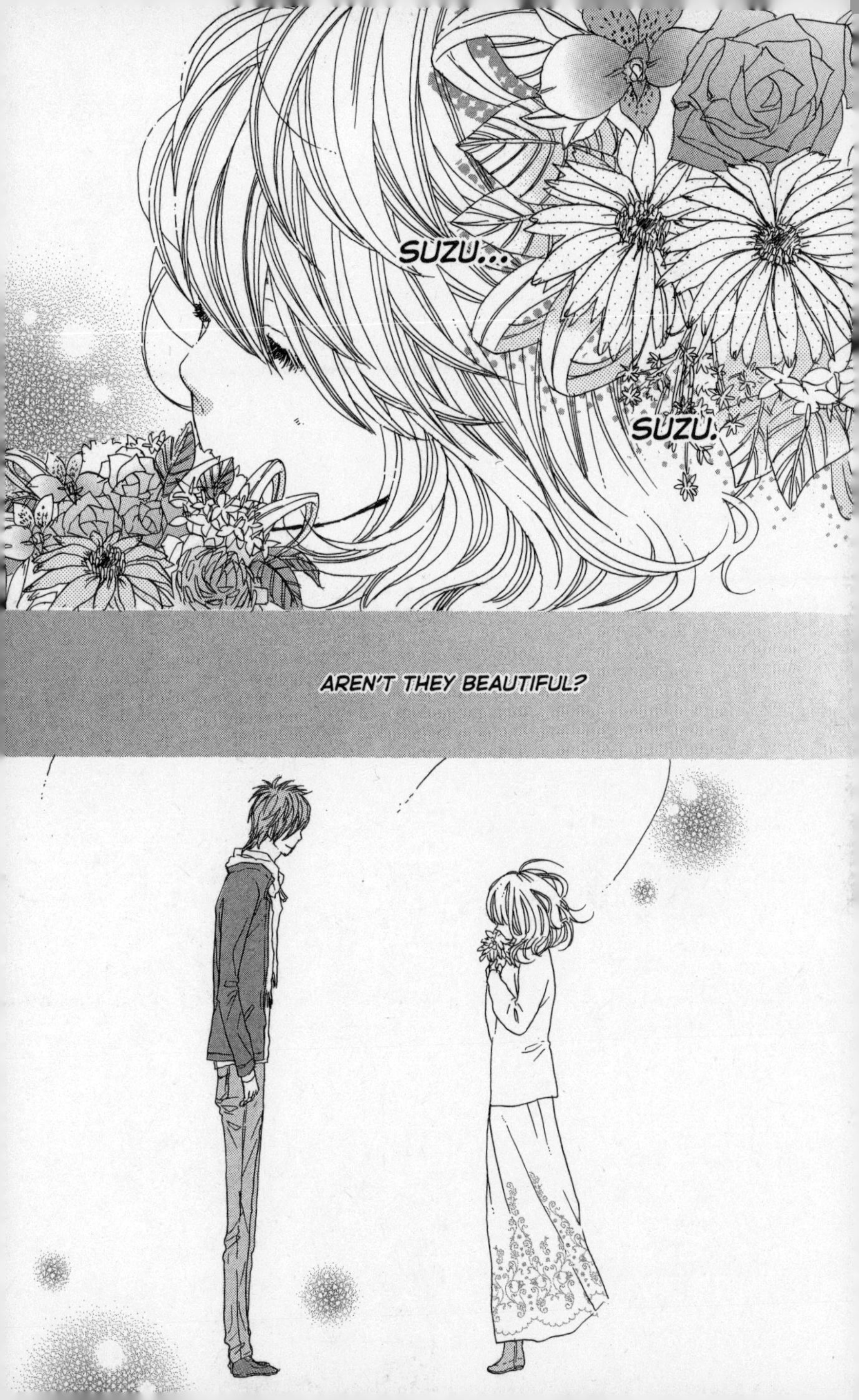
SUZU...
SUZU.
AREN'T THEY BEAUTIFUL?

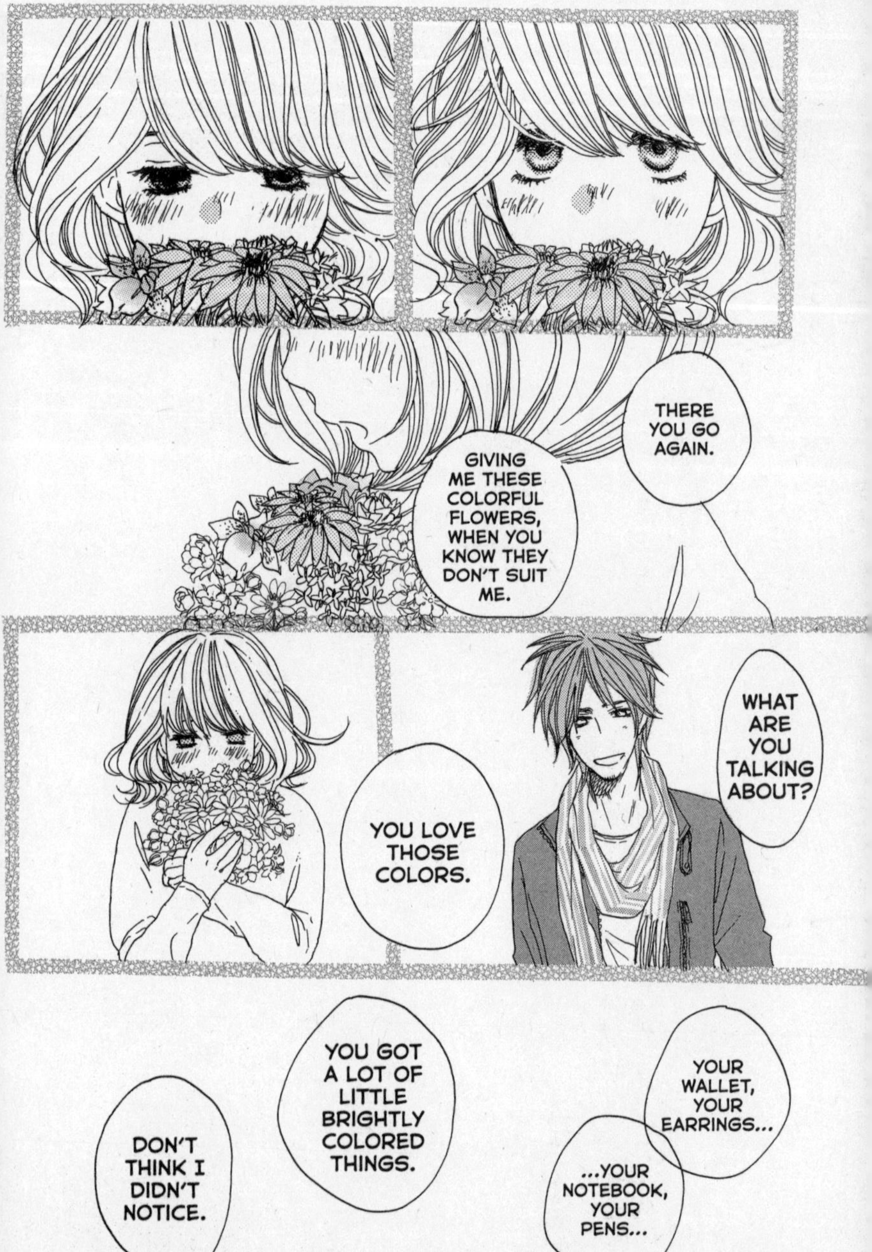
THERE YOU GO AGAIN.
GIVING ME THESE COLORFUL FLOWERS, WHEN YOU KNOW THEY DON'T SUIT ME.
WHAT ARE YOU TALKING ABOUT?
YOU LOVE THOSE COLORS.
YOUR WALLET, YOUR EARRINGS...
...YOUR NOTEBOOK, YOUR PENS...
YOU GOT A LOT OF LITTLE BRIGHTLY COLORED THINGS.
DON'T THINK I DIDN'T NOTICE.

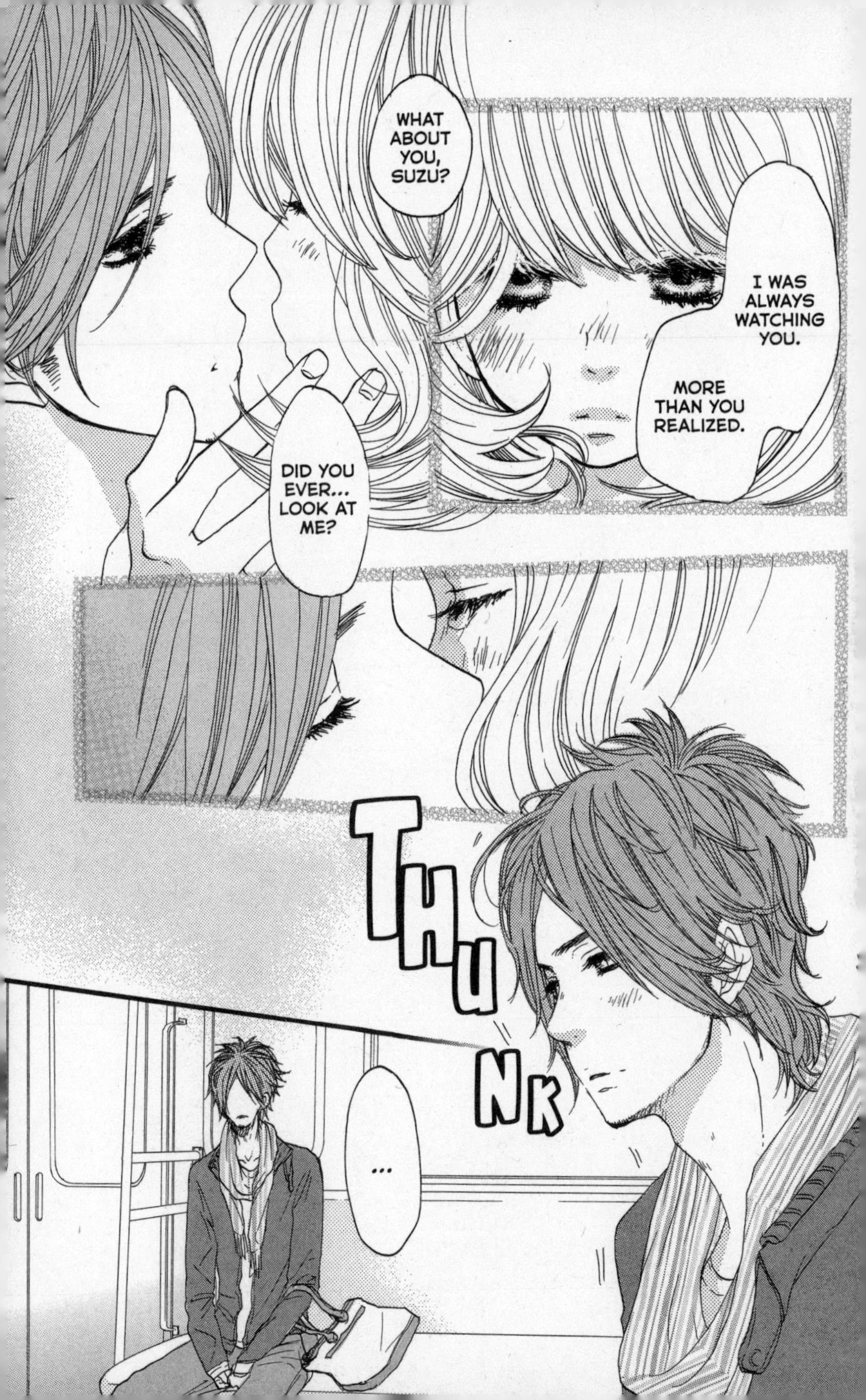
I WAS ALWAYS WATCHING YOU.
MORE THAN YOU REALIZED.
WHAT ABOUT YOU, SUZU?
DID YOU EVER... LOOK AT ME?
THUNK
...

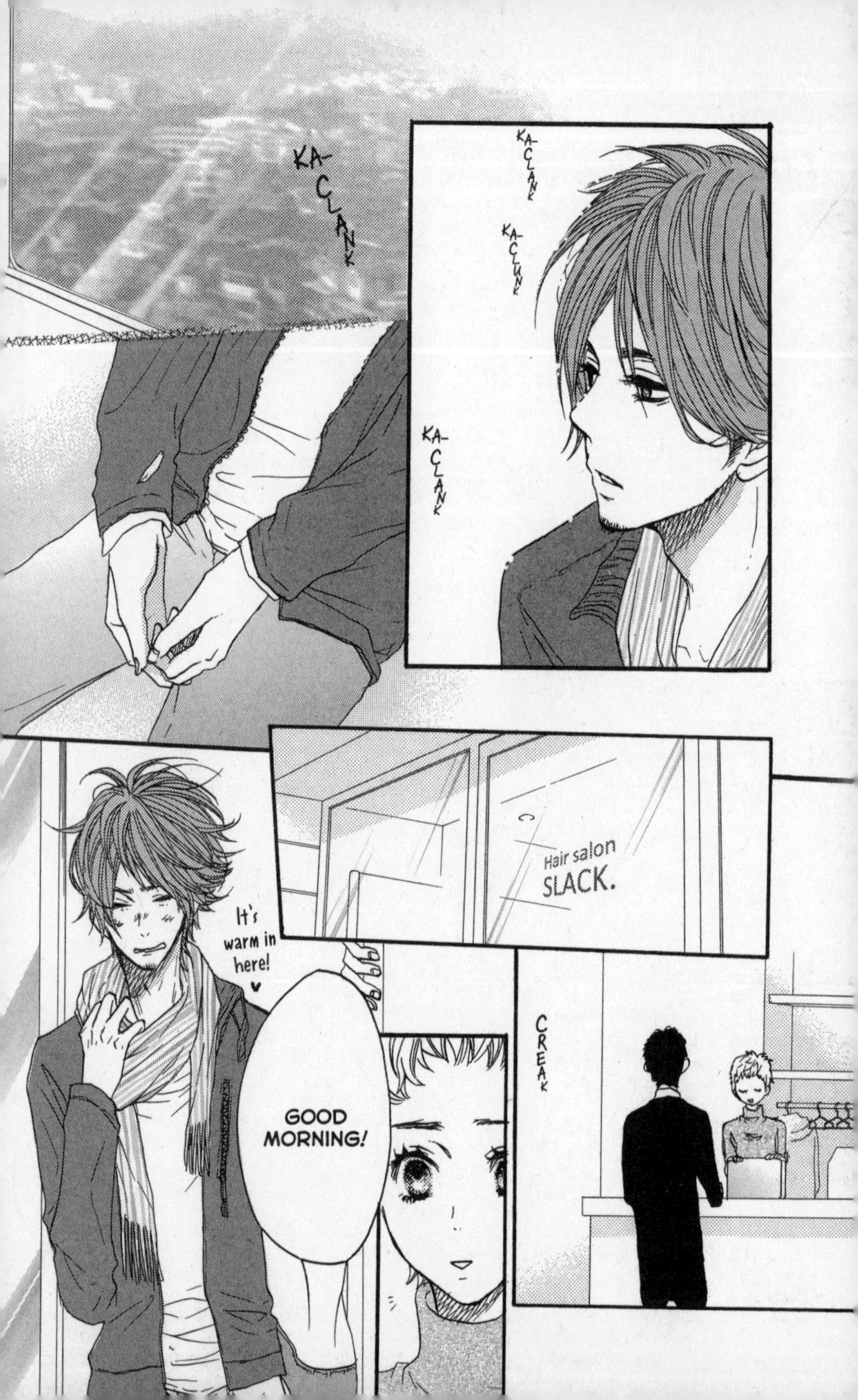
KA-CLANK
KA-CLUNK
KA-CLANK
KA-CLANK
Hair salon SLACK.
CREAK
GOOD MORNING!
It's warm in here! ♥

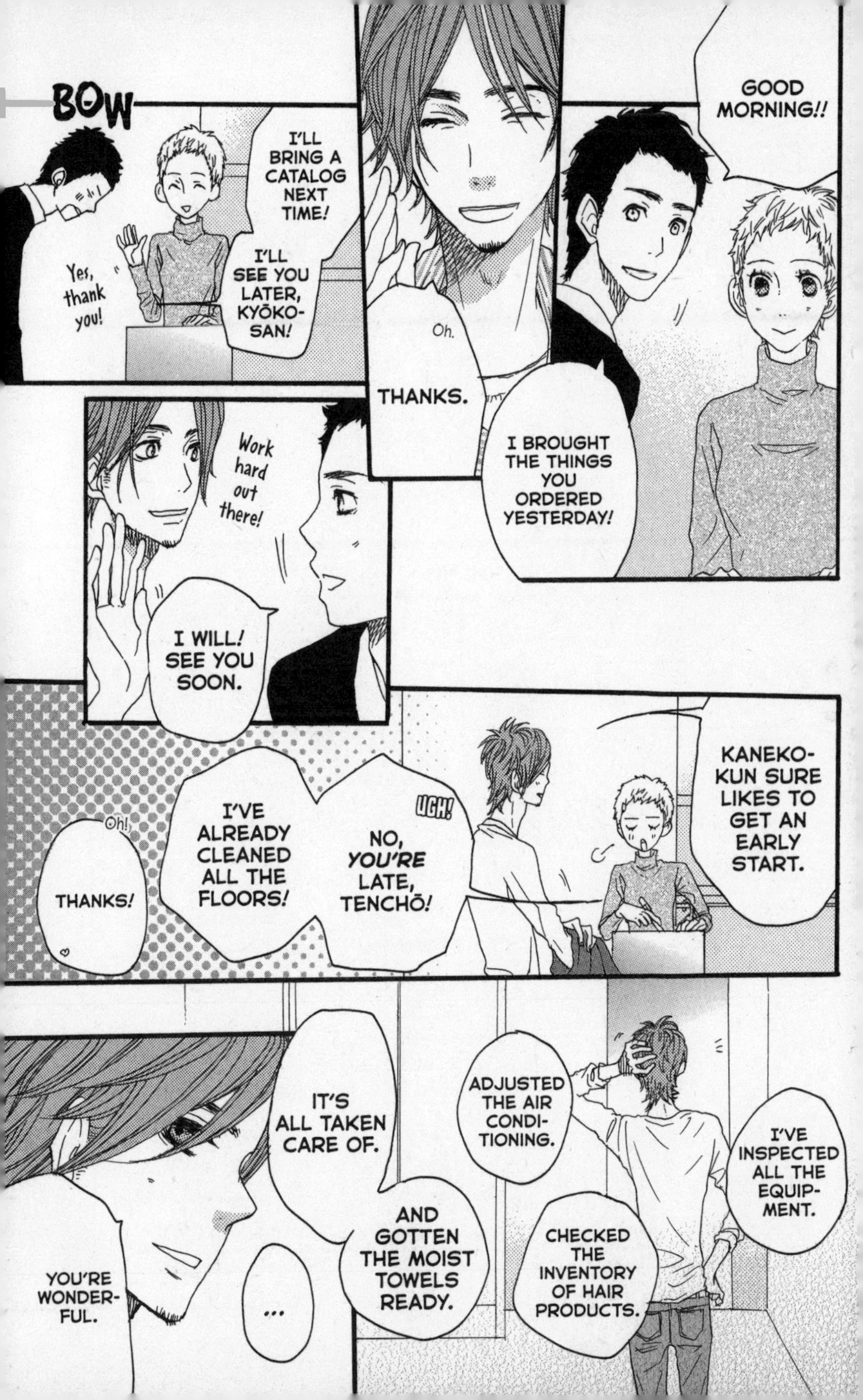
GOOD MORNING!!
I BROUGHT THE THINGS YOU ORDERED YESTERDAY!
Oh.
THANKS.
I'LL BRING A CATALOG NEXT TIME!
I'LL SEE YOU LATER, KYŌKO-SAN!
BOW
Yes, thank you!
Work hard out there!
I WILL! SEE YOU SOON.
KANEKO-KUN SURE LIKES TO GET AN EARLY START.
UGH!
NO, *YOU'RE* LATE, TENCHŌ!
I'VE ALREADY CLEANED ALL THE FLOORS!
Oh!
THANKS!
I'VE INSPECTED ALL THE EQUIPMENT.
ADJUSTED THE AIR CONDITIONING.
CHECKED THE INVENTORY OF HAIR PRODUCTS.
AND GOTTEN THE MOIST TOWELS READY.
IT'S ALL TAKEN CARE OF.
...
YOU'RE WONDERFUL.

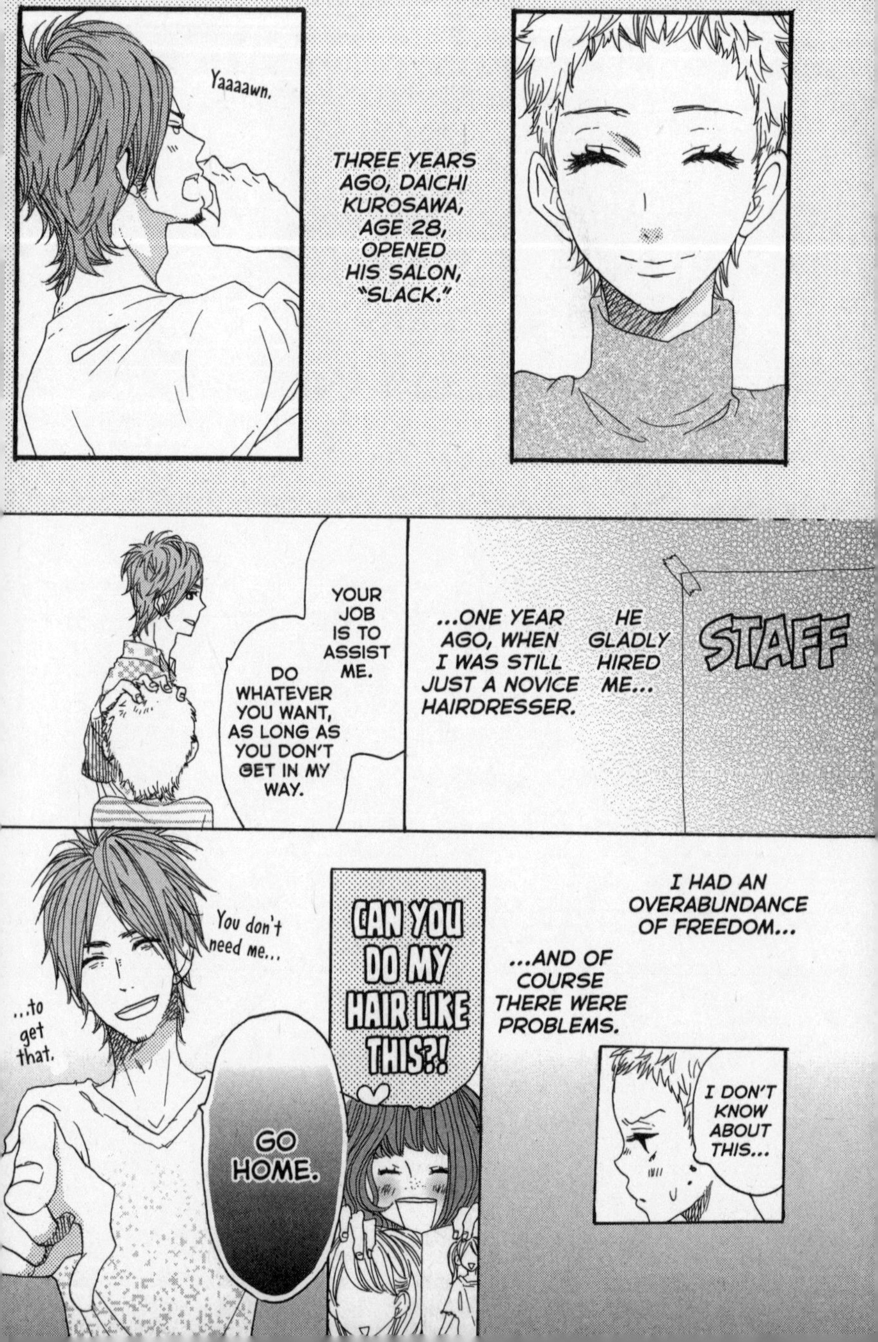
THREE YEARS AGO, DAICHI KUROSAWA, AGE 28, OPENED HIS SALON, "SLACK."
Yaaaawn.
STAFF
HE GLADLY HIRED ME...
...ONE YEAR AGO, WHEN I WAS STILL JUST A NOVICE HAIRDRESSER.
YOUR JOB IS TO ASSIST ME.
DO WHATEVER YOU WANT, AS LONG AS YOU DON'T GET IN MY WAY.
I HAD AN OVERABUNDANCE OF FREEDOM...
...AND OF COURSE THERE WERE PROBLEMS.
I DON'T KNOW ABOUT THIS...
CAN YOU DO MY HAIR LIKE THIS?!
You don't need me...
...to get that.
GO HOME.

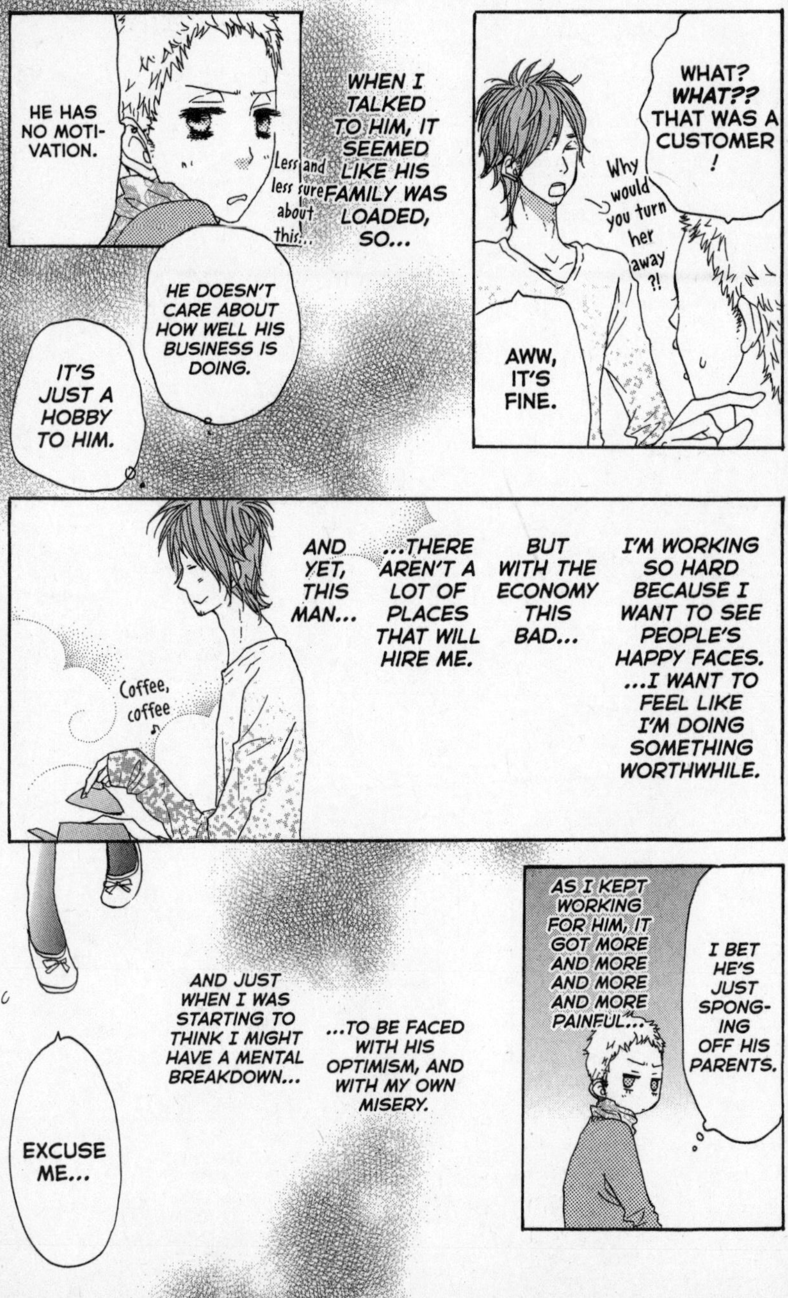
WHAT? WHAT?? THAT WAS A CUSTOMER!
Why would you turn her away?!
AWW, IT'S FINE.
WHEN I TALKED TO HIM, IT SEEMED LIKE HIS FAMILY WAS LOADED, SO...
Less and less sure about this...
HE HAS NO MOTI-VATION.
HE DOESN'T CARE ABOUT HOW WELL HIS BUSINESS IS DOING.
IT'S JUST A HOBBY TO HIM.
I'M WORKING SO HARD BECAUSE I WANT TO SEE PEOPLE'S HAPPY FACES. ...I WANT TO FEEL LIKE I'M DOING SOMETHING WORTHWHILE.
BUT WITH THE ECONOMY THIS BAD...
...THERE AREN'T A LOT OF PLACES THAT WILL HIRE ME.
AND YET, THIS MAN...
Coffee, coffee ♪
AS I KEPT WORKING FOR HIM, IT GOT MORE AND MORE AND MORE AND MORE PAINFUL...
I BET HE'S JUST SPONG-ING OFF HIS PARENTS.
...TO BE FACED WITH HIS OPTIMISM, AND WITH MY OWN MISERY.
AND JUST WHEN I WAS STARTING TO THINK I MIGHT HAVE A MENTAL BREAKDOWN...
EXCUSE ME...

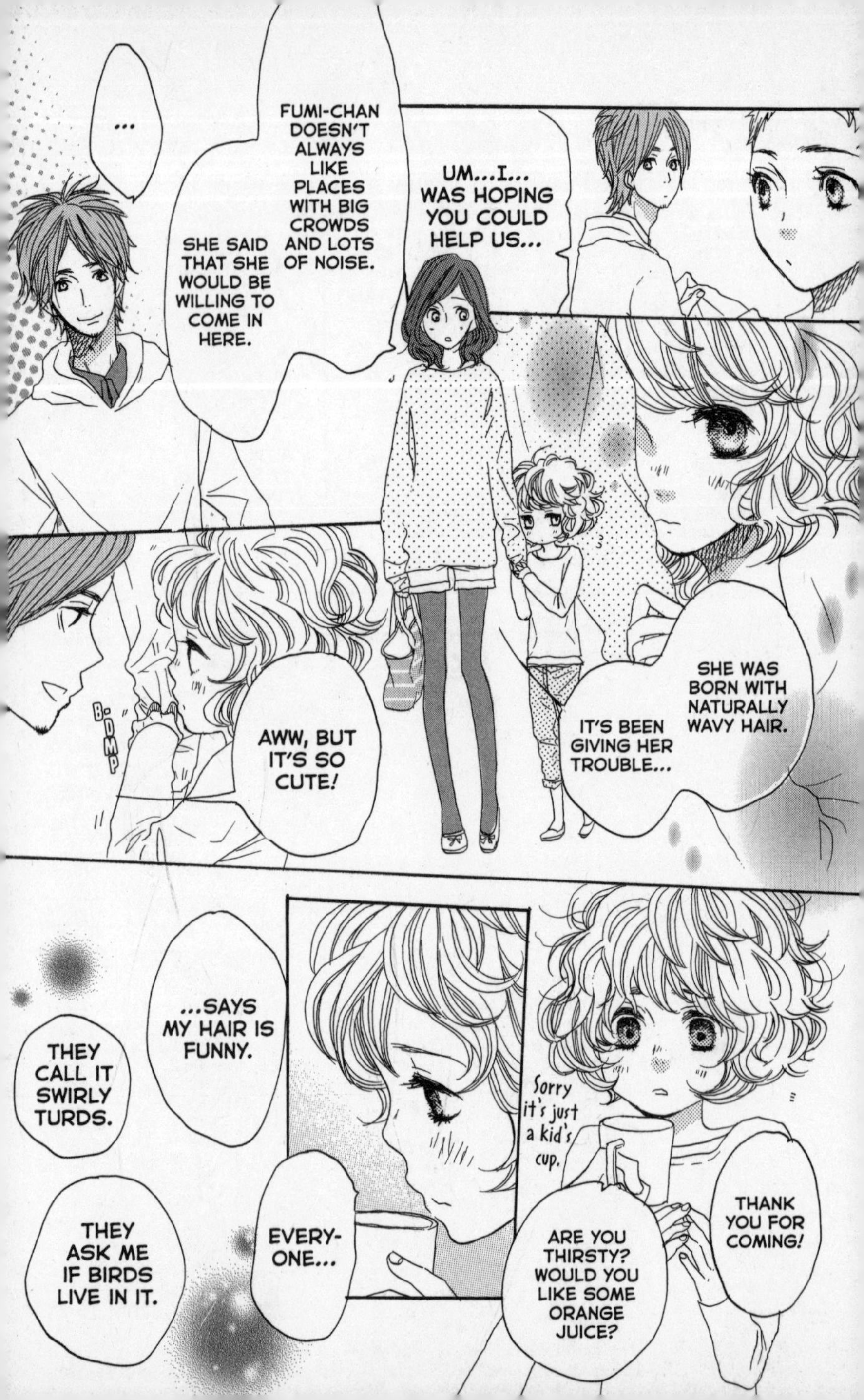
UM...I... WAS HOPING YOU COULD HELP US...
FUMI-CHAN DOESN'T ALWAYS LIKE PLACES WITH BIG CROWDS AND LOTS OF NOISE.
SHE SAID THAT SHE WOULD BE WILLING TO COME IN HERE.
...
SHE WAS BORN WITH NATURALLY WAVY HAIR.
IT'S BEEN GIVING HER TROUBLE...
AWW, BUT IT'S SO CUTE!
B-DMP
THANK YOU FOR COMING!
Sorry it's just a kid's cup.
ARE YOU THIRSTY? WOULD YOU LIKE SOME ORANGE JUICE?
EVERY-ONE...
...SAYS MY HAIR IS FUNNY.
THEY CALL IT SWIRLY TURDS.
THEY ASK ME IF BIRDS LIVE IN IT.

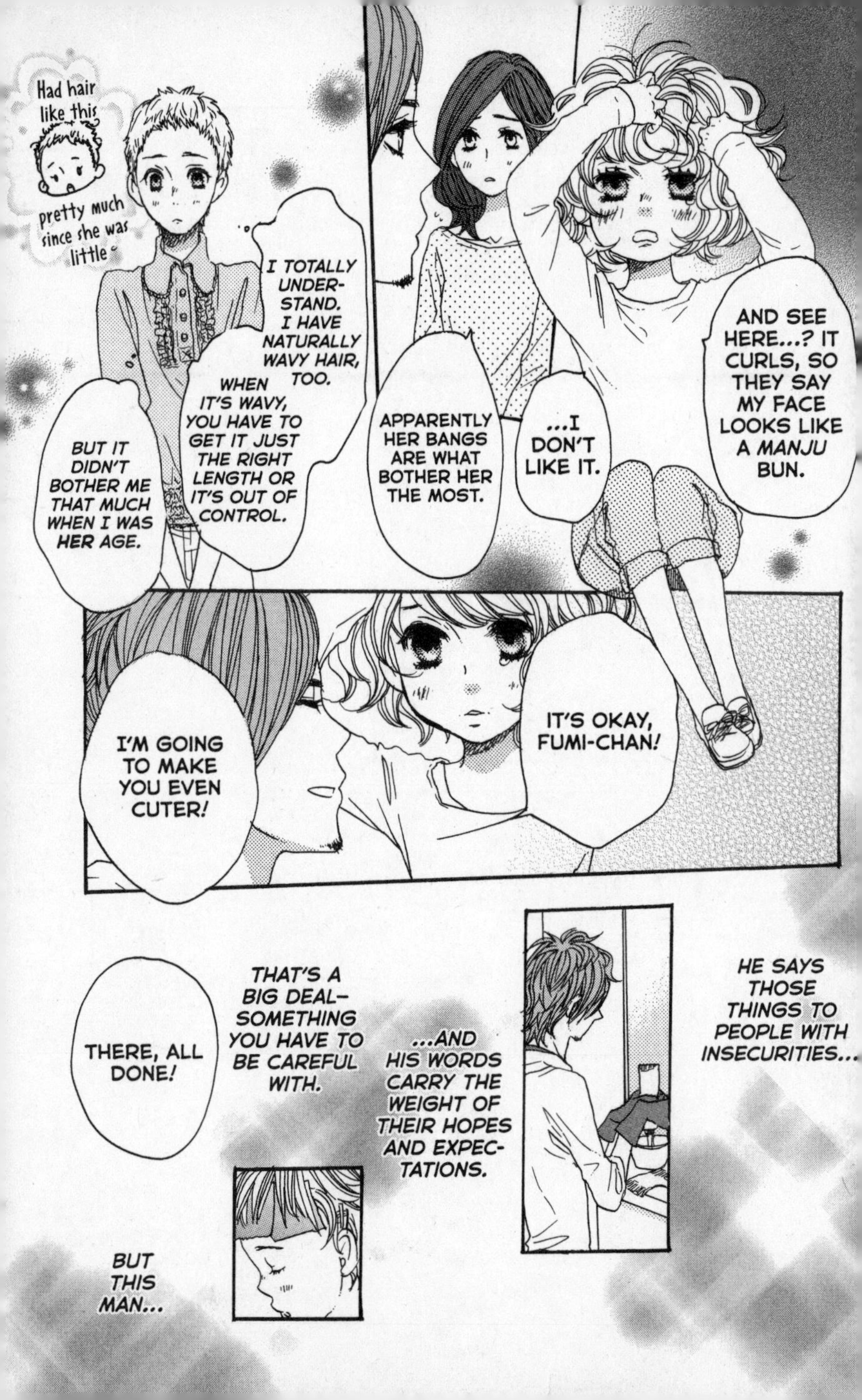
AND SEE HERE...? IT CURLS, SO THEY SAY MY FACE LOOKS LIKE A MANJU BUN.
...I DON'T LIKE IT.
APPARENTLY HER BANGS ARE WHAT BOTHER HER THE MOST.
I TOTALLY UNDERSTAND. I HAVE NATURALLY WAVY HAIR, TOO.
WHEN IT'S WAVY, YOU HAVE TO GET IT JUST THE RIGHT LENGTH OR IT'S OUT OF CONTROL.
BUT IT DIDN'T BOTHER ME THAT MUCH WHEN I WAS HER AGE.
Had hair like this pretty much since she was little
IT'S OKAY, FUMI-CHAN!
I'M GOING TO MAKE YOU EVEN CUTER!
HE SAYS THOSE THINGS TO PEOPLE WITH INSECURITIES...
...AND HIS WORDS CARRY THE WEIGHT OF THEIR HOPES AND EXPECTATIONS.
THAT'S A BIG DEAL—SOMETHING YOU HAVE TO BE CAREFUL WITH.
THERE, ALL DONE!
BUT THIS MAN...

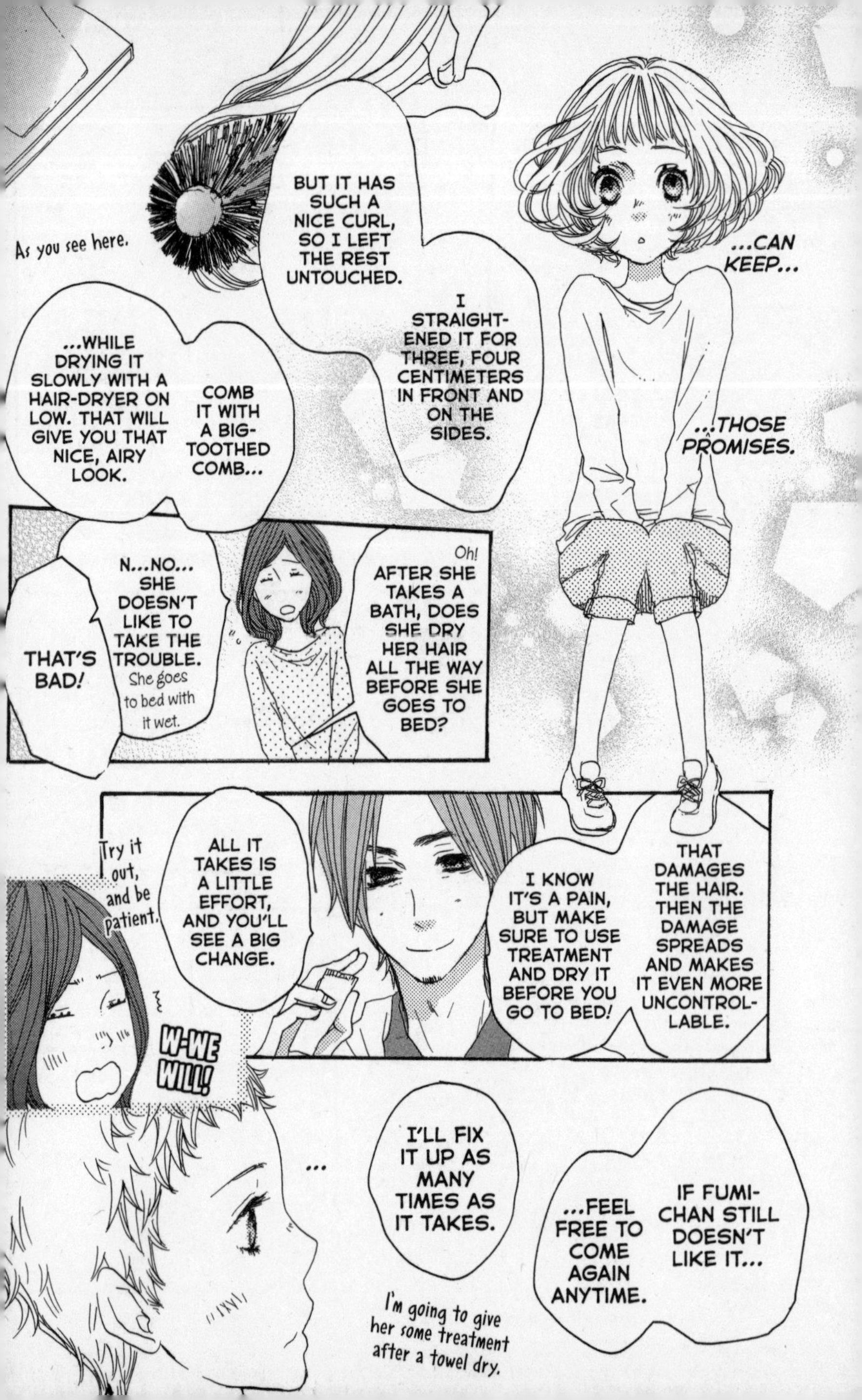
...CAN KEEP...
...THOSE PROMISES.
I STRAIGHTENED IT FOR THREE, FOUR CENTIMETERS IN FRONT AND ON THE SIDES.
BUT IT HAS SUCH A NICE CURL, SO I LEFT THE REST UNTOUCHED.
As you see here.
COMB IT WITH A BIG-TOOTHED COMB...
...WHILE DRYING IT SLOWLY WITH A HAIR-DRYER ON LOW. THAT WILL GIVE YOU THAT NICE, AIRY LOOK.
Oh!
AFTER SHE TAKES A BATH, DOES SHE DRY HER HAIR ALL THE WAY BEFORE SHE GOES TO BED?
N...NO... SHE DOESN'T LIKE TO TAKE THE TROUBLE.
She goes to bed with it wet.
THAT'S BAD!
THAT DAMAGES THE HAIR. THEN THE DAMAGE SPREADS AND MAKES IT EVEN MORE UNCONTROLLABLE.
I KNOW IT'S A PAIN, BUT MAKE SURE TO USE TREATMENT AND DRY IT BEFORE YOU GO TO BED!
ALL IT TAKES IS A LITTLE EFFORT, AND YOU'LL SEE A BIG CHANGE.
Try it out, and be patient.
W-WE WILL!
IF FUMI-CHAN STILL DOESN'T LIKE IT...
...FEEL FREE TO COME AGAIN ANYTIME.
I'LL FIX IT UP AS MANY TIMES AS IT TAKES.
I'm going to give her some treatment after a towel dry.
...

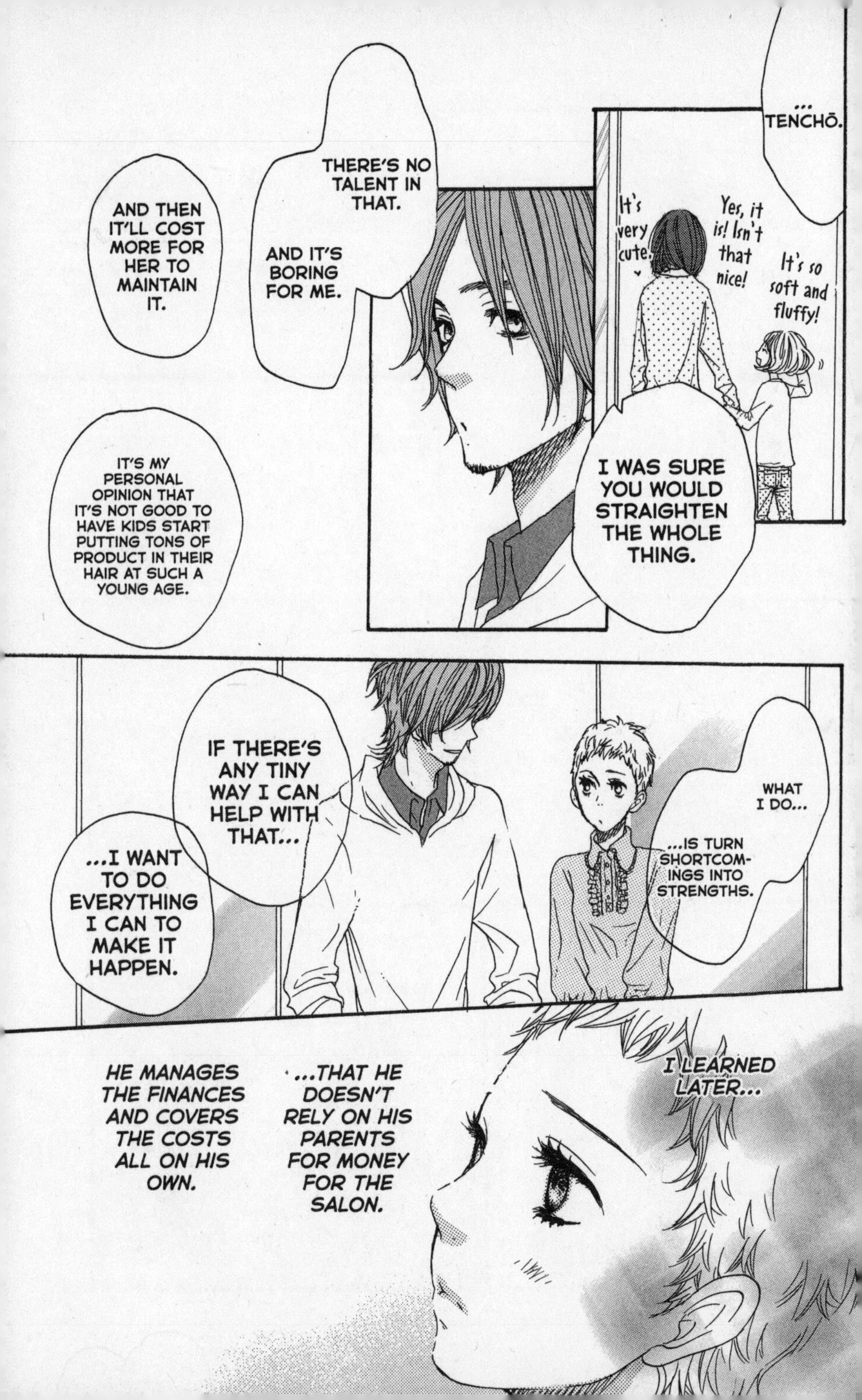
...TENCHŌ.
It's so soft and fluffy!
Yes, it is! Isn't that nice!
It's very cute.
I WAS SURE YOU WOULD STRAIGHTEN THE WHOLE THING.
THERE'S NO TALENT IN THAT.
AND IT'S BORING FOR ME.
AND THEN IT'LL COST MORE FOR HER TO MAINTAIN IT.
IT'S MY PERSONAL OPINION THAT IT'S NOT GOOD TO HAVE KIDS START PUTTING TONS OF PRODUCT IN THEIR HAIR AT SUCH A YOUNG AGE.
WHAT I DO...
...IS TURN SHORTCOMINGS INTO STRENGTHS.
IF THERE'S ANY TINY WAY I CAN HELP WITH THAT...
...I WANT TO DO EVERYTHING I CAN TO MAKE IT HAPPEN.
I LEARNED LATER...
...THAT HE DOESN'T RELY ON HIS PARENTS FOR MONEY FOR THE SALON.
HE MANAGES THE FINANCES AND COVERS THE COSTS ALL ON HIS OWN.

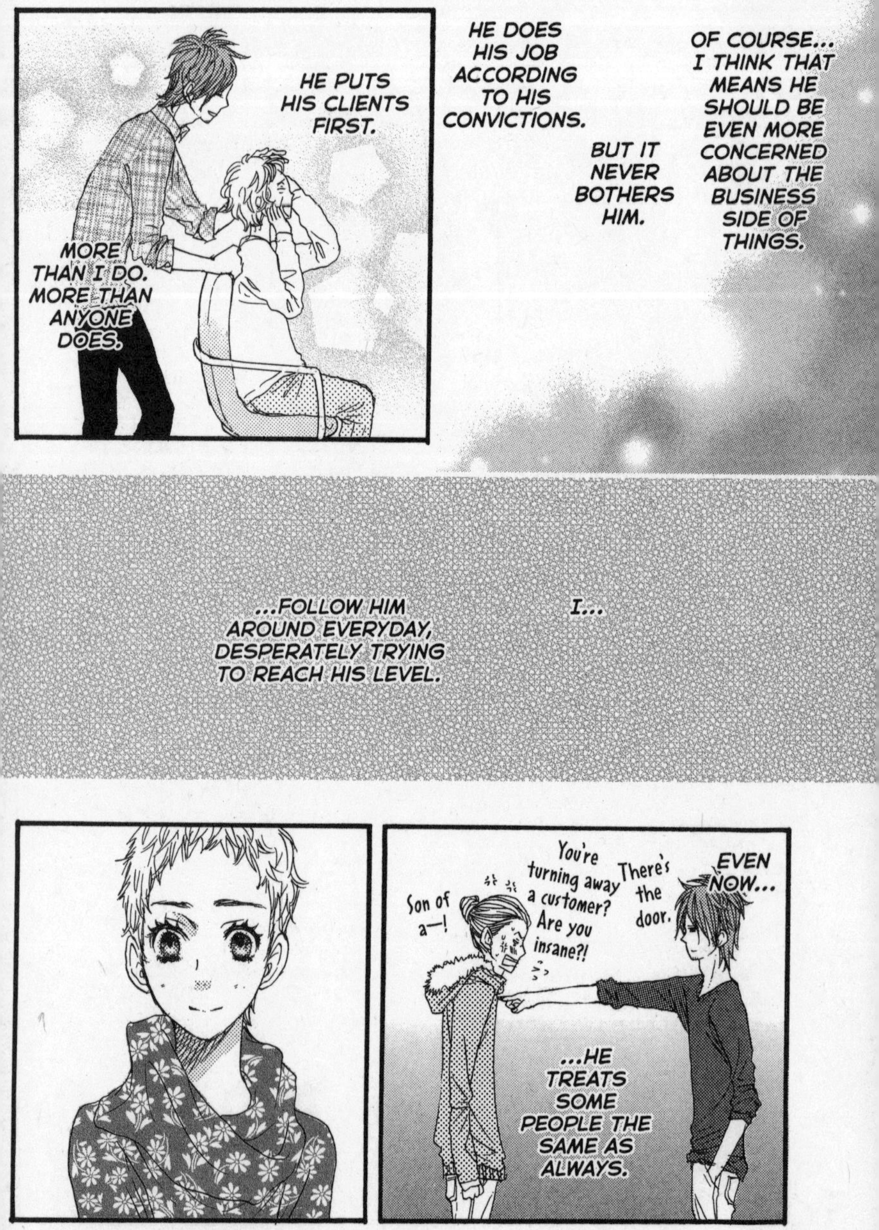
OF COURSE... I THINK THAT MEANS HE SHOULD BE EVEN MORE CONCERNED ABOUT THE BUSINESS SIDE OF THINGS.
BUT IT NEVER BOTHERS HIM.
HE DOES HIS JOB ACCORDING TO HIS CONVICTIONS.
HE PUTS HIS CLIENTS FIRST.
MORE THAN I DO. MORE THAN ANYONE DOES.
I...
...FOLLOW HIM AROUND EVERYDAY, DESPERATELY TRYING TO REACH HIS LEVEL.
EVEN NOW...
There's the door.
You're turning away a customer? Are you insane?!
Son of a—!
...HE TREATS SOME PEOPLE THE SAME AS ALWAYS.

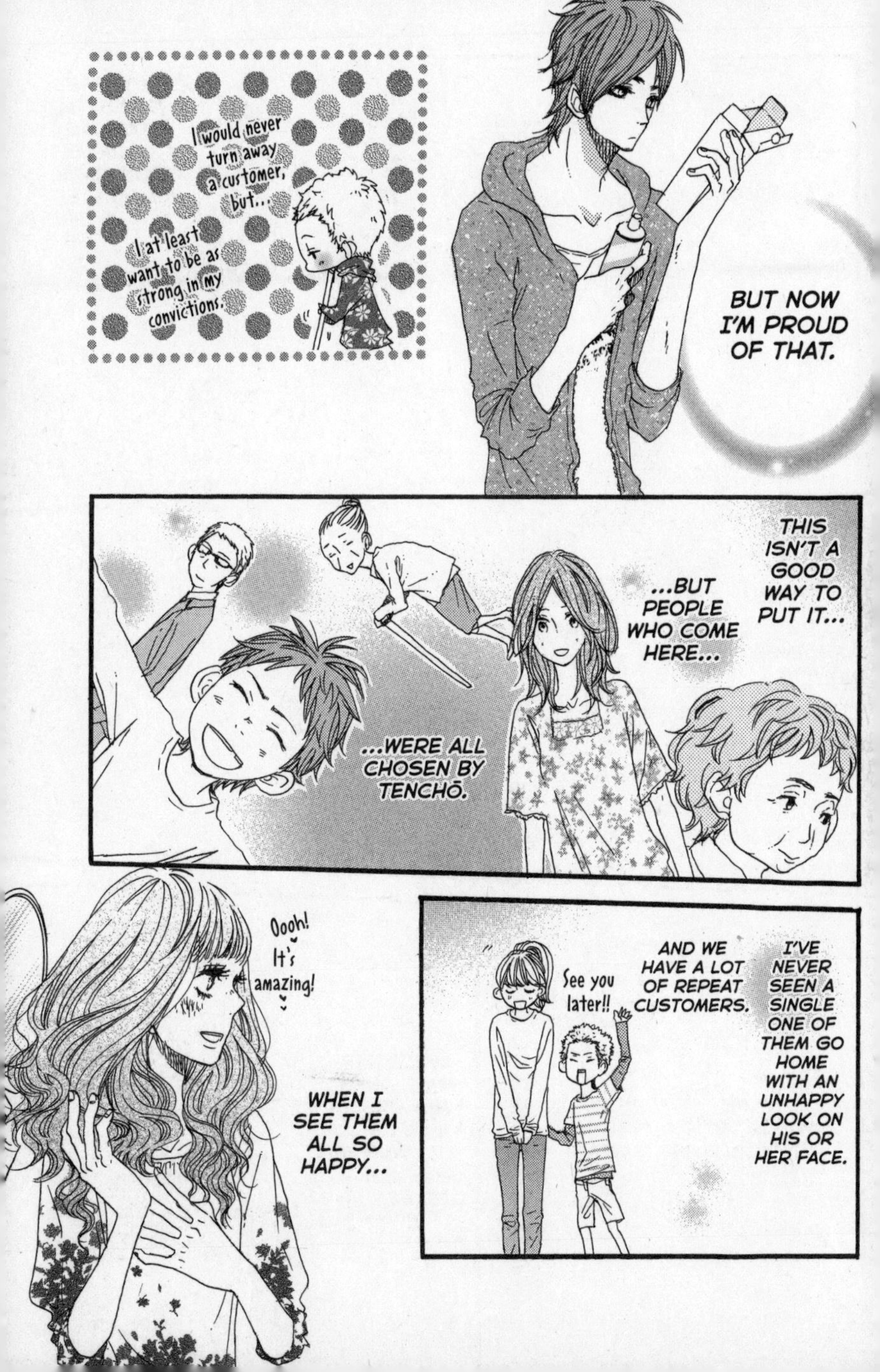
BUT NOW I'M PROUD OF THAT.
I would never turn away a customer, but...
I at least want to be as strong in my convictions.
THIS ISN'T A GOOD WAY TO PUT IT...
...BUT PEOPLE WHO COME HERE...
...WERE ALL CHOSEN BY TENCHŌ.
I'VE NEVER SEEN A SINGLE ONE OF THEM GO HOME WITH AN UNHAPPY LOOK ON HIS OR HER FACE.
AND WE HAVE A LOT OF REPEAT CUSTOMERS.
See you later!!
Oooh! It's amazing!
WHEN I SEE THEM ALL SO HAPPY...

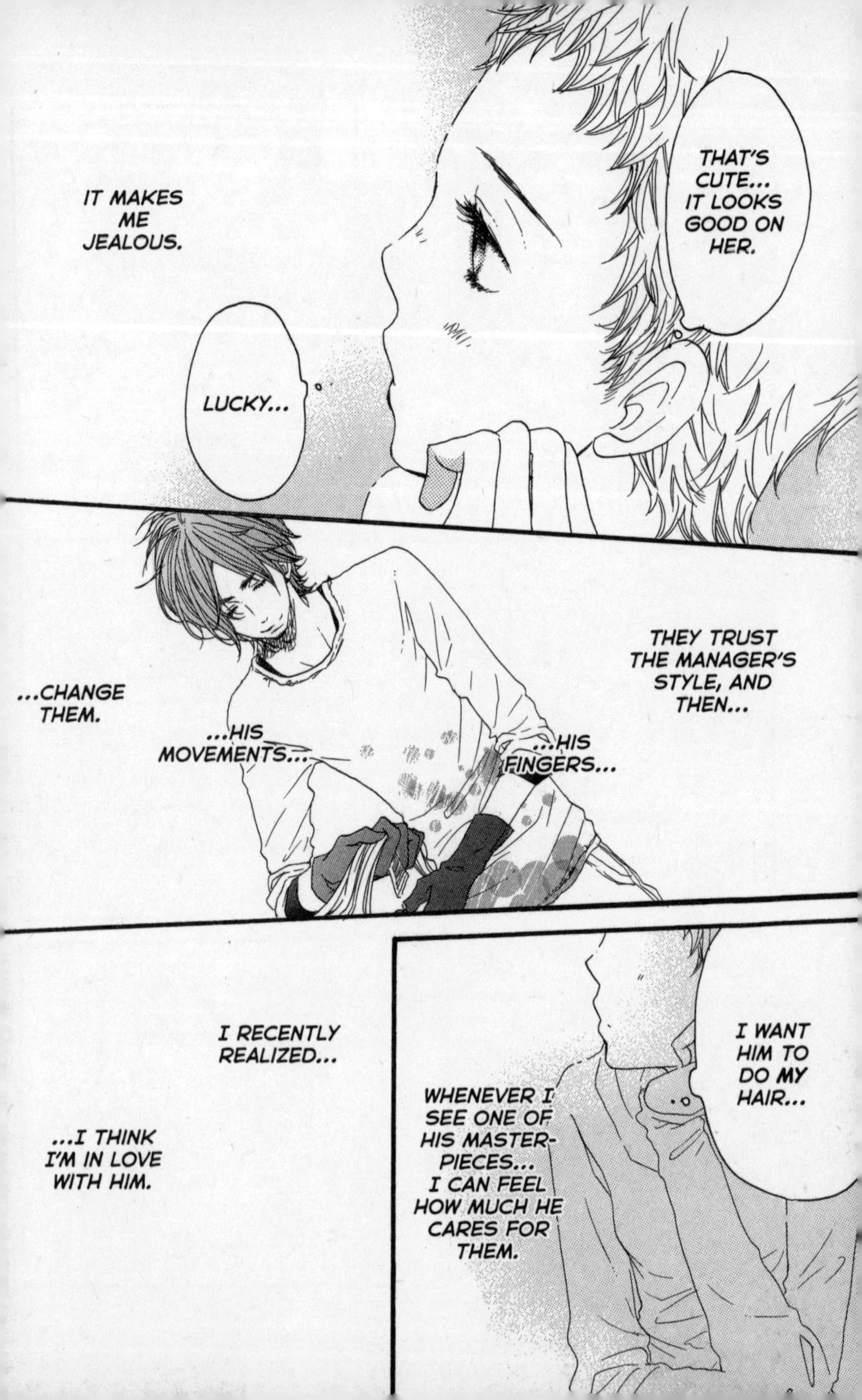

THAT'S CUTE... IT LOOKS GOOD ON HER.
IT MAKES ME JEALOUS.
LUCKY...
THEY TRUST THE MANAGER'S STYLE, AND THEN...
...HIS FINGERS...
...HIS MOVEMENTS...
...CHANGE THEM.
I WANT HIM TO DO MY HAIR...
WHENEVER I SEE ONE OF HIS MASTER-PIECES... I CAN FEEL HOW MUCH HE CARES FOR THEM.
I RECENTLY REALIZED...
...I THINK I'M IN LOVE WITH HIM.

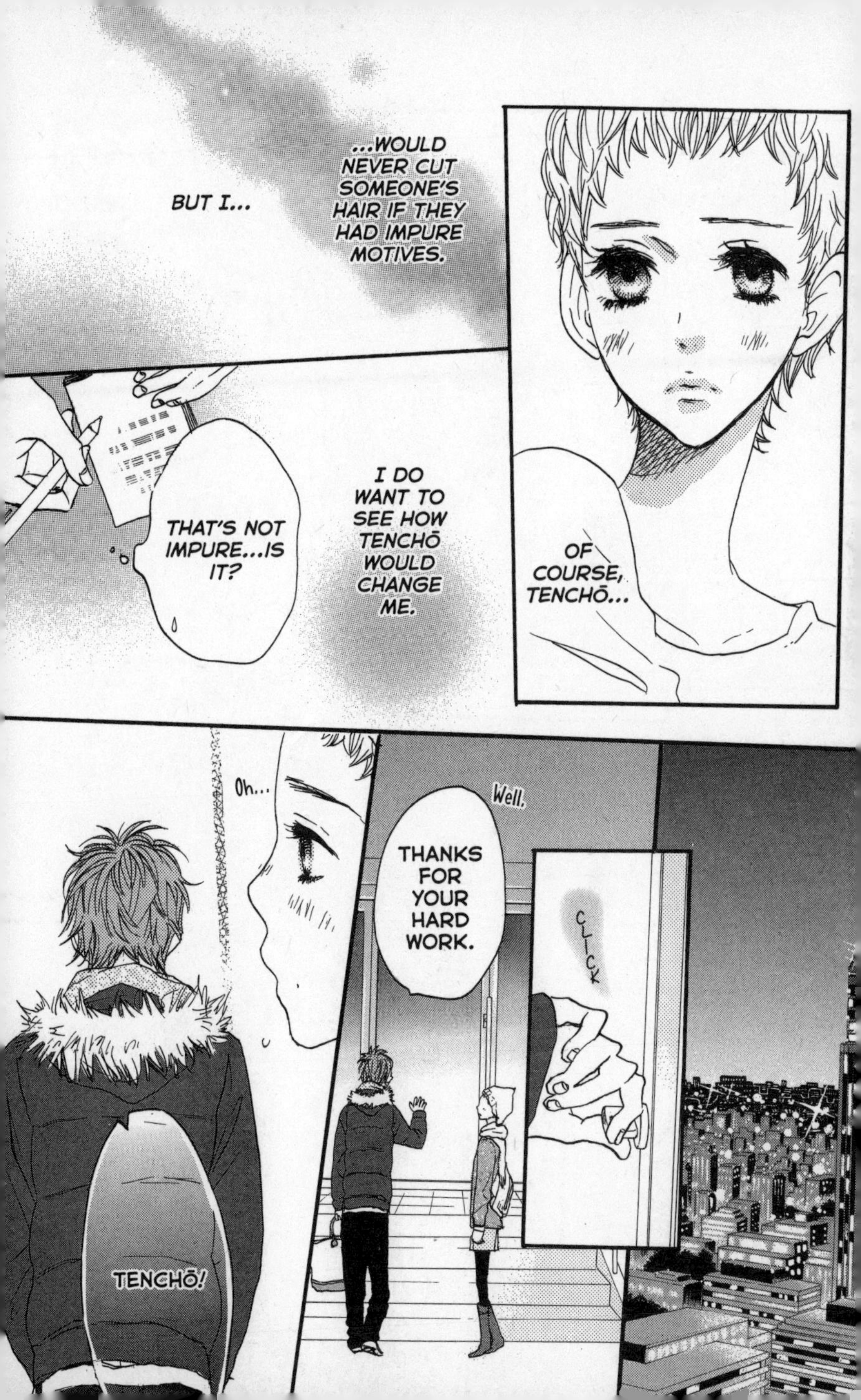
OF COURSE, TENCHŌ...
...WOULD NEVER CUT SOMEONE'S HAIR IF THEY HAD IMPURE MOTIVES.
BUT I...
I DO WANT TO SEE HOW TENCHŌ WOULD CHANGE ME.
THAT'S NOT IMPURE...IS IT?
CLICK
Well.
THANKS FOR YOUR HARD WORK.
Oh...
TENCHŌ!

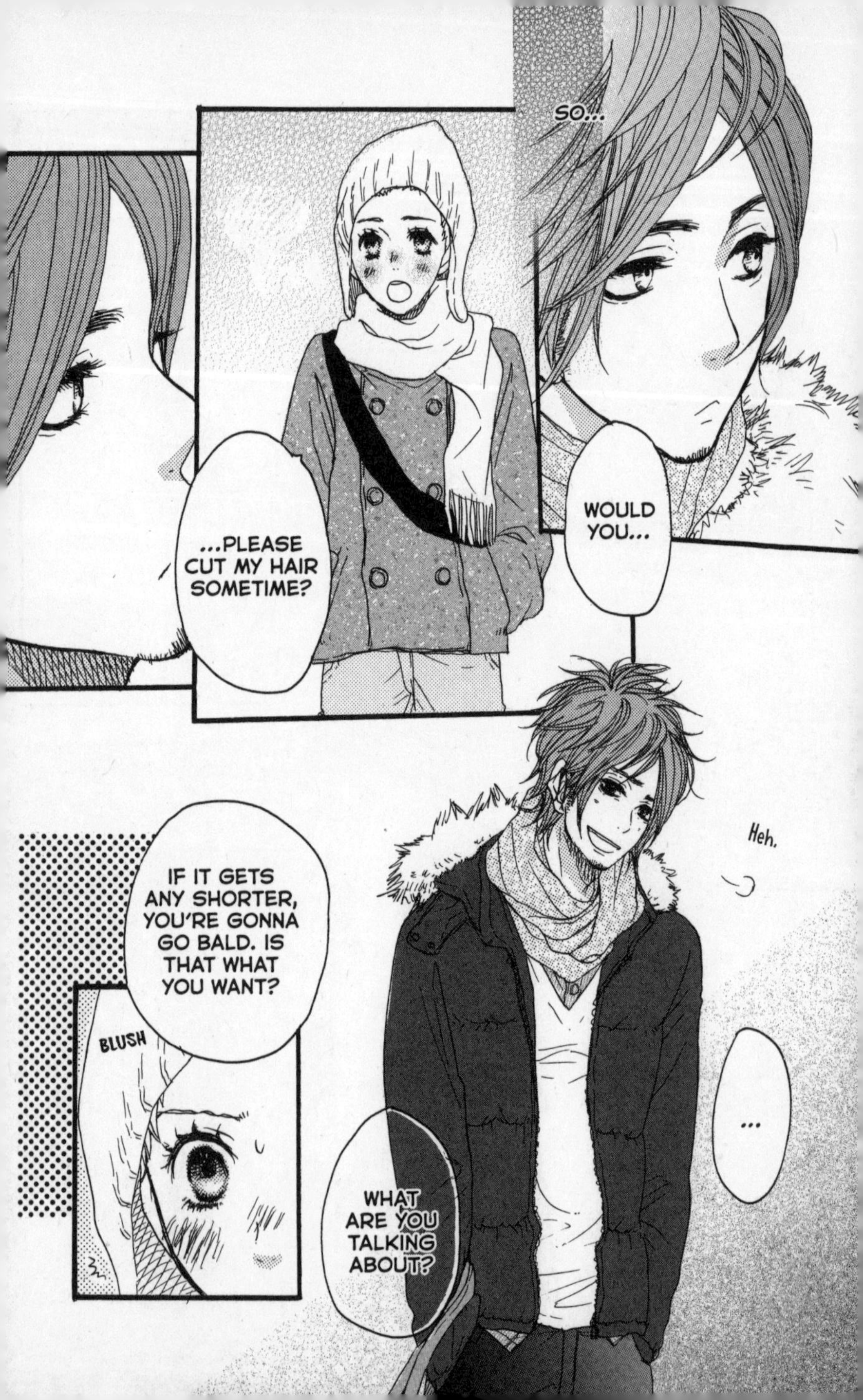
SO...
WOULD YOU...
...PLEASE CUT MY HAIR SOMETIME?
Heh.
IF IT GETS ANY SHORTER, YOU'RE GONNA GO BALD. IS THAT WHAT YOU WANT?
...
BLUSH
WHAT ARE YOU TALKING ABOUT?

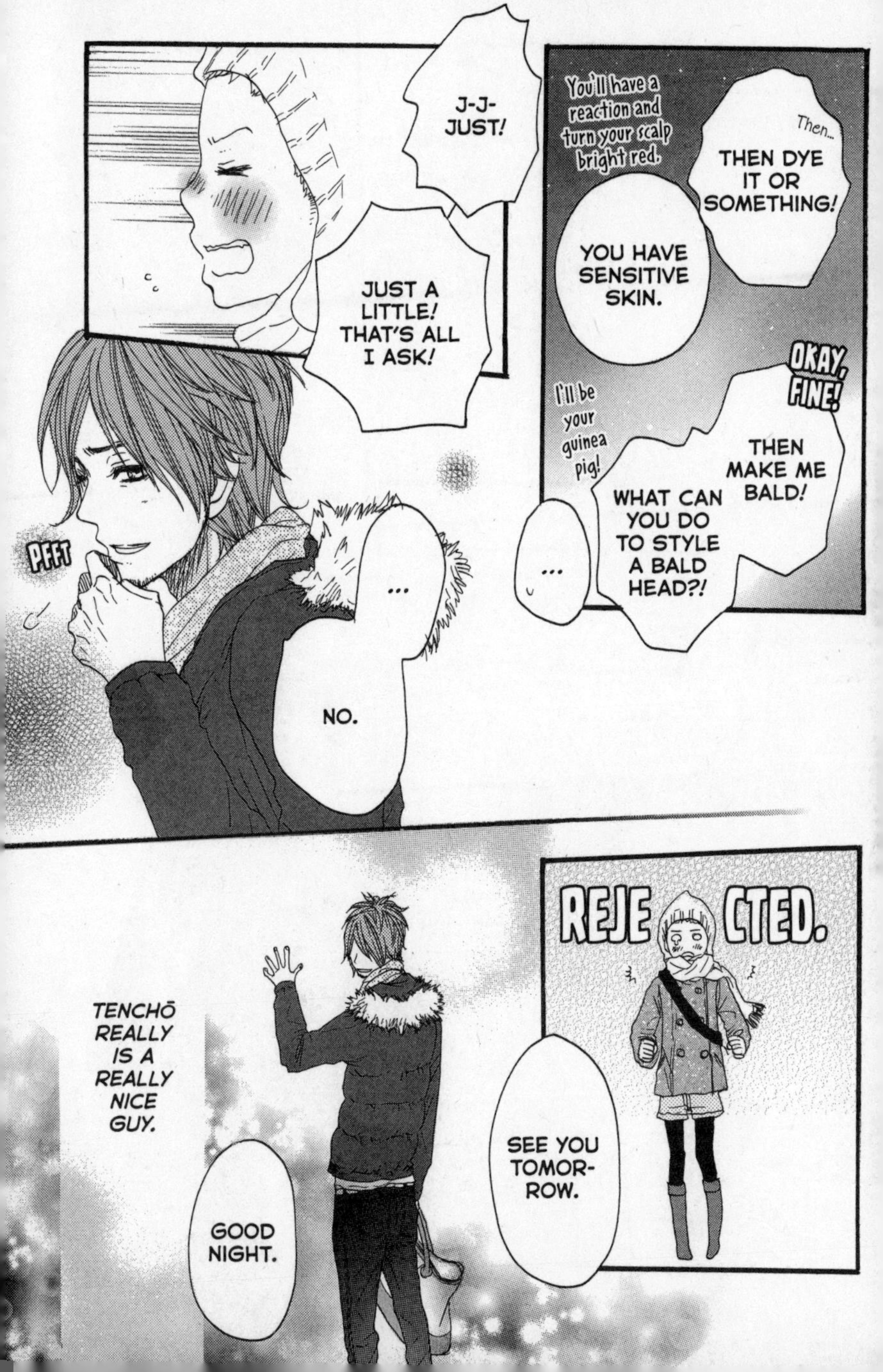
Then...
THEN DYE IT OR SOMETHING!
YOU HAVE SENSITIVE SKIN.
You'll have a reaction and turn your scalp bright red.
OKAY, FINE!
THEN MAKE ME BALD!
I'll be your guinea pig!
WHAT CAN YOU DO TO STYLE A BALD HEAD?!
...
J-J-JUST!
JUST A LITTLE! THAT'S ALL I ASK!
...
NO.
PFFT
REJECTED.
SEE YOU TOMOR-ROW.
GOOD NIGHT.
TENCHŌ REALLY IS A REALLY NICE GUY.

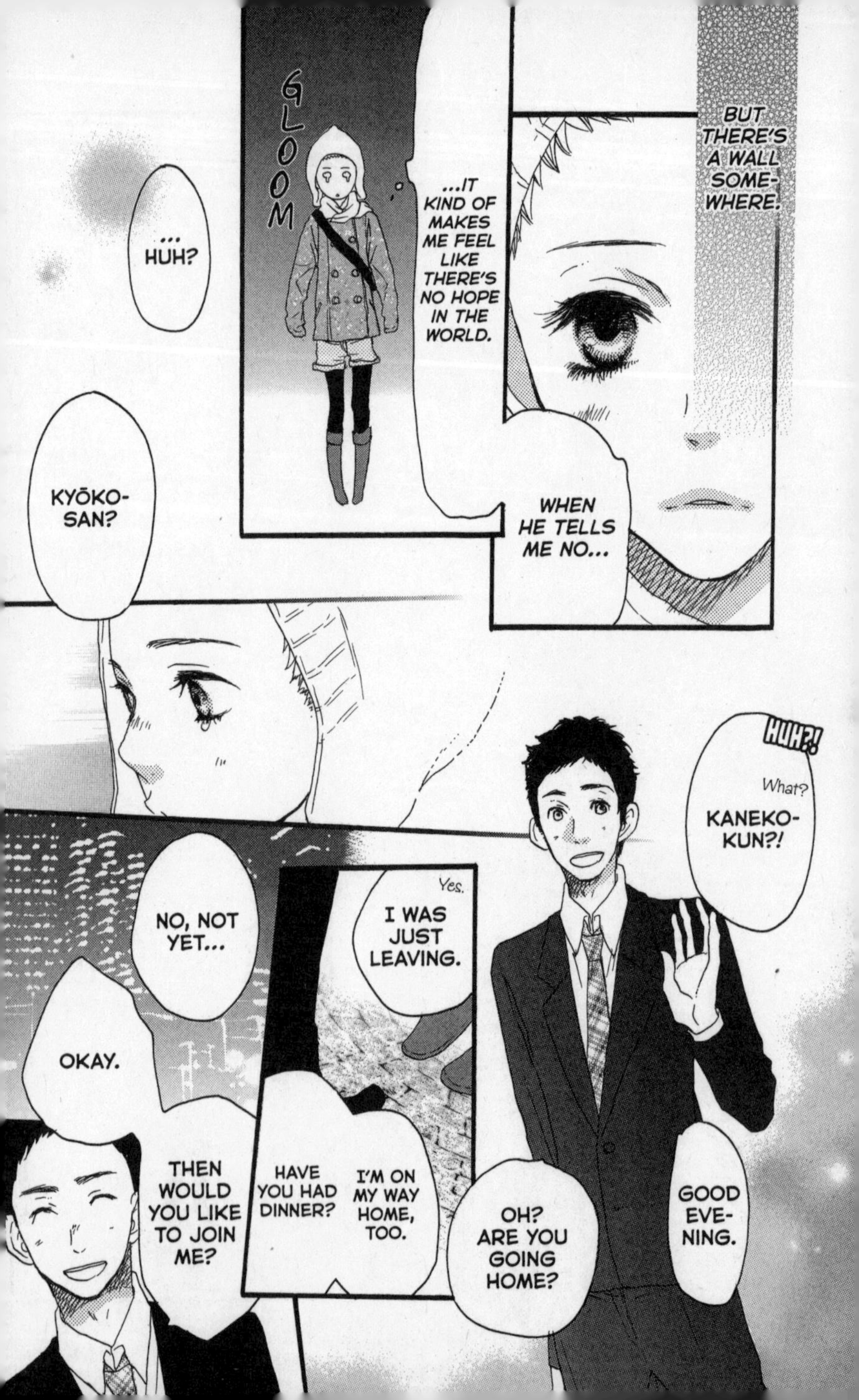
BUT THERE'S A WALL SOME-WHERE.
WHEN HE TELLS ME NO...
GLOOM
...IT KIND OF MAKES ME FEEL LIKE THERE'S NO HOPE IN THE WORLD.
...HUH?
KYŌKO-SAN?
HUH?!
What?
KANEKO-KUN?!
GOOD EVE-NING.
OH? ARE YOU GOING HOME?
Yes.
I WAS JUST LEAVING.
I'M ON MY WAY HOME, TOO.
HAVE YOU HAD DINNER?
NO, NOT YET...
OKAY.
THEN WOULD YOU LIKE TO JOIN ME?

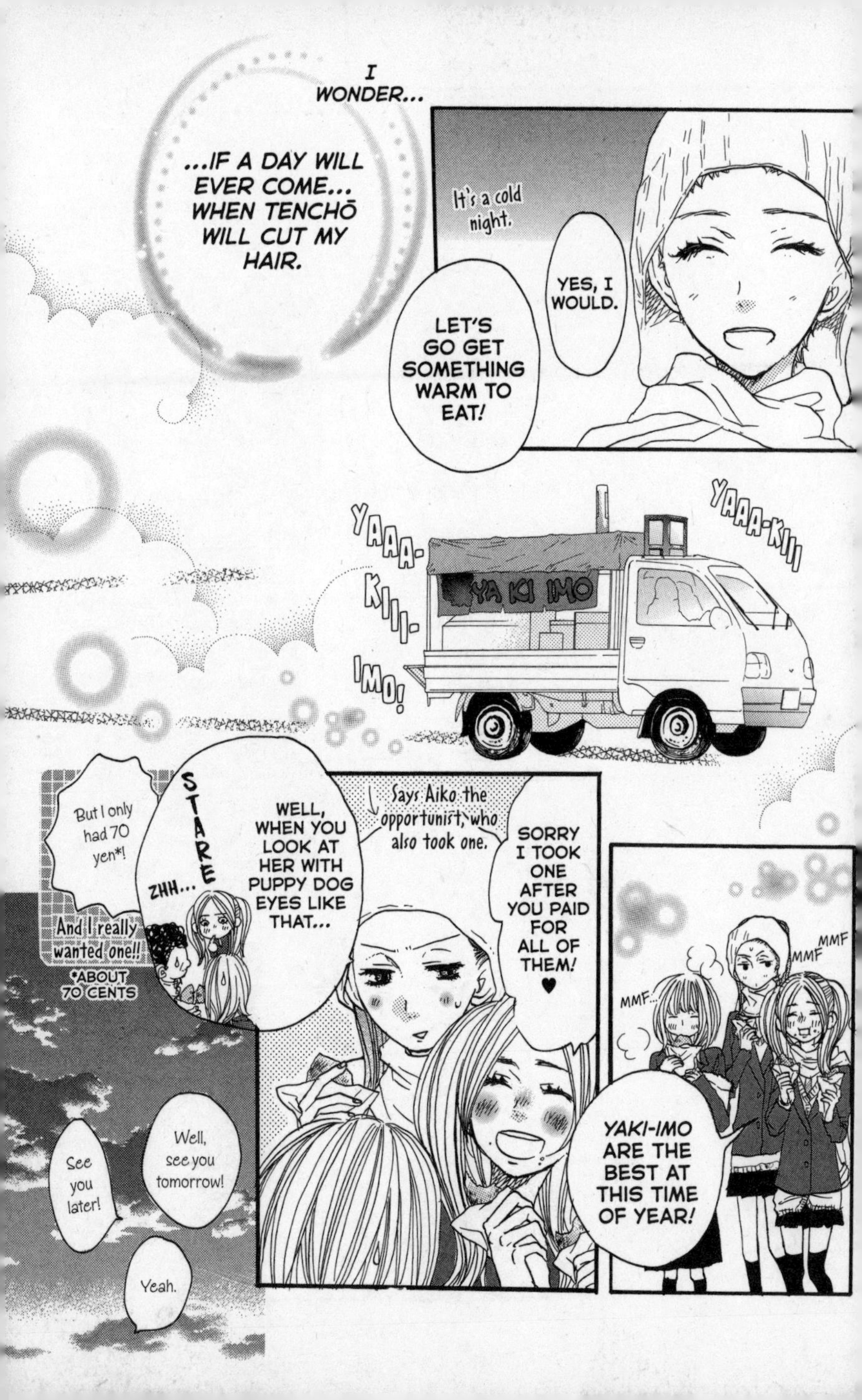
It's a cold night.
YES, I WOULD.
LET'S GO GET SOMETHING WARM TO EAT!
I WONDER...
...IF A DAY WILL EVER COME... WHEN TENCHŌ WILL CUT MY HAIR.
YAAA-KIII
YA KI IMO
YAAA-KIII-IMO!
MMF MMF
MMF...
YAKI-IMO ARE THE BEST AT THIS TIME OF YEAR!
SORRY I TOOK ONE AFTER YOU PAID FOR ALL OF THEM! ♥
Says Aiko the opportunist, who also took one.
WELL, WHEN YOU LOOK AT HER WITH PUPPY DOG EYES LIKE THAT...
STARE
ZHH...
But I only had 70 yen*!
And I really wanted one!!
*ABOUT 70 CENTS
Well, see you tomorrow!
See you later!
Yeah.

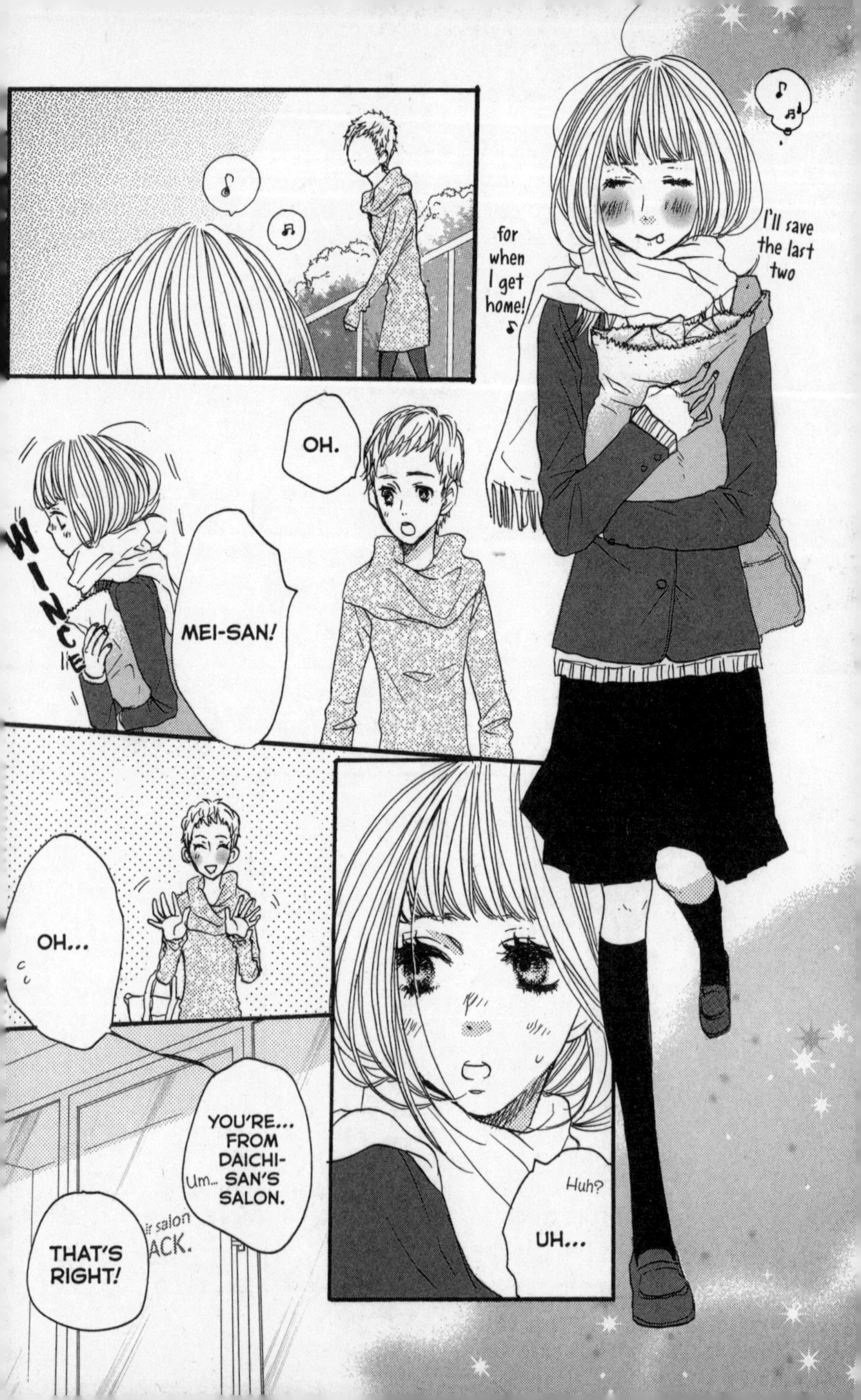

I'll save the last two
for when I get home!
OH.
MEI-SAN!
WINCE
Huh?
UH...
YOU'RE... FROM DAICHI-SAN'S SALON.
Um...
OH...
THAT'S RIGHT!
ir salon
ACK.

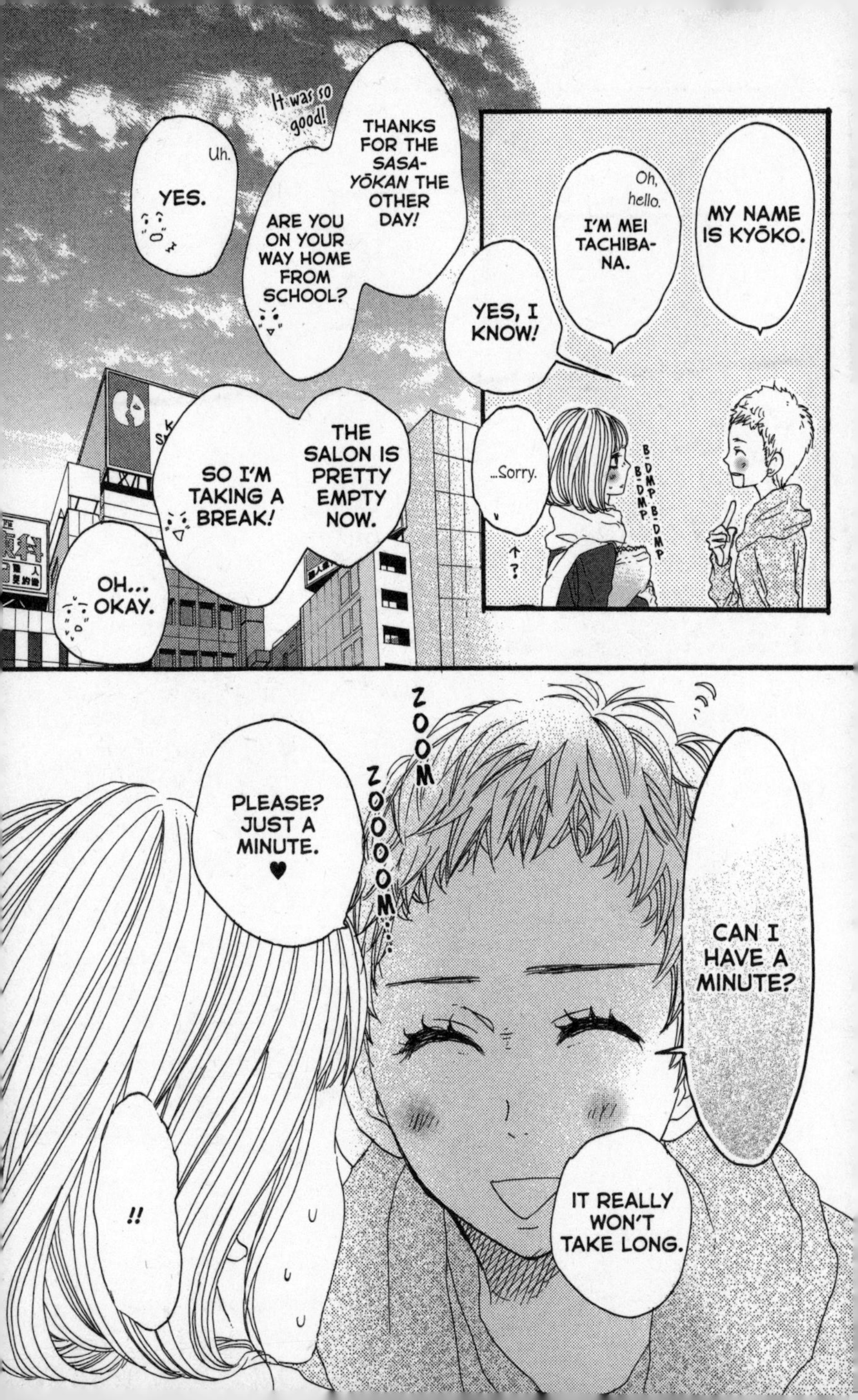
MY NAME IS KYŌKO.
Oh, hello.
I'M MEI TACHIBANA.
YES, I KNOW!
B-DMP B-DMP B-DMP B-DMP
...Sorry.
?
THANKS FOR THE SASA-YŌKAN THE OTHER DAY!
It was so good!
ARE YOU ON YOUR WAY HOME FROM SCHOOL?
Uh.
YES.
THE SALON IS PRETTY EMPTY NOW.
SO I'M TAKING A BREAK!
OH... OKAY.
CAN I HAVE A MINUTE?
ZOOM
ZOOOOOM...
PLEASE? JUST A MINUTE. ♥
IT REALLY WON'T TAKE LONG.
!!

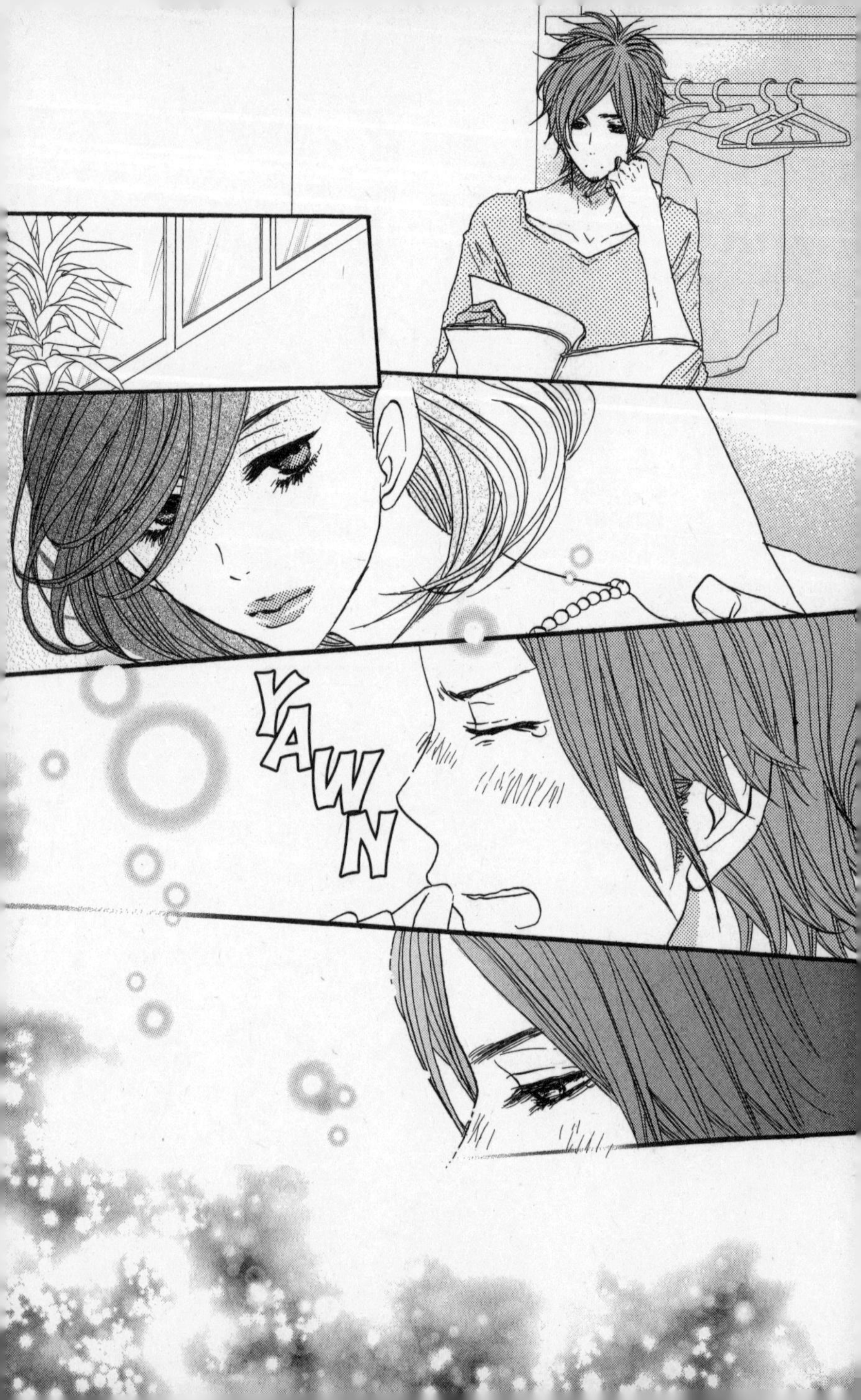
YAWN

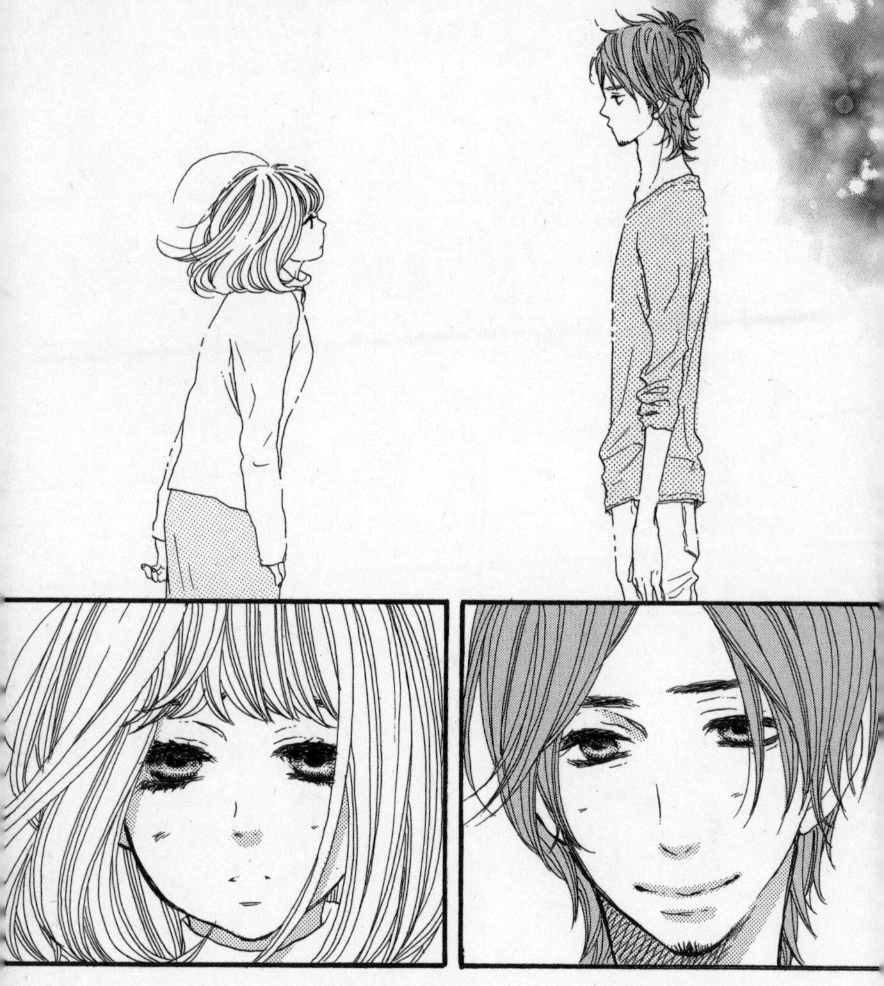

EVERY TIME I SEE YOU...

...YOU LOOK SAD...

...FOR JUST A SECOND...

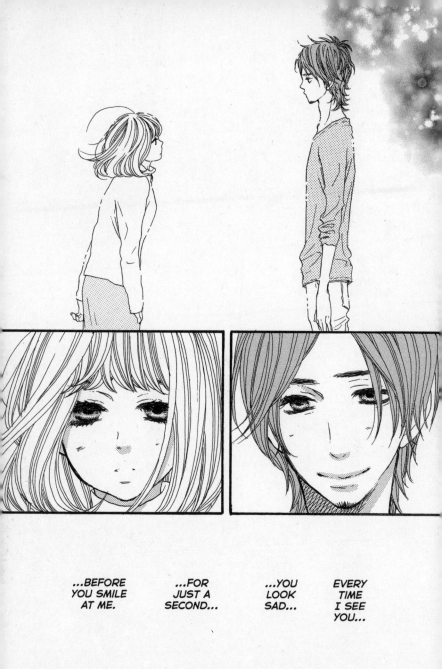

...BEFORE YOU SMILE AT ME.

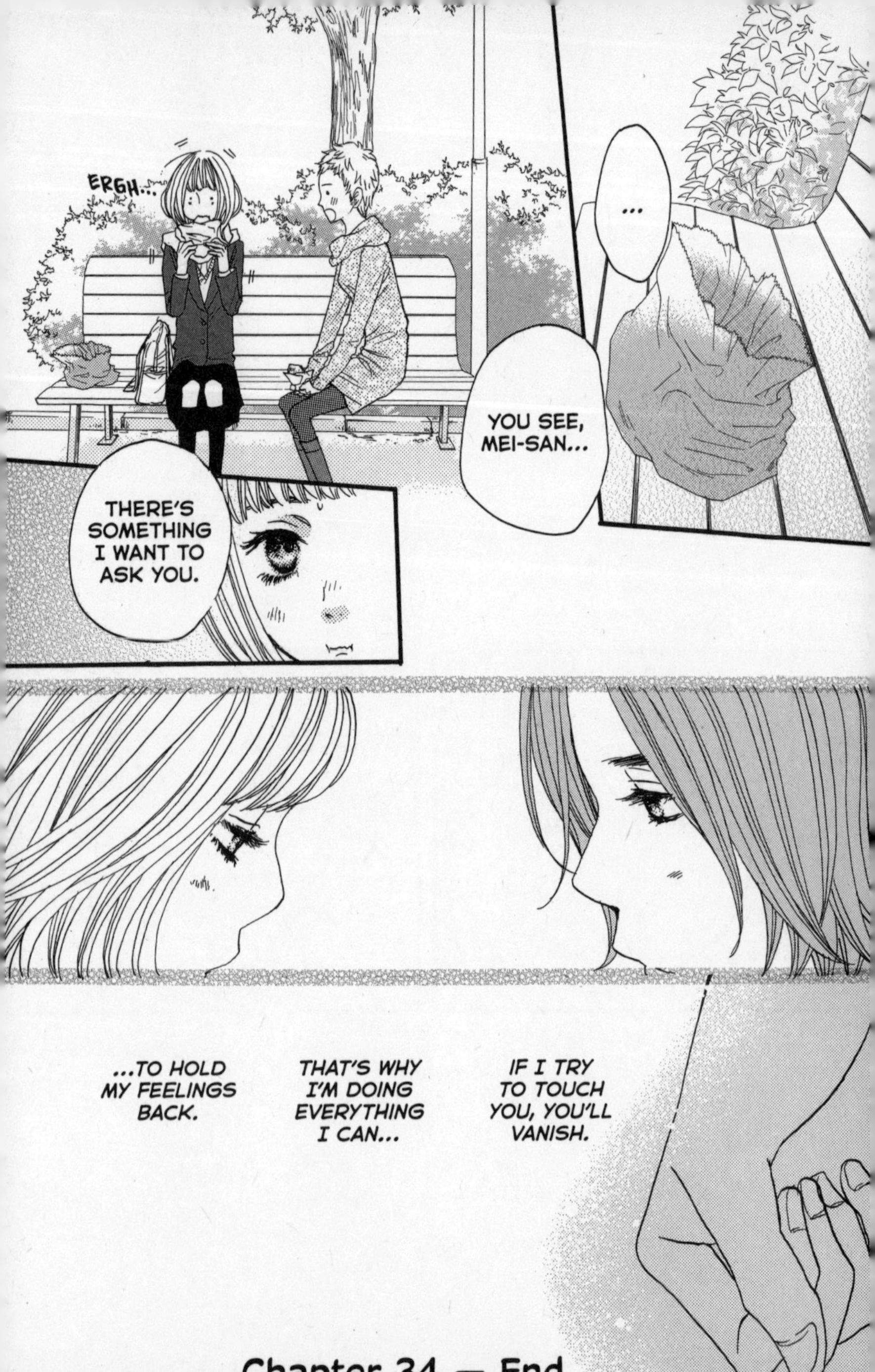
...
YOU SEE, MEI-SAN...
ERGH...
THERE'S SOMETHING I WANT TO ASK YOU.
IF I TRY TO TOUCH YOU, YOU'LL VANISH.
THAT'S WHY I'M DOING EVERYTHING I CAN...
...TO HOLD MY FEELINGS BACK.

Chapter 34 — End

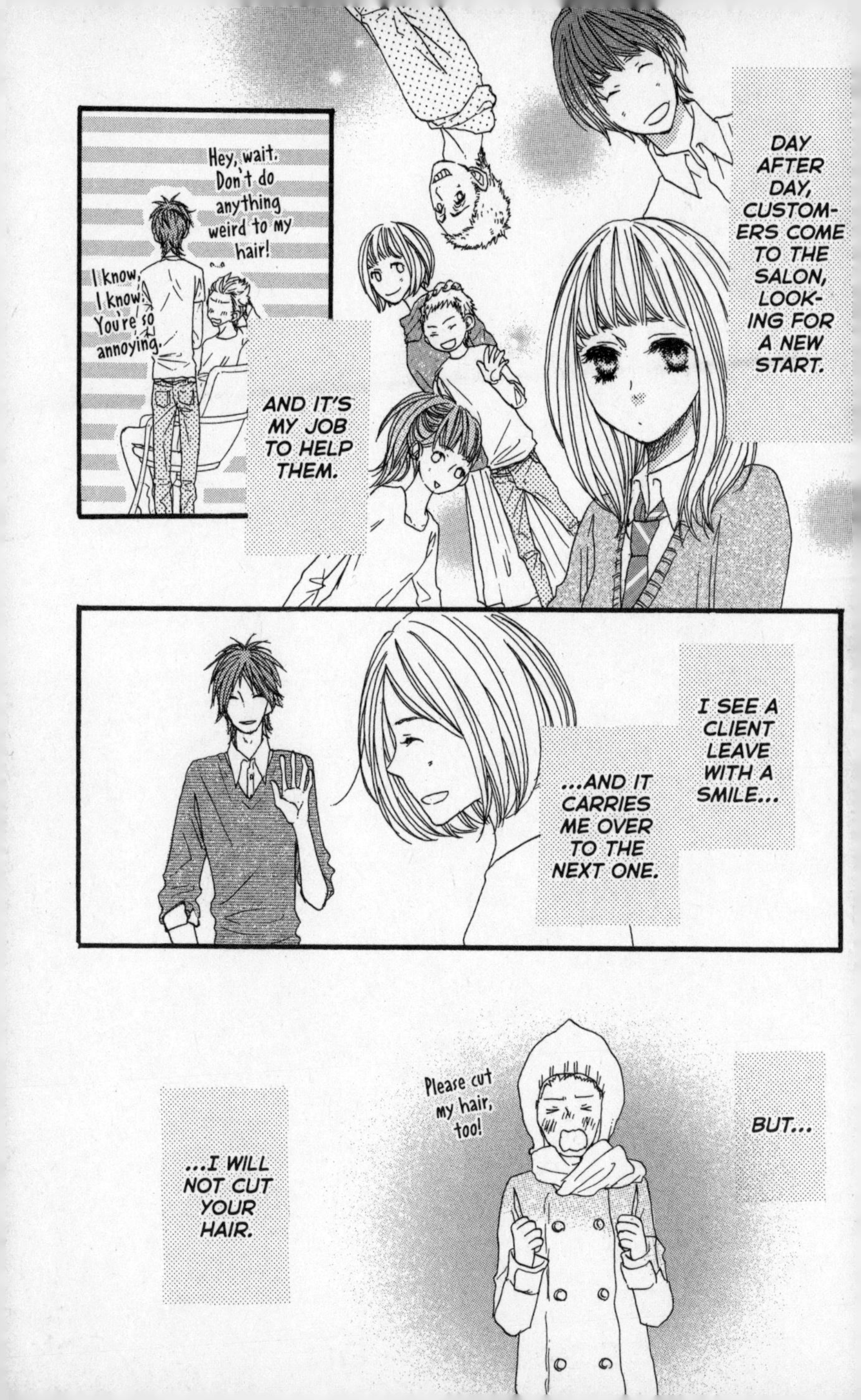
DAY AFTER DAY, CUSTOMERS COME TO THE SALON, LOOKING FOR A NEW START.
AND IT'S MY JOB TO HELP THEM.
Hey, wait. Don't do anything weird to my hair!
I know, I know. You're so annoying.
I SEE A CLIENT LEAVE WITH A SMILE...
...AND IT CARRIES ME OVER TO THE NEXT ONE.
BUT...
Please cut my hair, too!
...I WILL NOT CUT YOUR HAIR.

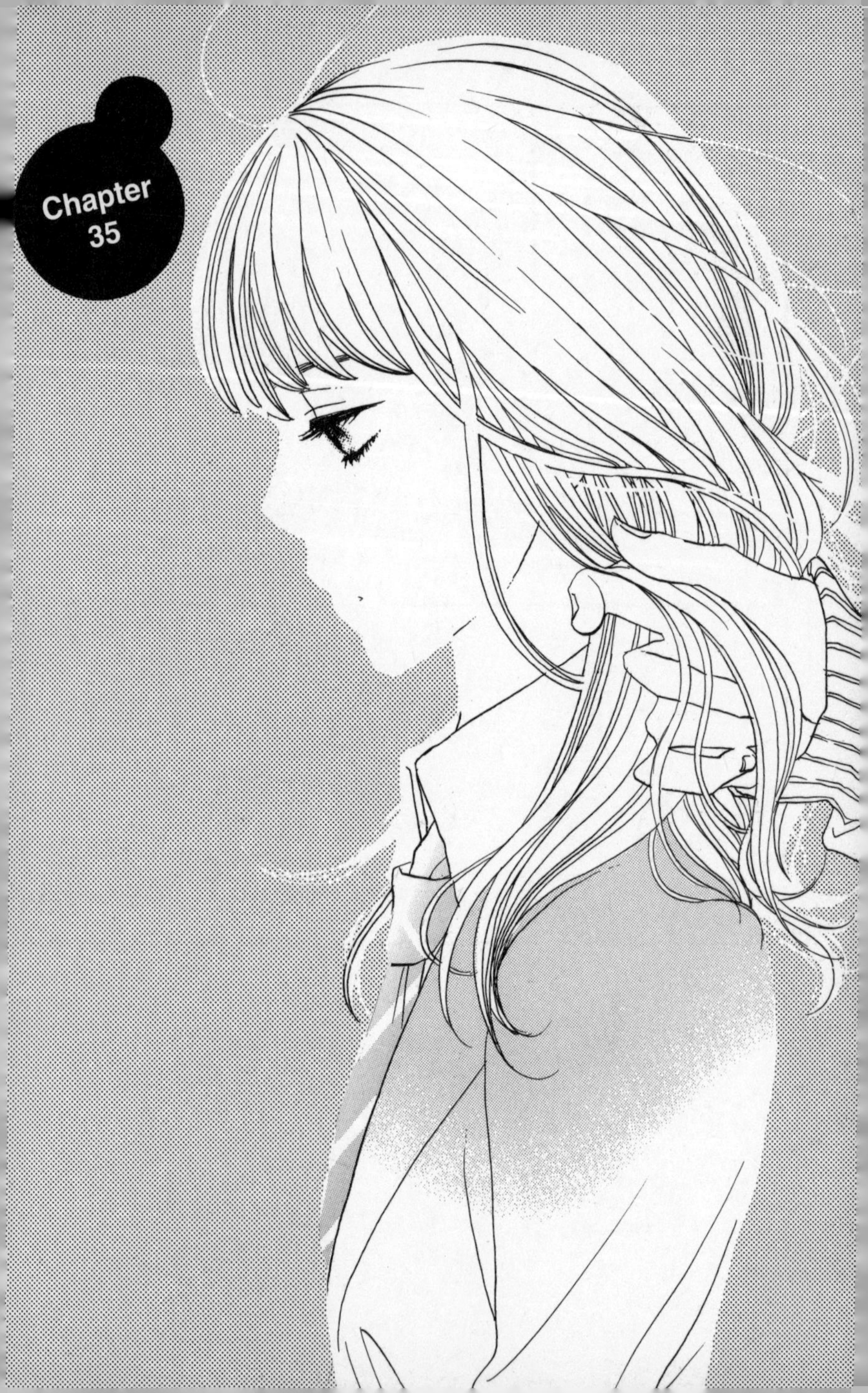
Chapter 35

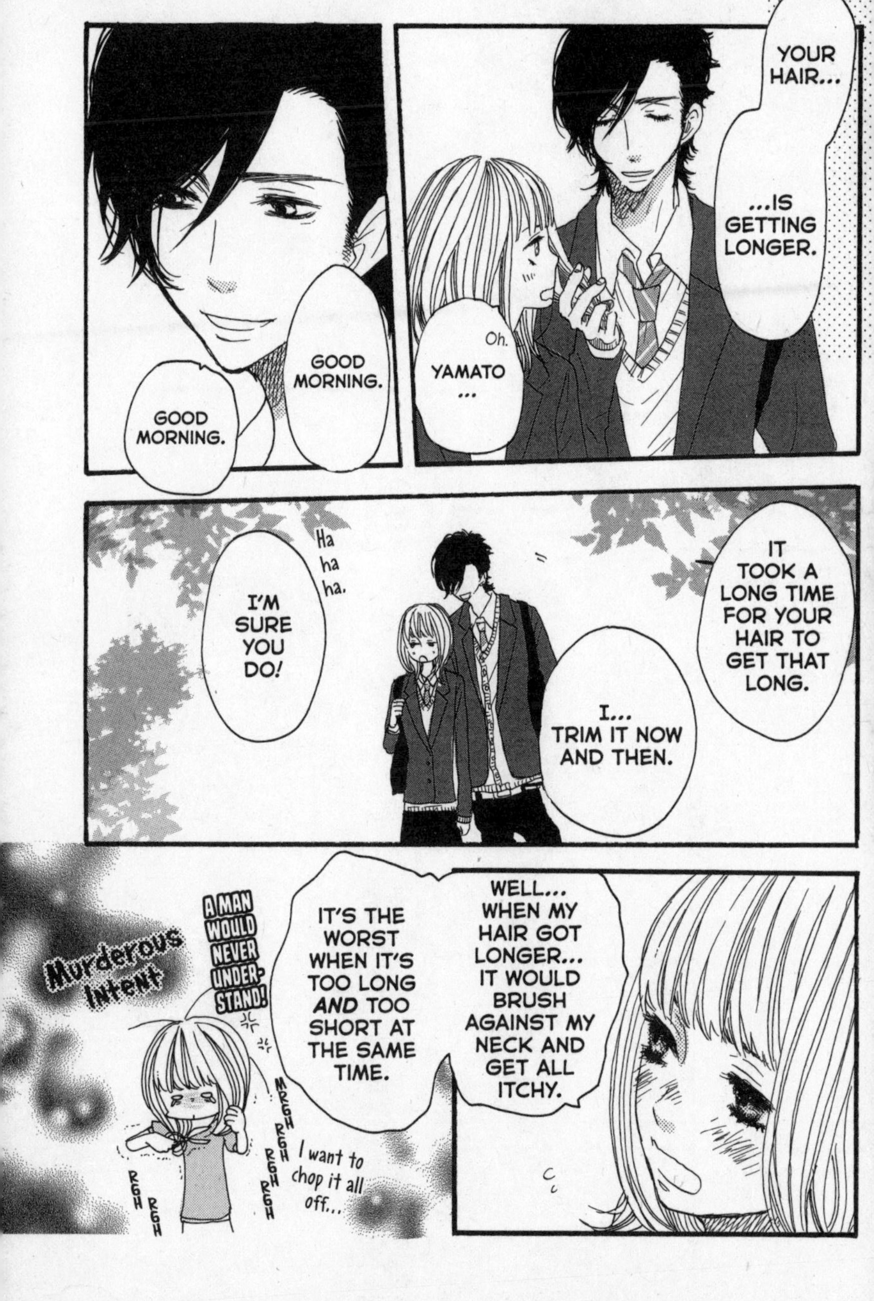
YOUR HAIR...
...IS GETTING LONGER.
Oh.
YAMATO ...
GOOD MORNING.
GOOD MORNING.
IT TOOK A LONG TIME FOR YOUR HAIR TO GET THAT LONG.
I... TRIM IT NOW AND THEN.
Ha ha ha.
I'M SURE YOU DO!
WELL... WHEN MY HAIR GOT LONGER... IT WOULD BRUSH AGAINST MY NECK AND GET ALL ITCHY.
IT'S THE WORST WHEN IT'S TOO LONG *AND* TOO SHORT AT THE SAME TIME.
A MAN WOULD NEVER UNDER-STAND!
Murderous Intent
MRGH RGH RGH RGH
I want to chop it all off...
RGH RGH

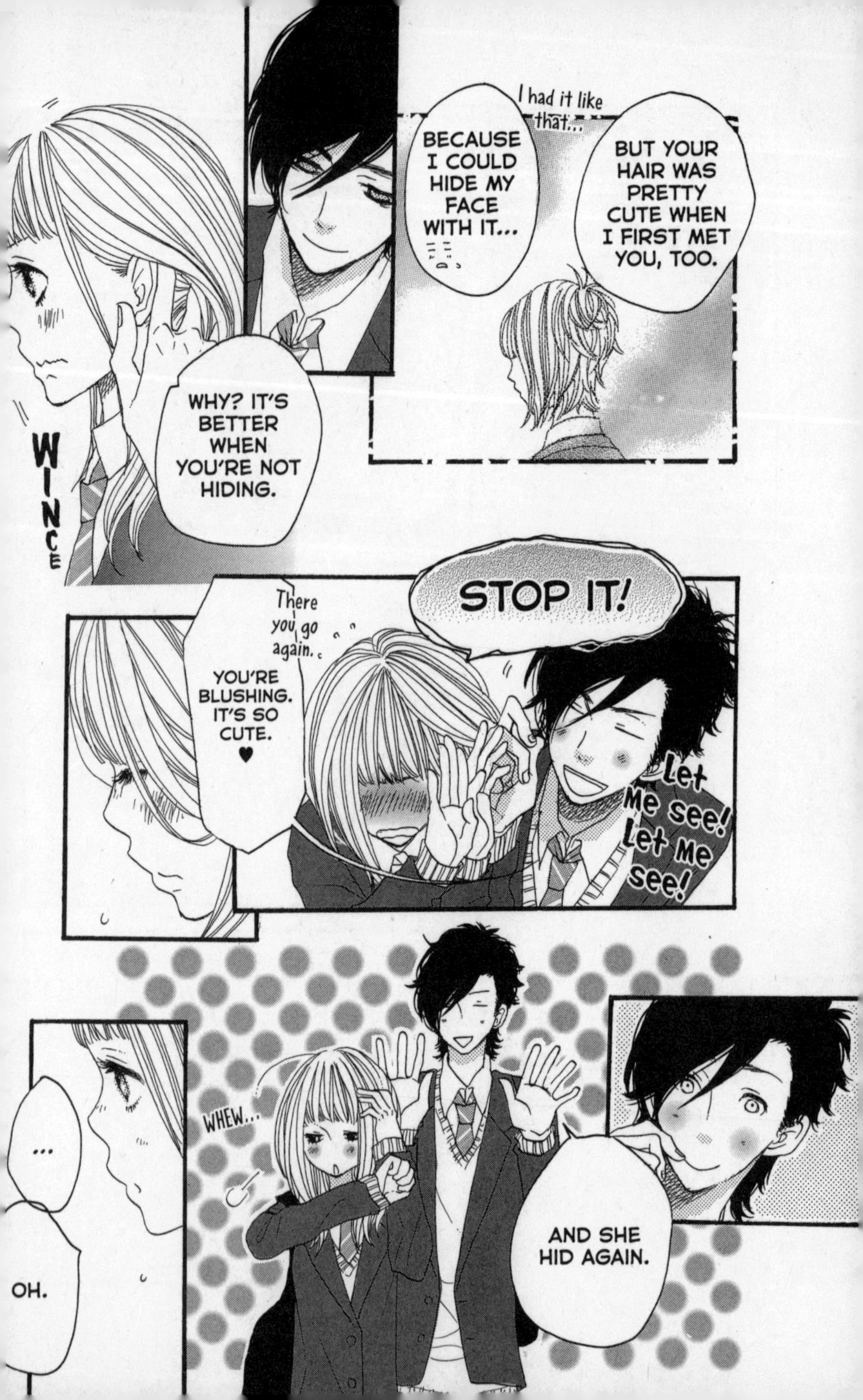
BUT YOUR HAIR WAS PRETTY CUTE WHEN I FIRST MET YOU, TOO.
I had it like that...
BECAUSE I COULD HIDE MY FACE WITH IT...
WHY? IT'S BETTER WHEN YOU'RE NOT HIDING.
WINCE
STOP IT!
Let me see! Let me see!
There you go again.
YOU'RE BLUSHING. IT'S SO CUTE. ♥
AND SHE HID AGAIN.
WHEW...
...
OH.

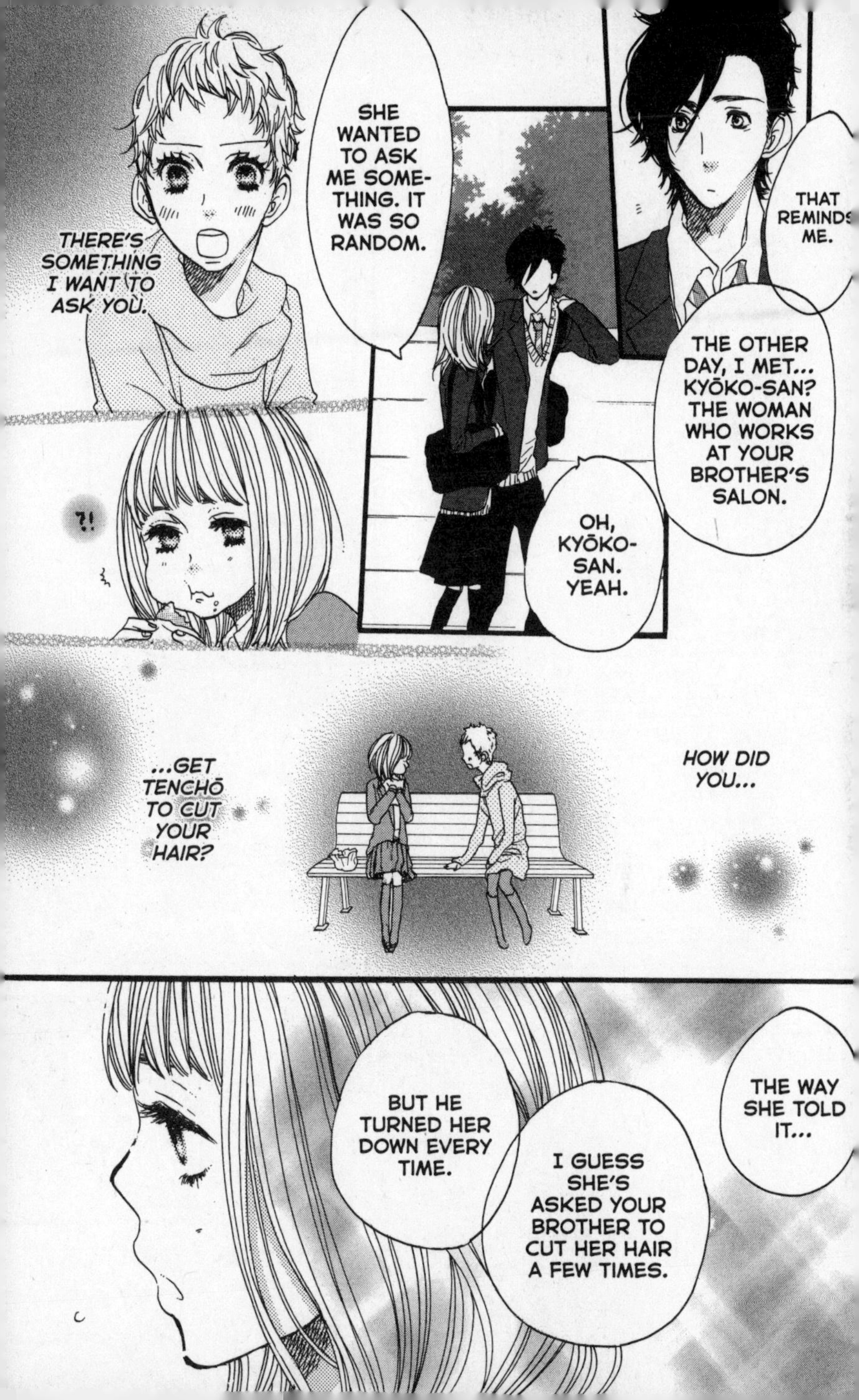
THAT REMINDS ME.
THE OTHER DAY, I MET... KYŌKO-SAN? THE WOMAN WHO WORKS AT YOUR BROTHER'S SALON.
OH, KYŌKO-SAN. YEAH.
SHE WANTED TO ASK ME SOME-THING. IT WAS SO RANDOM.
THERE'S SOMETHING I WANT TO ASK YOU.
?!
HOW DID YOU...
...GET TENCHŌ TO CUT YOUR HAIR?
THE WAY SHE TOLD IT...
I GUESS SHE'S ASKED YOUR BROTHER TO CUT HER HAIR A FEW TIMES.
BUT HE TURNED HER DOWN EVERY TIME.

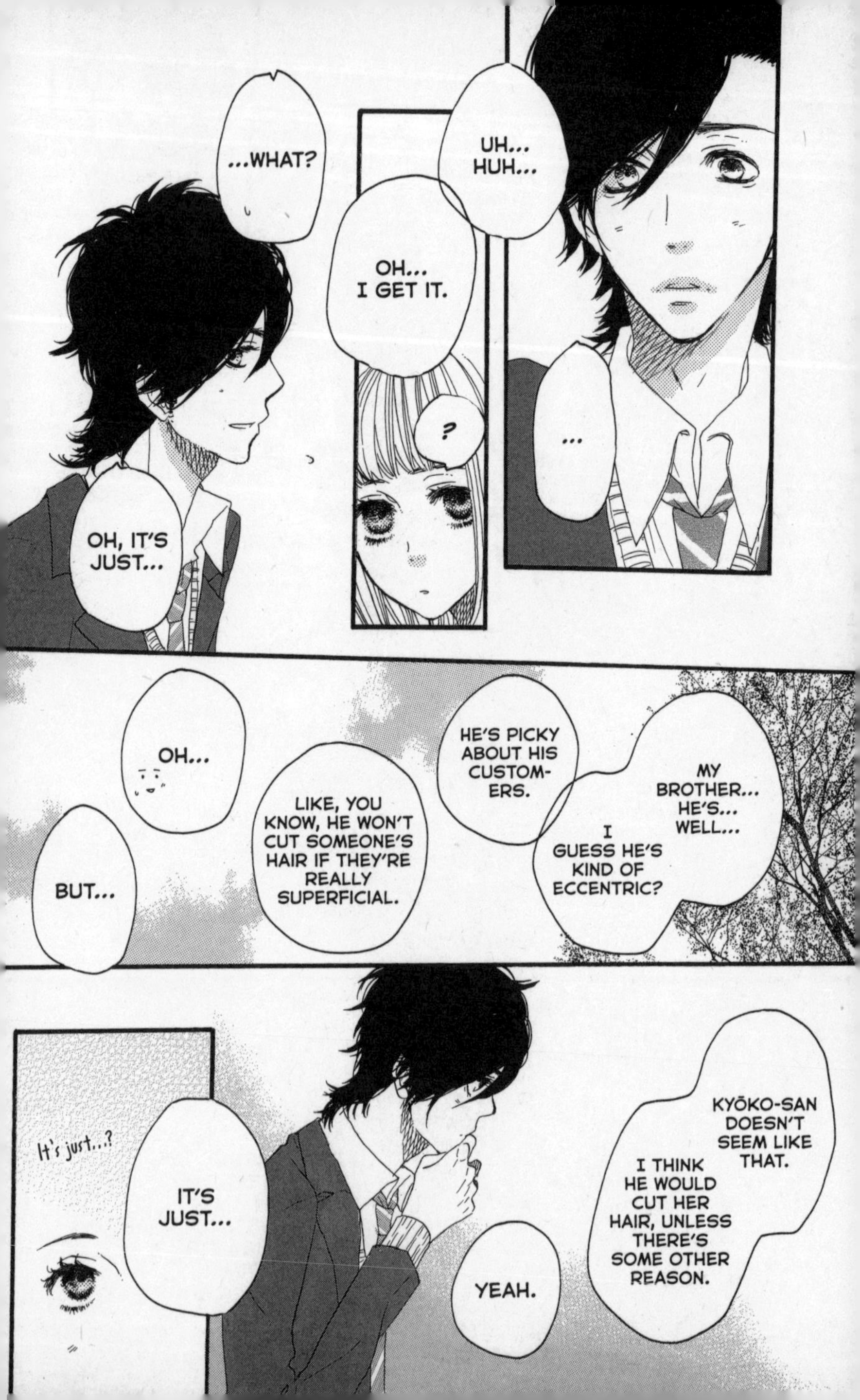
UH... HUH...
...
OH... I GET IT.
?
...WHAT?
OH, IT'S JUST...
MY BROTHER... HE'S... WELL...
I GUESS HE'S KIND OF ECCENTRIC?
HE'S PICKY ABOUT HIS CUSTOMERS.
LIKE, YOU KNOW, HE WON'T CUT SOMEONE'S HAIR IF THEY'RE REALLY SUPERFICIAL.
OH...
BUT...
KYŌKO-SAN DOESN'T SEEM LIKE THAT.
I THINK HE WOULD CUT HER HAIR, UNLESS THERE'S SOME OTHER REASON.
YEAH.
IT'S JUST...
It's just...?

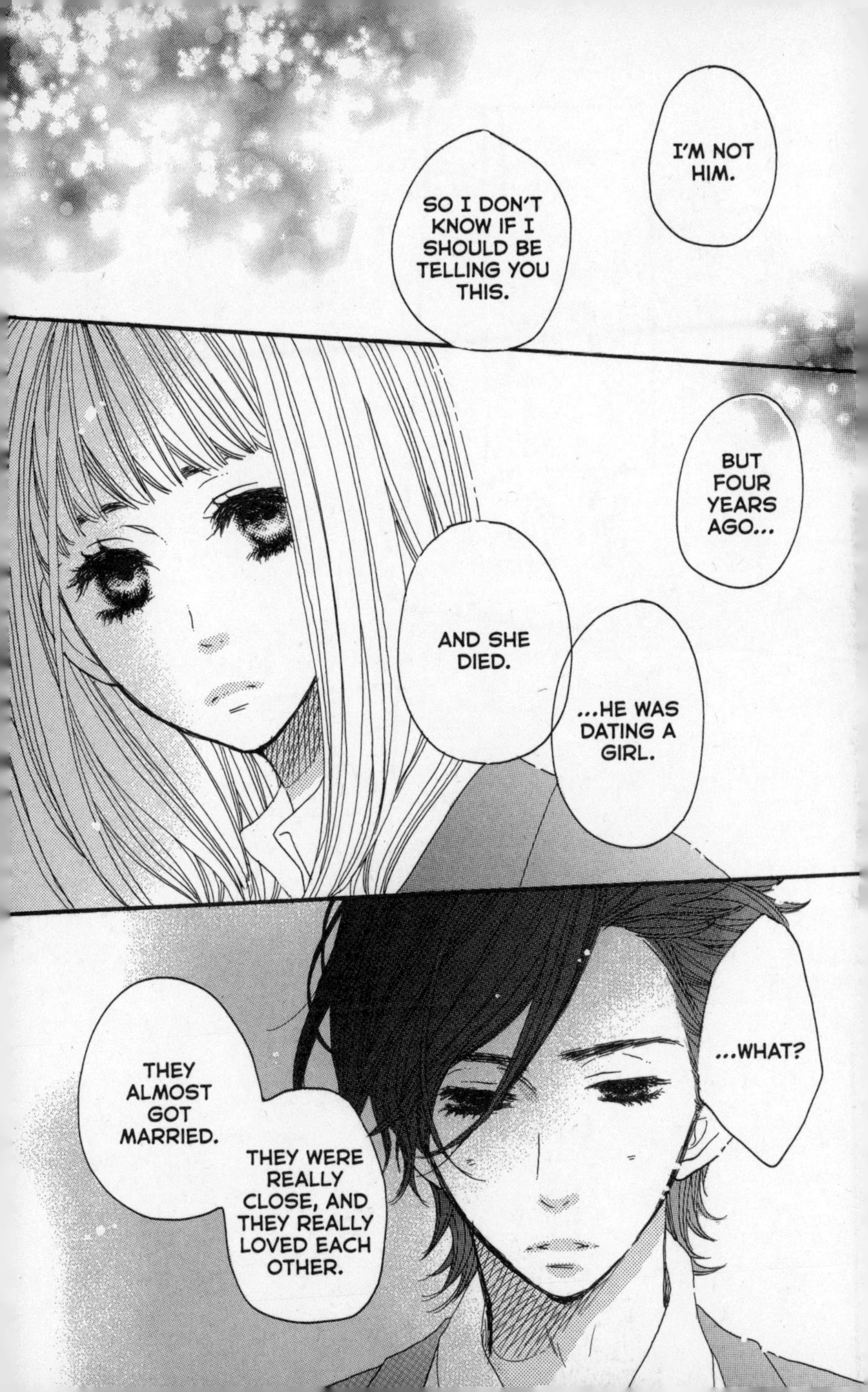
I'M NOT HIM.
SO I DON'T KNOW IF I SHOULD BE TELLING YOU THIS.
BUT FOUR YEARS AGO...
...HE WAS DATING A GIRL.
AND SHE DIED.
...WHAT?
THEY ALMOST GOT MARRIED.
THEY WERE REALLY CLOSE, AND THEY REALLY LOVED EACH OTHER.

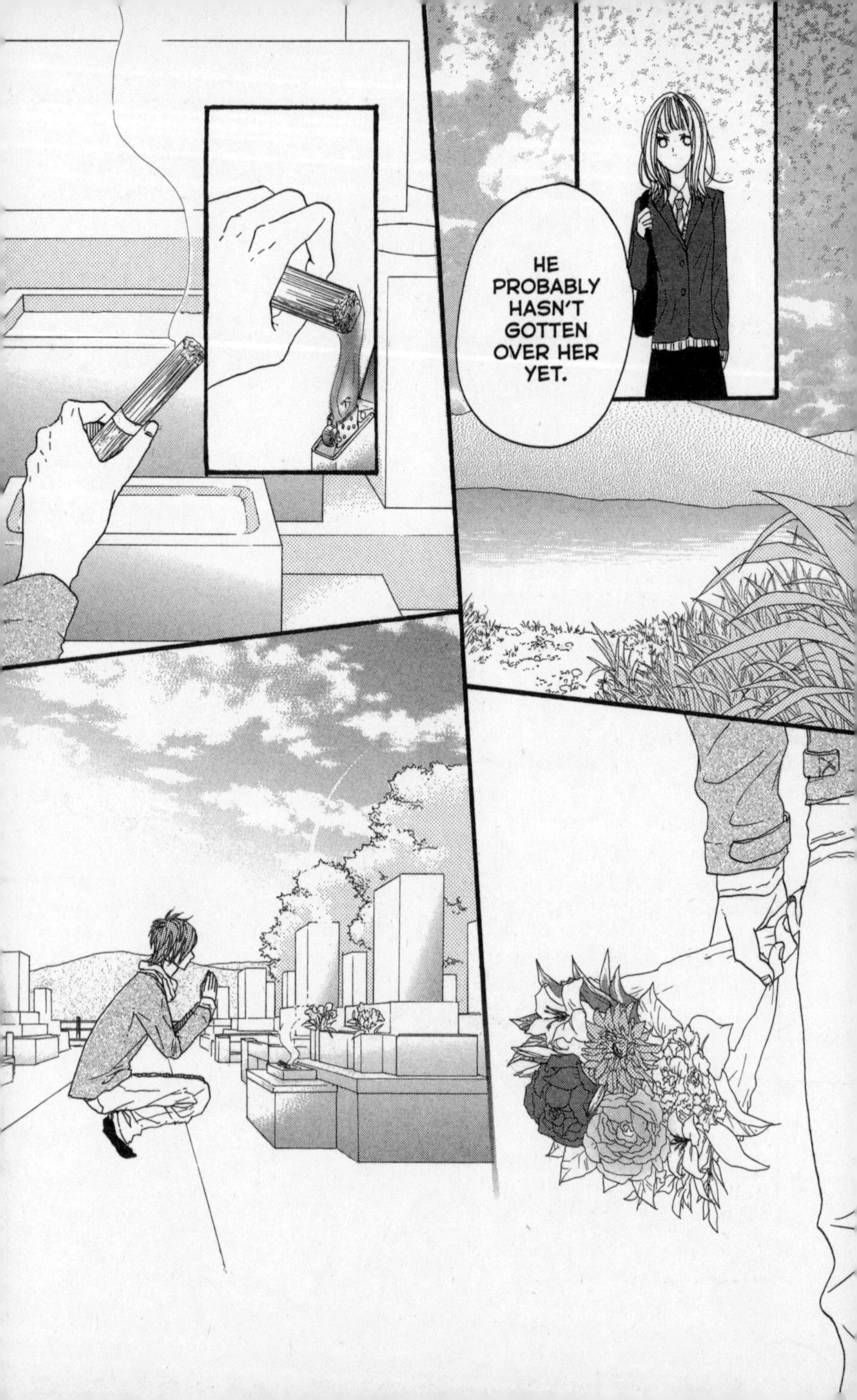
HE PROBABLY HASN'T GOTTEN OVER HER YET.

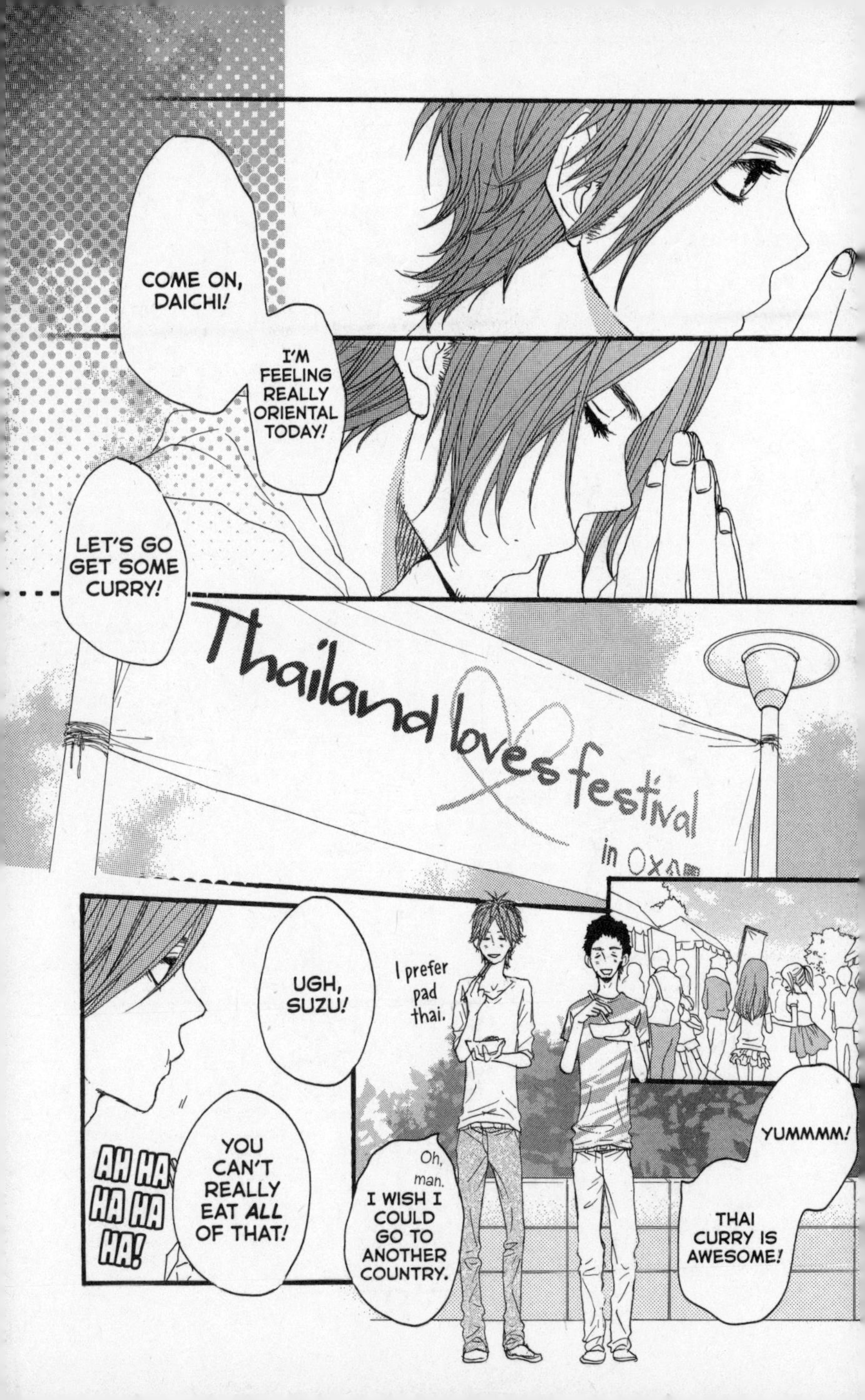
COME ON, DAICHI!
I'M FEELING REALLY ORIENTAL TODAY!
LET'S GO GET SOME CURRY!
Thailand loves festival
YUMMMM!
THAI CURRY IS AWESOME!
Oh, man.
I WISH I COULD GO TO ANOTHER COUNTRY.
I prefer pad thai.
UGH, SUZU!
YOU CAN'T REALLY EAT ALL OF THAT!
AH HA HA HA HA!

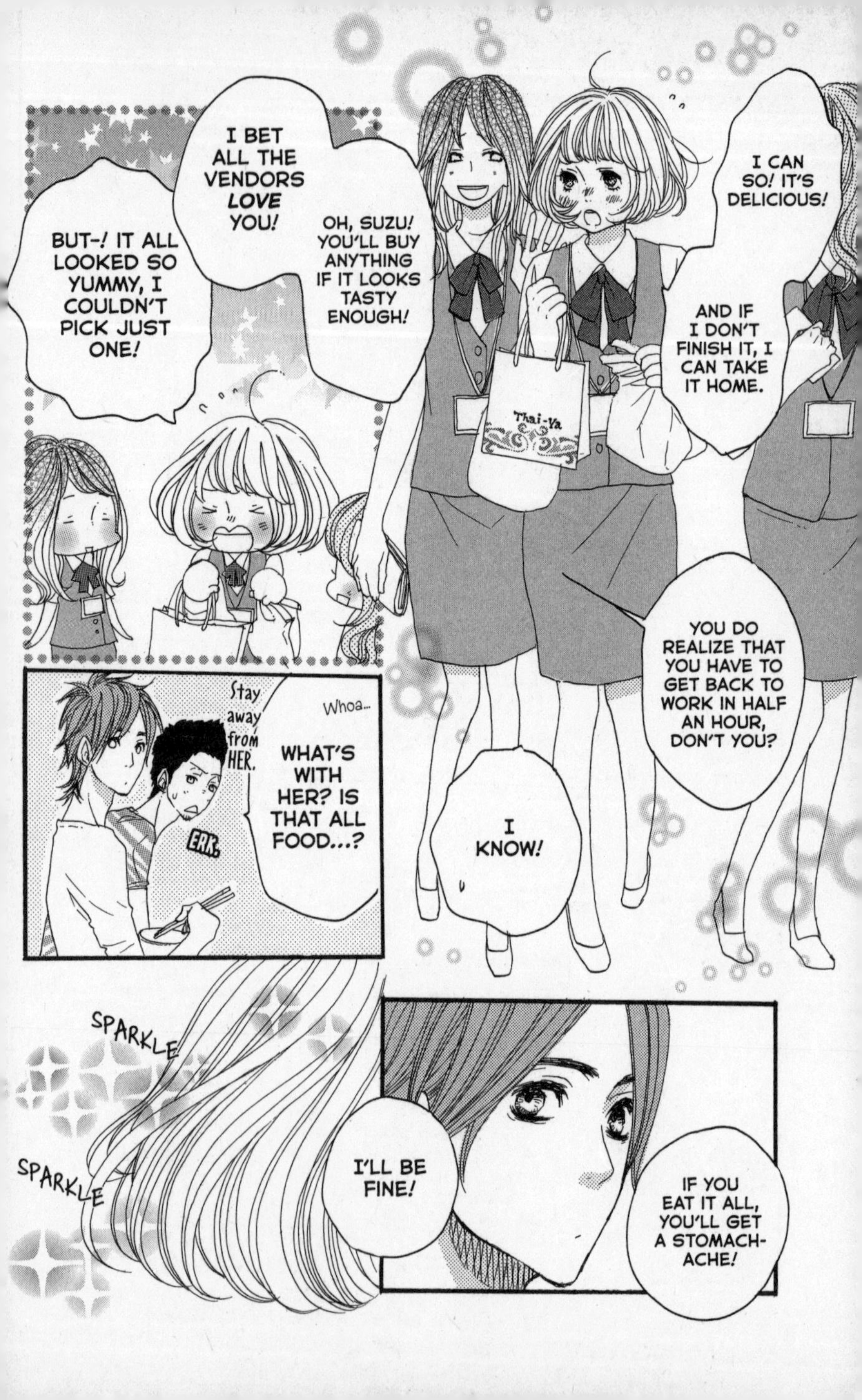
I CAN SO! IT'S DELICIOUS!
AND IF I DON'T FINISH IT, I CAN TAKE IT HOME.
OH, SUZU! YOU'LL BUY ANYTHING IF IT LOOKS TASTY ENOUGH!
YOU DO REALIZE THAT YOU HAVE TO GET BACK TO WORK IN HALF AN HOUR, DON'T YOU?
I KNOW!
I BET ALL THE VENDORS LOVE YOU!
BUT-! IT ALL LOOKED SO YUMMY, I COULDN'T PICK JUST ONE!
Stay away from HER.
Whoa...
WHAT'S WITH HER? IS THAT ALL FOOD...?
ERK.
IF YOU EAT IT ALL, YOU'LL GET A STOMACH-ACHE!
I'LL BE FINE!
SPARKLE
SPARKLE

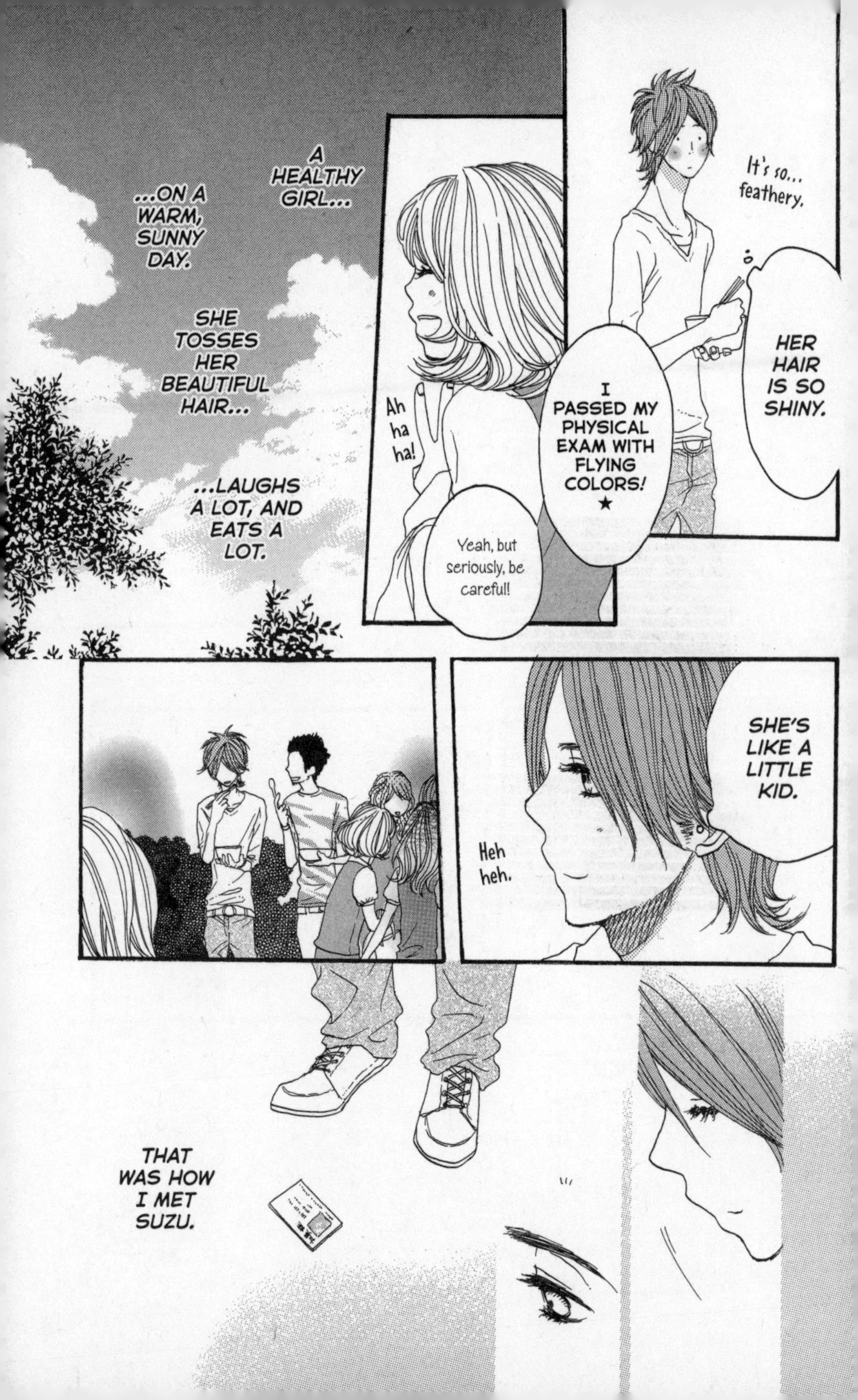
It's so... feathery.
HER HAIR IS SO SHINY.
I PASSED MY PHYSICAL EXAM WITH FLYING COLORS! ★
Ah ha ha!
Yeah, but seriously, be careful!
A HEALTHY GIRL...
...ON A WARM, SUNNY DAY.
SHE TOSSES HER BEAUTIFUL HAIR...
...LAUGHS A LOT, AND EATS A LOT.
SHE'S LIKE A LITTLE KID.
Heh heh.
THAT WAS HOW I MET SUZU.

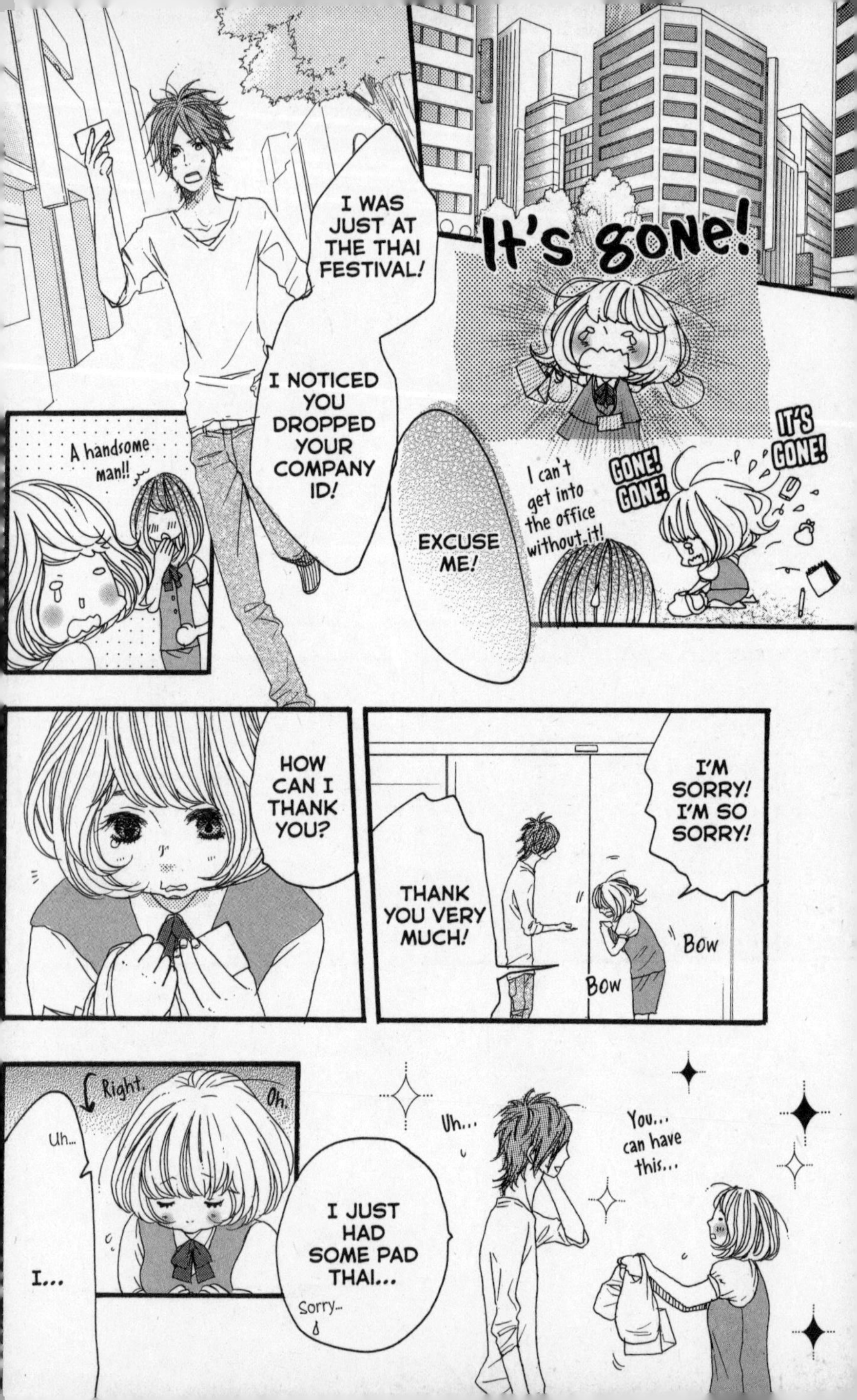
It's gone!
IT'S GONE!
GONE! GONE!
I can't get into the office without it!
EXCUSE ME!
I WAS JUST AT THE THAI FESTIVAL!
I NOTICED YOU DROPPED YOUR COMPANY ID!
A handsome man!!
I'M SORRY! I'M SO SORRY!
Bow
Bow
THANK YOU VERY MUCH!
HOW CAN I THANK YOU?
You... can have this...
Uh...
Oh.
Right.
Uh...
I JUST HAD SOME PAD THAI...
Sorry...
I...

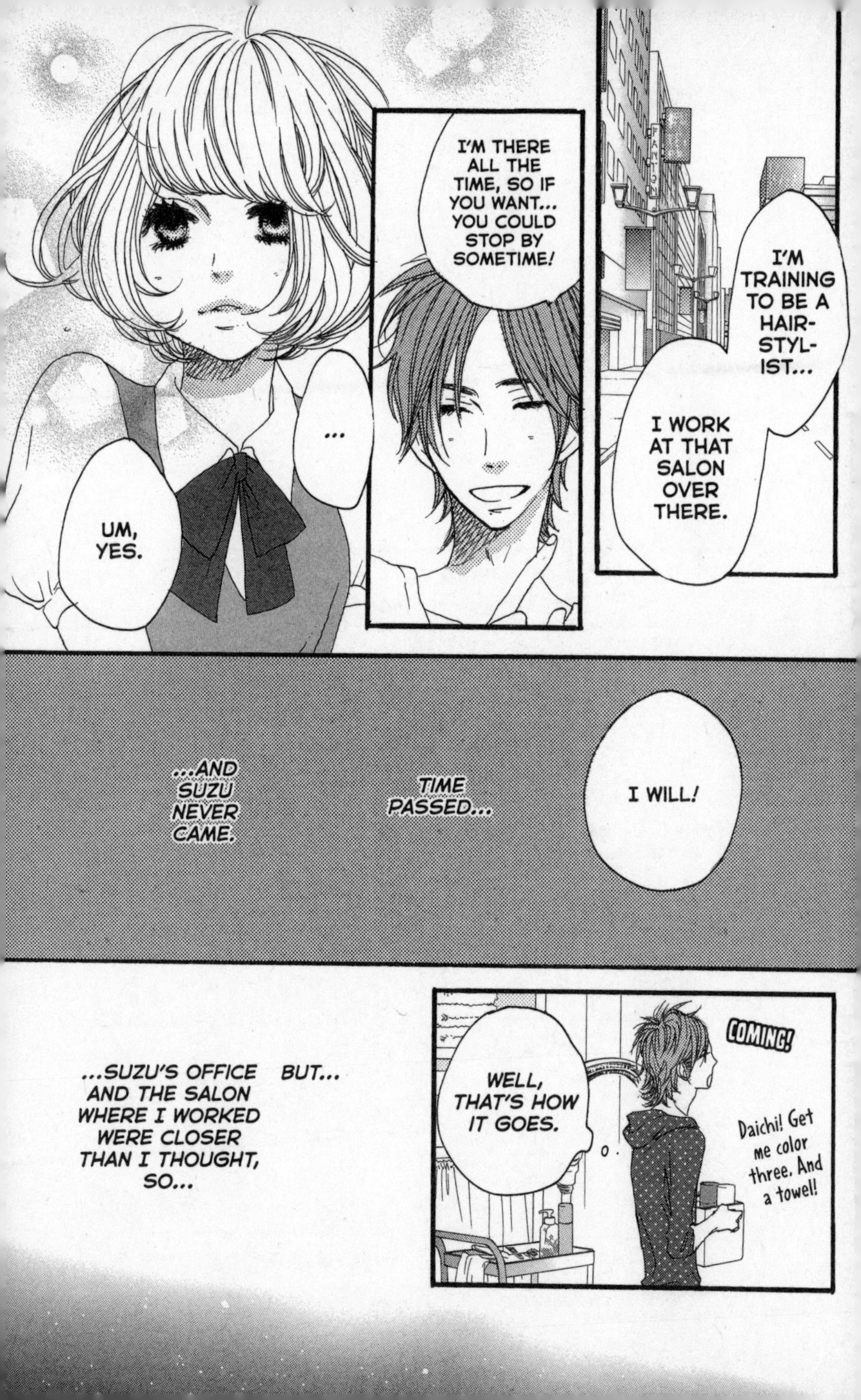
I'M TRAINING TO BE A HAIR-STYL-IST...
I WORK AT THAT SALON OVER THERE.
I'M THERE ALL THE TIME, SO IF YOU WANT... YOU COULD STOP BY SOMETIME!
...
UM, YES.
I WILL!
TIME PASSED...
...AND SUZU NEVER CAME.
COMING!
Daichi! Get me color three. And a towel!
WELL, THAT'S HOW IT GOES.
BUT...
...SUZU'S OFFICE AND THE SALON WHERE I WORKED WERE CLOSER THAN I THOUGHT, SO...

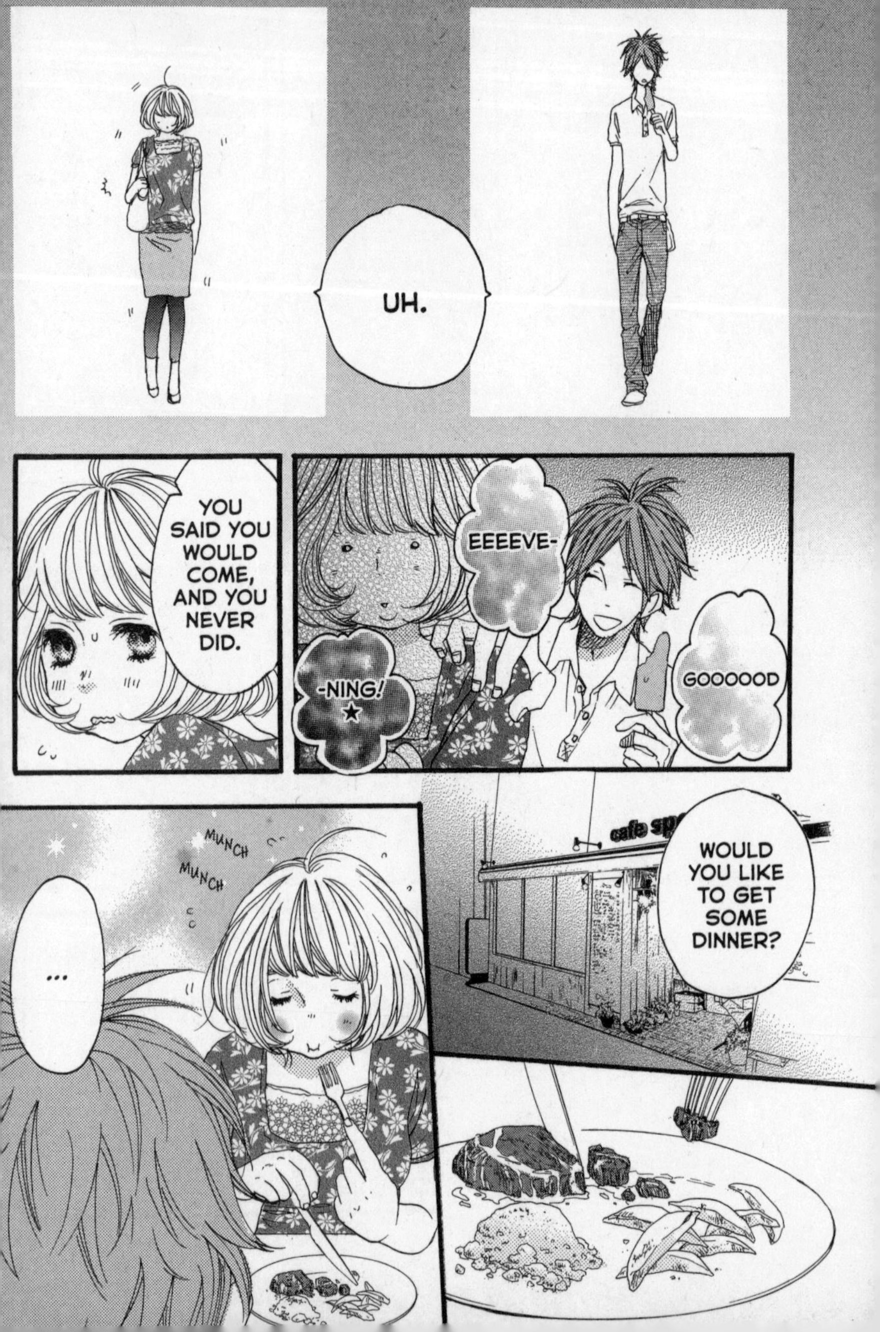
UH.
GOOOOOD
EEEEVE-
-NING! ★
YOU SAID YOU WOULD COME, AND YOU NEVER DID.
WOULD YOU LIKE TO GET SOME DINNER?
cafe sp
MUNCH
MUNCH
...

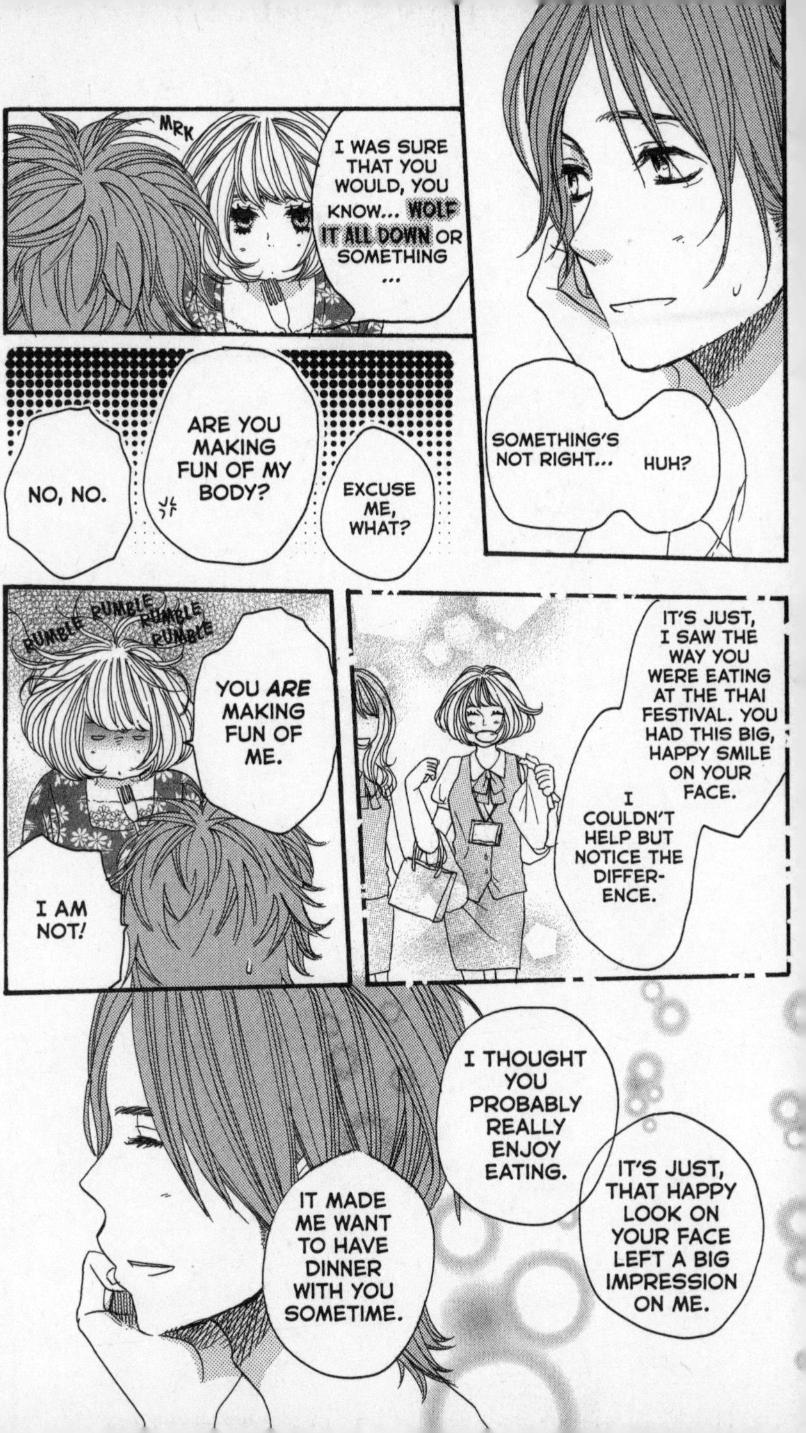

SOMETHING'S NOT RIGHT...
HUH?
MRK
I WAS SURE THAT YOU WOULD, YOU KNOW... WOLF IT ALL DOWN OR SOMETHING ...
EXCUSE ME, WHAT?
ARE YOU MAKING FUN OF MY BODY?
NO, NO.
IT'S JUST, I SAW THE WAY YOU WERE EATING AT THE THAI FESTIVAL. YOU HAD THIS BIG, HAPPY SMILE ON YOUR FACE.
I COULDN'T HELP BUT NOTICE THE DIFFER-ENCE.
RUMBLE RUMBLE RUMBLE RUMBLE
YOU ARE MAKING FUN OF ME.
I AM NOT!
IT'S JUST, THAT HAPPY LOOK ON YOUR FACE LEFT A BIG IMPRESSION ON ME.
I THOUGHT YOU PROBABLY REALLY ENJOY EATING.
IT MADE ME WANT TO HAVE DINNER WITH YOU SOMETIME.

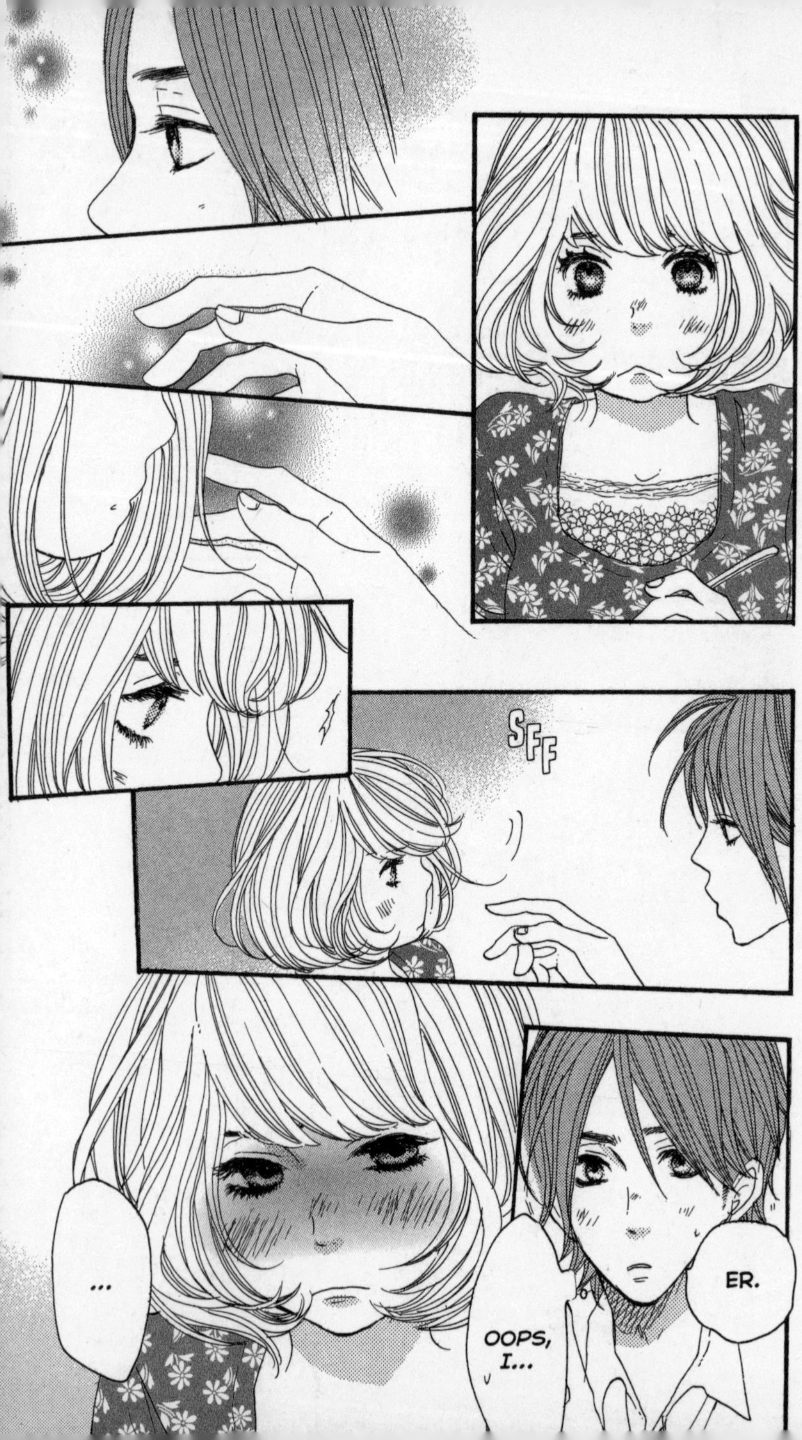
SFF
ER.
OOPS, I...
...

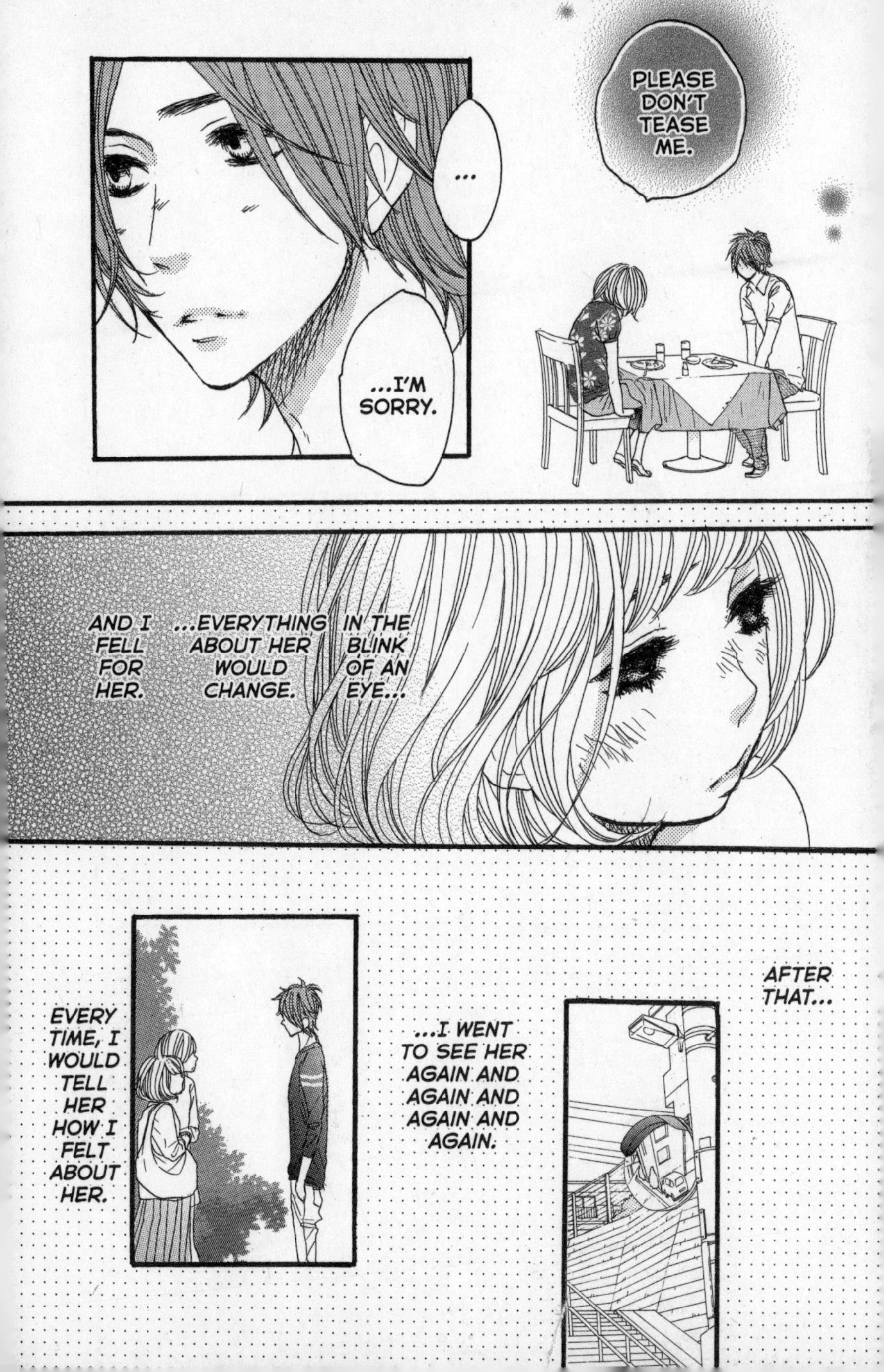
PLEASE DON'T TEASE ME.
...
...I'M SORRY.
IN THE BLINK OF AN EYE...
...EVERYTHING ABOUT HER WOULD CHANGE.
AND I FELL FOR HER.
AFTER THAT...
...I WENT TO SEE HER AGAIN AND AGAIN AND AGAIN AND AGAIN.
EVERY TIME, I WOULD TELL HER HOW I FELT ABOUT HER.

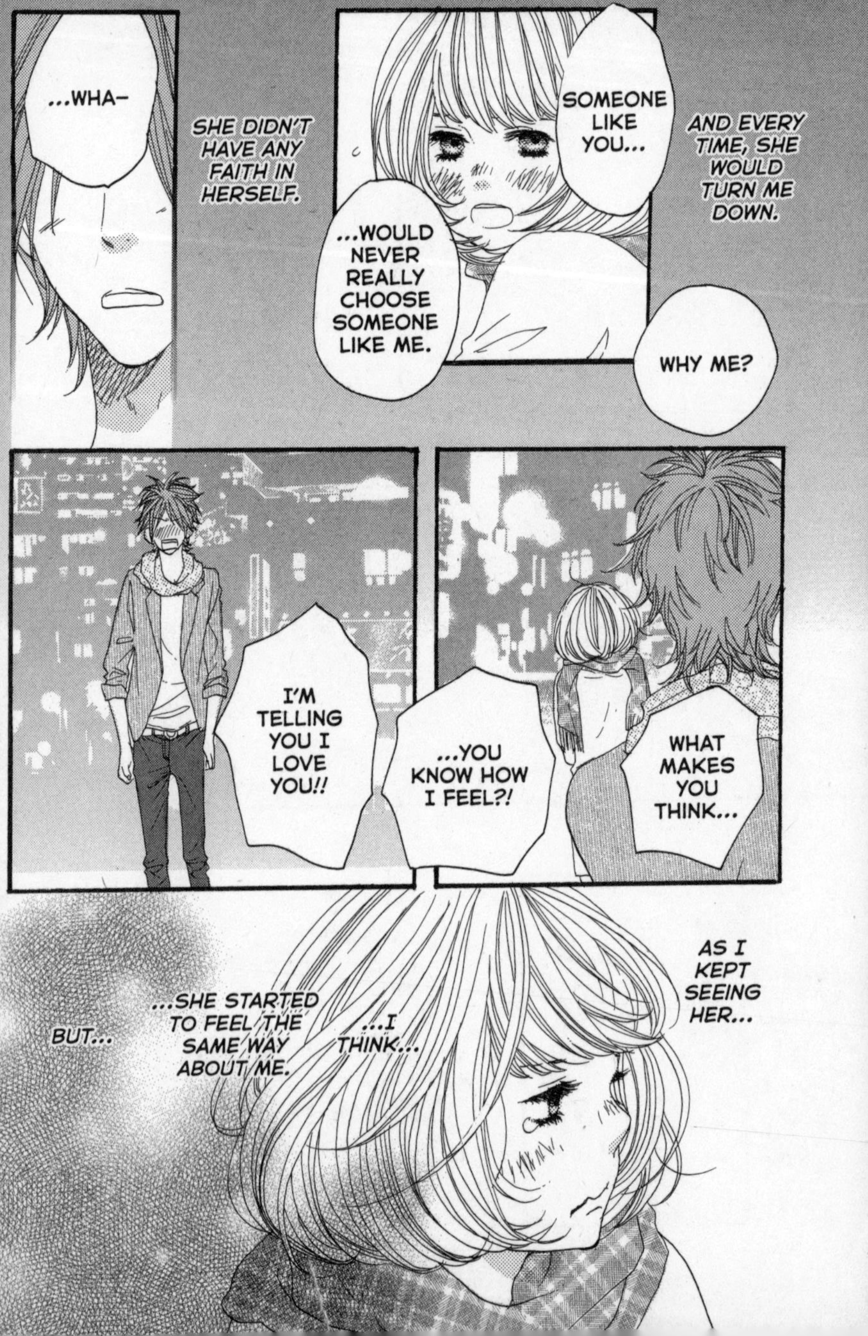
AND EVERY TIME, SHE WOULD TURN ME DOWN.
SOMEONE LIKE YOU...
...WOULD NEVER REALLY CHOOSE SOMEONE LIKE ME.
WHY ME?
SHE DIDN'T HAVE ANY FAITH IN HERSELF.
...WHA–
WHAT MAKES YOU THINK...
...YOU KNOW HOW I FEEL?!
I'M TELLING YOU I LOVE YOU!!
AS I KEPT SEEING HER...
...I THINK...
...SHE STARTED TO FEEL THE SAME WAY ABOUT ME.
BUT...

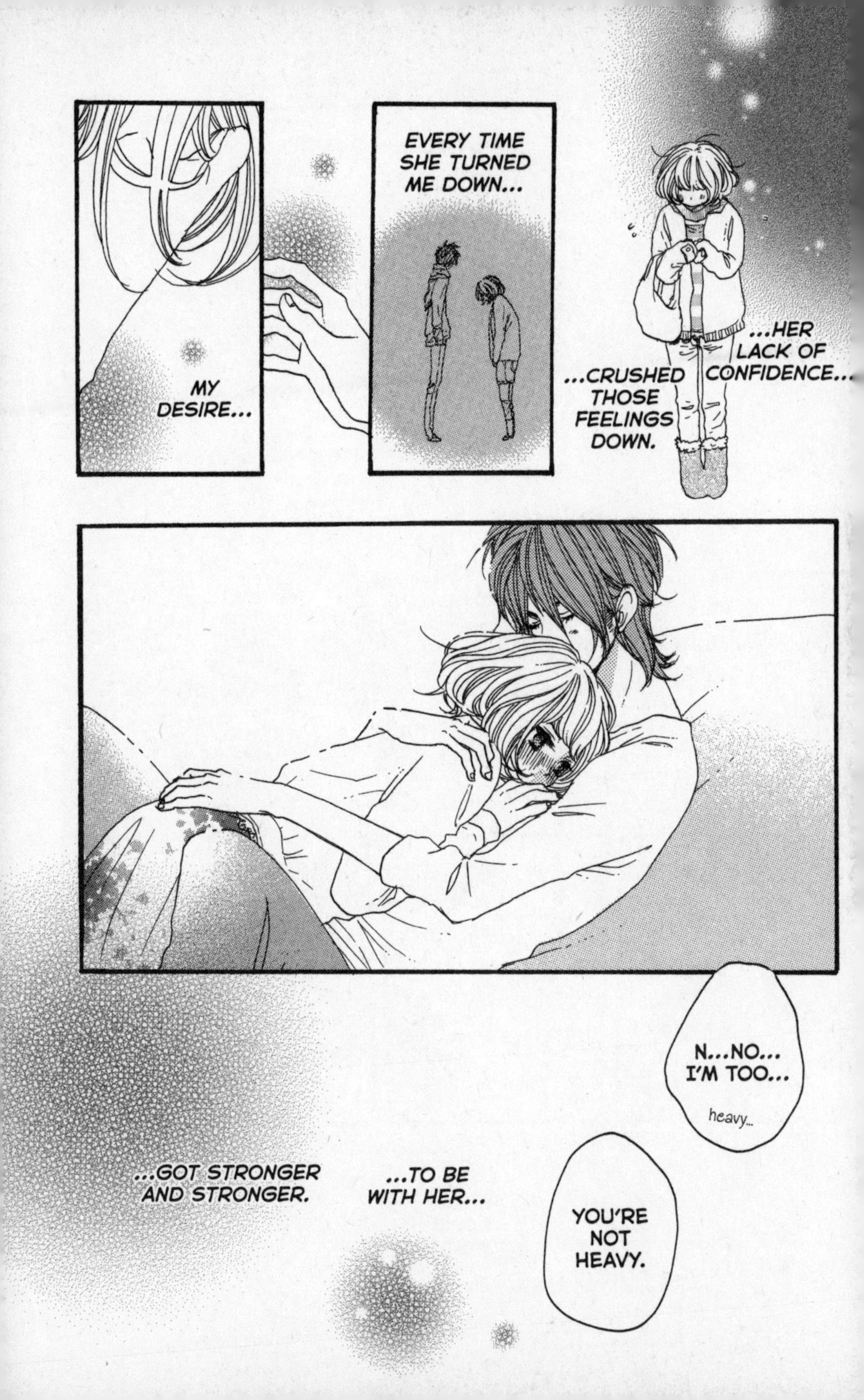
...HER LACK OF CONFIDENCE...
...CRUSHED THOSE FEELINGS DOWN.
EVERY TIME SHE TURNED ME DOWN...
MY DESIRE...
N...NO... I'M TOO...
heavy...
YOU'RE NOT HEAVY.
...TO BE WITH HER...
...GOT STRONGER AND STRONGER.

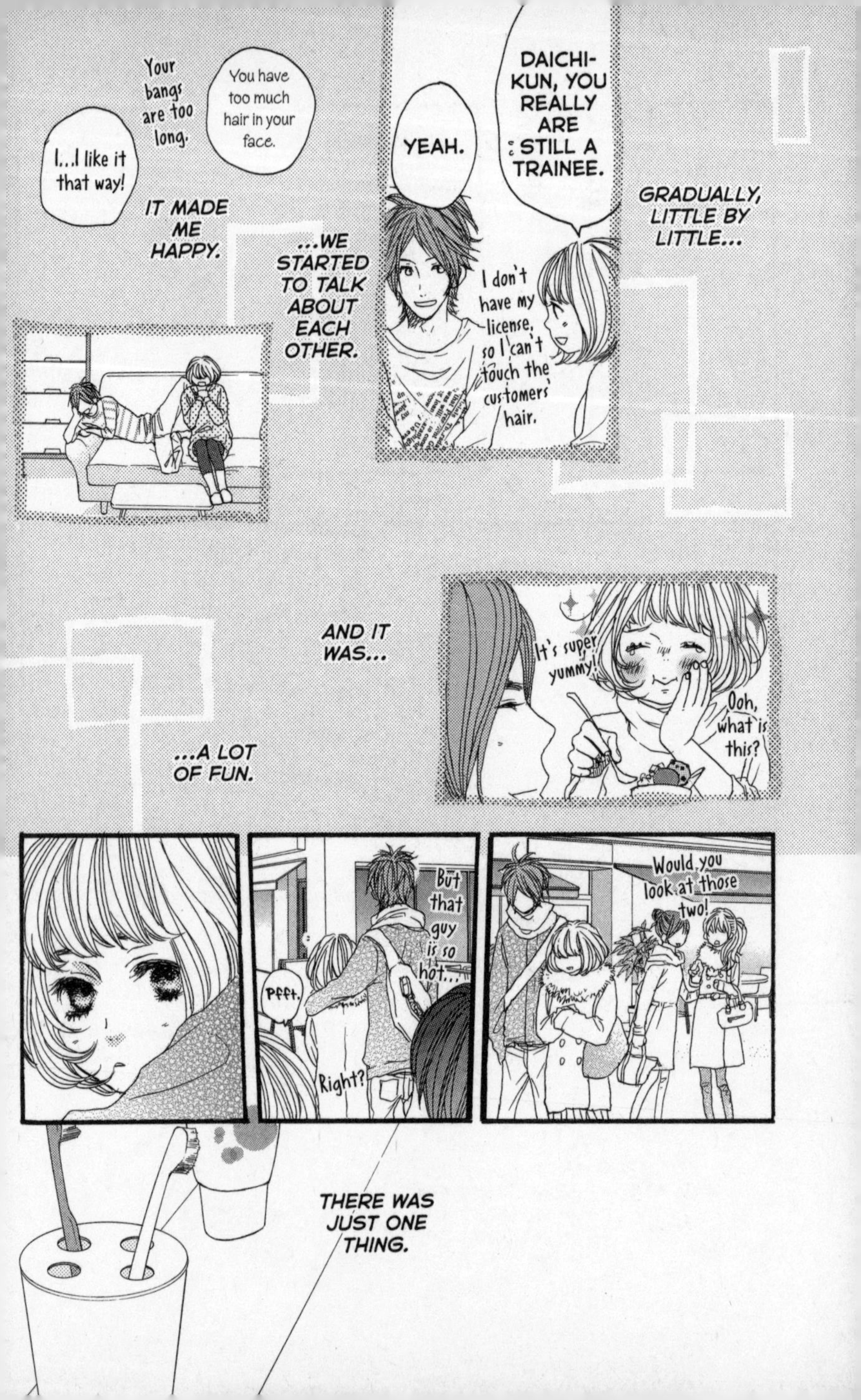
GRADUALLY, LITTLE BY LITTLE...
DAICHI-KUN, YOU REALLY ARE STILL A TRAINEE.
YEAH.
I don't have my license, so I can't touch the customers' hair.
...WE STARTED TO TALK ABOUT EACH OTHER.
IT MADE ME HAPPY.
You have too much hair in your face.
Your bangs are too long.
I...I like it that way!
Ooh, what is this?
It's super yummy!
AND IT WAS...
...A LOT OF FUN.
Would you look at those two!
But that guy is so hot...
Pfft.
Right?
THERE WAS JUST ONE THING.

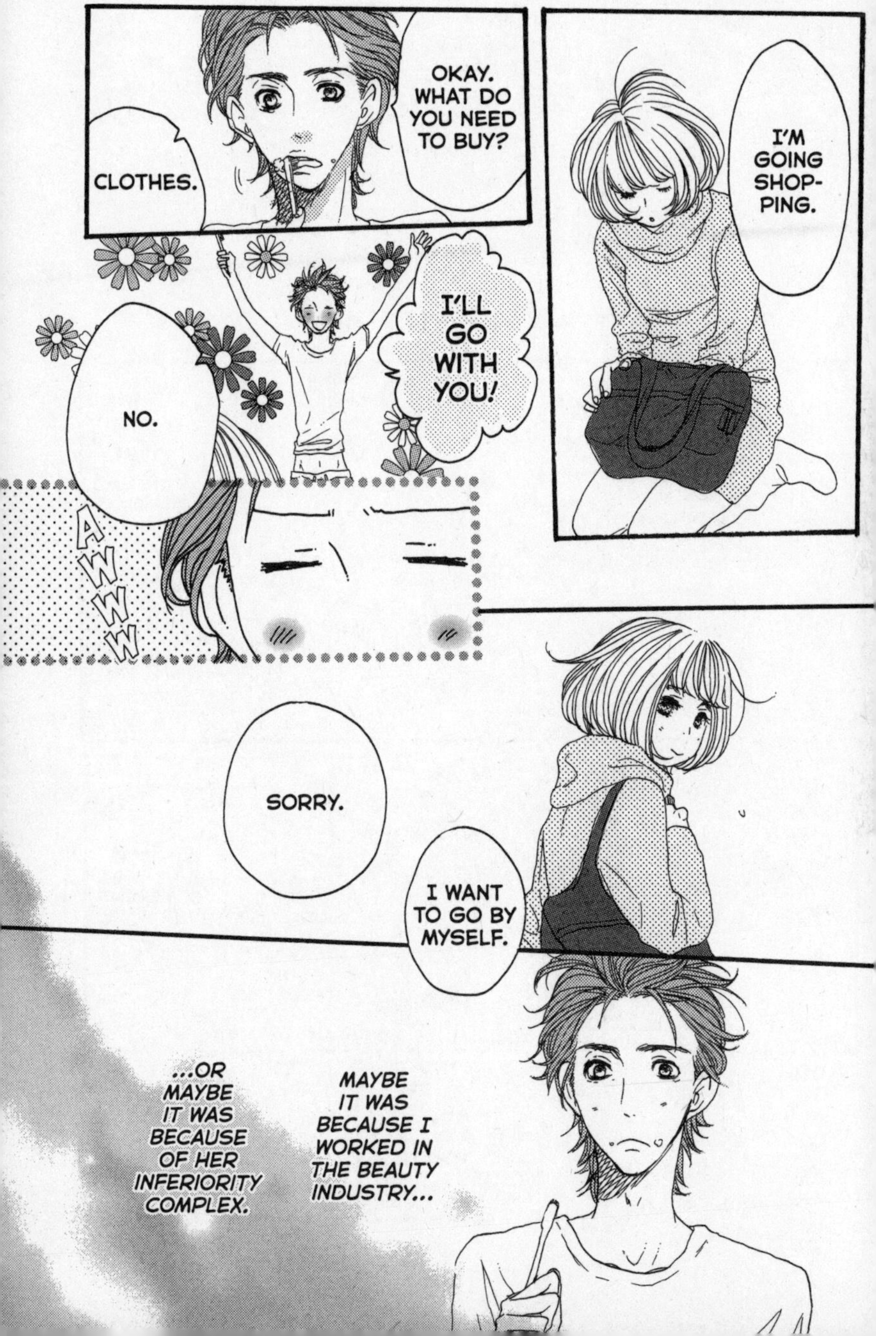
I'M GOING SHOP-PING.
OKAY. WHAT DO YOU NEED TO BUY?
CLOTHES.
I'LL GO WITH YOU!
NO.
AWWW
SORRY.
I WANT TO GO BY MYSELF.
MAYBE IT WAS BECAUSE I WORKED IN THE BEAUTY INDUSTRY...
...OR MAYBE IT WAS BECAUSE OF HER INFERIORITY COMPLEX.

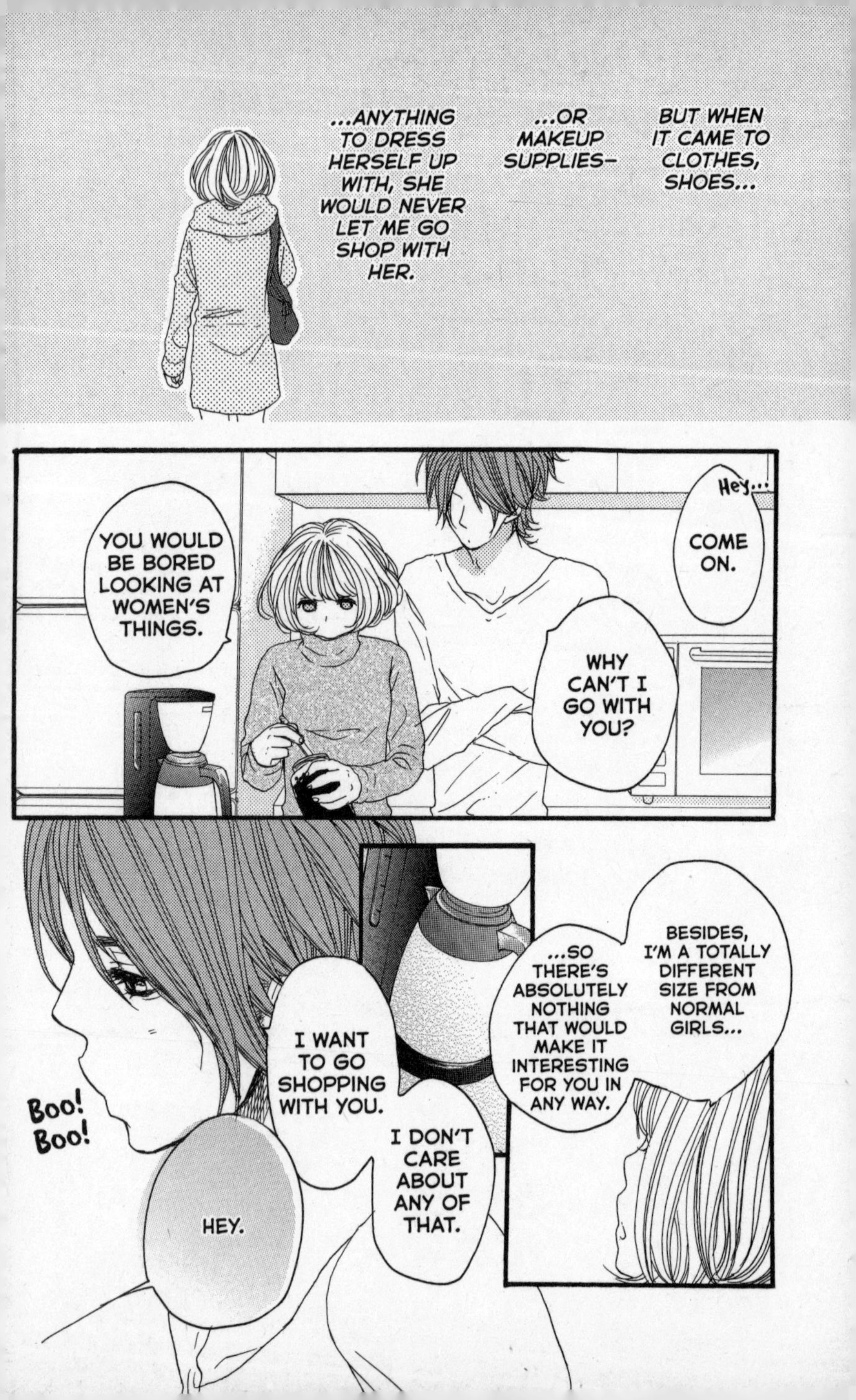
BUT WHEN IT CAME TO CLOTHES, SHOES...
...OR MAKEUP SUPPLIES—
...ANYTHING TO DRESS HERSELF UP WITH, SHE WOULD NEVER LET ME GO SHOP WITH HER.
Hey...
COME ON.
WHY CAN'T I GO WITH YOU?
YOU WOULD BE BORED LOOKING AT WOMEN'S THINGS.
BESIDES, I'M A TOTALLY DIFFERENT SIZE FROM NORMAL GIRLS...
...SO THERE'S ABSOLUTELY NOTHING THAT WOULD MAKE IT INTERESTING FOR YOU IN ANY WAY.
I WANT TO GO SHOPPING WITH YOU.
I DON'T CARE ABOUT ANY OF THAT.
Boo! Boo!
HEY.

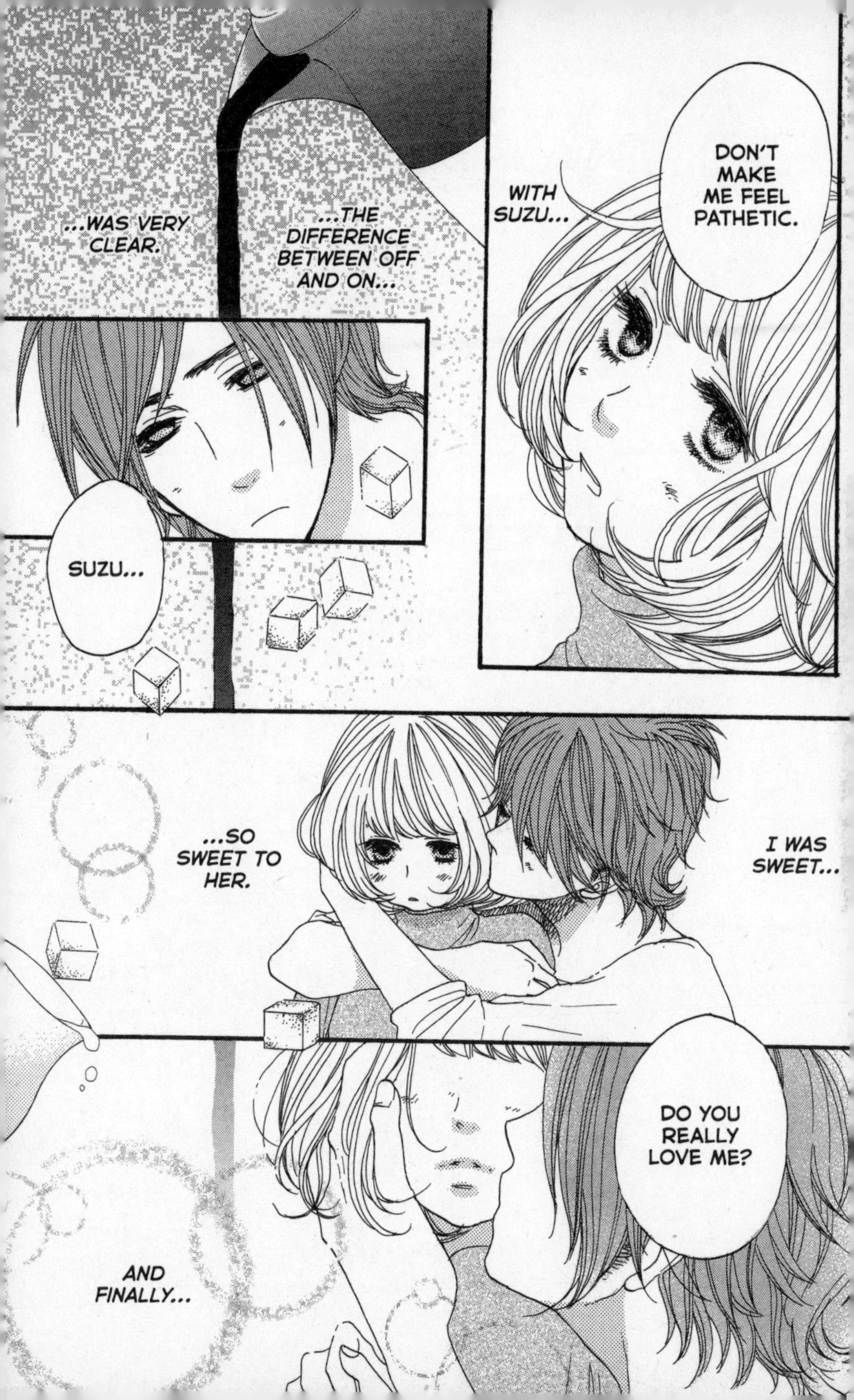
DON'T MAKE ME FEEL PATHETIC.
WITH SUZU...
...THE DIFFERENCE BETWEEN OFF AND ON...
...WAS VERY CLEAR.
SUZU...
I WAS SWEET...
...SO SWEET TO HER.
DO YOU REALLY LOVE ME?
AND FINALLY...

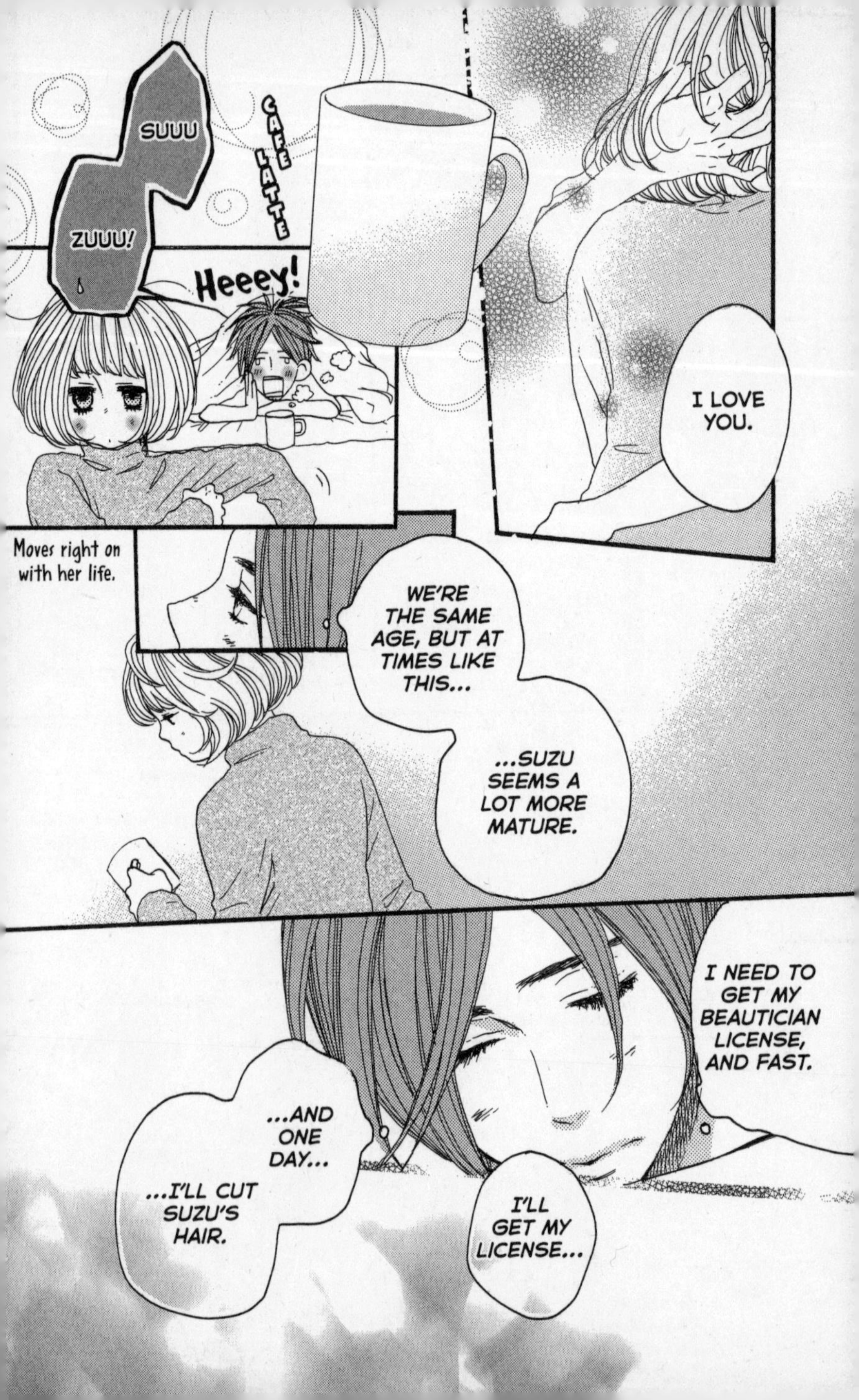
I LOVE YOU.
CAFE LATTE
Heeey!
SUUU
ZUUU!
Moves right on with her life.
WE'RE THE SAME AGE, BUT AT TIMES LIKE THIS...
...SUZU SEEMS A LOT MORE MATURE.
I NEED TO GET MY BEAUTICIAN LICENSE, AND FAST.
I'LL GET MY LICENSE...
...AND ONE DAY...
...I'LL CUT SUZU'S HAIR.

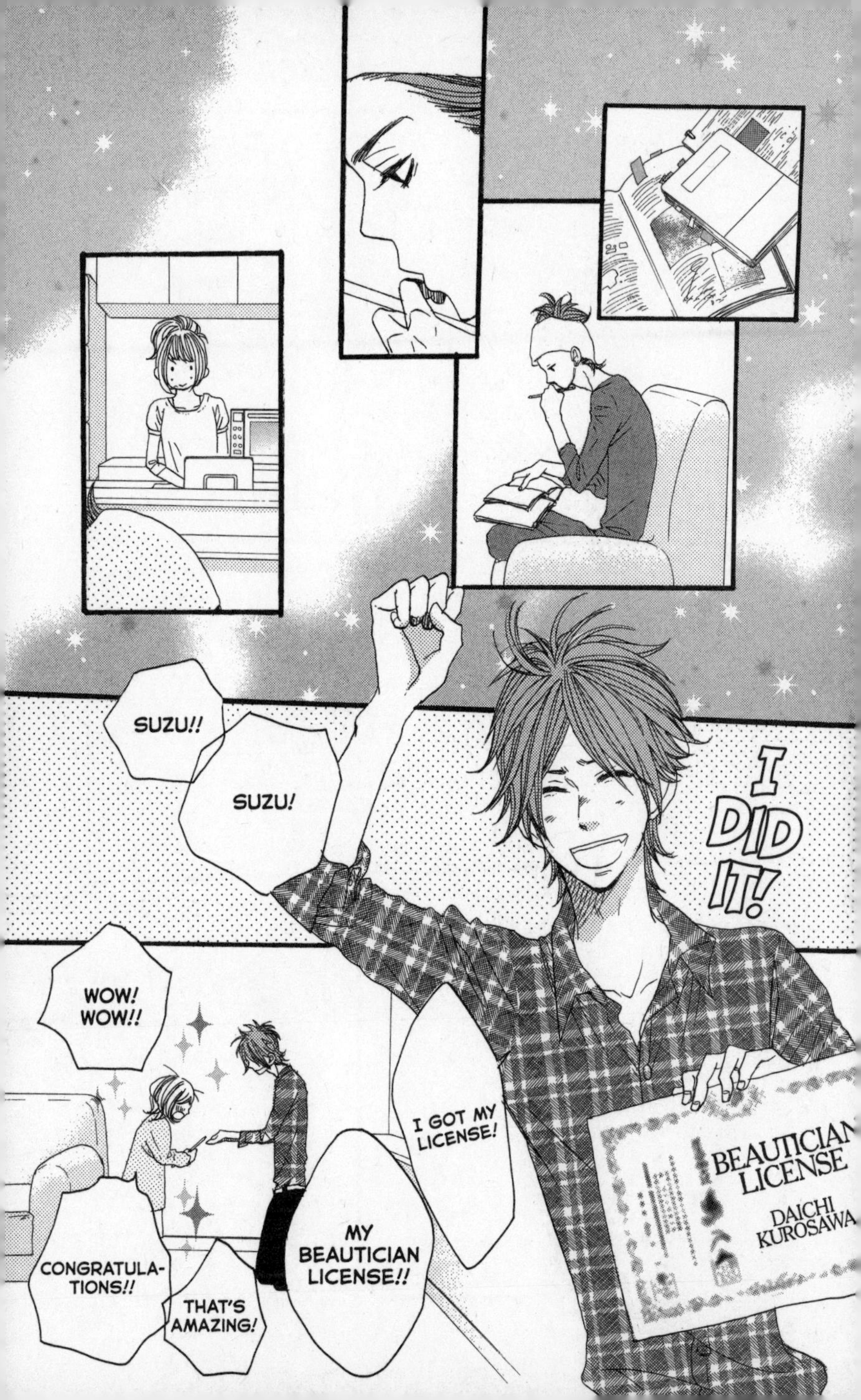
I DID IT!
SUZU!!
SUZU!
I GOT MY LICENSE!
MY BEAUTICIAN LICENSE!!
BEAUTICIAN LICENSE
DAICHI KUROSAWA
WOW! WOW!!
THAT'S AMAZING!
CONGRATULA-TIONS!!

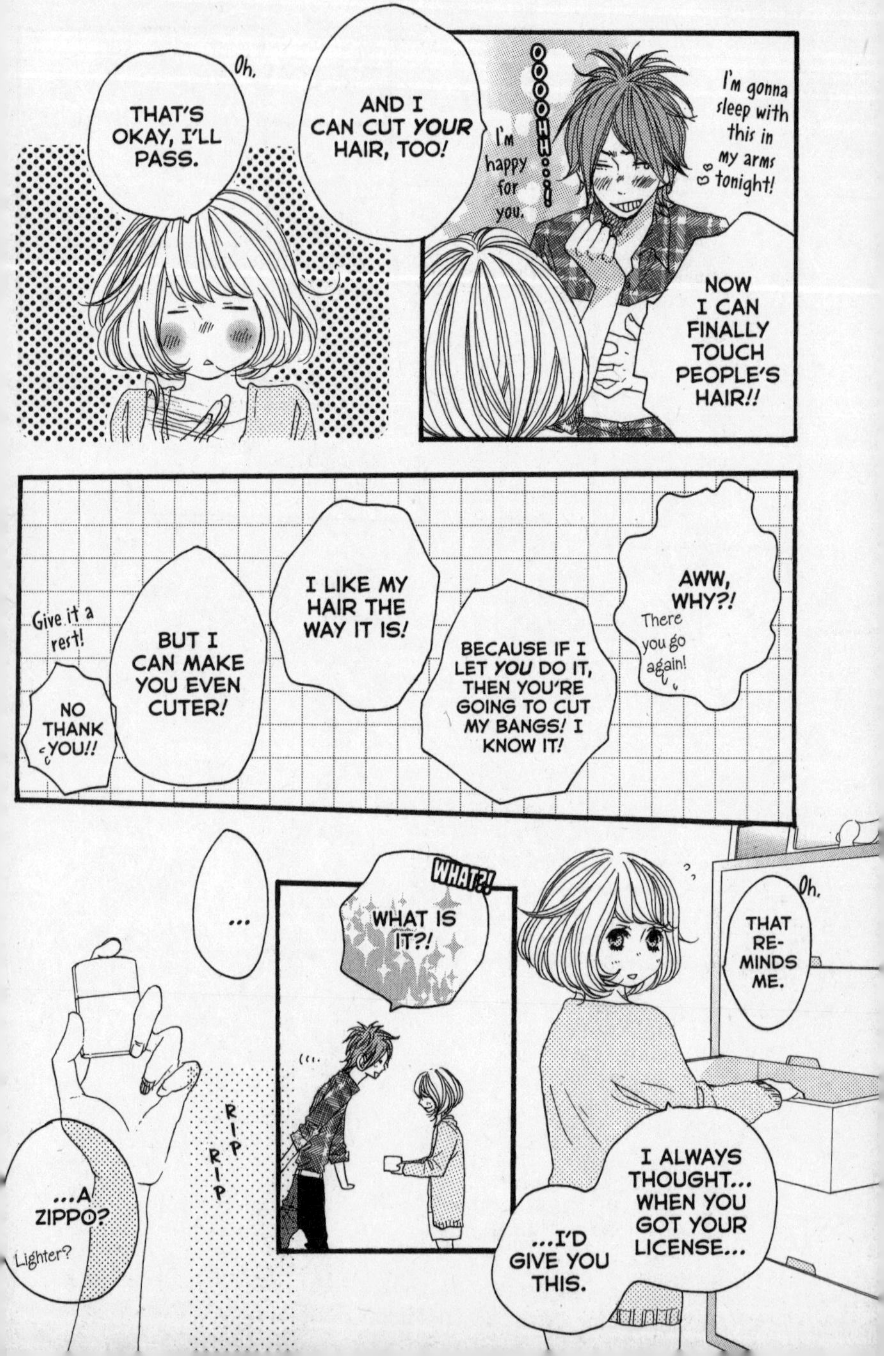

OOOOOHH...!!
I'm gonna sleep with this in my arms tonight!
NOW I CAN FINALLY TOUCH PEOPLE'S HAIR!!
I'm happy for you.
AND I CAN CUT *YOUR* HAIR, TOO!
Oh.
THAT'S OKAY, I'LL PASS.
AWW, WHY?!
There you go again!
BECAUSE IF I LET *YOU* DO IT, THEN YOU'RE GOING TO CUT MY BANGS! I KNOW IT!
I LIKE MY HAIR THE WAY IT IS!
BUT I CAN MAKE YOU EVEN CUTER!
Give it a rest!
NO THANK YOU!!
Oh.
THAT RE-MINDS ME.
I ALWAYS THOUGHT... WHEN YOU GOT YOUR LICENSE...
...I'D GIVE YOU THIS.
WHAT?!
WHAT IS IT?!
...
RIP RIP
...A ZIPPO?
Lighter?

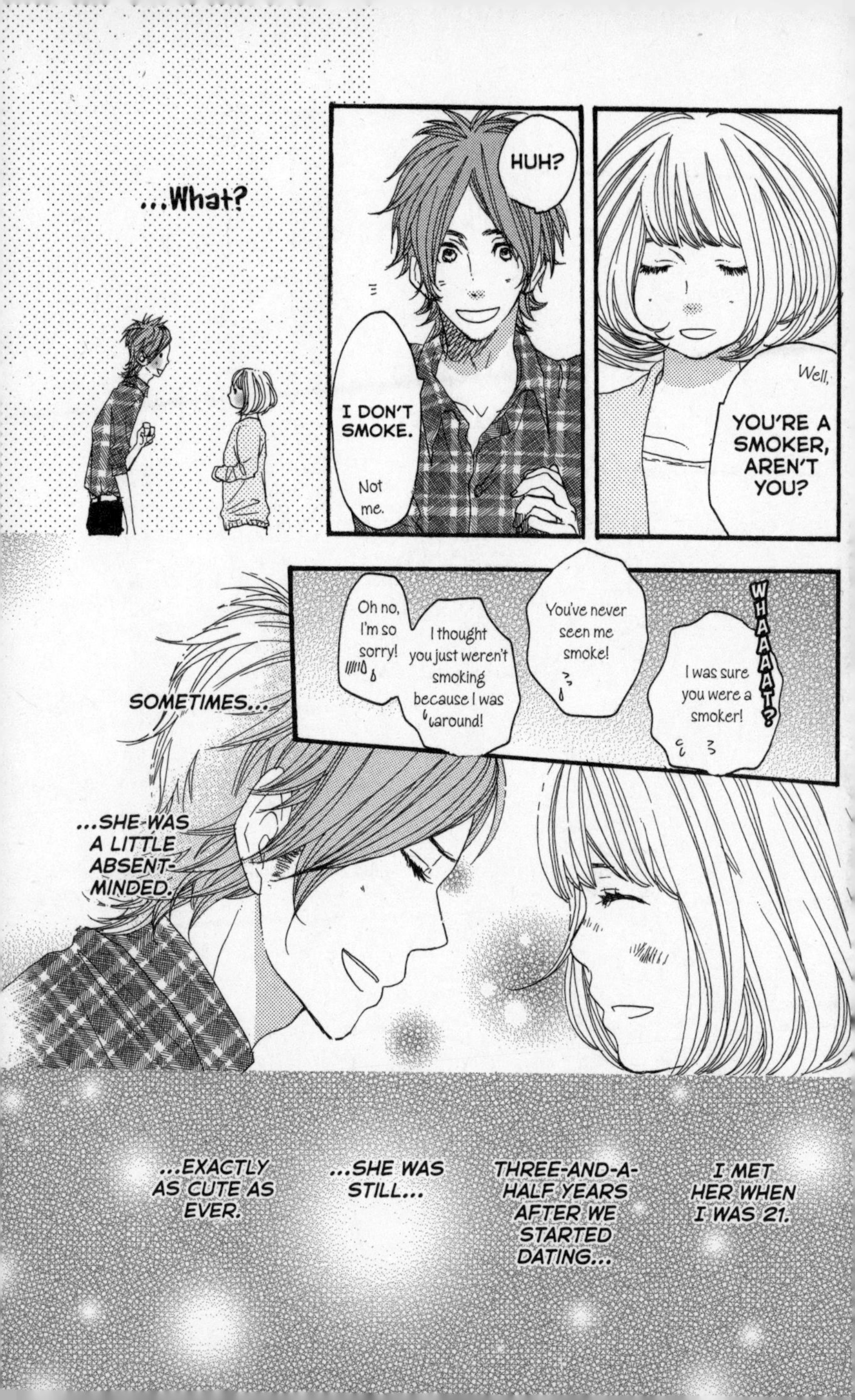
Well,
YOU'RE A SMOKER, AREN'T YOU?
HUH?
I DON'T SMOKE.
Not me.
...What?
WHAAAAT?!
I was sure you were a smoker!
You've never seen me smoke!
I thought you just weren't smoking because I was around!
Oh no, I'm so sorry!
SOMETIMES...
...SHE WAS A LITTLE ABSENT-MINDED.
I MET HER WHEN I WAS 21.
THREE-AND-A-HALF YEARS AFTER WE STARTED DATING...
...SHE WAS STILL...
...EXACTLY AS CUTE AS EVER.

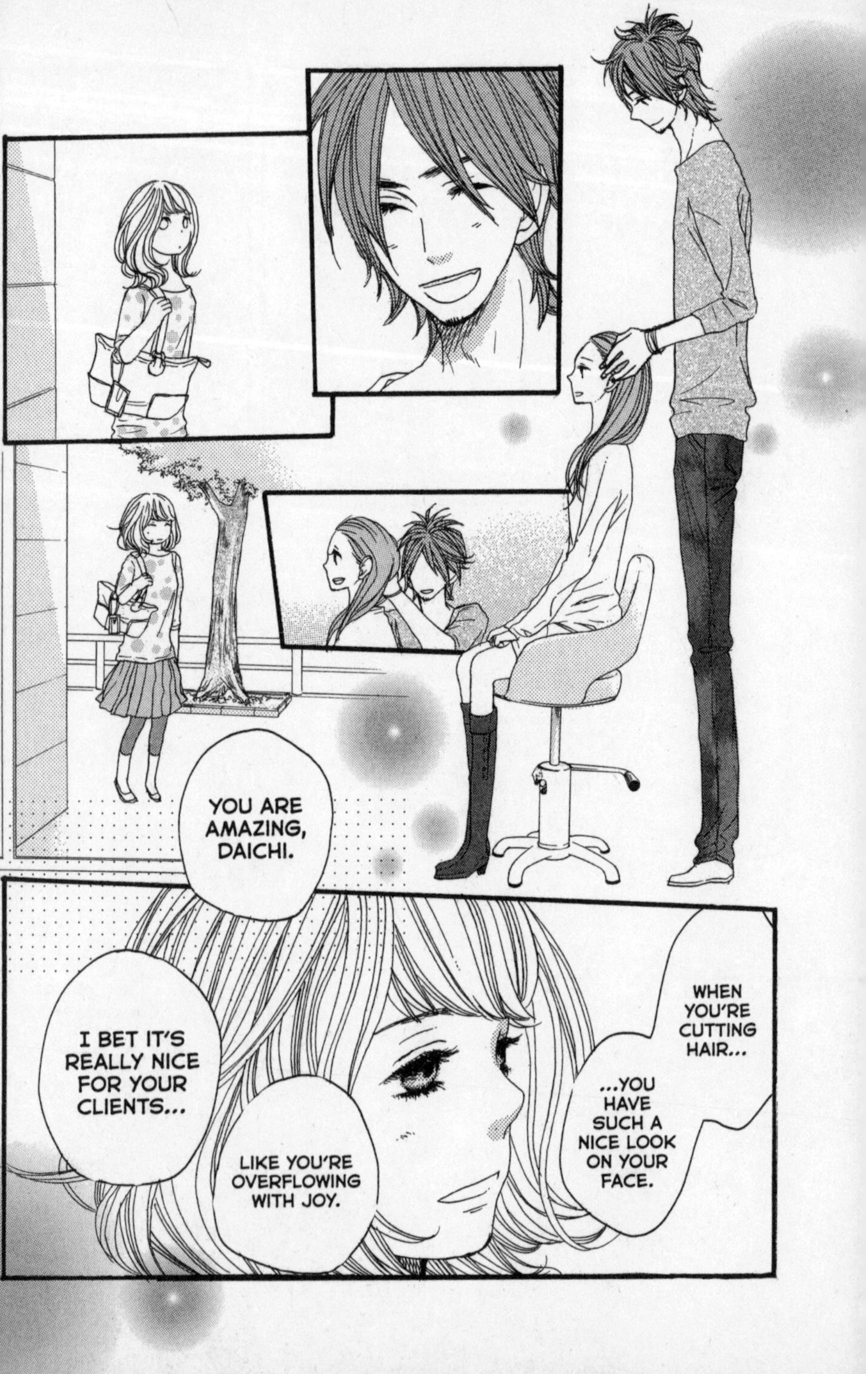
YOU ARE AMAZING, DAICHI.
WHEN YOU'RE CUTTING HAIR...
...YOU HAVE SUCH A NICE LOOK ON YOUR FACE.
LIKE YOU'RE OVERFLOWING WITH JOY.
I BET IT'S REALLY NICE FOR YOUR CLIENTS...

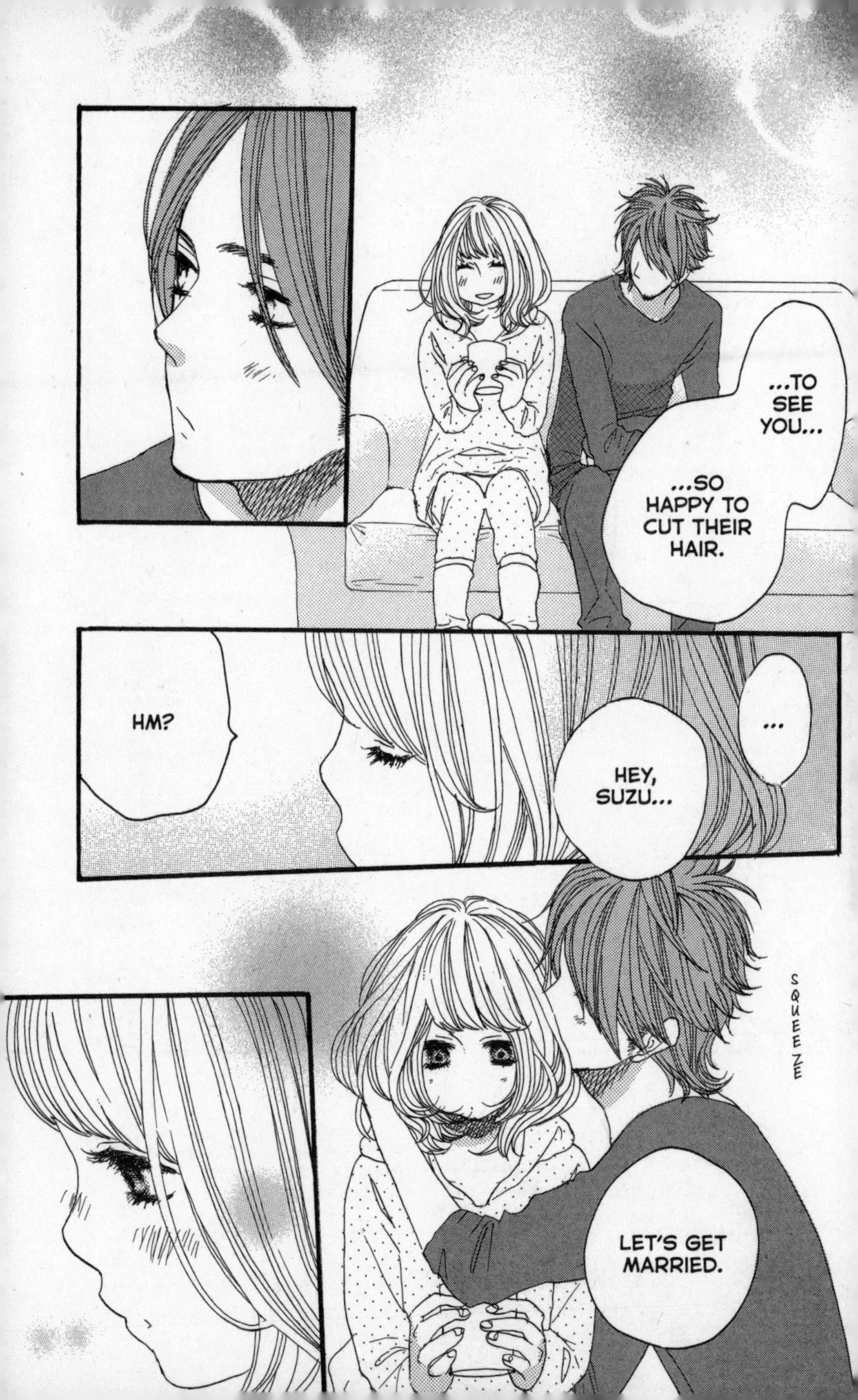
...TO SEE YOU...
...SO HAPPY TO CUT THEIR HAIR.
...
HEY, SUZU...
HM?
SQUEEZE
LET'S GET MARRIED.

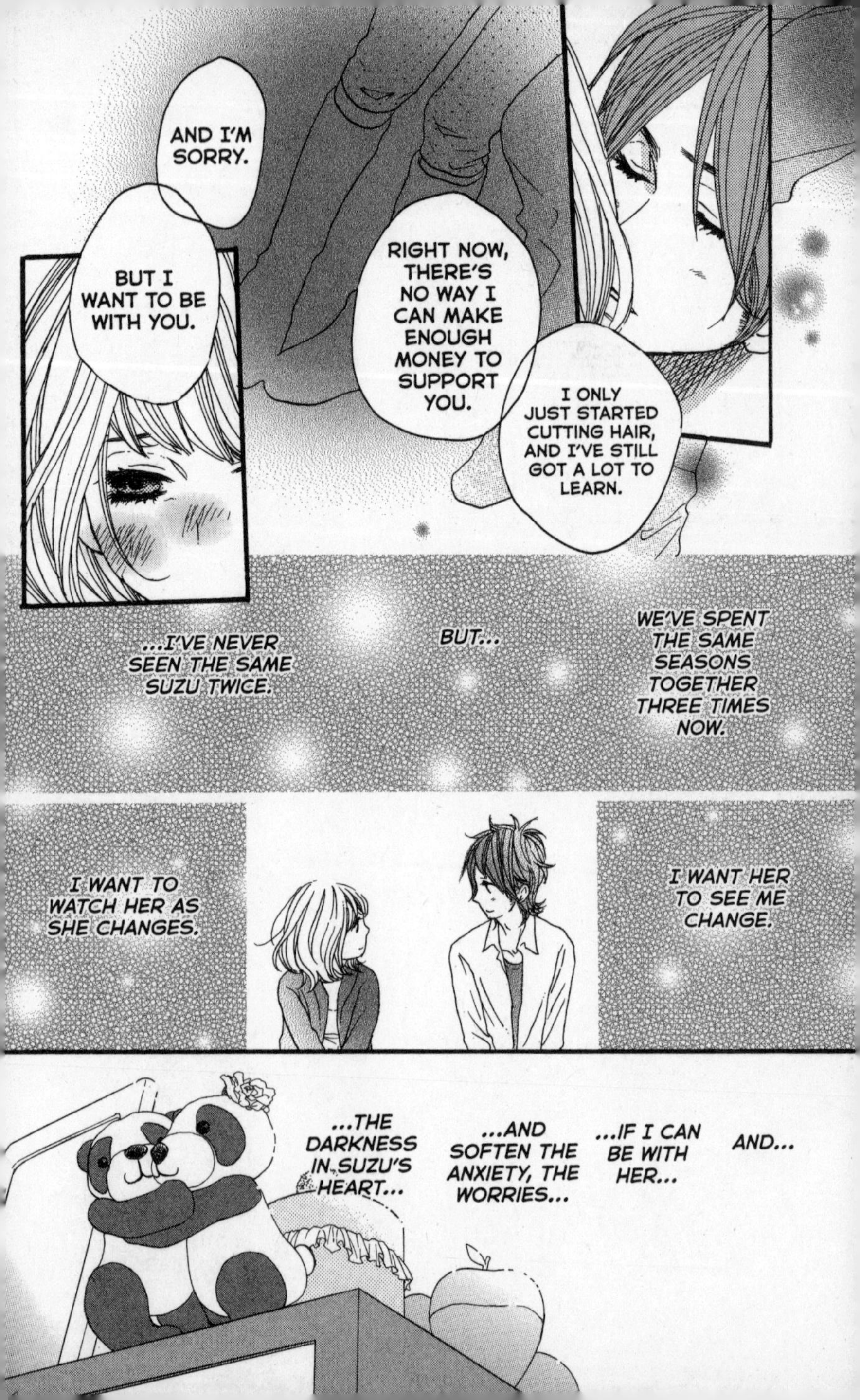
I ONLY JUST STARTED CUTTING HAIR, AND I'VE STILL GOT A LOT TO LEARN.
RIGHT NOW, THERE'S NO WAY I CAN MAKE ENOUGH MONEY TO SUPPORT YOU.
AND I'M SORRY.
BUT I WANT TO BE WITH YOU.
WE'VE SPENT THE SAME SEASONS TOGETHER THREE TIMES NOW.
BUT...
...I'VE NEVER SEEN THE SAME SUZU TWICE.
I WANT HER TO SEE ME CHANGE.
I WANT TO WATCH HER AS SHE CHANGES.
AND...
...IF I CAN BE WITH HER...
...AND SOFTEN THE ANXIETY, THE WORRIES...
...THE DARKNESS IN SUZU'S HEART...

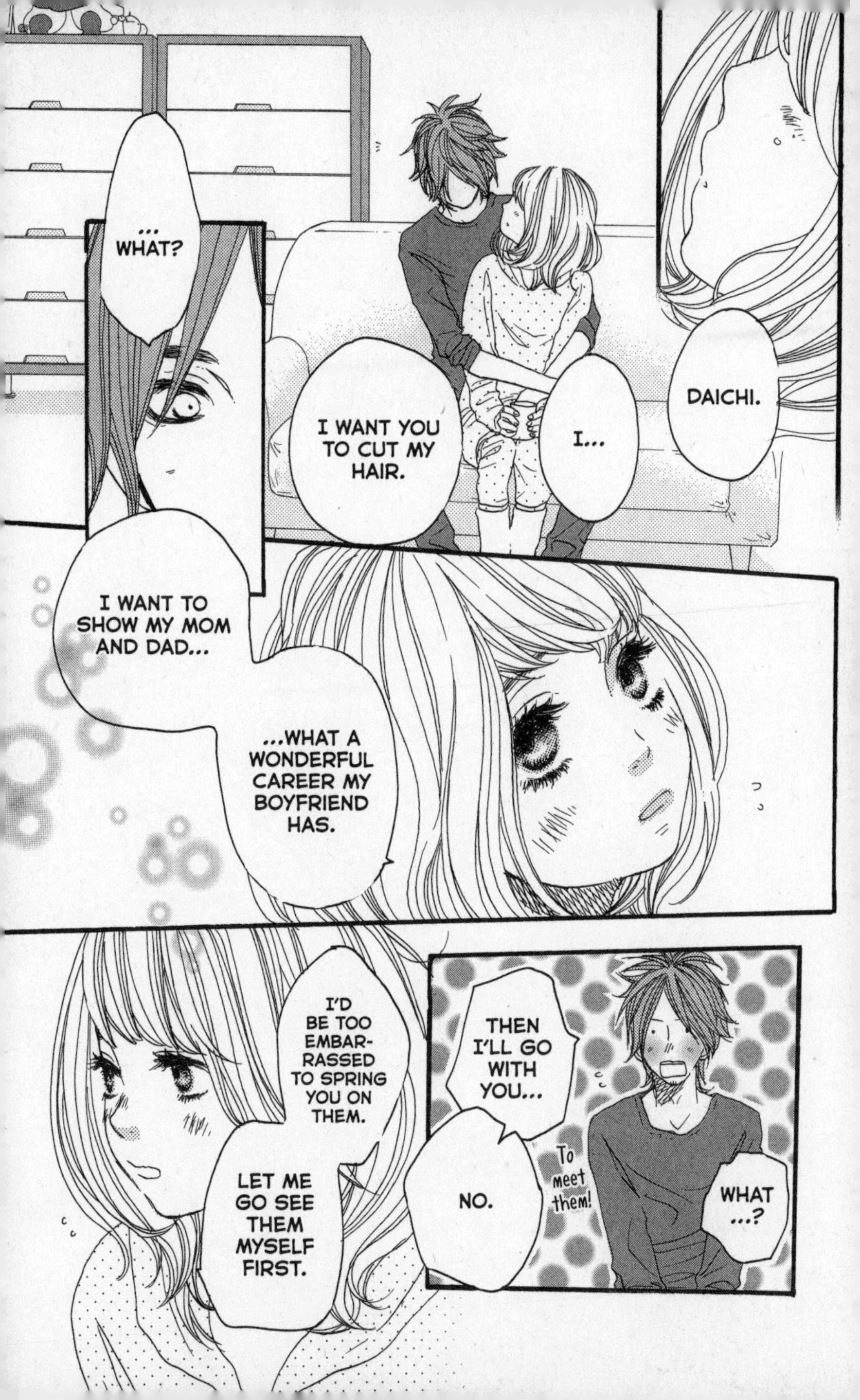

DAICHI.
I...
I WANT YOU TO CUT MY HAIR.
...WHAT?
I WANT TO SHOW MY MOM AND DAD...
...WHAT A WONDERFUL CAREER MY BOYFRIEND HAS.
THEN I'LL GO WITH YOU...
To meet them!
NO.
WHAT ...?
I'D BE TOO EMBAR-RASSED TO SPRING YOU ON THEM.
LET ME GO SEE THEM MYSELF FIRST.

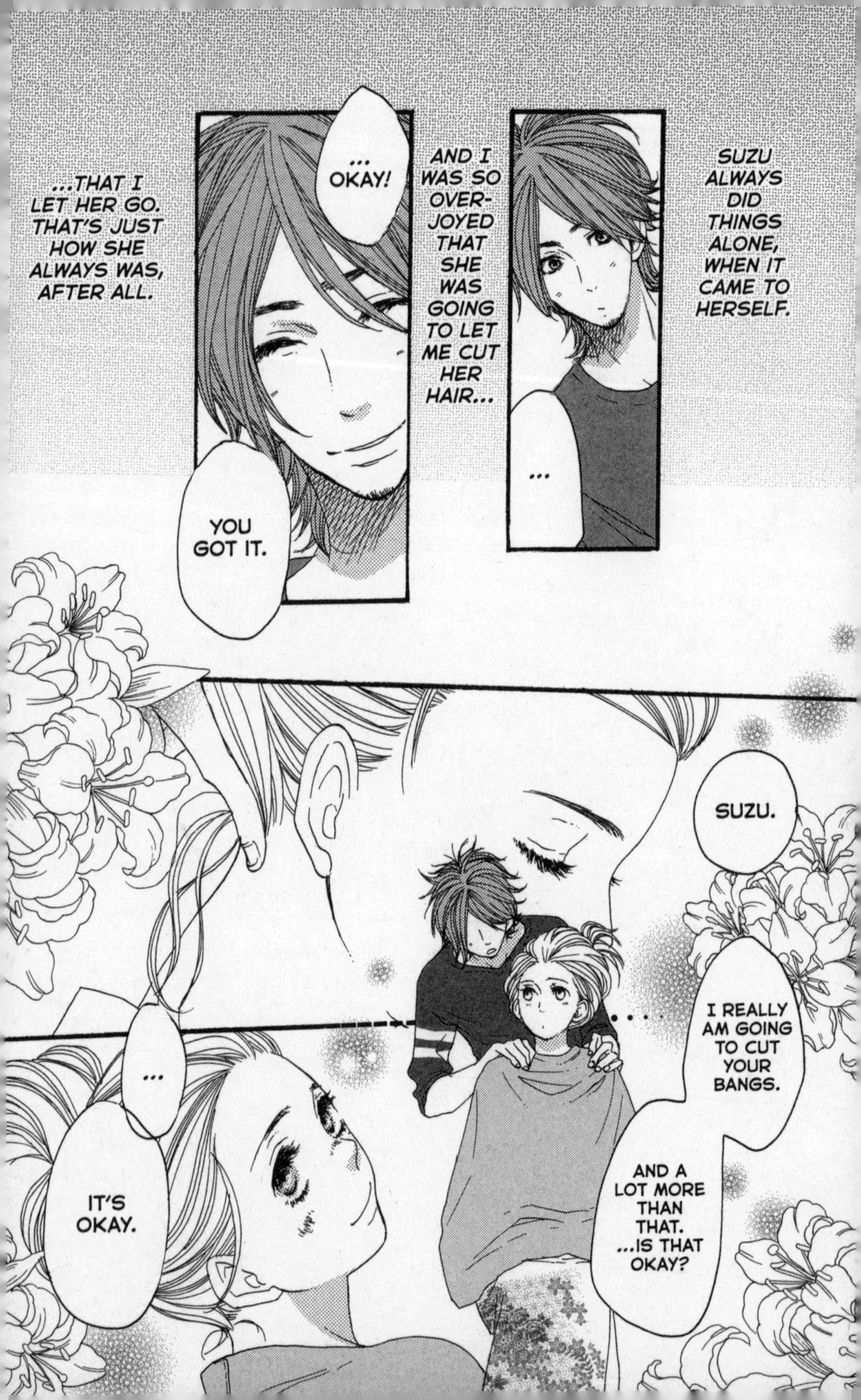
SUZU ALWAYS DID THINGS ALONE, WHEN IT CAME TO HERSELF.
...
AND I WAS SO OVER-JOYED THAT SHE WAS GOING TO LET ME CUT HER HAIR...
... OKAY!
YOU GOT IT.
...THAT I LET HER GO. THAT'S JUST HOW SHE ALWAYS WAS, AFTER ALL.
SUZU.
I REALLY AM GOING TO CUT YOUR BANGS.
AND A LOT MORE THAN THAT. ...IS THAT OKAY?
...
...
IT'S OKAY.

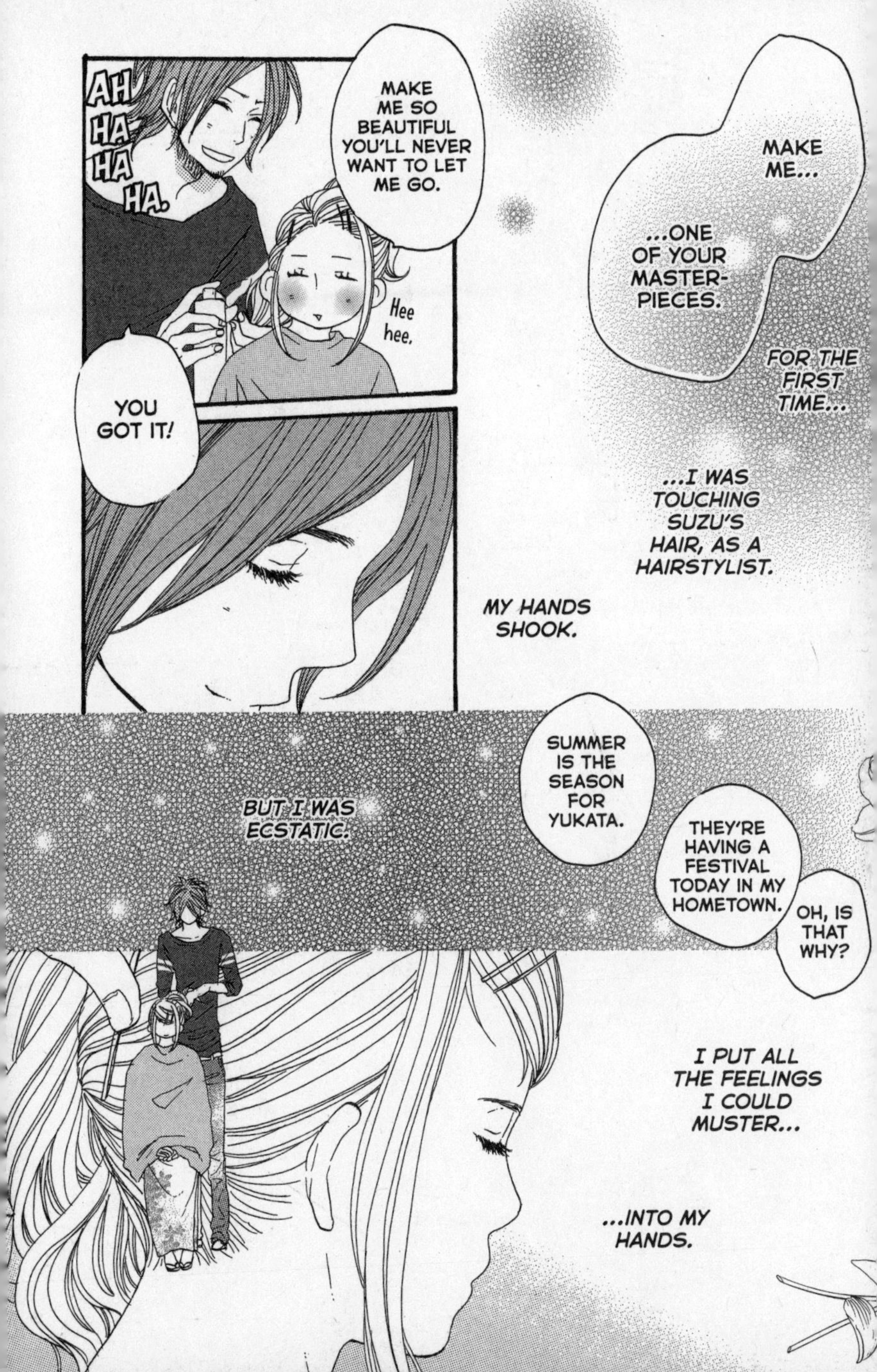
MAKE ME...
...ONE OF YOUR MASTERPIECES.
MAKE ME SO BEAUTIFUL YOU'LL NEVER WANT TO LET ME GO.
AH HA HA HA.
Hee hee.
YOU GOT IT!
FOR THE FIRST TIME...
...I WAS TOUCHING SUZU'S HAIR, AS A HAIRSTYLIST.
MY HANDS SHOOK.
BUT I WAS ECSTATIC.
SUMMER IS THE SEASON FOR YUKATA.
THEY'RE HAVING A FESTIVAL TODAY IN MY HOMETOWN.
OH, IS THAT WHY?
I PUT ALL THE FEELINGS I COULD MUSTER...
...INTO MY HANDS.

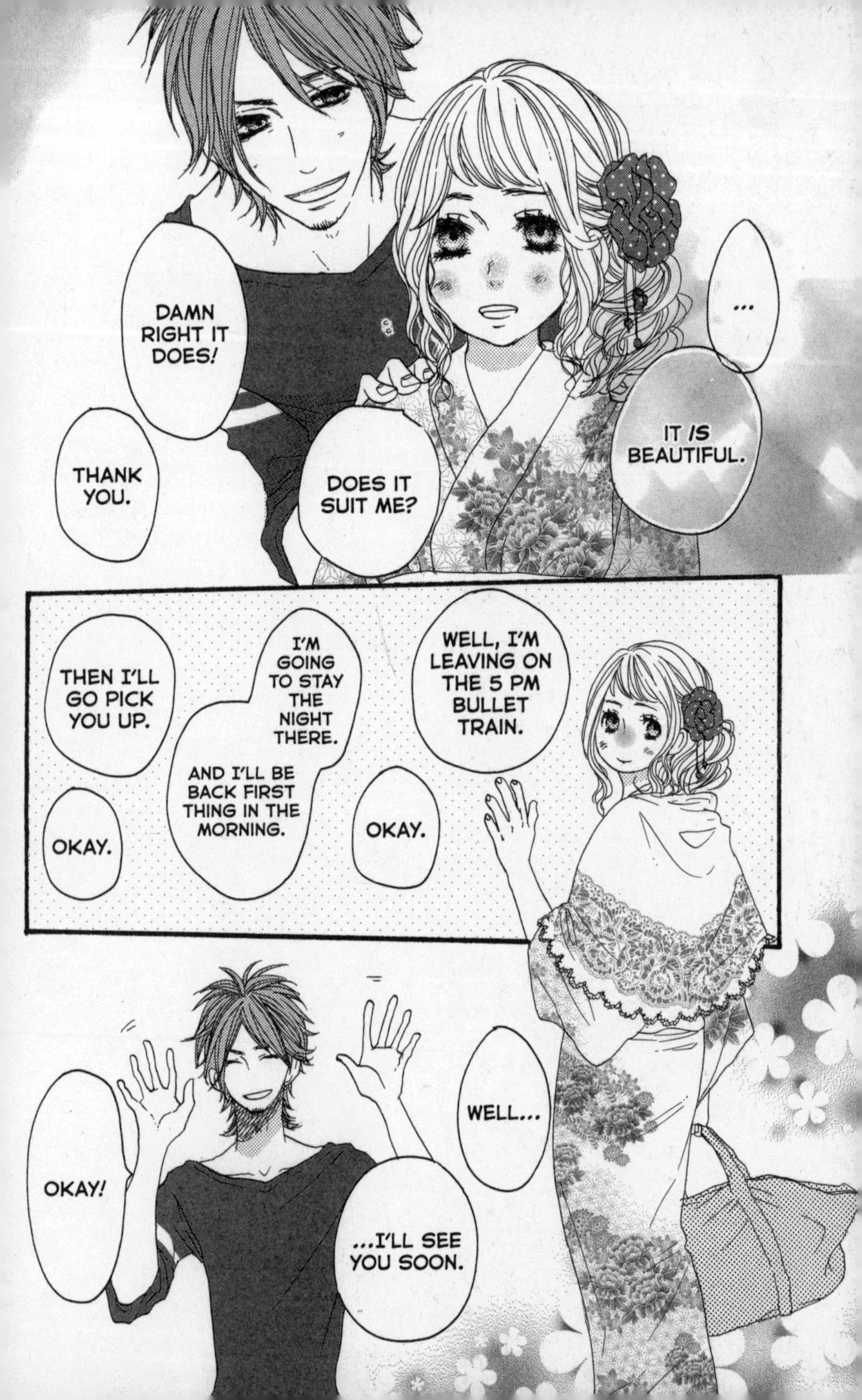
...
IT IS BEAUTIFUL.
DOES IT SUIT ME?
DAMN RIGHT IT DOES!
THANK YOU.
WELL, I'M LEAVING ON THE 5 PM BULLET TRAIN.
OKAY.
I'M GOING TO STAY THE NIGHT THERE.
AND I'LL BE BACK FIRST THING IN THE MORNING.
THEN I'LL GO PICK YOU UP.
OKAY.
WELL...
...I'LL SEE YOU SOON.
OKAY!

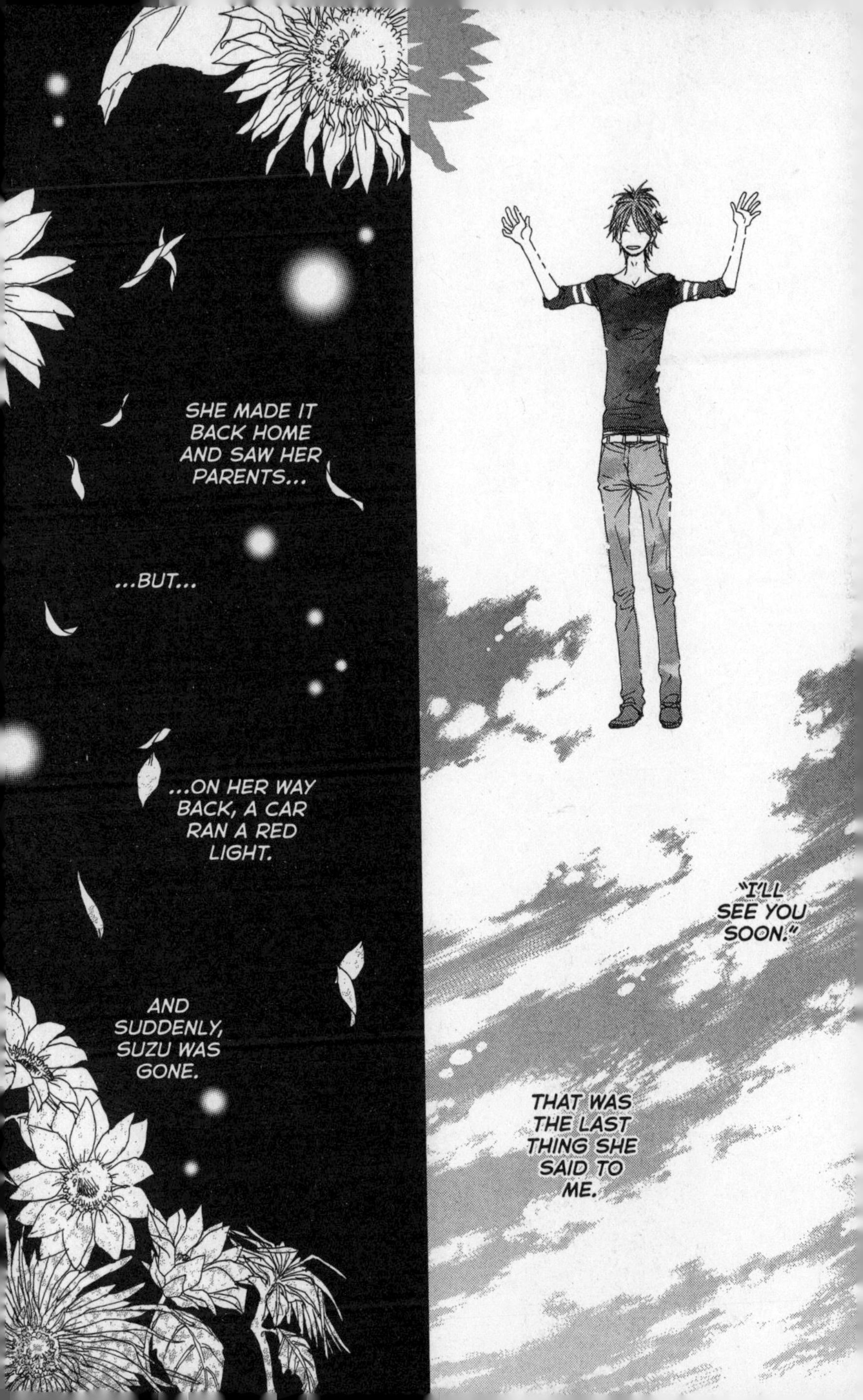
SHE MADE IT BACK HOME AND SAW HER PARENTS...
...BUT...
...ON HER WAY BACK, A CAR RAN A RED LIGHT.
AND SUDDENLY, SUZU WAS GONE.
"I'LL SEE YOU SOON."
THAT WAS THE LAST THING SHE SAID TO ME.

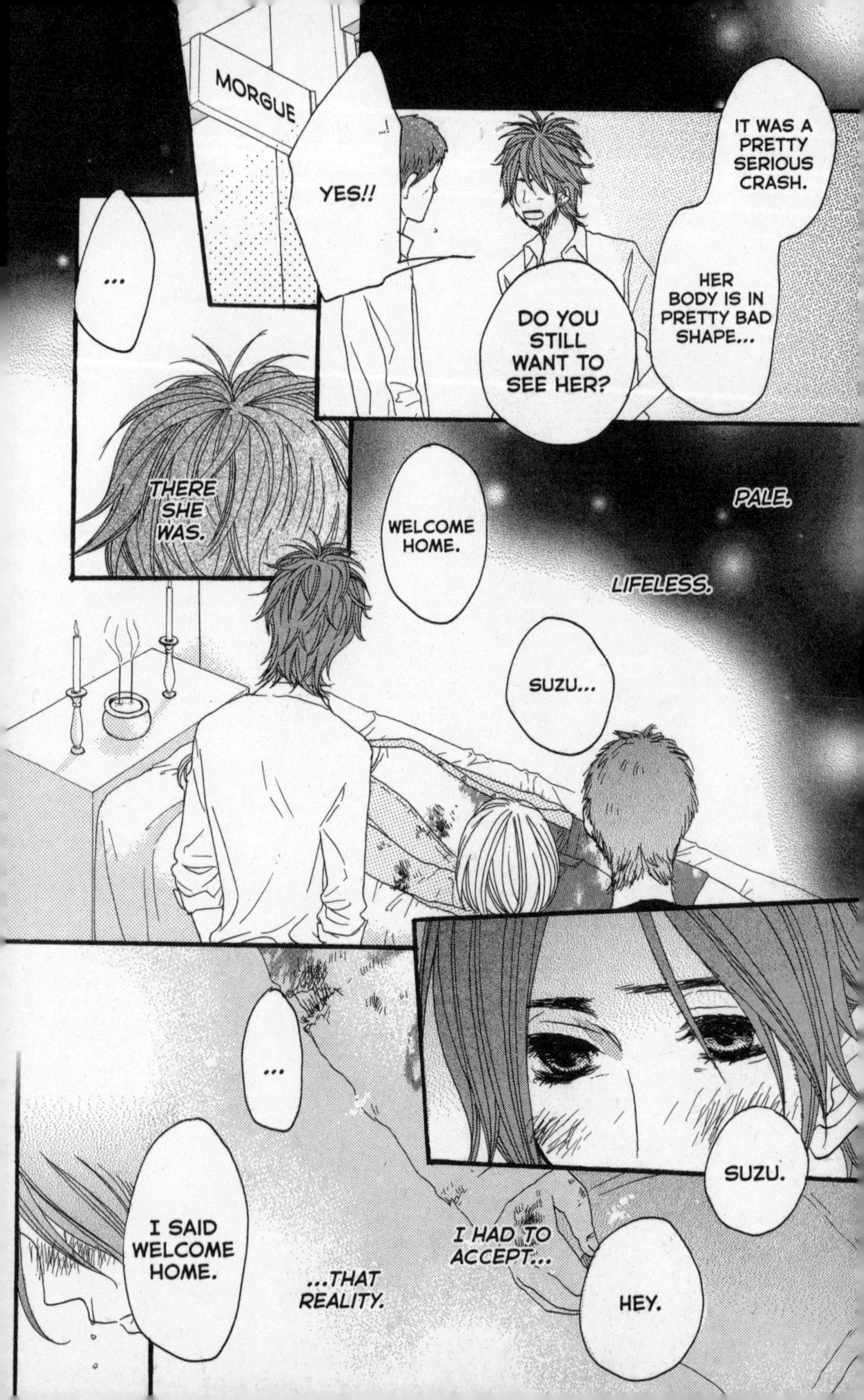
IT WAS A PRETTY SERIOUS CRASH.
HER BODY IS IN PRETTY BAD SHAPE...
DO YOU STILL WANT TO SEE HER?
YES!!
MORGUE
...
THERE SHE WAS.
PALE.
LIFELESS.
WELCOME HOME.
SUZU...
SUZU.
HEY.
I HAD TO ACCEPT...
...THAT REALITY.
...
I SAID WELCOME HOME.

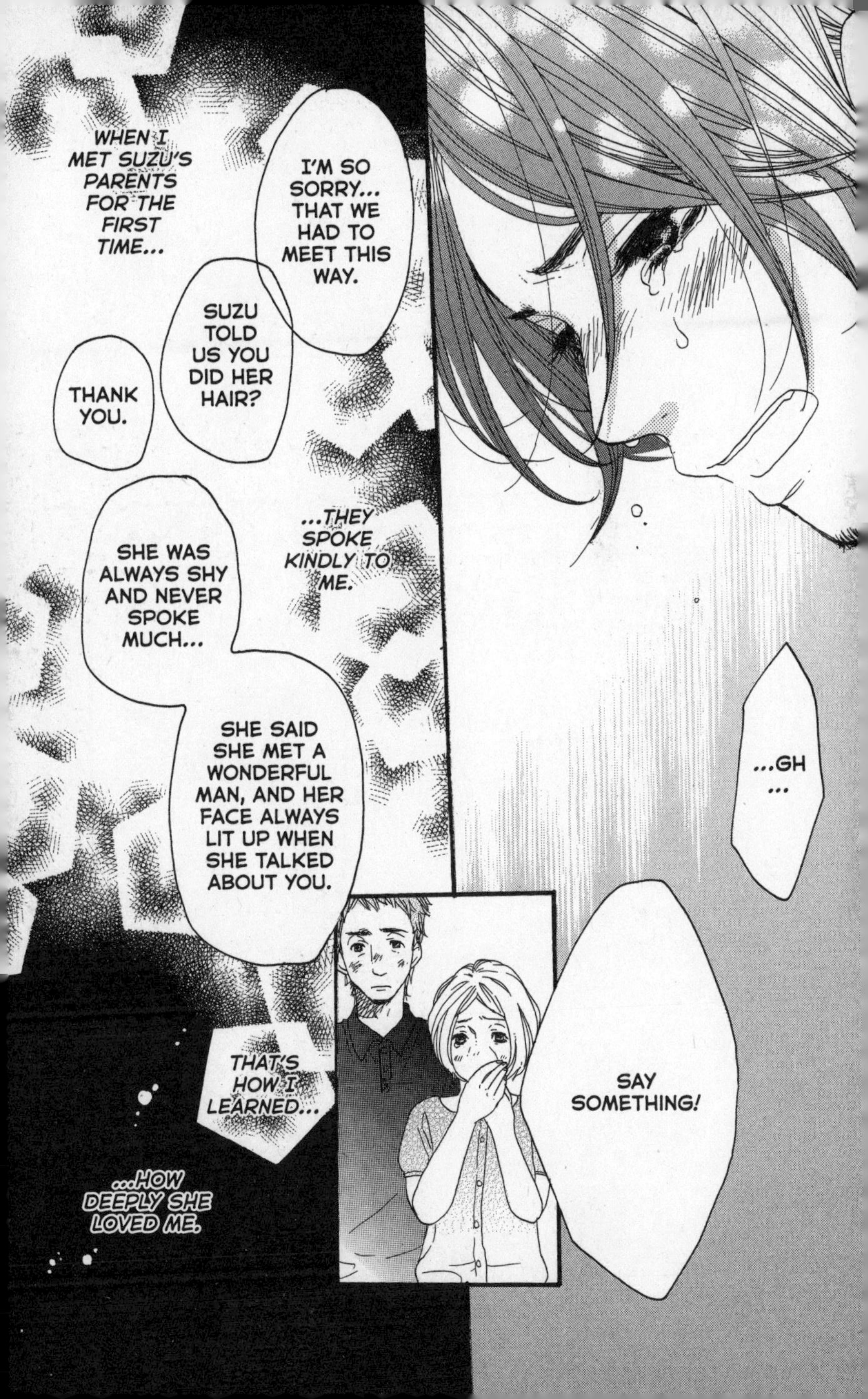
...GH...
SAY SOMETHING!
WHEN I MET SUZU'S PARENTS FOR THE FIRST TIME...
I'M SO SORRY... THAT WE HAD TO MEET THIS WAY.
SUZU TOLD US YOU DID HER HAIR?
THANK YOU.
...THEY SPOKE KINDLY TO ME.
SHE WAS ALWAYS SHY AND NEVER SPOKE MUCH...
SHE SAID SHE MET A WONDERFUL MAN, AND HER FACE ALWAYS LIT UP WHEN SHE TALKED ABOUT YOU.
THAT'S HOW I LEARNED...
...HOW DEEPLY SHE LOVED ME.

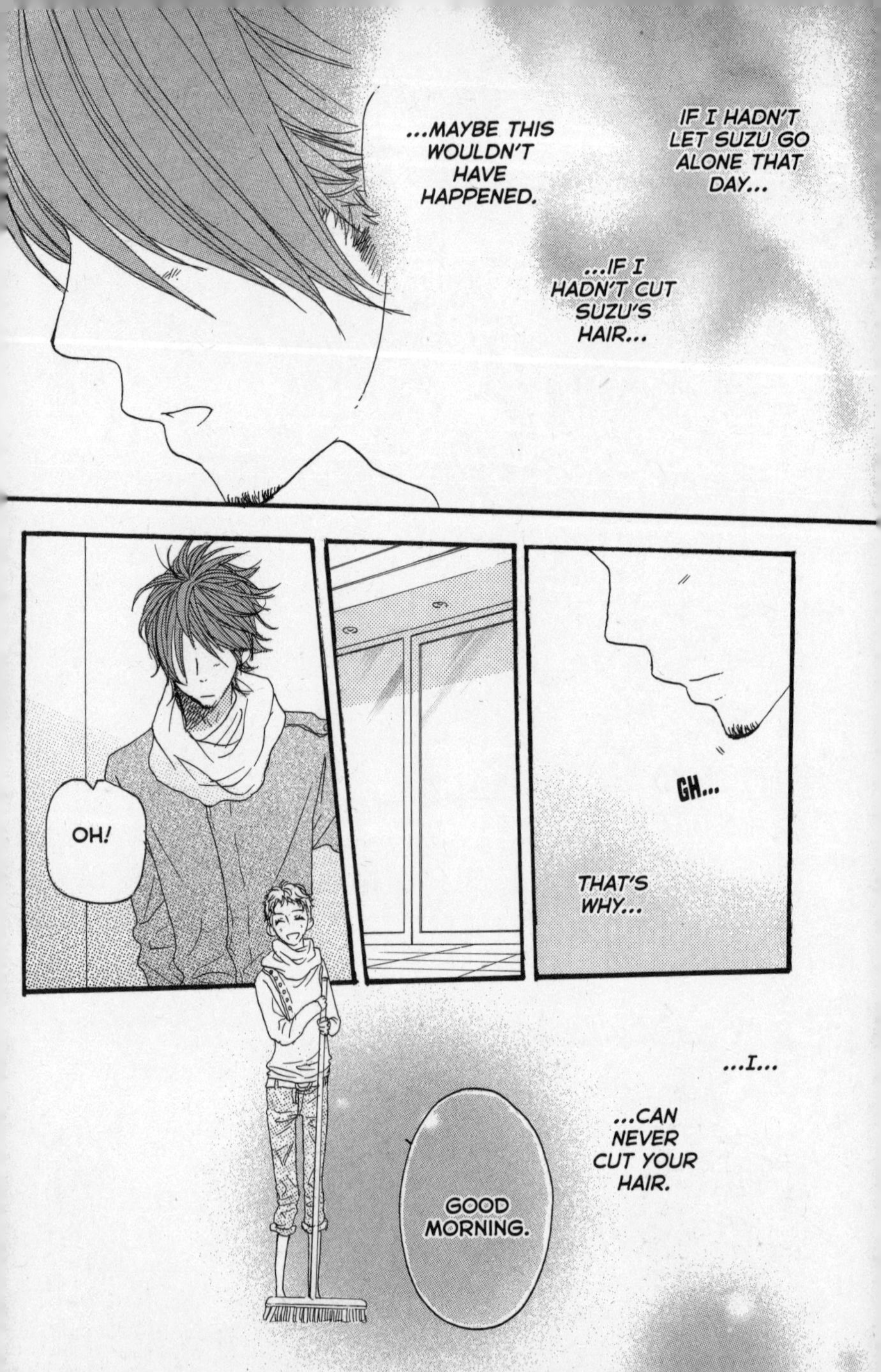
IF I HADN'T LET SUZU GO ALONE THAT DAY...
...IF I HADN'T CUT SUZU'S HAIR...
...MAYBE THIS WOULDN'T HAVE HAPPENED.
GH...
THAT'S WHY...
OH!
...I...
...CAN NEVER CUT YOUR HAIR.
GOOD MORNING.

Chapter 35 — End

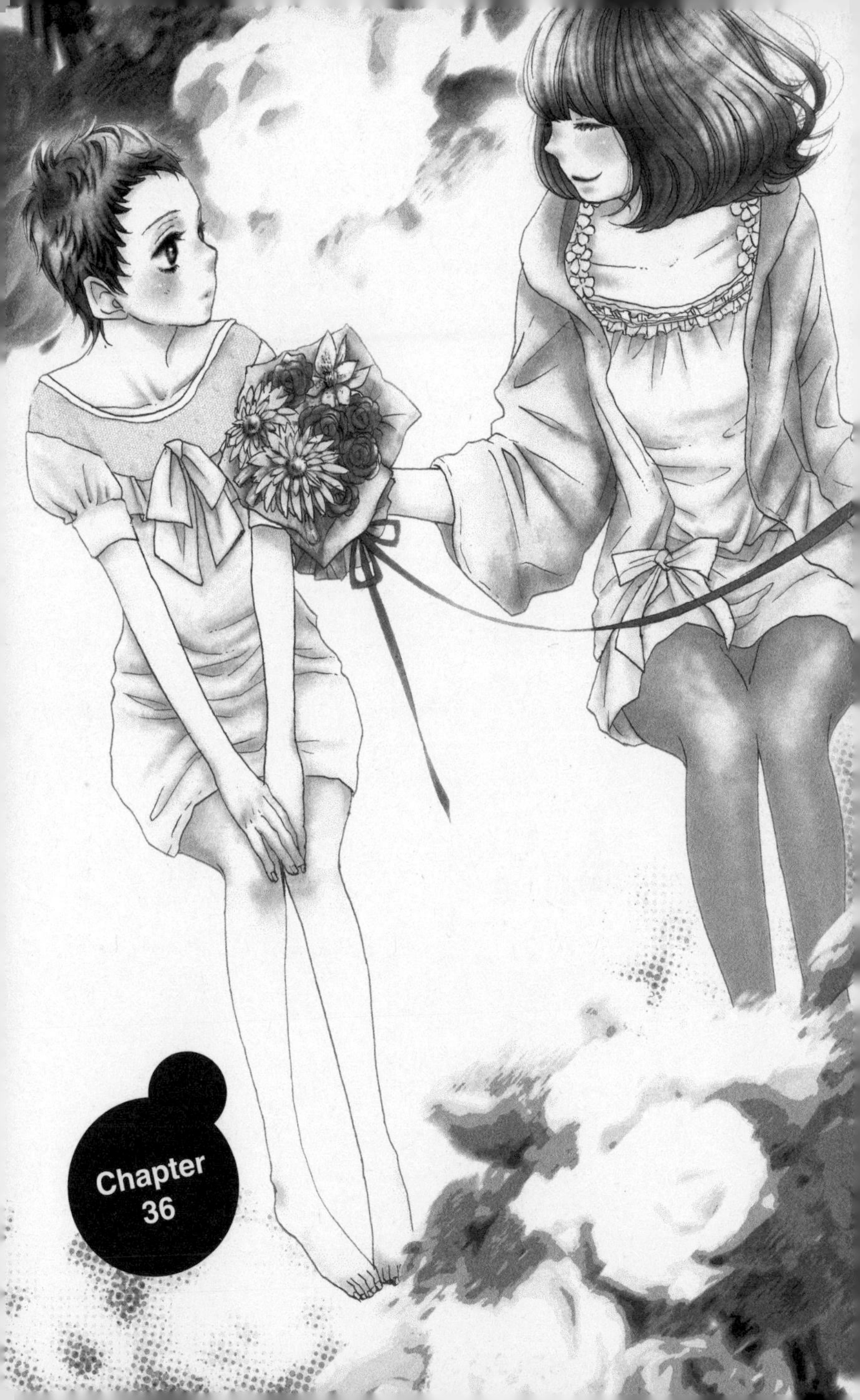
Chapter 36

Say "I love you".

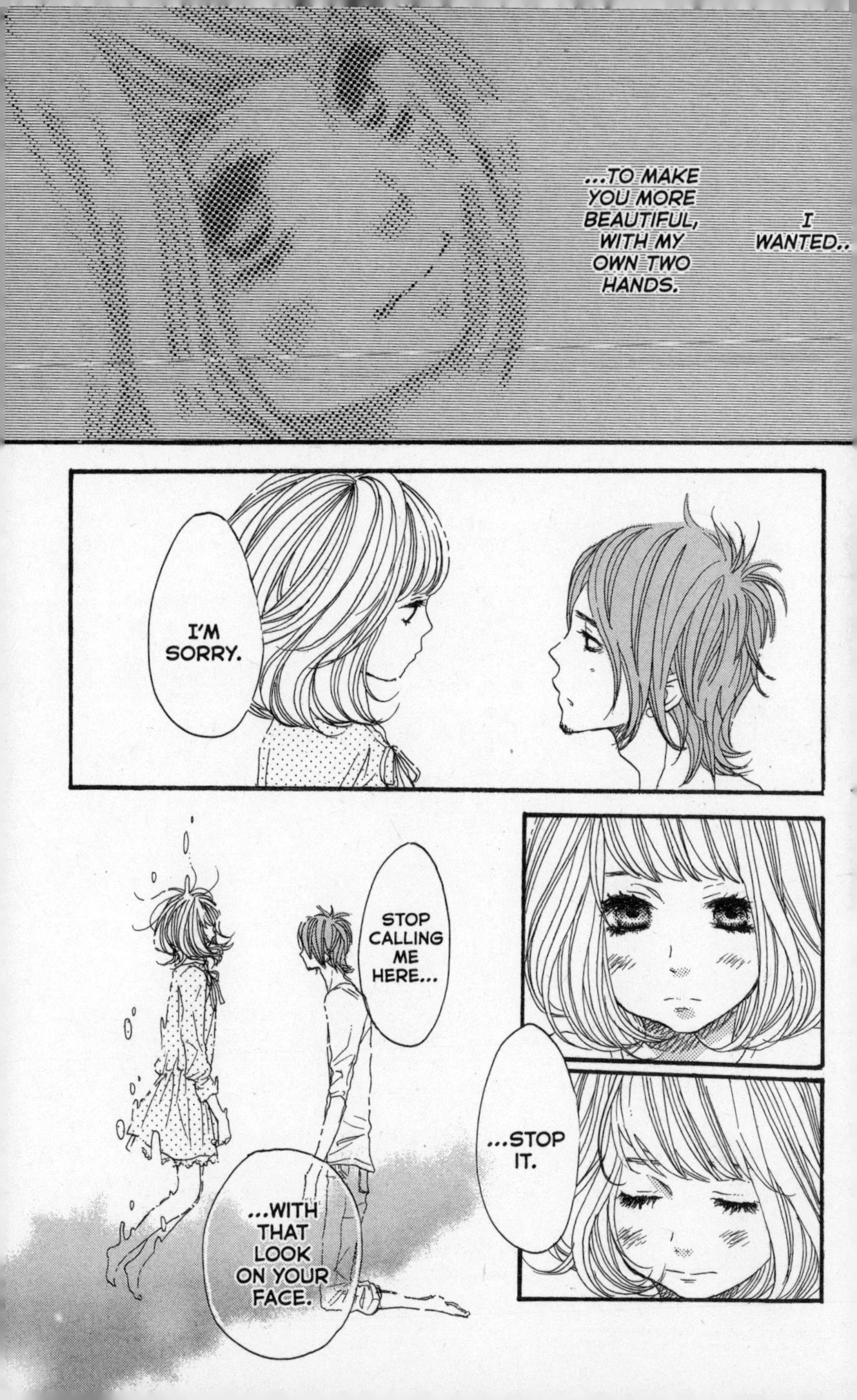
I WANTED..
...TO MAKE YOU MORE BEAUTIFUL, WITH MY OWN TWO HANDS.
I'M SORRY.
...STOP IT.
STOP CALLING ME HERE...
...WITH THAT LOOK ON YOUR FACE.

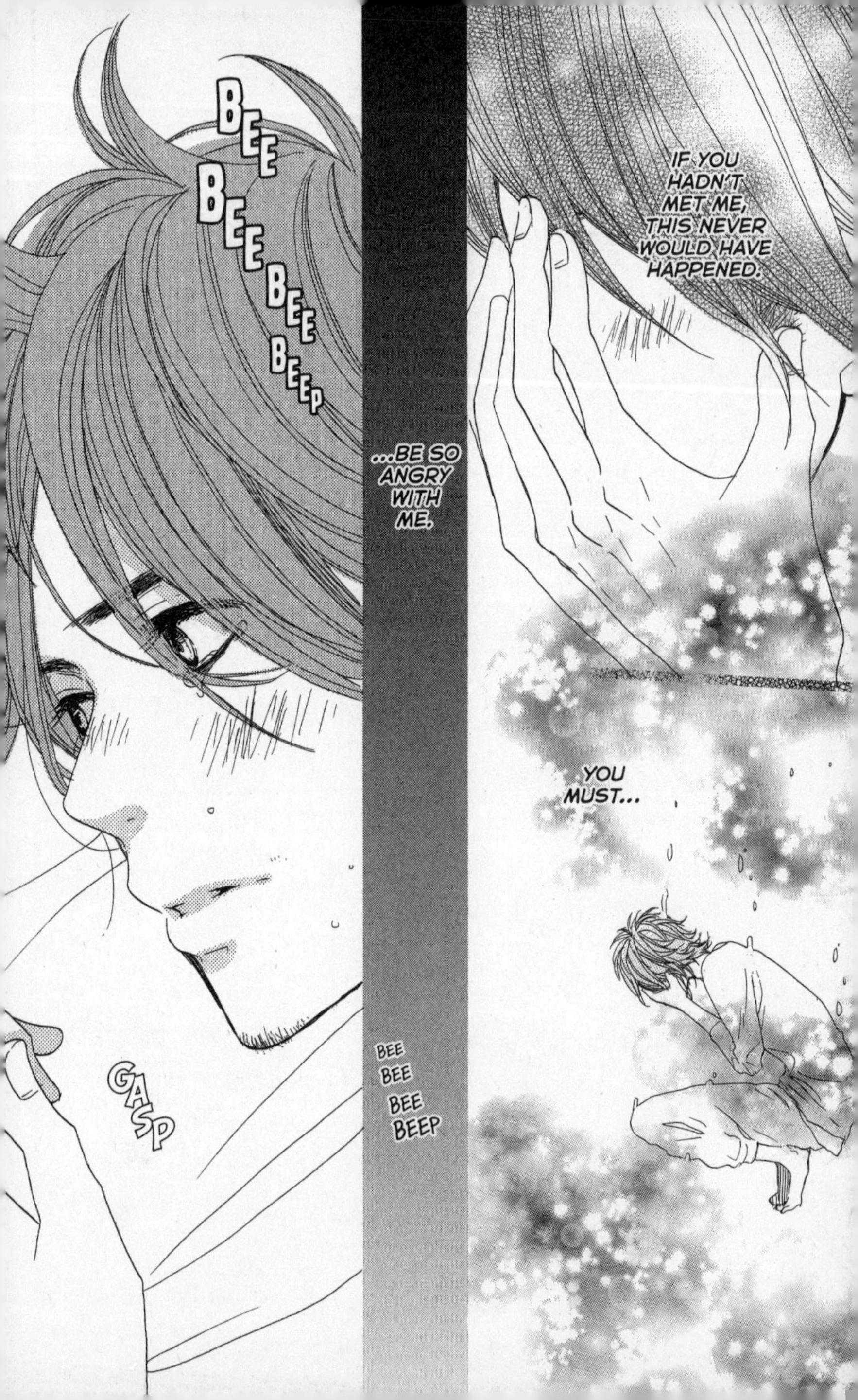
IF YOU HADN'T MET ME, THIS NEVER WOULD HAVE HAPPENED.
YOU MUST...
...BE SO ANGRY WITH ME.
BEE BEE BEE BEEP
BEE BEE BEE BEEP
GASP

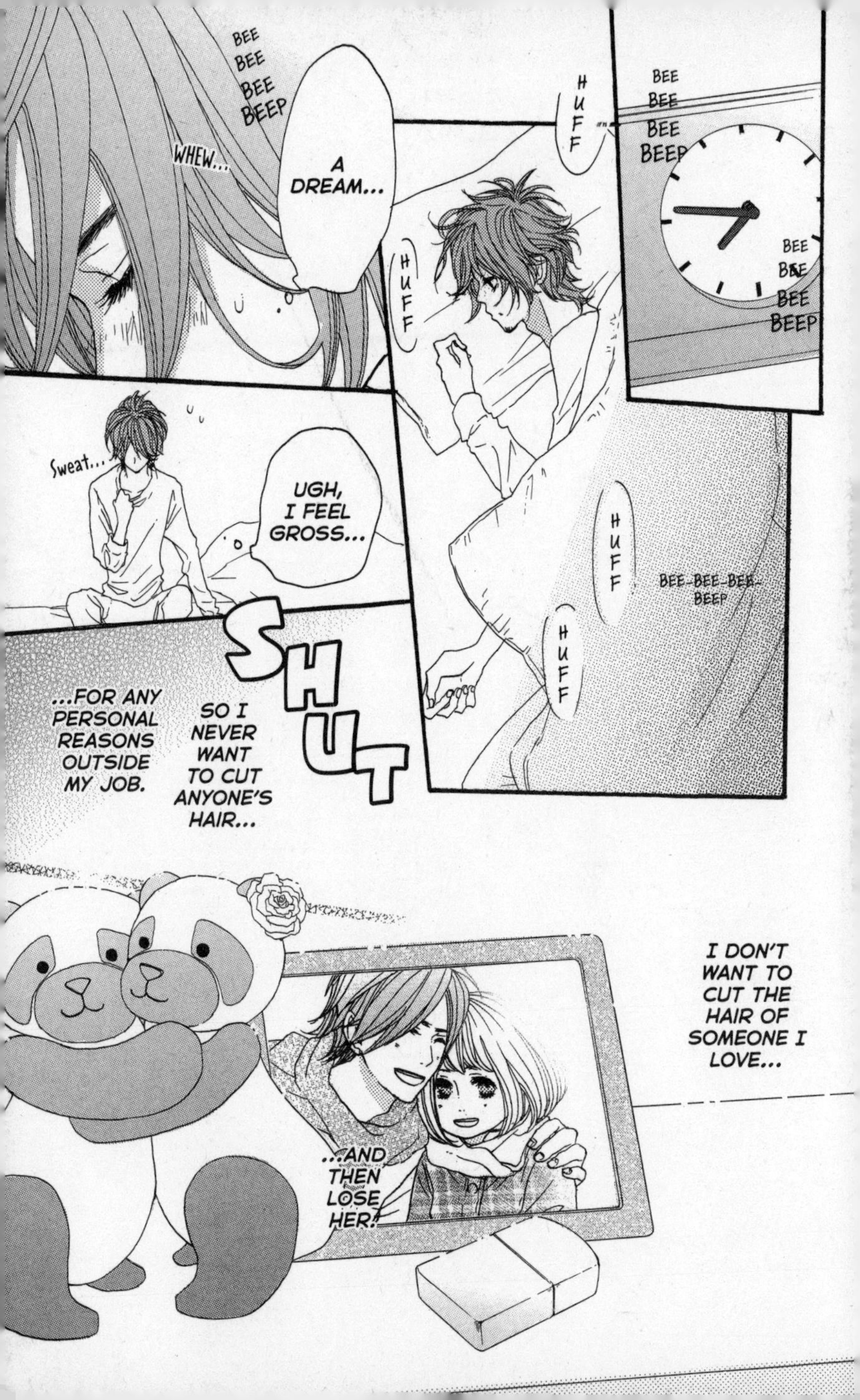
BEE BEE BEE BEEP
BEE BEE BEE BEEP
HUFF
HUFF
HUFF
HUFF
BEE-BEE-BEE-BEEP
BEE BEE BEE BEEP
A DREAM...
WHEW...
Sweat...
UGH, I FEEL GROSS...
SHUT
SO I NEVER WANT TO CUT ANYONE'S HAIR...
...FOR ANY PERSONAL REASONS OUTSIDE MY JOB.
I DON'T WANT TO CUT THE HAIR OF SOMEONE I LOVE...
...AND THEN LOSE HER!

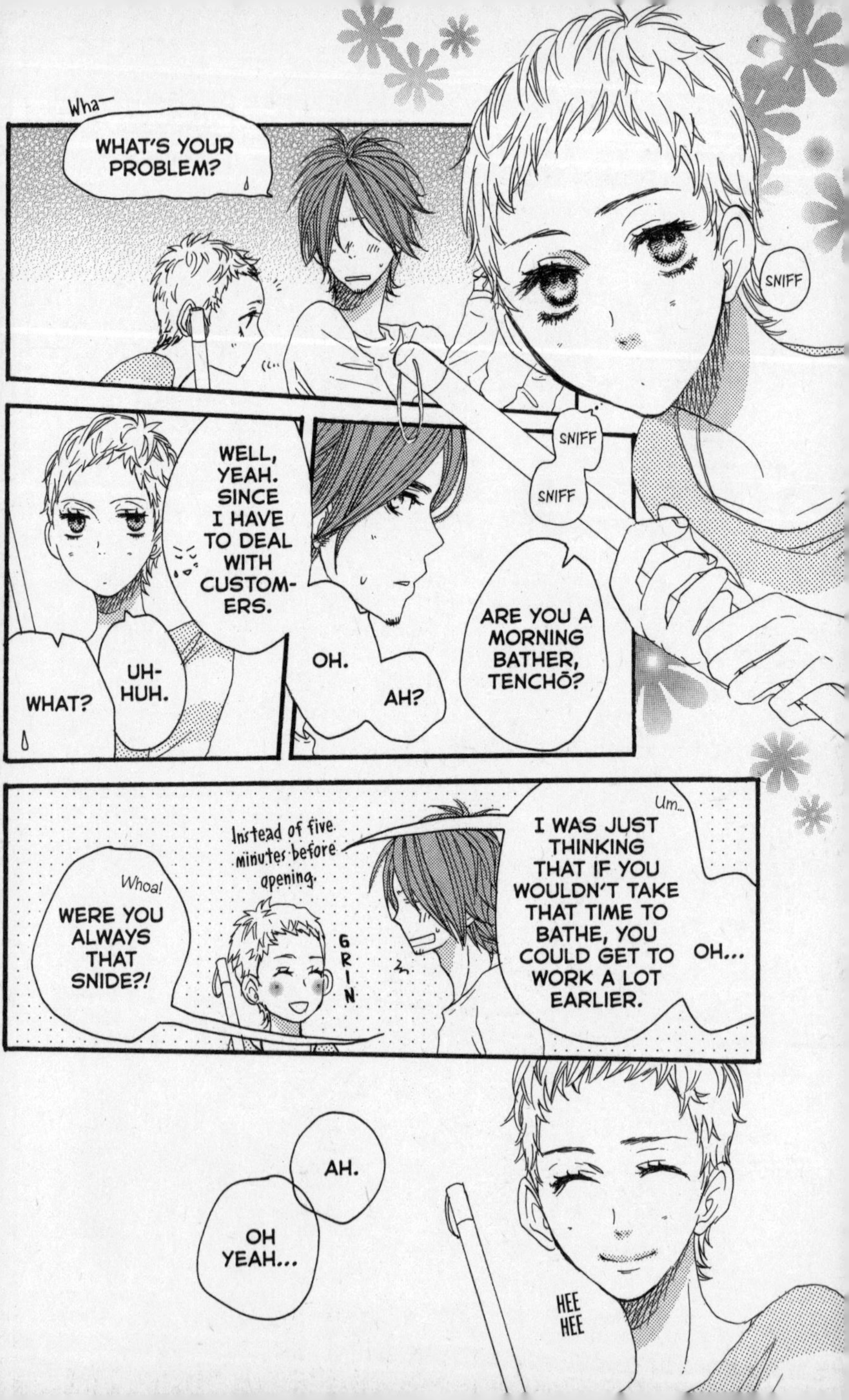
SNIFF
SNIFF
SNIFF
Wha—
WHAT'S YOUR PROBLEM?
ARE YOU A MORNING BATHER, TENCHŌ?
AH?
OH.
WELL, YEAH. SINCE I HAVE TO DEAL WITH CUSTOMERS.
UH-HUH.
WHAT?
Um...
I WAS JUST THINKING THAT IF YOU WOULDN'T TAKE THAT TIME TO BATHE, YOU COULD GET TO WORK A LOT EARLIER.
OH...
Instead of five minutes before opening.
GRIN
Whoa!
WERE YOU ALWAYS THAT SNIDE?!
HEE HEE
AH.
OH YEAH...

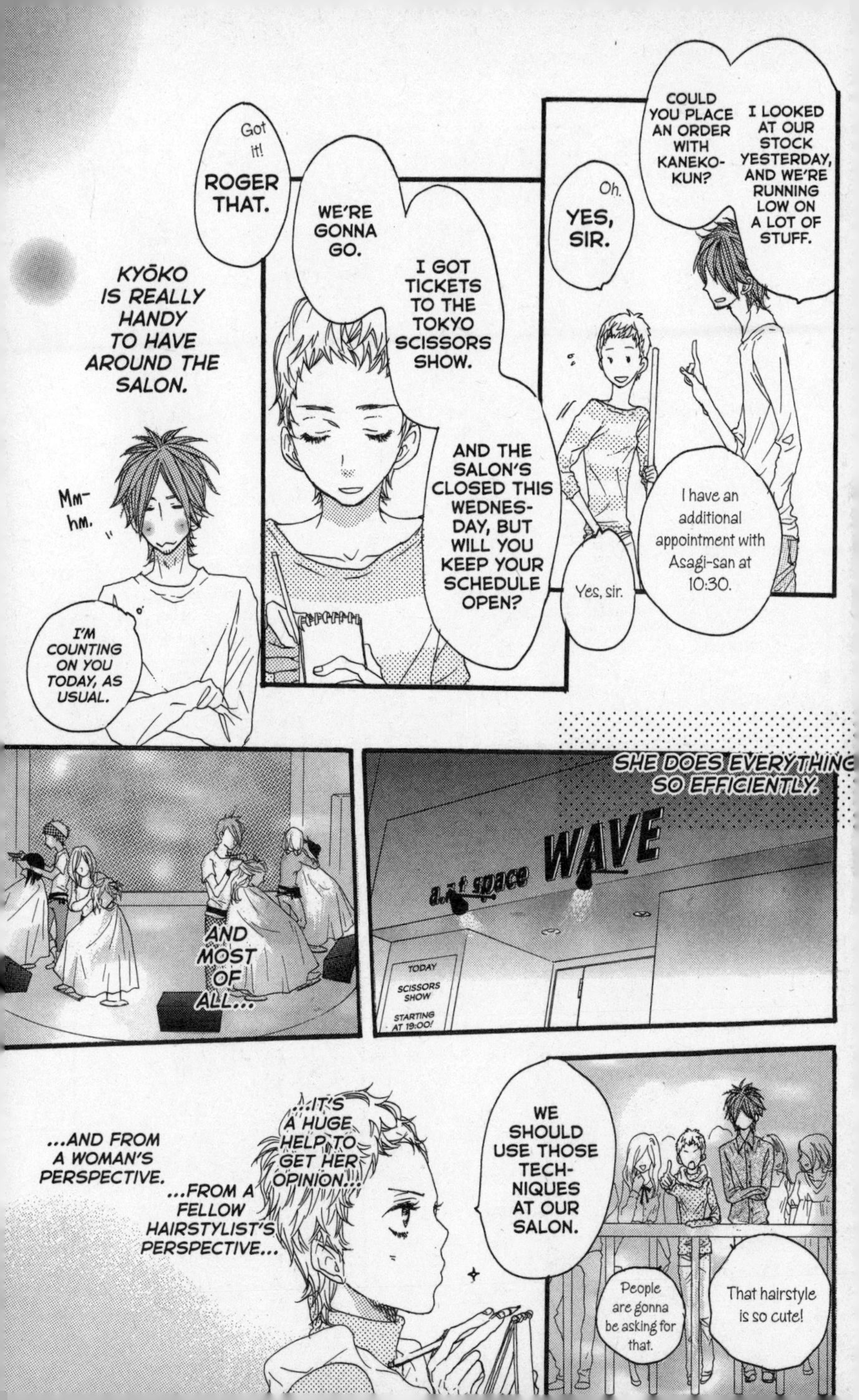
I LOOKED AT OUR STOCK YESTERDAY, AND WE'RE RUNNING LOW ON A LOT OF STUFF.
COULD YOU PLACE AN ORDER WITH KANEKO-KUN?
Oh. YES, SIR.
I have an additional appointment with Asagi-san at 10:30.
Yes, sir.
WE'RE GONNA GO.
I GOT TICKETS TO THE TOKYO SCISSORS SHOW.
AND THE SALON'S CLOSED THIS WEDNES-DAY, BUT WILL YOU KEEP YOUR SCHEDULE OPEN?
Got it! ROGER THAT.
KYŌKO IS REALLY HANDY TO HAVE AROUND THE SALON.
Mm-hm.
I'M COUNTING ON YOU TODAY, AS USUAL.
SHE DOES EVERYTHING SO EFFICIENTLY.
WAVE
TODAY SCISSORS SHOW STARTING AT 19:00!
AND MOST OF ALL...
WE SHOULD USE THOSE TECH-NIQUES AT OUR SALON.
That hairstyle is so cute!
People are gonna be asking for that.
...IT'S A HUGE HELP TO GET HER OPINION...
...FROM A FELLOW HAIRSTYLIST'S PERSPECTIVE...
...AND FROM A WOMAN'S PERSPECTIVE.

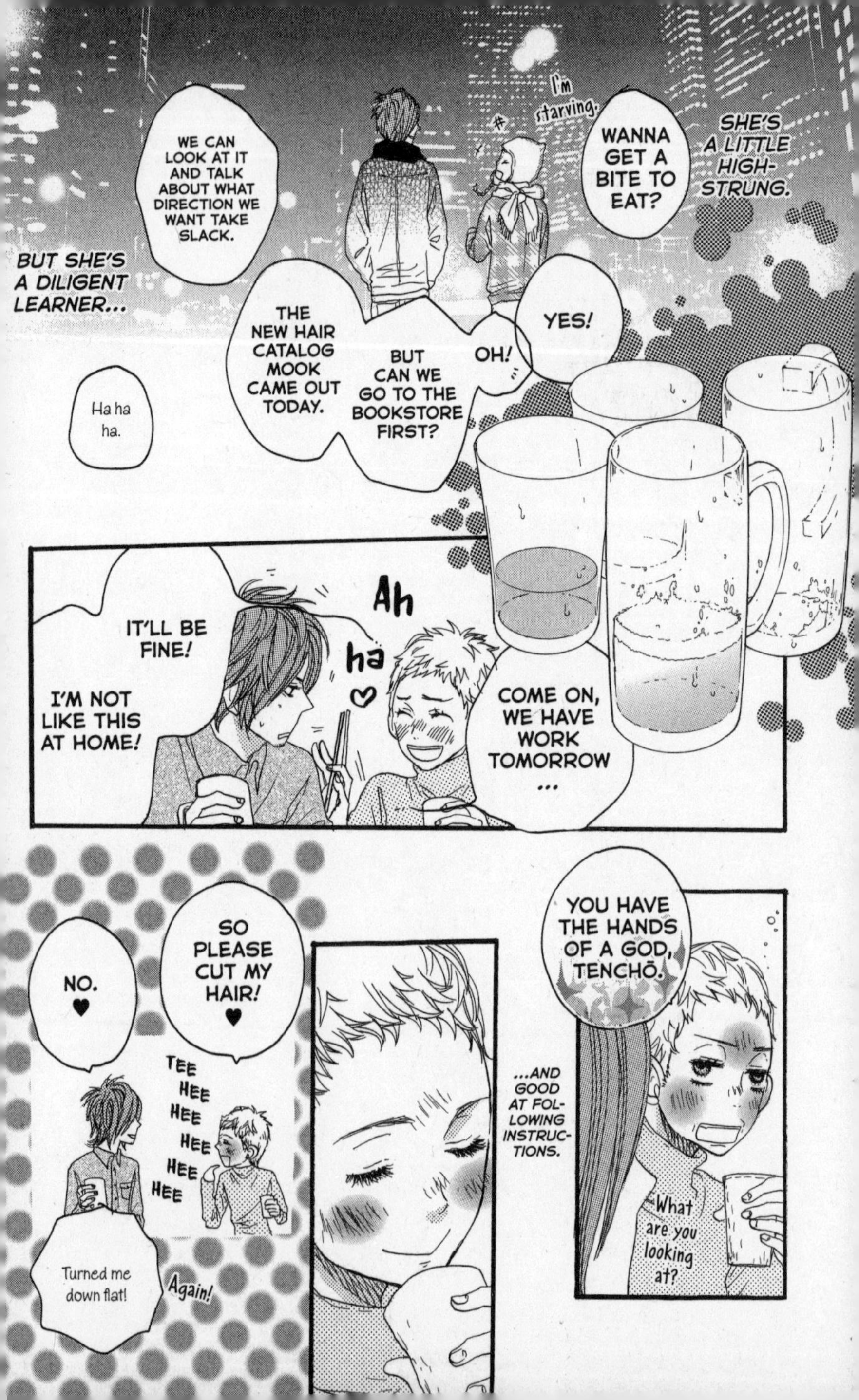
SHE'S A LITTLE HIGH-STRUNG.
I'm starving.
WANNA GET A BITE TO EAT?
YES!
OH!
BUT CAN WE GO TO THE BOOKSTORE FIRST?
THE NEW HAIR CATALOG MOOK CAME OUT TODAY.
WE CAN LOOK AT IT AND TALK ABOUT WHAT DIRECTION WE WANT TAKE SLACK.
Ha ha ha.
BUT SHE'S A DILIGENT LEARNER...
COME ON, WE HAVE WORK TOMORROW...
Ah ha ♥
IT'LL BE FINE!
I'M NOT LIKE THIS AT HOME!
YOU HAVE THE HANDS OF A GOD, TENCHŌ.
What are you looking at?
...AND GOOD AT FOL-LOWING INSTRUC-TIONS.
SO PLEASE CUT MY HAIR! ♥
NO. ♥
TEE HEE HEE HEE HEE HEE
Turned me down flat!
Again!

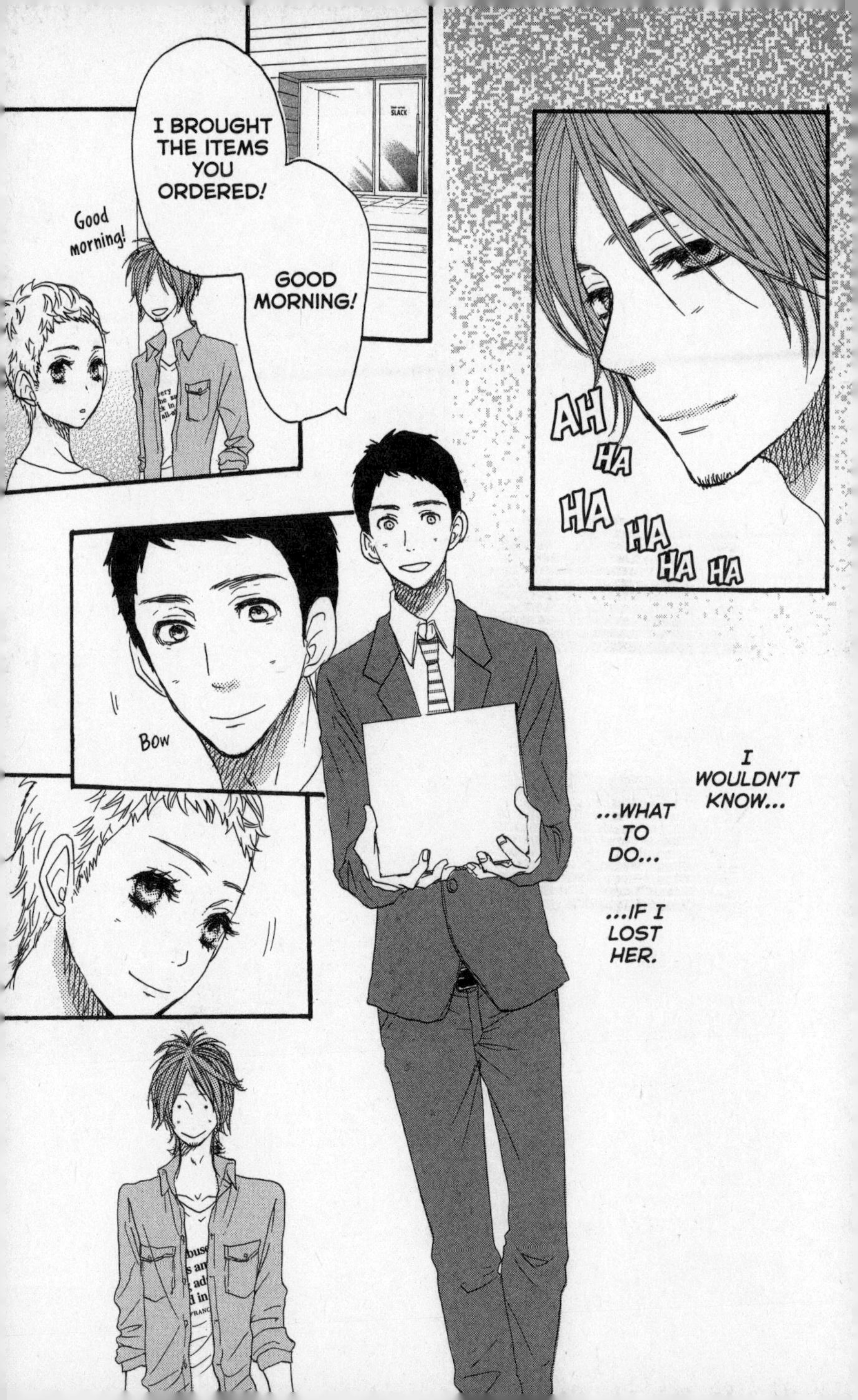
AH HA HA HA HA HA
I BROUGHT THE ITEMS YOU ORDERED!
GOOD MORNING!
Good morning!
Bow
I WOULDN'T KNOW...
...WHAT TO DO...
...IF I LOST HER.

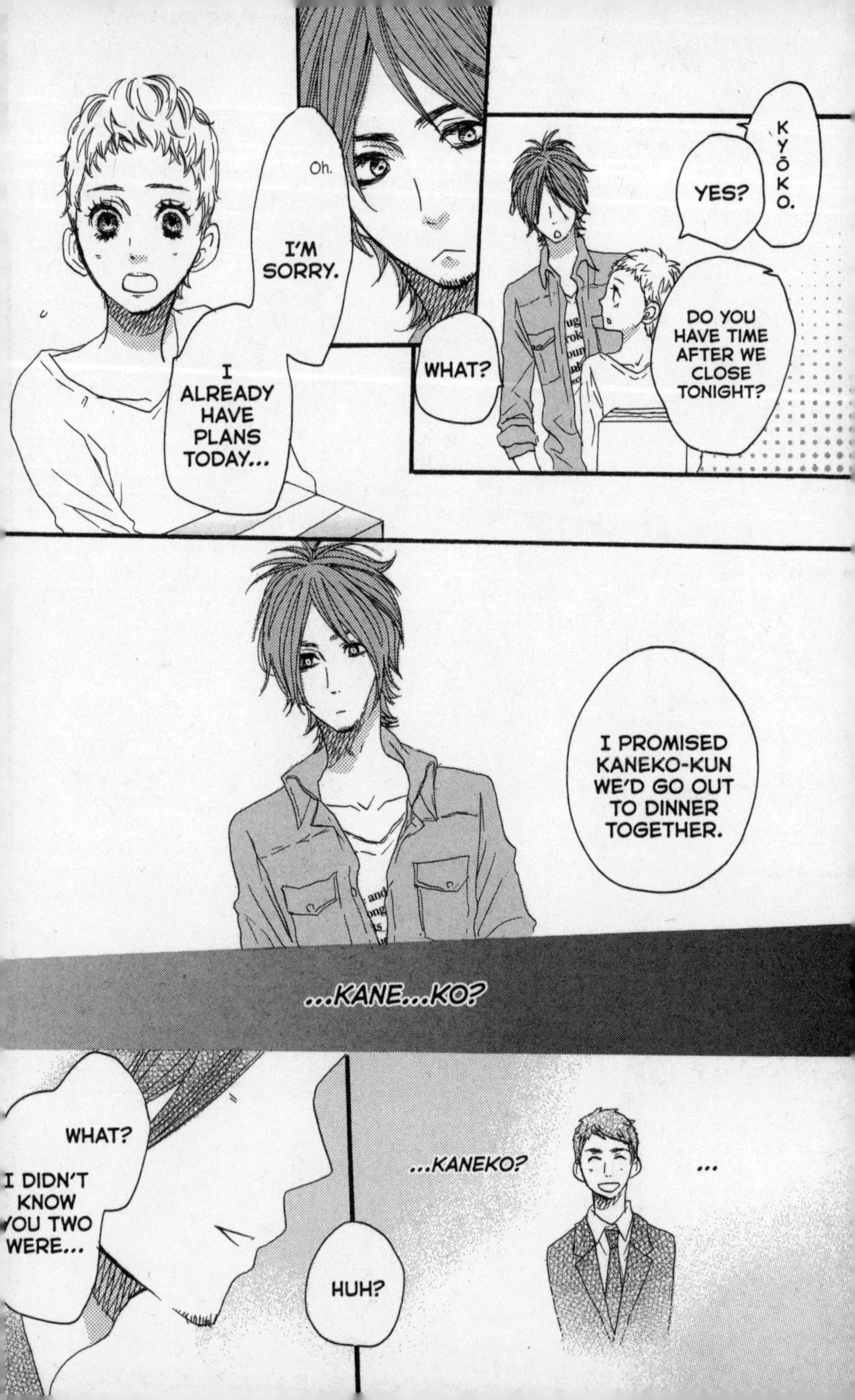
KYŌKO.
YES?
DO YOU HAVE TIME AFTER WE CLOSE TONIGHT?
WHAT?
Oh.
I'M SORRY.
I ALREADY HAVE PLANS TODAY...
I PROMISED KANEKO-KUN WE'D GO OUT TO DINNER TOGETHER.
...KANE...KO?
...
...KANEKO?
HUH?
WHAT?
I DIDN'T KNOW YOU TWO WERE...

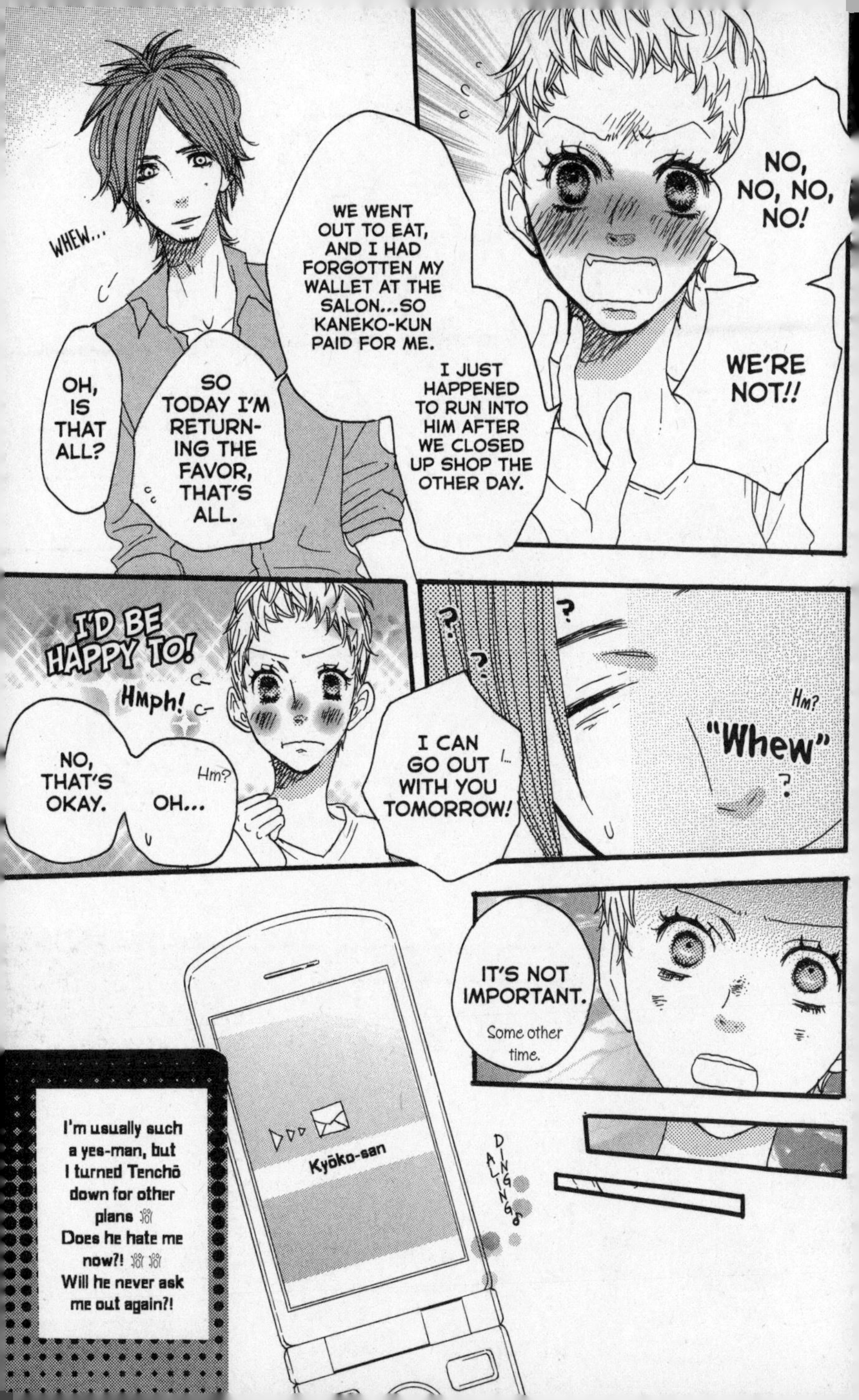
NO, NO, NO, NO!
WE'RE NOT!!
I JUST HAPPENED TO RUN INTO HIM AFTER WE CLOSED UP SHOP THE OTHER DAY.
WE WENT OUT TO EAT, AND I HAD FORGOTTEN MY WALLET AT THE SALON...SO KANEKO-KUN PAID FOR ME.
SO TODAY I'M RETURNING THE FAVOR, THAT'S ALL.
WHEW...
OH, IS THAT ALL?
Hm?
"Whew"
I...
I CAN GO OUT WITH YOU TOMORROW!
Hm?
OH...
NO, THAT'S OKAY.
I'D BE HAPPY TO!
Hmph!
IT'S NOT IMPORTANT.
Some other time.
DING A LING
Kyōko-san
I'm usually such a yes-man, but I turned Tenchō down for other plans
Does he hate me now?!
Will he never ask me out again?!

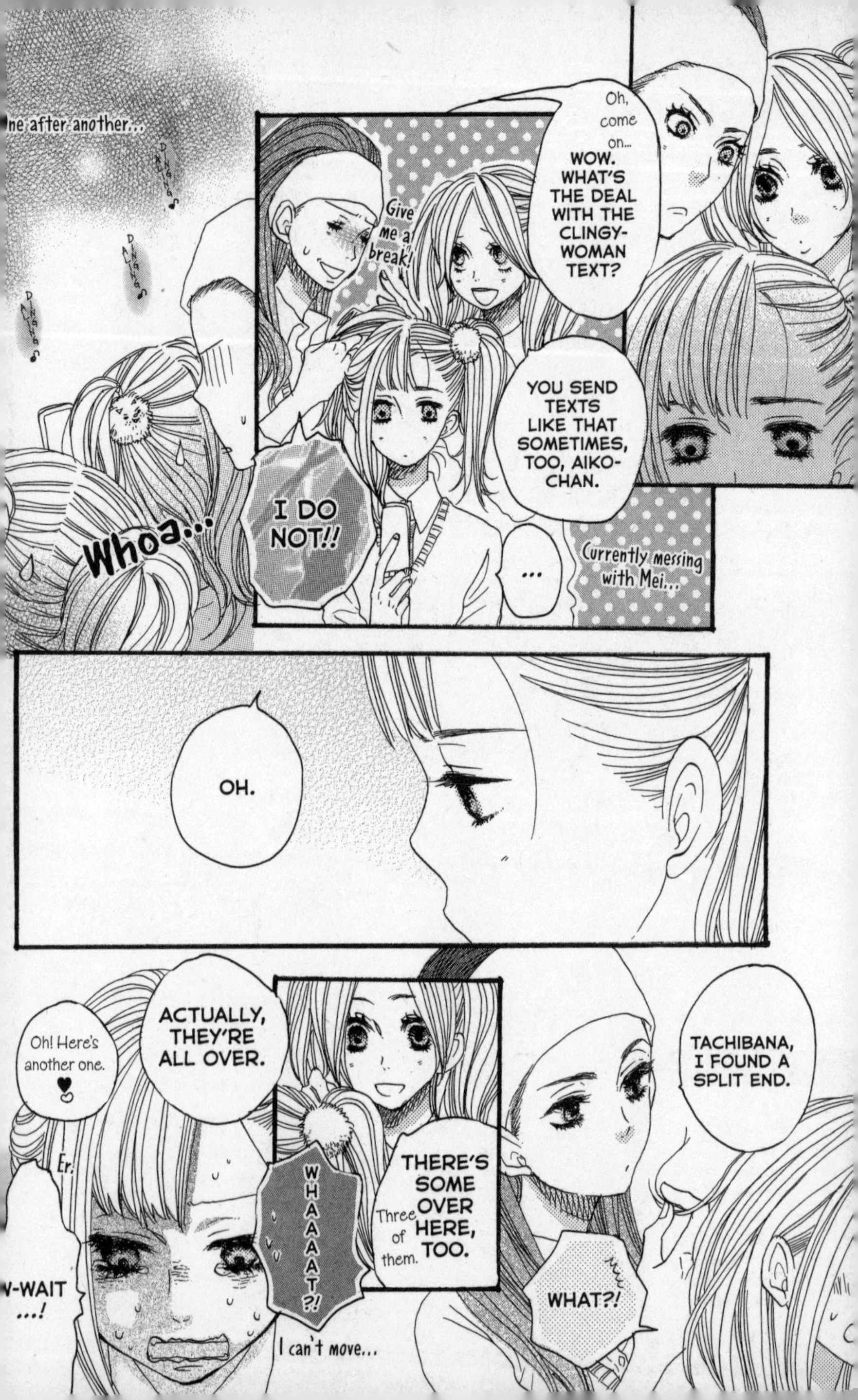

Oh, come on...
WOW. WHAT'S THE DEAL WITH THE CLINGY-WOMAN TEXT?
YOU SEND TEXTS LIKE THAT SOMETIMES, TOO, AIKO-CHAN.
Currently messing with Mei...
...
I DO NOT!!
Give me a break!
ne after another...
Whoa...
OH.
TACHIBANA, I FOUND A SPLIT END.
WHAT?!
THERE'S SOME OVER HERE, TOO.
Three of them.
WHAAAAT?!
I can't move...
ACTUALLY, THEY'RE ALL OVER.
Oh! Here's another one.
Er.
W-WAIT...!

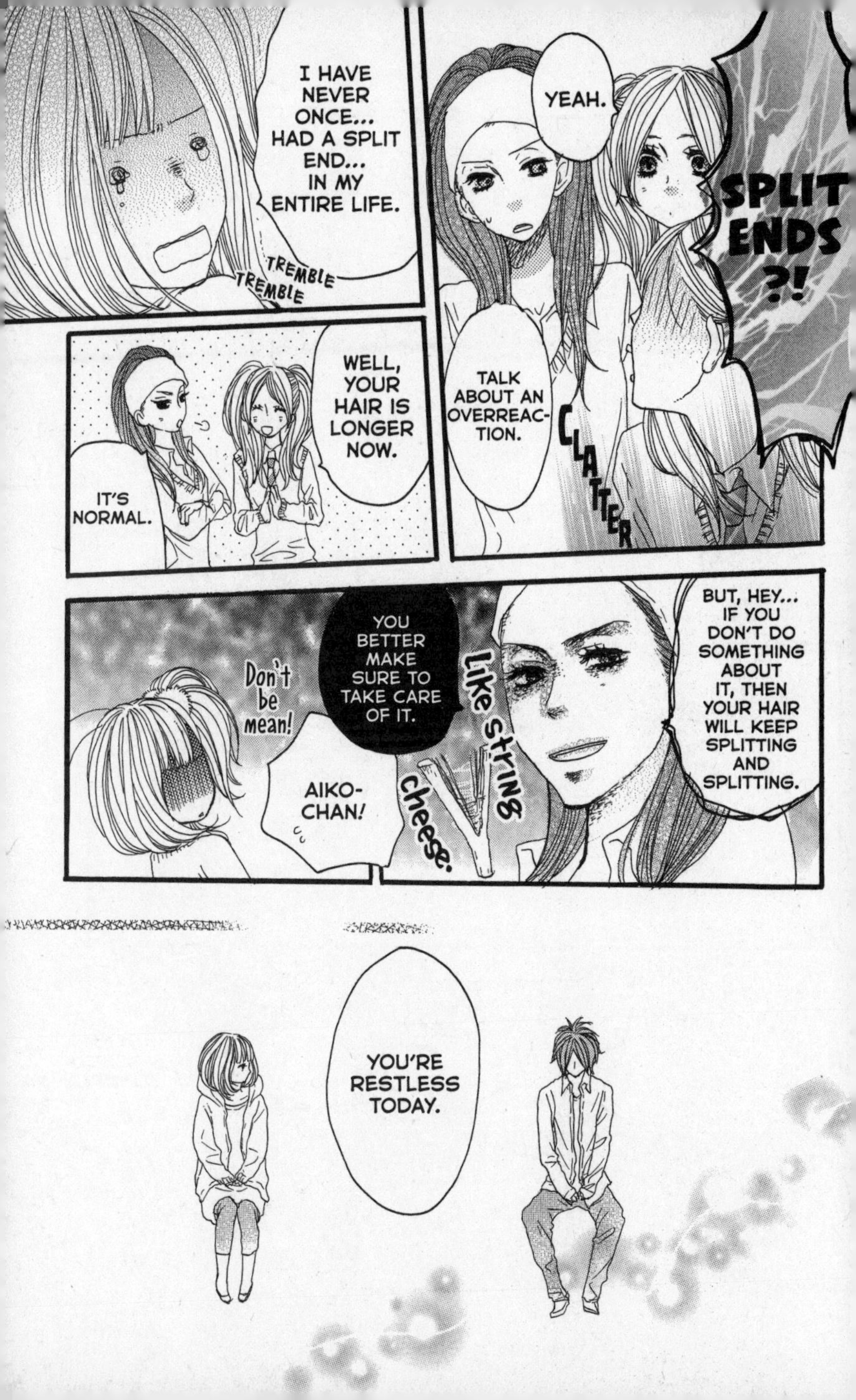

SPLIT ENDS ?!
YEAH.
CLATTER
TALK ABOUT AN OVERREAC-TION.
I HAVE NEVER ONCE... HAD A SPLIT END... IN MY ENTIRE LIFE.
TREMBLE TREMBLE
WELL, YOUR HAIR IS LONGER NOW.
IT'S NORMAL.
BUT, HEY... IF YOU DON'T DO SOMETHING ABOUT IT, THEN YOUR HAIR WILL KEEP SPLITTING AND SPLITTING.
Like string cheese.
YOU BETTER MAKE SURE TO TAKE CARE OF IT.
Don't be mean!
AIKO-CHAN!
YOU'RE RESTLESS TODAY.

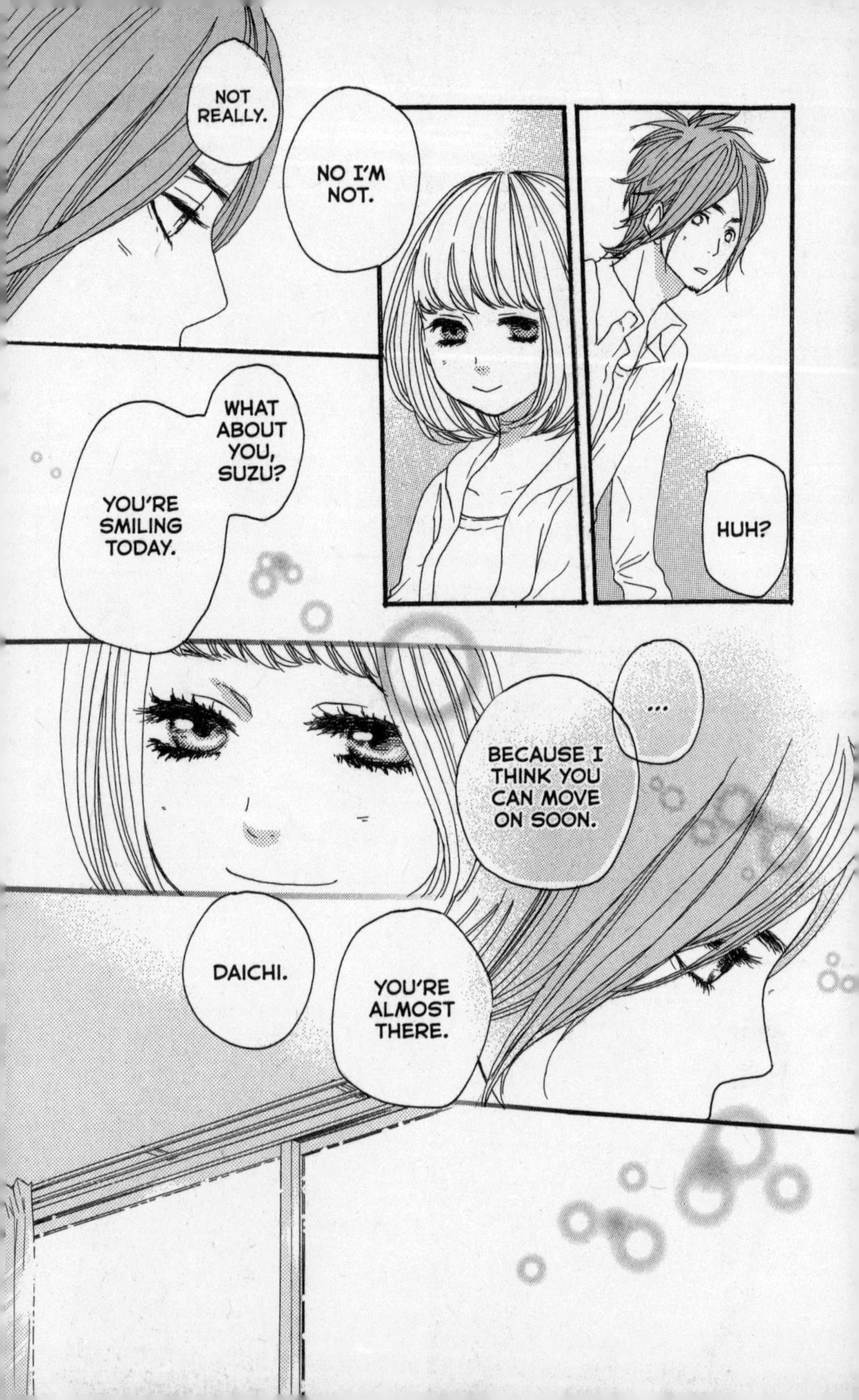
HUH?
NO I'M NOT.
NOT REALLY.
WHAT ABOUT YOU, SUZU?
YOU'RE SMILING TODAY.
...
BECAUSE I THINK YOU CAN MOVE ON SOON.
DAICHI.
YOU'RE ALMOST THERE.

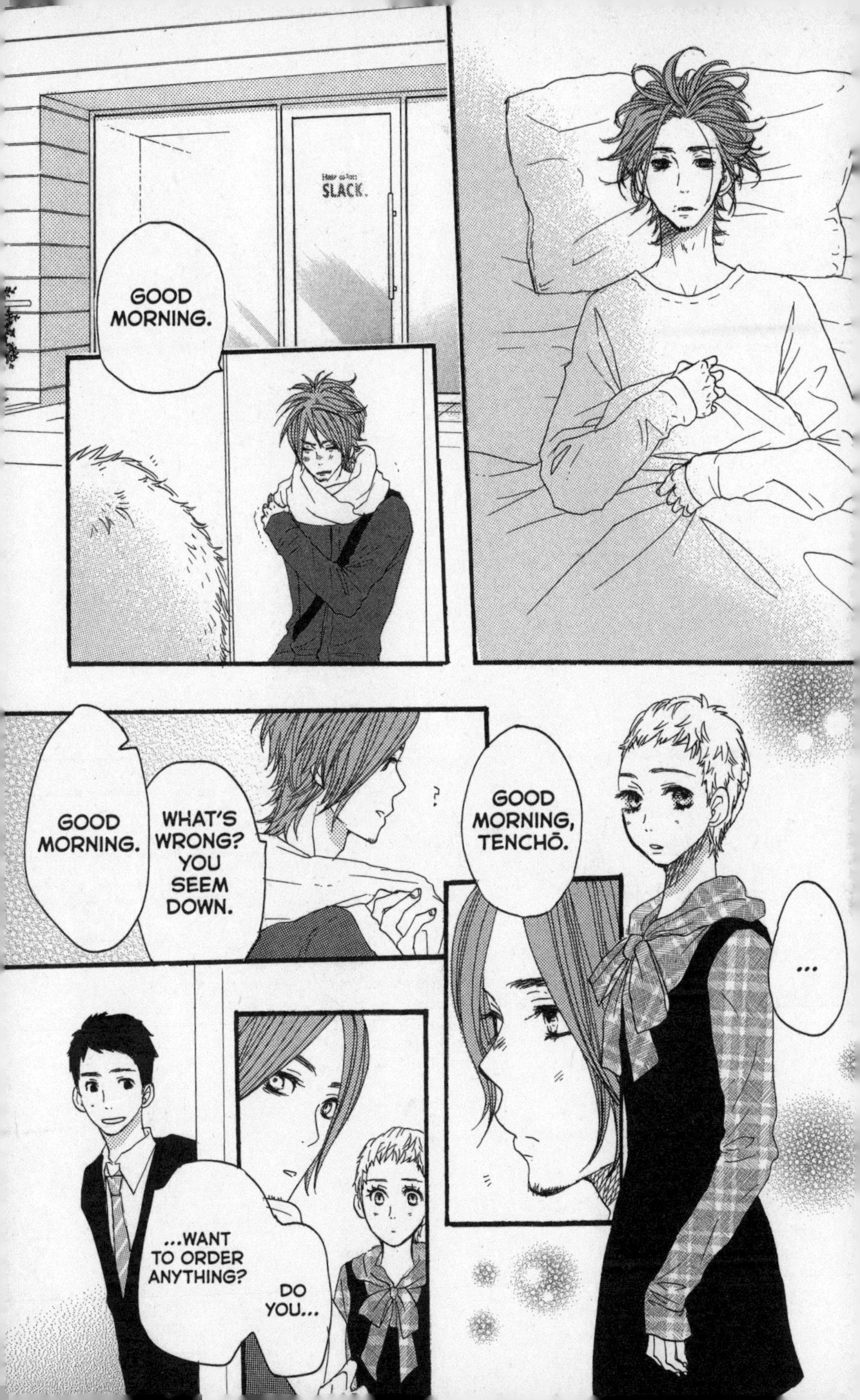
SLACK.
GOOD MORNING.
GOOD MORNING, TENCHŌ.
...
GOOD MORNING.
WHAT'S WRONG? YOU SEEM DOWN.
DO YOU...
...WANT TO ORDER ANYTHING?

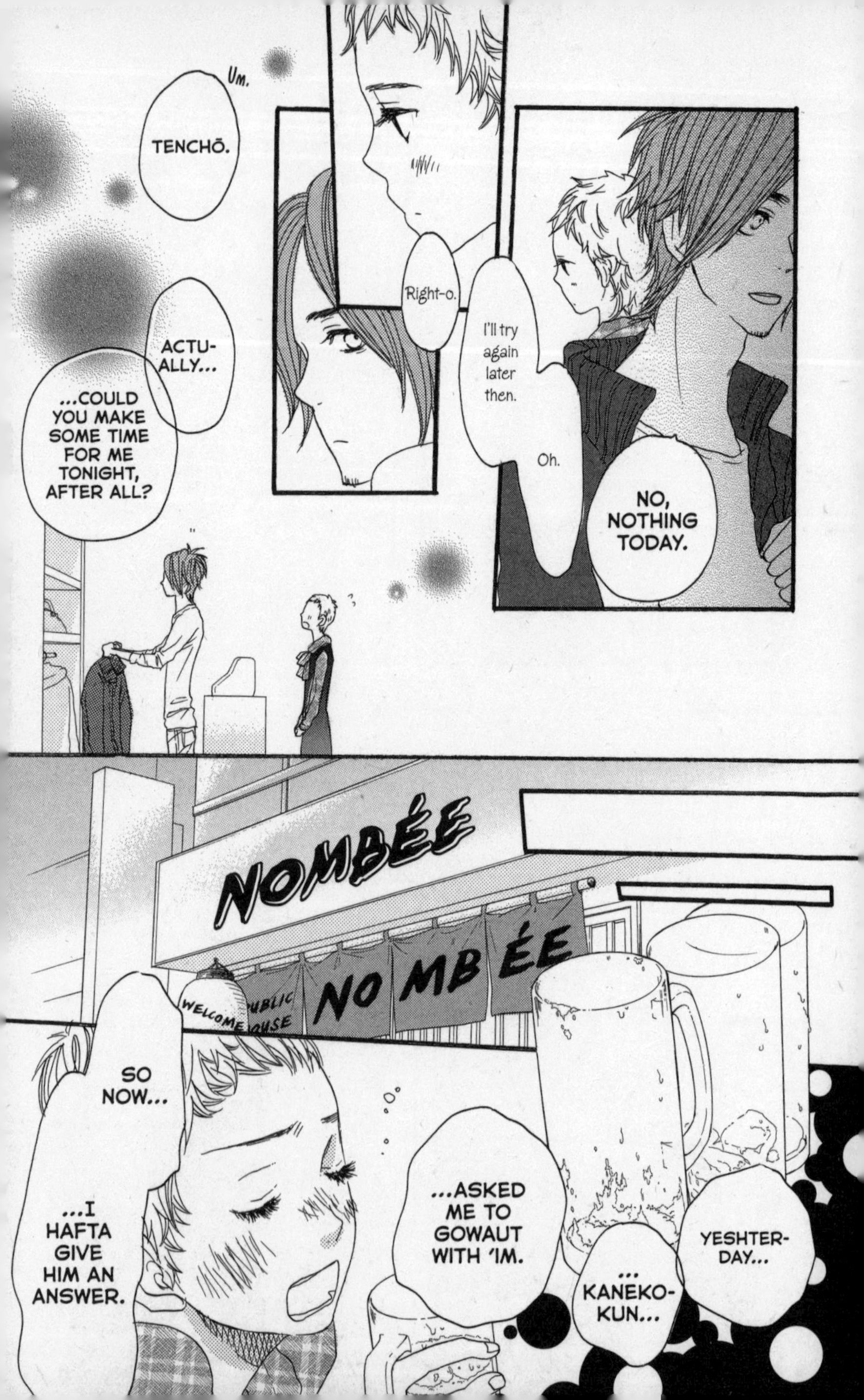
NO, NOTHING TODAY.
Oh.
I'll try again later then.
Right-o.
UM.
TENCHŌ.
ACTU-ALLY...
...COULD YOU MAKE SOME TIME FOR ME TONIGHT, AFTER ALL?
NOMBÉE
NO MB ÉE
WELCOME
YESHTER-DAY...
...KANEKO-KUN...
...ASKED ME TO GOWAUT WITH 'IM.
SO NOW...
...I HAFTA GIVE HIM AN ANSWER.

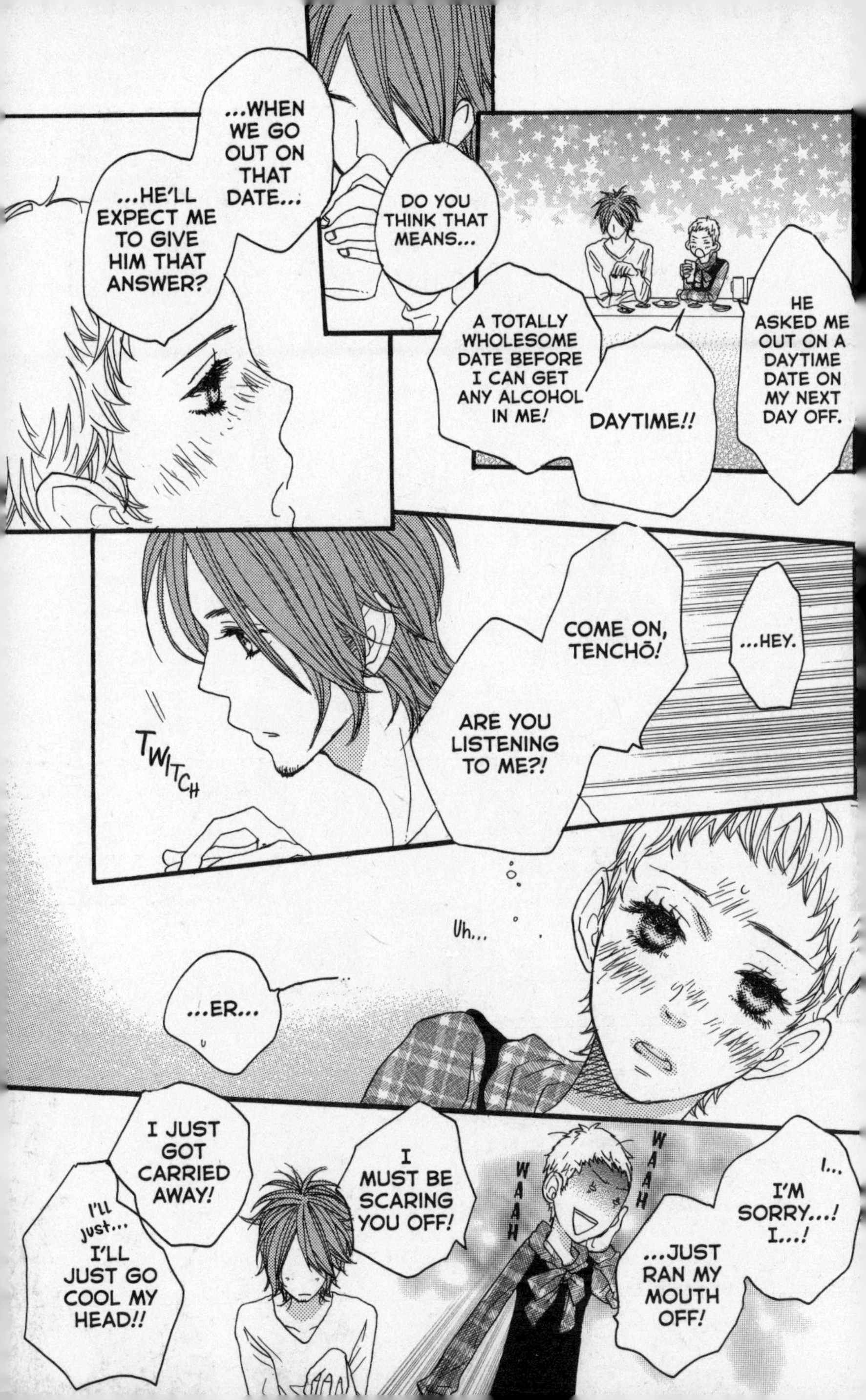
HE ASKED ME OUT ON A DAYTIME DATE ON MY NEXT DAY OFF.
DAYTIME!!
A TOTALLY WHOLESOME DATE BEFORE I CAN GET ANY ALCOHOL IN ME!
DO YOU THINK THAT MEANS...
...WHEN WE GO OUT ON THAT DATE...
...HE'LL EXPECT ME TO GIVE HIM THAT ANSWER?
...HEY.
COME ON, TENCHŌ!
ARE YOU LISTENING TO ME?!
TWITCH
Uh...
...ER...
I... I'M SORRY...! I...!
...JUST RAN MY MOUTH OFF!
WAAH
WAAH
I MUST BE SCARING YOU OFF!
I JUST GOT CARRIED AWAY!
I'll just...
I'LL JUST GO COOL MY HEAD!!

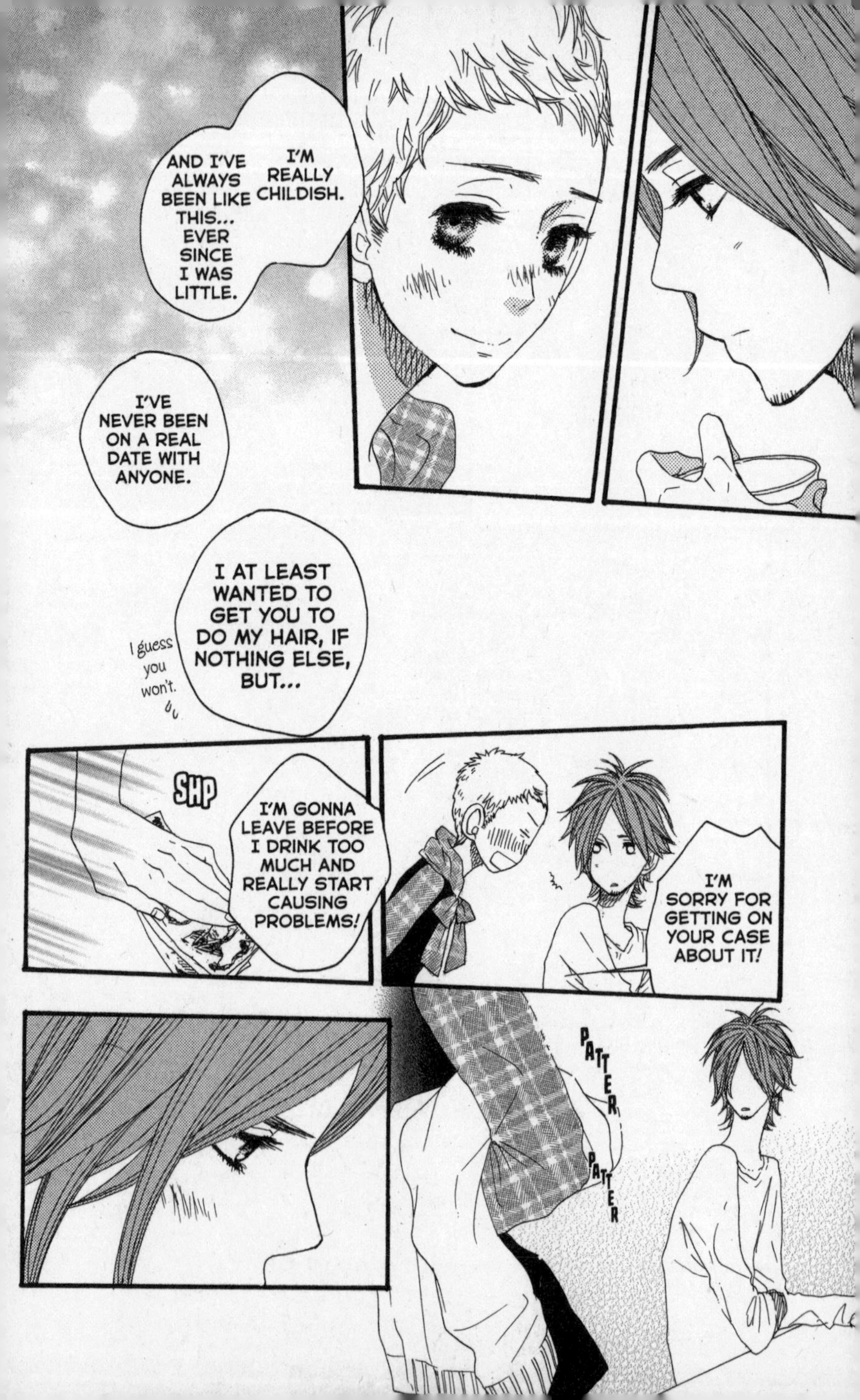
I'M REALLY CHILDISH.
AND I'VE ALWAYS BEEN LIKE THIS... EVER SINCE I WAS LITTLE.
I'VE NEVER BEEN ON A REAL DATE WITH ANYONE.
I AT LEAST WANTED TO GET YOU TO DO MY HAIR, IF NOTHING ELSE, BUT...
I guess you won't.
I'M SORRY FOR GETTING ON YOUR CASE ABOUT IT!
SHP
I'M GONNA LEAVE BEFORE I DRINK TOO MUCH AND REALLY START CAUSING PROBLEMS!
PATTER
PATTER

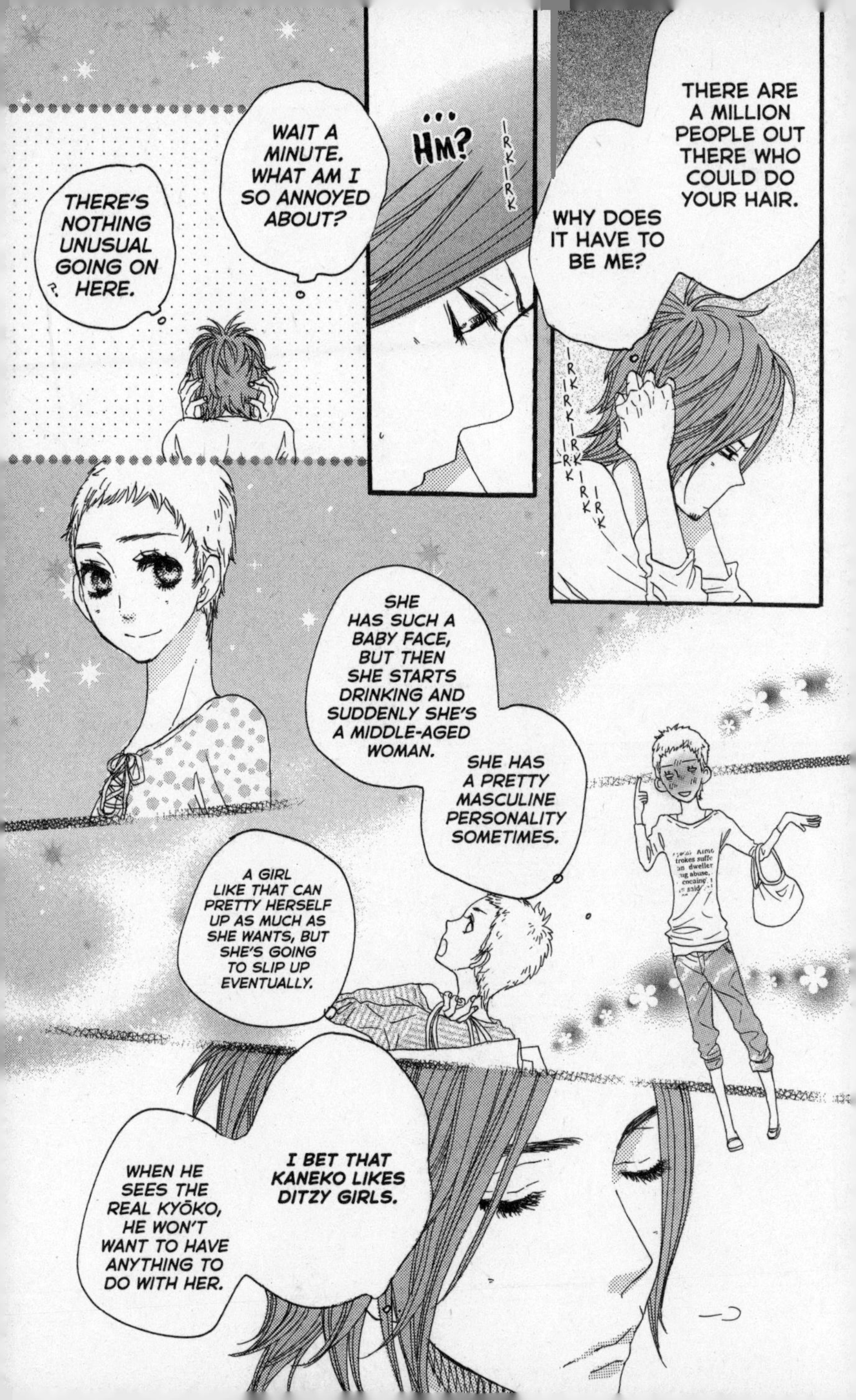
THERE ARE A MILLION PEOPLE OUT THERE WHO COULD DO YOUR HAIR.
WHY DOES IT HAVE TO BE ME?
IRK IRK IRK IRK IRK
...HM?
IRK IRK
WAIT A MINUTE. WHAT AM I SO ANNOYED ABOUT?
THERE'S NOTHING UNUSUAL GOING ON HERE.
SHE HAS SUCH A BABY FACE, BUT THEN SHE STARTS DRINKING AND SUDDENLY SHE'S A MIDDLE-AGED WOMAN.
SHE HAS A PRETTY MASCULINE PERSONALITY SOMETIMES.
A GIRL LIKE THAT CAN PRETTY HERSELF UP AS MUCH AS SHE WANTS, BUT SHE'S GOING TO SLIP UP EVENTUALLY.
I BET THAT KANEKO LIKES DITZY GIRLS.
WHEN HE SEES THE REAL KYŌKO, HE WON'T WANT TO HAVE ANYTHING TO DO WITH HER.

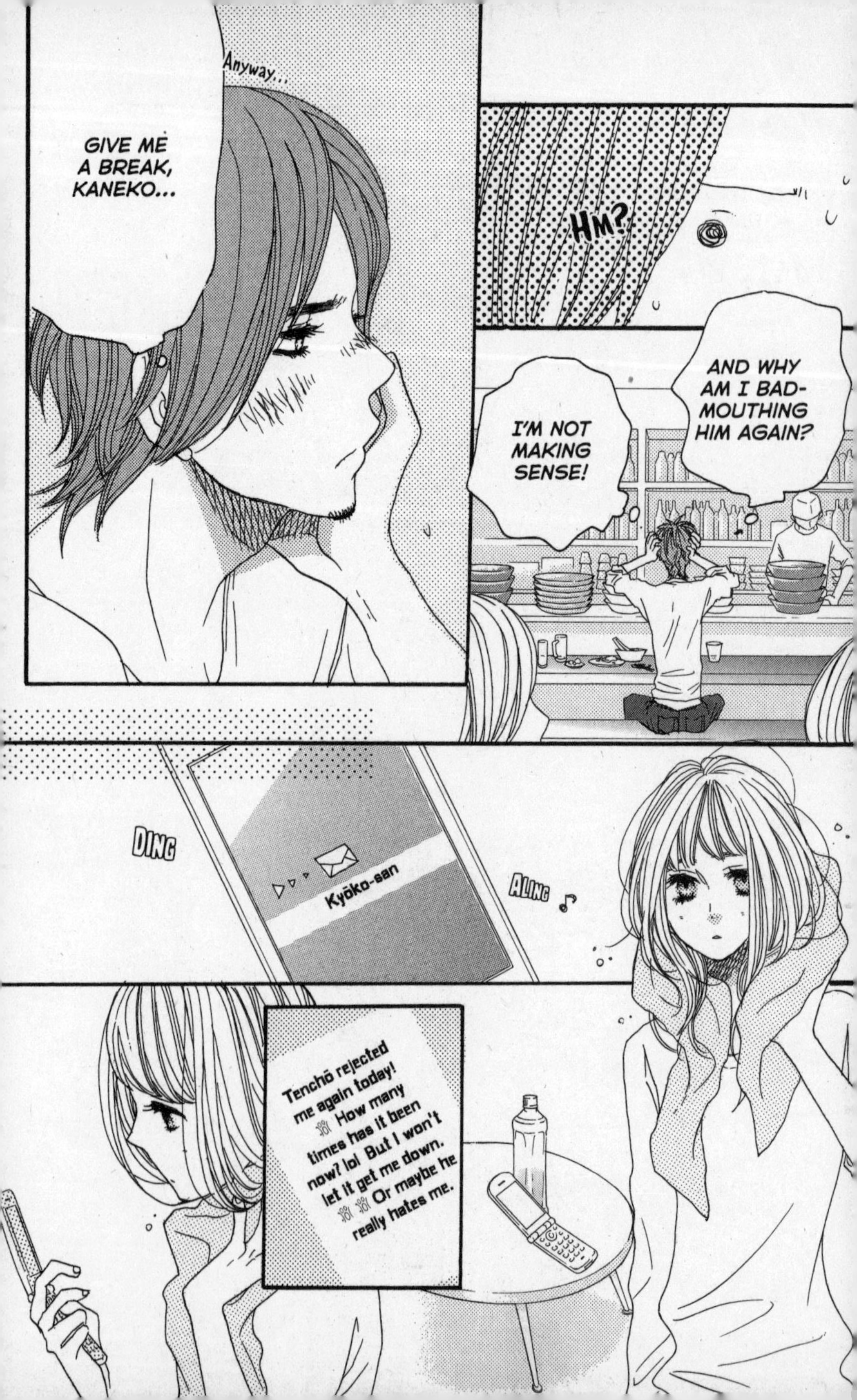
HM?
AND WHY AM I BAD-MOUTHING HIM AGAIN?
I'M NOT MAKING SENSE!
Anyway...
GIVE ME A BREAK, KANEKO...
ALING
DING
Kyōko-san
Tenchō rejected me again today! How many times has it been now? lol But I won't let it get me down. Or maybe he really hates me.

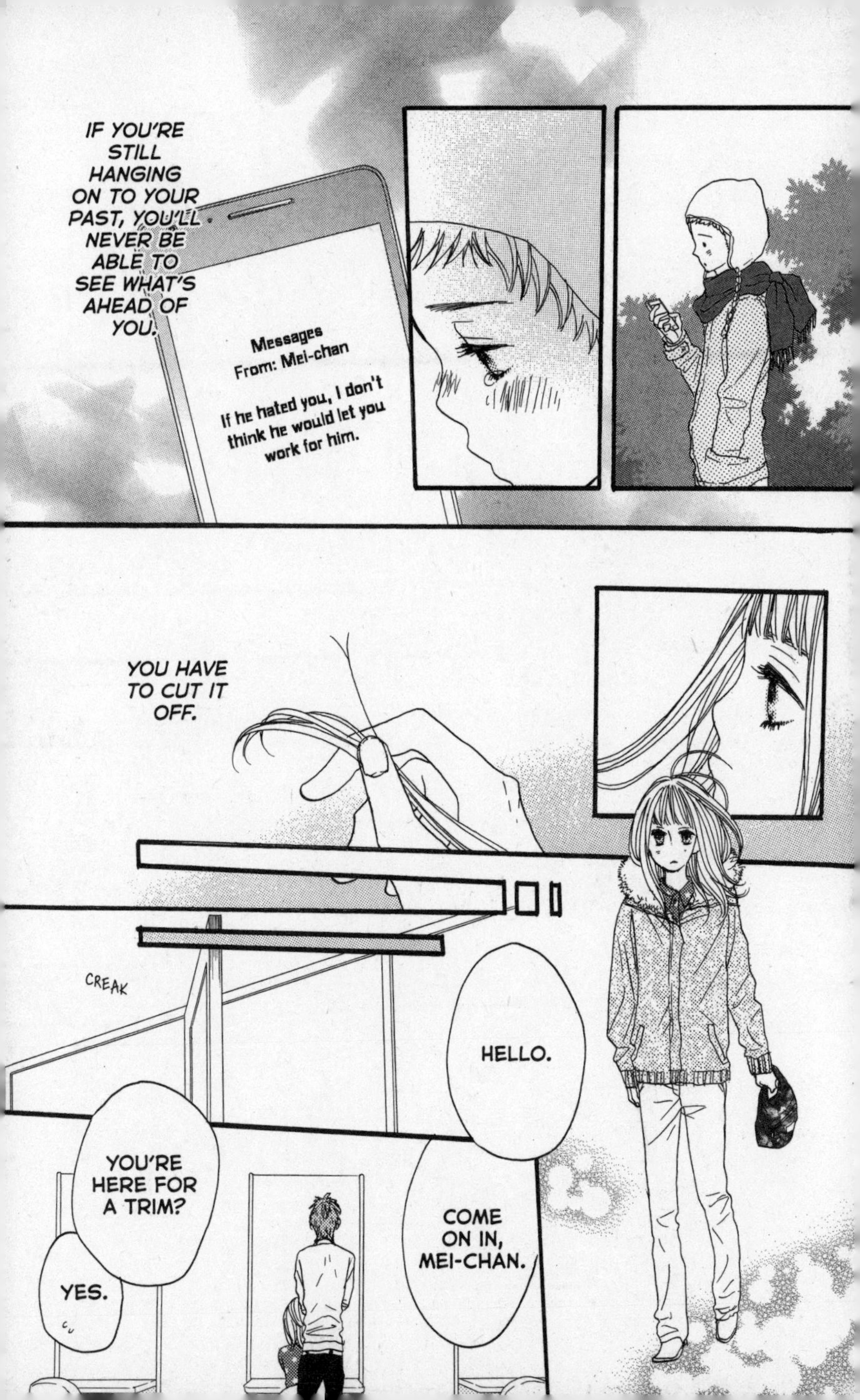
IF YOU'RE STILL HANGING ON TO YOUR PAST, YOU'LL NEVER BE ABLE TO SEE WHAT'S AHEAD OF YOU.
Messages
From: Mei-chan
If he hated you, I don't think he would let you work for him.
YOU HAVE TO CUT IT OFF.
CREAK
HELLO.
COME ON IN, MEI-CHAN.
YOU'RE HERE FOR A TRIM?
YES.

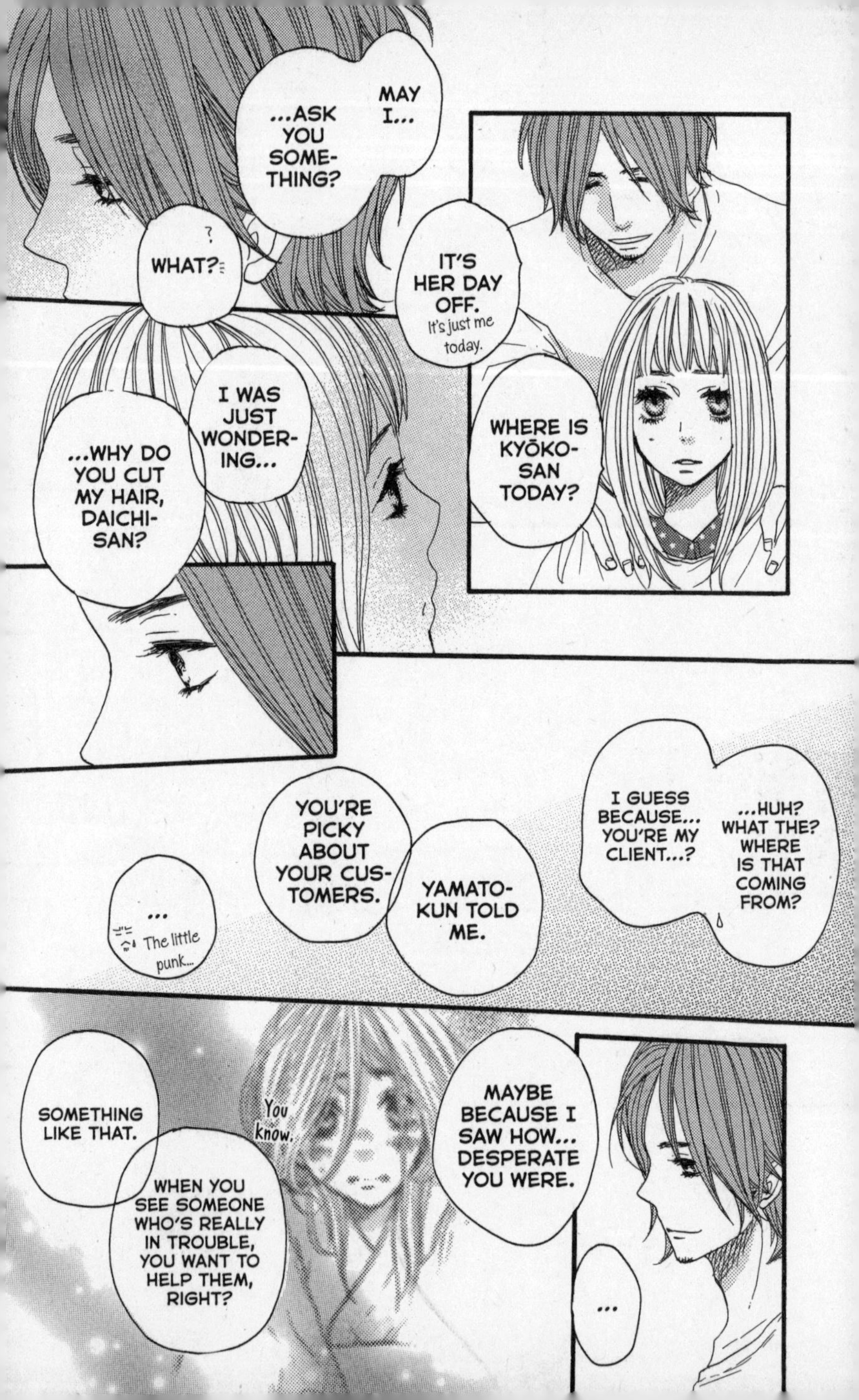
WHERE IS KYŌKO-SAN TODAY?
IT'S HER DAY OFF.
It's just me today.
MAY I...
...ASK YOU SOMETHING?
WHAT?
I WAS JUST WONDERING...
...WHY DO YOU CUT MY HAIR, DAICHI-SAN?
...HUH? WHAT THE? WHERE IS THAT COMING FROM?
I GUESS BECAUSE... YOU'RE MY CLIENT...?
YOU'RE PICKY ABOUT YOUR CUSTOMERS.
YAMATO-KUN TOLD ME.
...
The little punk...
...
MAYBE BECAUSE I SAW HOW... DESPERATE YOU WERE.
You know.
WHEN YOU SEE SOMEONE WHO'S REALLY IN TROUBLE, YOU WANT TO HELP THEM, RIGHT?
SOMETHING LIKE THAT.

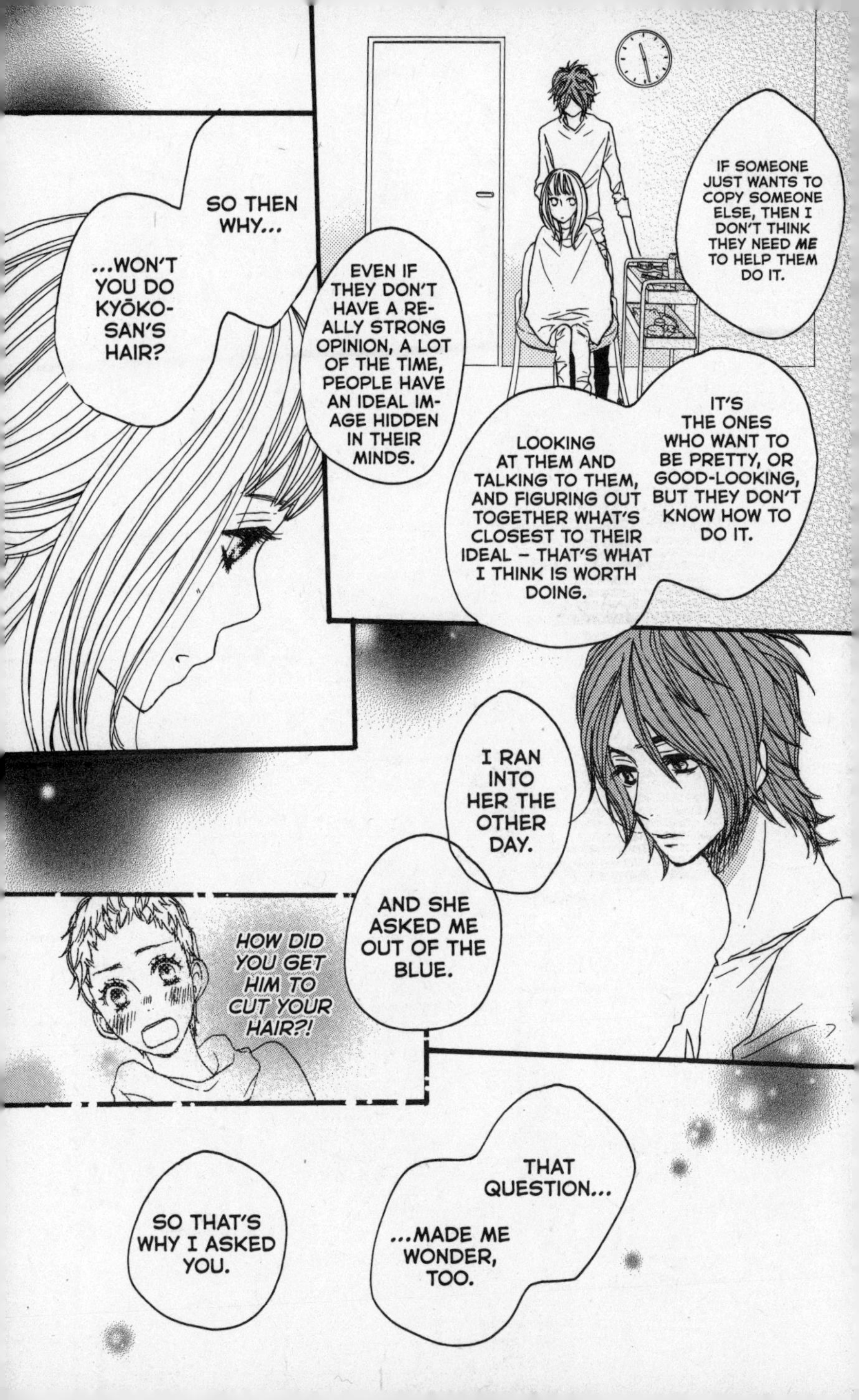
IF SOMEONE JUST WANTS TO COPY SOMEONE ELSE, THEN I DON'T THINK THEY NEED *ME* TO HELP THEM DO IT.
EVEN IF THEY DON'T HAVE A REALLY STRONG OPINION, A LOT OF THE TIME, PEOPLE HAVE AN IDEAL IMAGE HIDDEN IN THEIR MINDS.
IT'S THE ONES WHO WANT TO BE PRETTY, OR GOOD-LOOKING, BUT THEY DON'T KNOW HOW TO DO IT.
LOOKING AT THEM AND TALKING TO THEM, AND FIGURING OUT TOGETHER WHAT'S CLOSEST TO THEIR IDEAL – THAT'S WHAT I THINK IS WORTH DOING.
SO THEN WHY...
...WON'T YOU DO KYŌKO-SAN'S HAIR?
I RAN INTO HER THE OTHER DAY.
AND SHE ASKED ME OUT OF THE BLUE.
HOW DID YOU GET HIM TO CUT YOUR HAIR?!
THAT QUESTION...
...MADE ME WONDER, TOO.
SO THAT'S WHY I ASKED YOU.

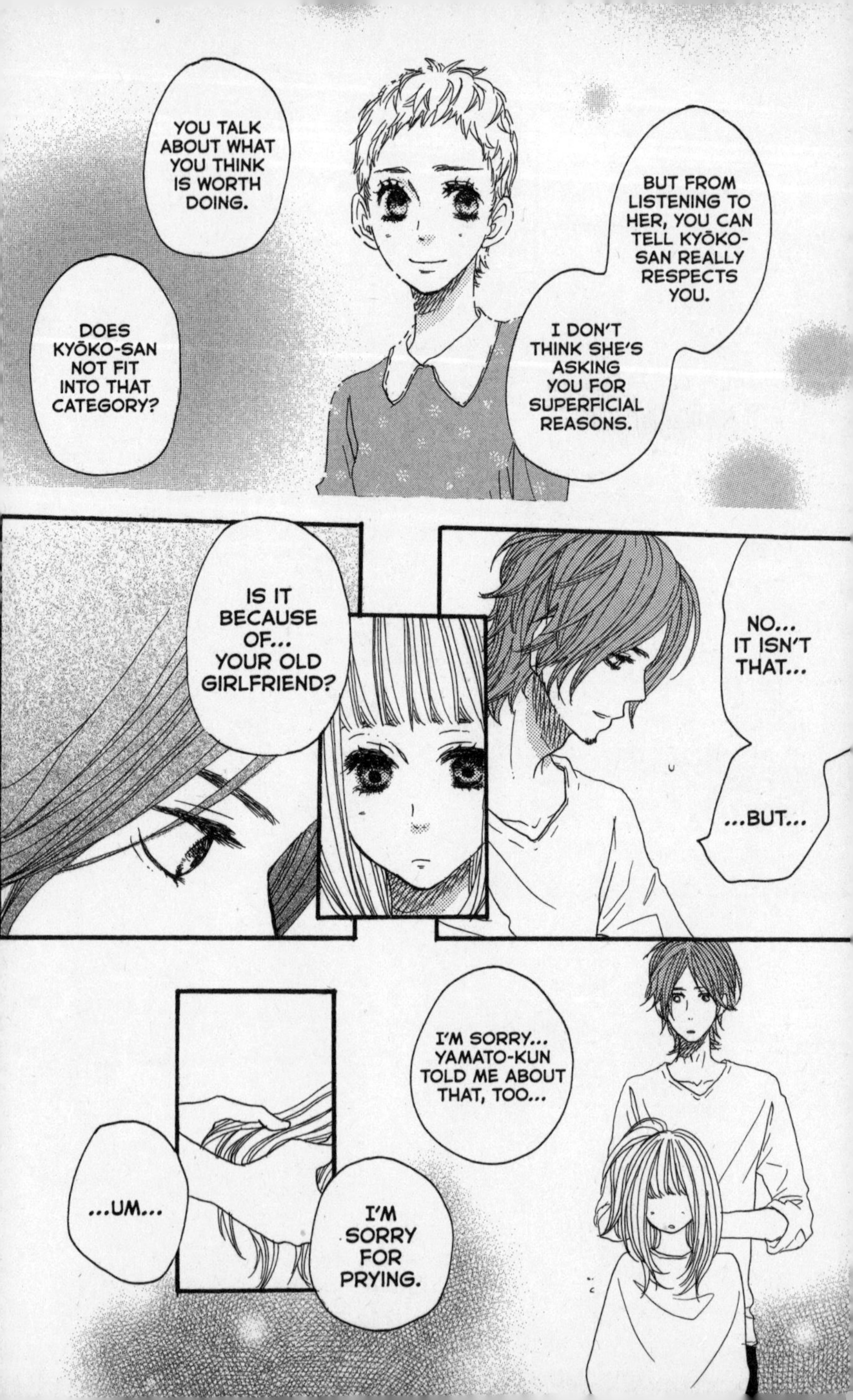
BUT FROM LISTENING TO HER, YOU CAN TELL KYŌKO-SAN REALLY RESPECTS YOU.
I DON'T THINK SHE'S ASKING YOU FOR SUPERFICIAL REASONS.
YOU TALK ABOUT WHAT YOU THINK IS WORTH DOING.
DOES KYŌKO-SAN NOT FIT INTO THAT CATEGORY?
IS IT BECAUSE OF... YOUR OLD GIRLFRIEND?
NO... IT ISN'T THAT...
...BUT...
I'M SORRY... YAMATO-KUN TOLD ME ABOUT THAT, TOO...
I'M SORRY FOR PRYING.
...UM...

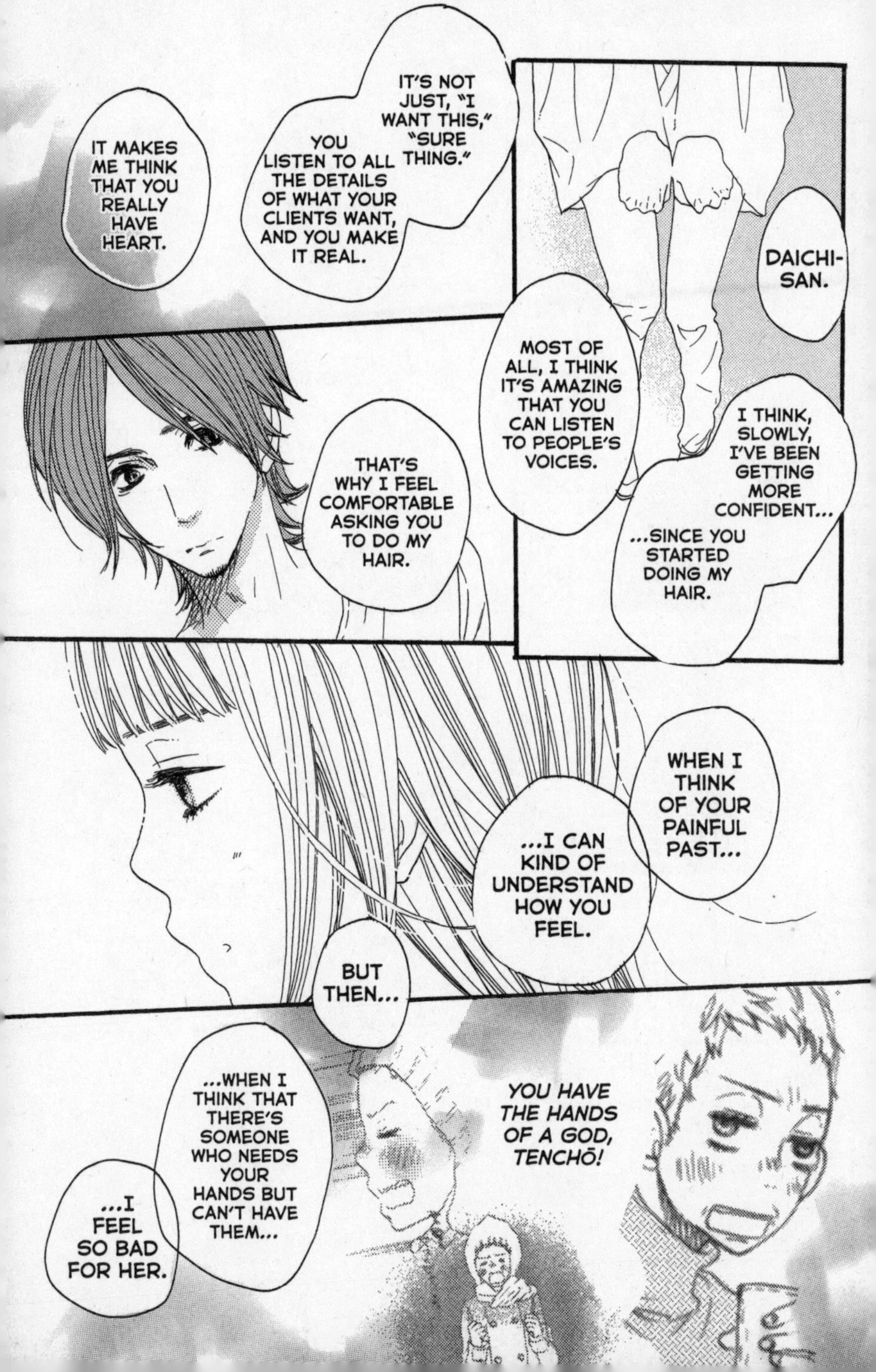
DAICHI-SAN.
I THINK, SLOWLY, I'VE BEEN GETTING MORE CONFIDENT...
...SINCE YOU STARTED DOING MY HAIR.
IT'S NOT JUST, "I WANT THIS," "SURE THING."
YOU LISTEN TO ALL THE DETAILS OF WHAT YOUR CLIENTS WANT, AND YOU MAKE IT REAL.
IT MAKES ME THINK THAT YOU REALLY HAVE HEART.
MOST OF ALL, I THINK IT'S AMAZING THAT YOU CAN LISTEN TO PEOPLE'S VOICES.
THAT'S WHY I FEEL COMFORTABLE ASKING YOU TO DO MY HAIR.
WHEN I THINK OF YOUR PAINFUL PAST...
...I CAN KIND OF UNDERSTAND HOW YOU FEEL.
BUT THEN...
YOU HAVE THE HANDS OF A GOD, TENCHŌ!
...WHEN I THINK THAT THERE'S SOMEONE WHO NEEDS YOUR HANDS BUT CAN'T HAVE THEM...
...I FEEL SO BAD FOR HER.

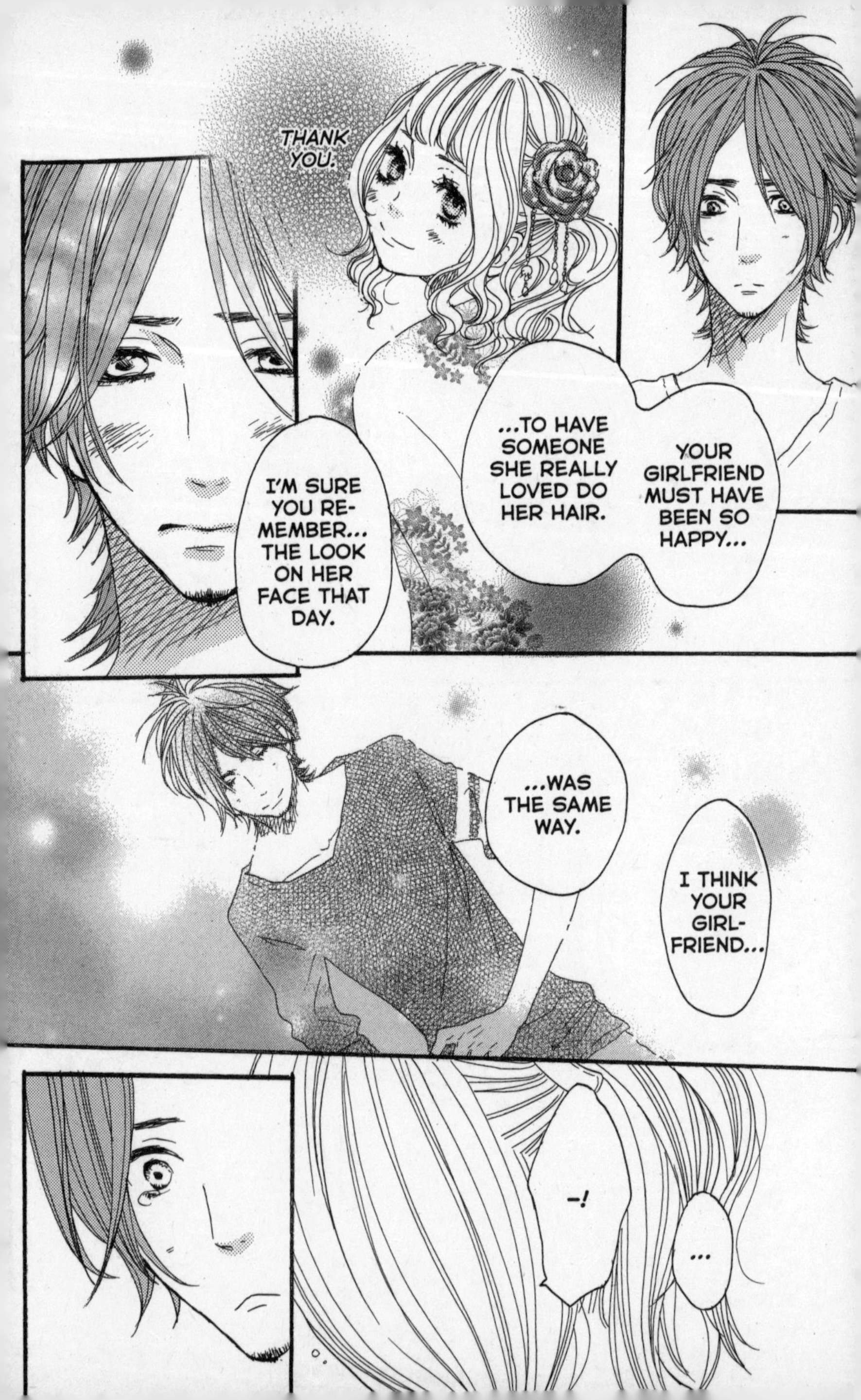
THANK YOU.
YOUR GIRLFRIEND MUST HAVE BEEN SO HAPPY...
...TO HAVE SOMEONE SHE REALLY LOVED DO HER HAIR.
I'M SURE YOU RE-MEMBER... THE LOOK ON HER FACE THAT DAY.
I THINK YOUR GIRL-FRIEND...
...WAS THE SAME WAY.
...
-!

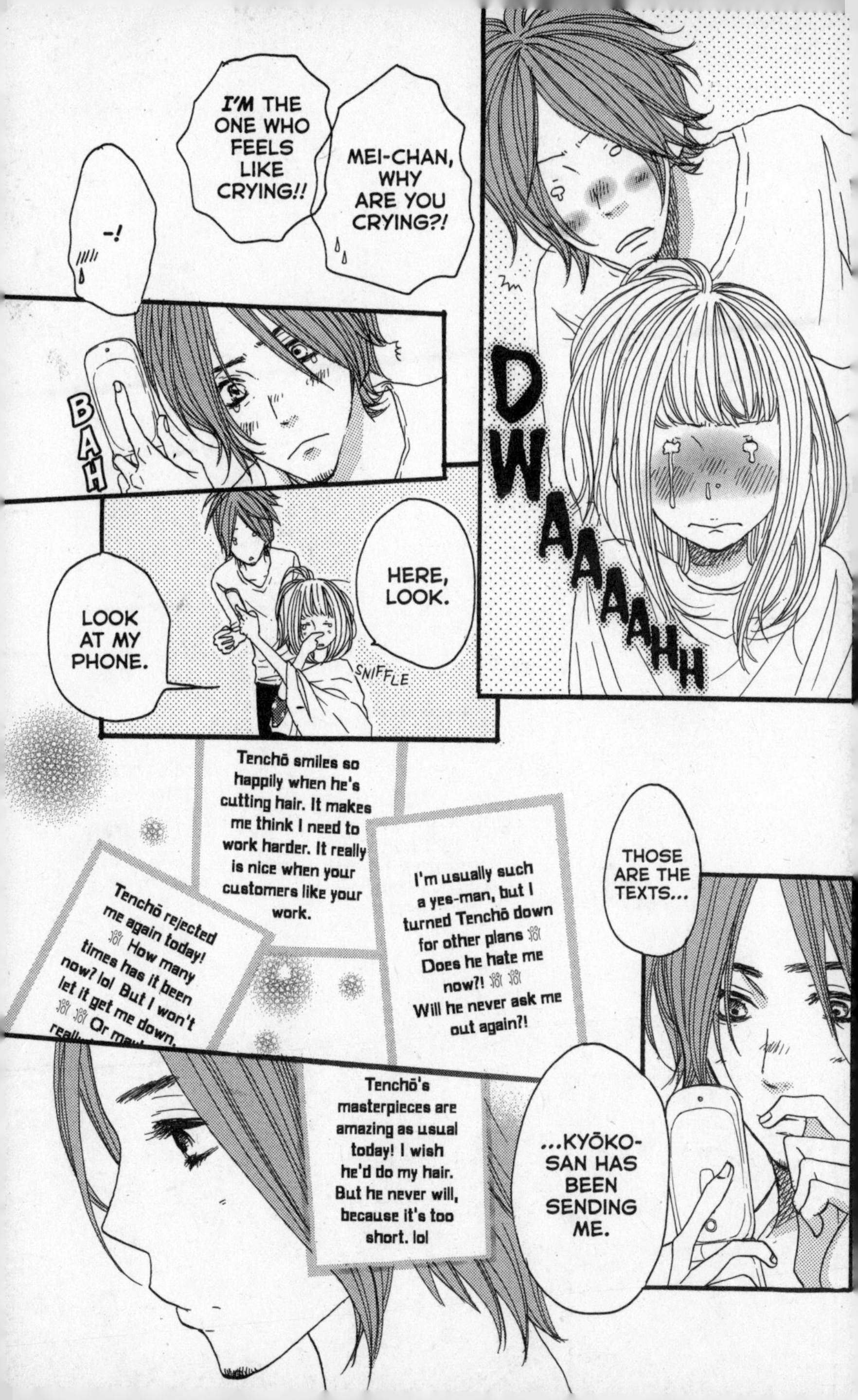
DWAAAAAHH
MEI-CHAN, WHY ARE YOU CRYING?!
I'M THE ONE WHO FEELS LIKE CRYING!!
–!
BAH
HERE, LOOK.
LOOK AT MY PHONE.
SNIFFLE
THOSE ARE THE TEXTS...
...KYŌKO-SAN HAS BEEN SENDING ME.
I'm usually such a yes-man, but I turned Tenchō down for other plans Does he hate me now?! Will he never ask me out again?!
Tenchō smiles so happily when he's cutting hair. It makes me think I need to work harder. It really is nice when your customers like your work.
Tenchō rejected me again today! How many times has it been now? lol But I won't let it get me down, Or
Tenchō's masterpieces are amazing as usual today! I wish he'd do my hair. But he never will, because it's too short. lol

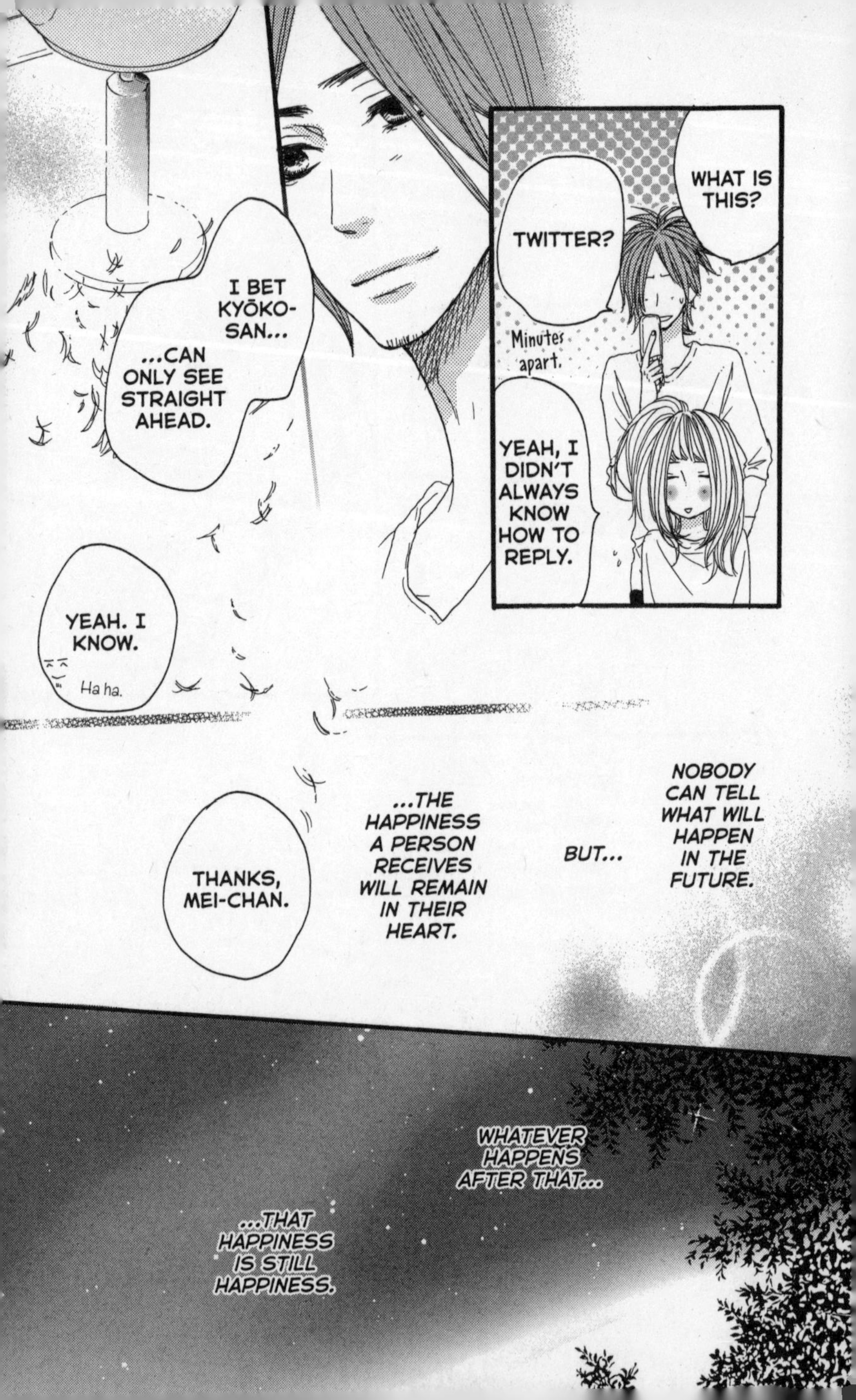
WHAT IS THIS?
TWITTER?
Minutes apart.
YEAH, I DIDN'T ALWAYS KNOW HOW TO REPLY.
I BET KYŌKO-SAN...
...CAN ONLY SEE STRAIGHT AHEAD.
YEAH. I KNOW.
Ha ha.
NOBODY CAN TELL WHAT WILL HAPPEN IN THE FUTURE.
BUT...
...THE HAPPINESS A PERSON RECEIVES WILL REMAIN IN THEIR HEART.
THANKS, MEI-CHAN.
WHATEVER HAPPENS AFTER THAT...
...THAT HAPPINESS IS STILL HAPPINESS.

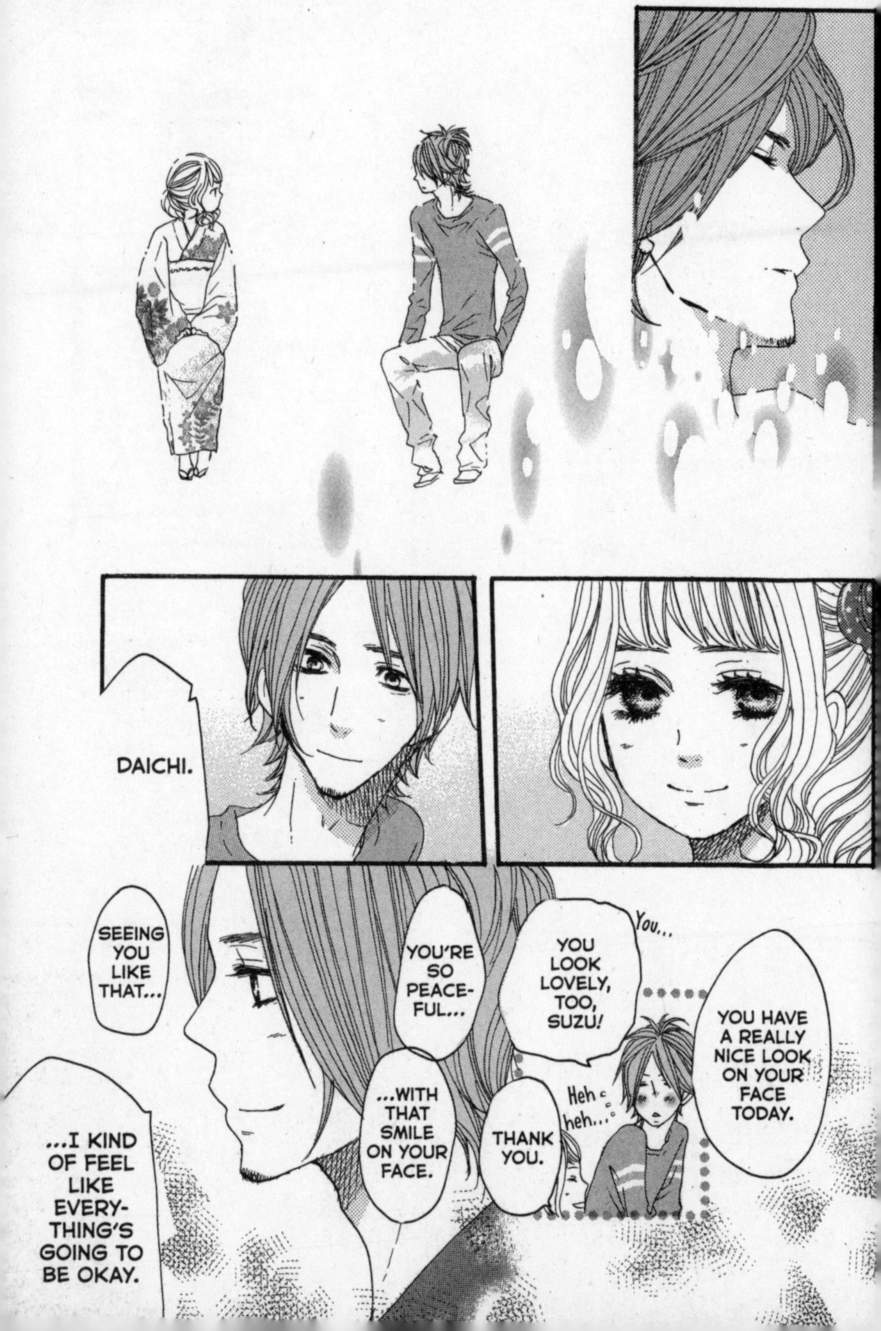
DAICHI.
You...
YOU HAVE A REALLY NICE LOOK ON YOUR FACE TODAY.
YOU LOOK LOVELY, TOO, SUZU!
Heh heh...
THANK YOU.
YOU'RE SO PEACE-FUL...
...WITH THAT SMILE ON YOUR FACE.
SEEING YOU LIKE THAT...
...I KIND OF FEEL LIKE EVERY-THING'S GOING TO BE OKAY.

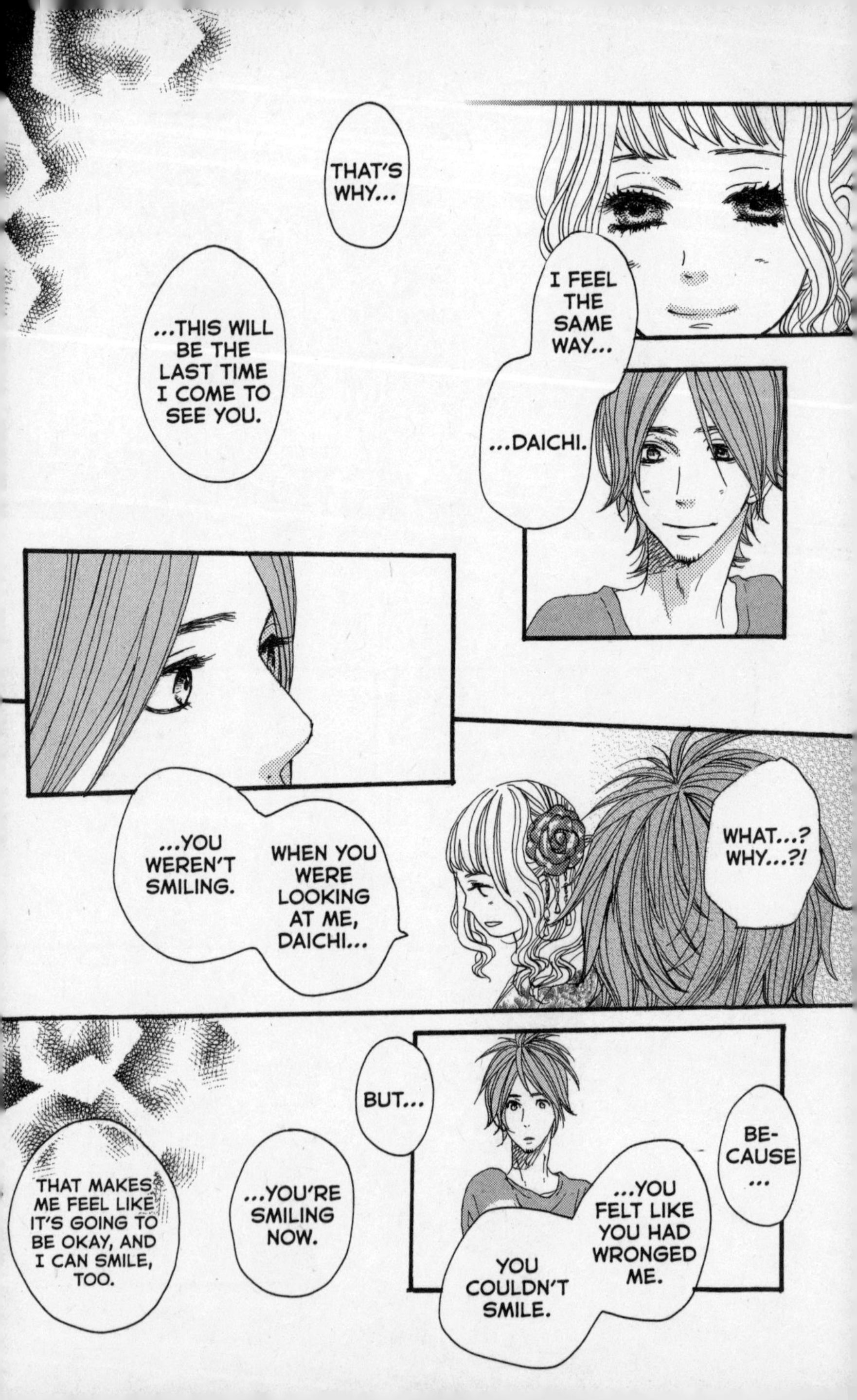
I FEEL THE SAME WAY...
...DAICHI.
THAT'S WHY...
...THIS WILL BE THE LAST TIME I COME TO SEE YOU.
WHAT...? WHY...?!
WHEN YOU WERE LOOKING AT ME, DAICHI...
...YOU WEREN'T SMILING.
BE-CAUSE...
...YOU FELT LIKE YOU HAD WRONGED ME.
YOU COULDN'T SMILE.
BUT...
...YOU'RE SMILING NOW.
THAT MAKES ME FEEL LIKE IT'S GOING TO BE OKAY, AND I CAN SMILE, TOO.

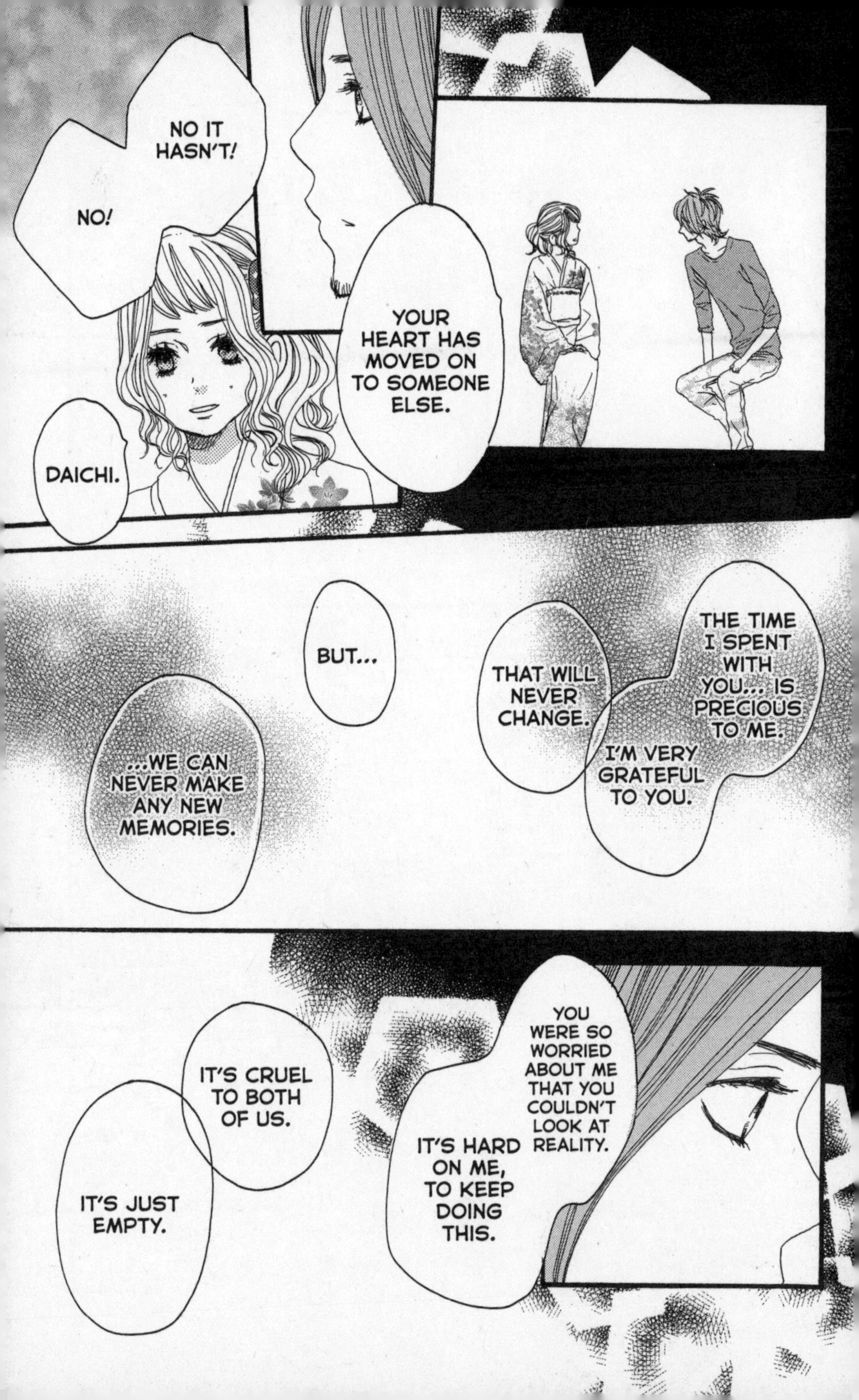
YOUR HEART HAS MOVED ON TO SOMEONE ELSE.
NO IT HASN'T!
NO!
DAICHI.
THE TIME I SPENT WITH YOU... IS PRECIOUS TO ME.
THAT WILL NEVER CHANGE.
I'M VERY GRATEFUL TO YOU.
BUT...
...WE CAN NEVER MAKE ANY NEW MEMORIES.
YOU WERE SO WORRIED ABOUT ME THAT YOU COULDN'T LOOK AT REALITY.
IT'S HARD ON ME, TO KEEP DOING THIS.
IT'S CRUEL TO BOTH OF US.
IT'S JUST EMPTY.

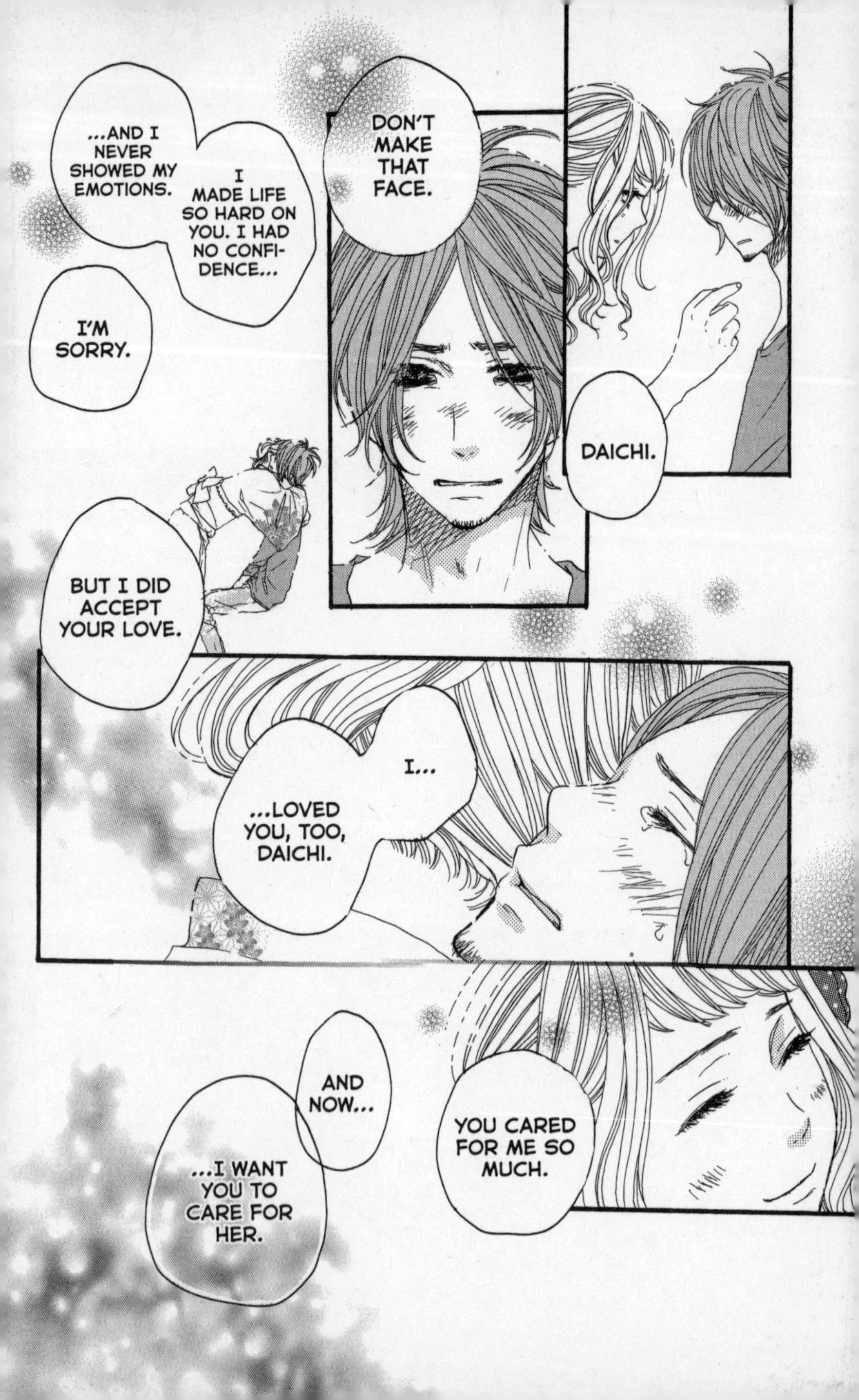
DAICHI.
DON'T MAKE THAT FACE.
I MADE LIFE SO HARD ON YOU. I HAD NO CONFIDENCE...
...AND I NEVER SHOWED MY EMOTIONS.
I'M SORRY.
BUT I DID ACCEPT YOUR LOVE.
I...
...LOVED YOU, TOO, DAICHI.
YOU CARED FOR ME SO MUCH.
AND NOW...
...I WANT YOU TO CARE FOR HER.

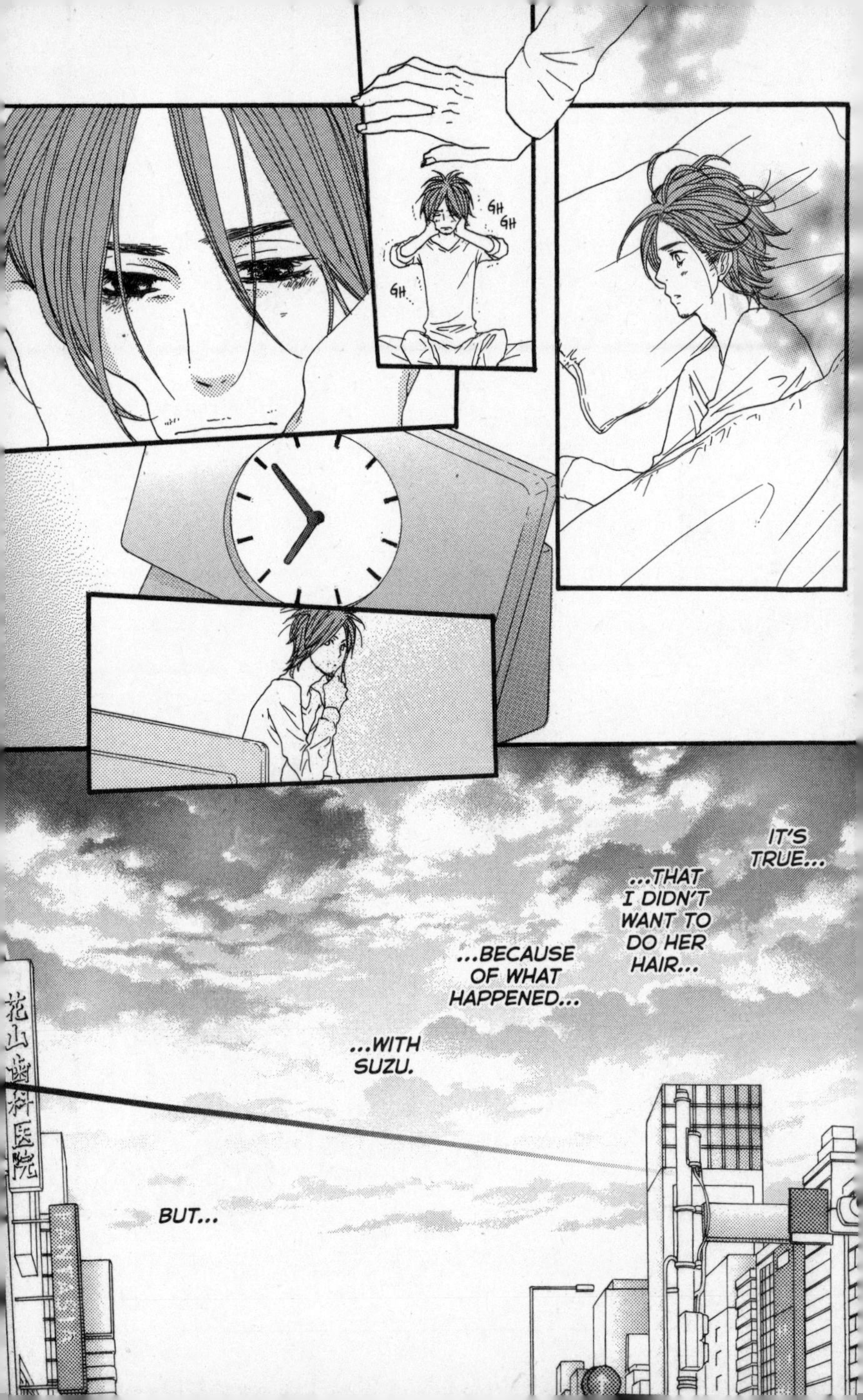
GH
GH
GH
IT'S TRUE...
...THAT I DIDN'T WANT TO DO HER HAIR...
...BECAUSE OF WHAT HAPPENED...
...WITH SUZU.
花山歯科医院
BUT...

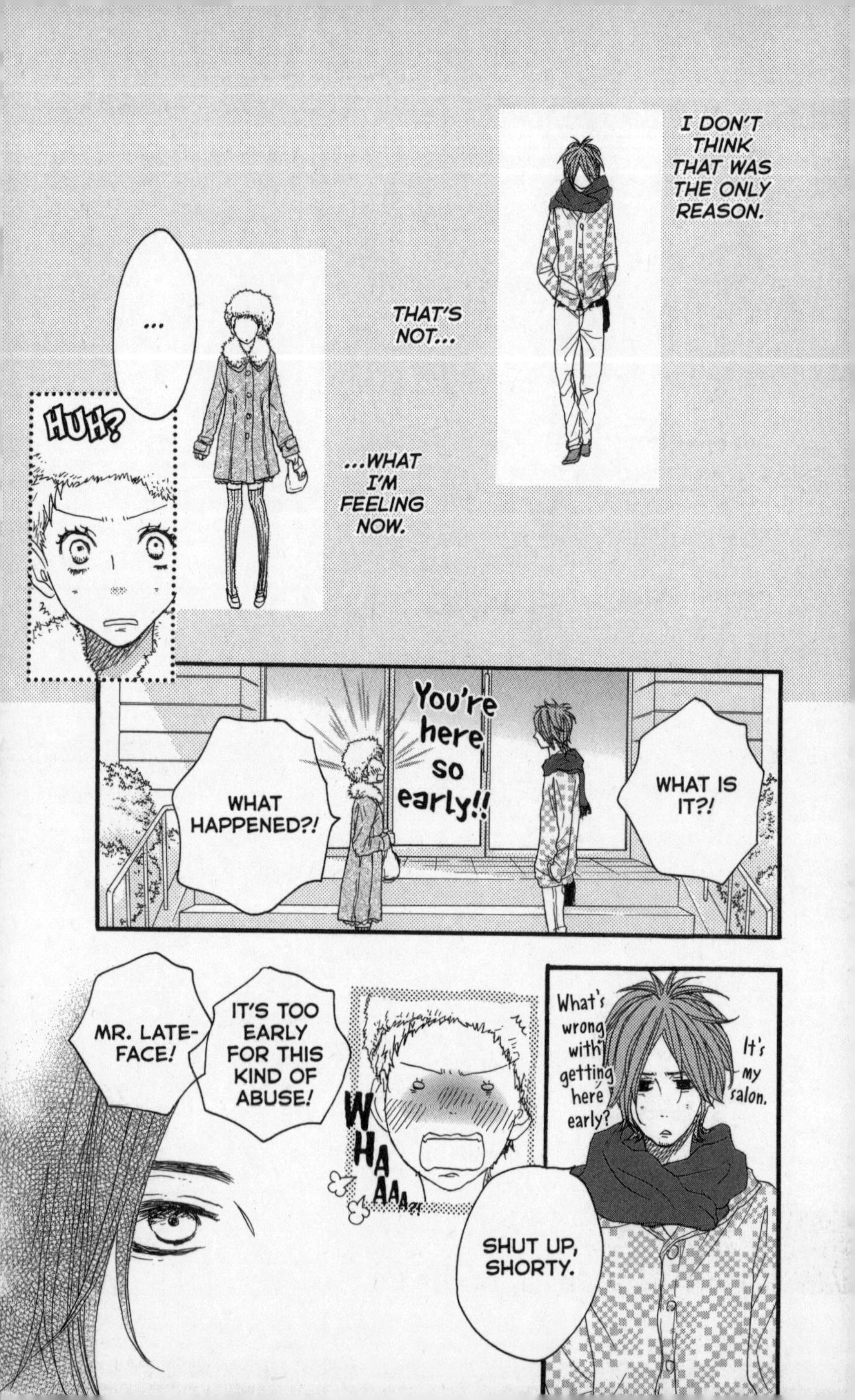

I DON'T THINK THAT WAS THE ONLY REASON.
THAT'S NOT...
...WHAT I'M FEELING NOW.
...
HUH?
WHAT IS IT?!
You're here so early!!
WHAT HAPPENED?!
What's wrong with getting here early?
It's my salon.
SHUT UP, SHORTY.
WHAAAA?!
IT'S TOO EARLY FOR THIS KIND OF ABUSE!
MR. LATE-FACE!

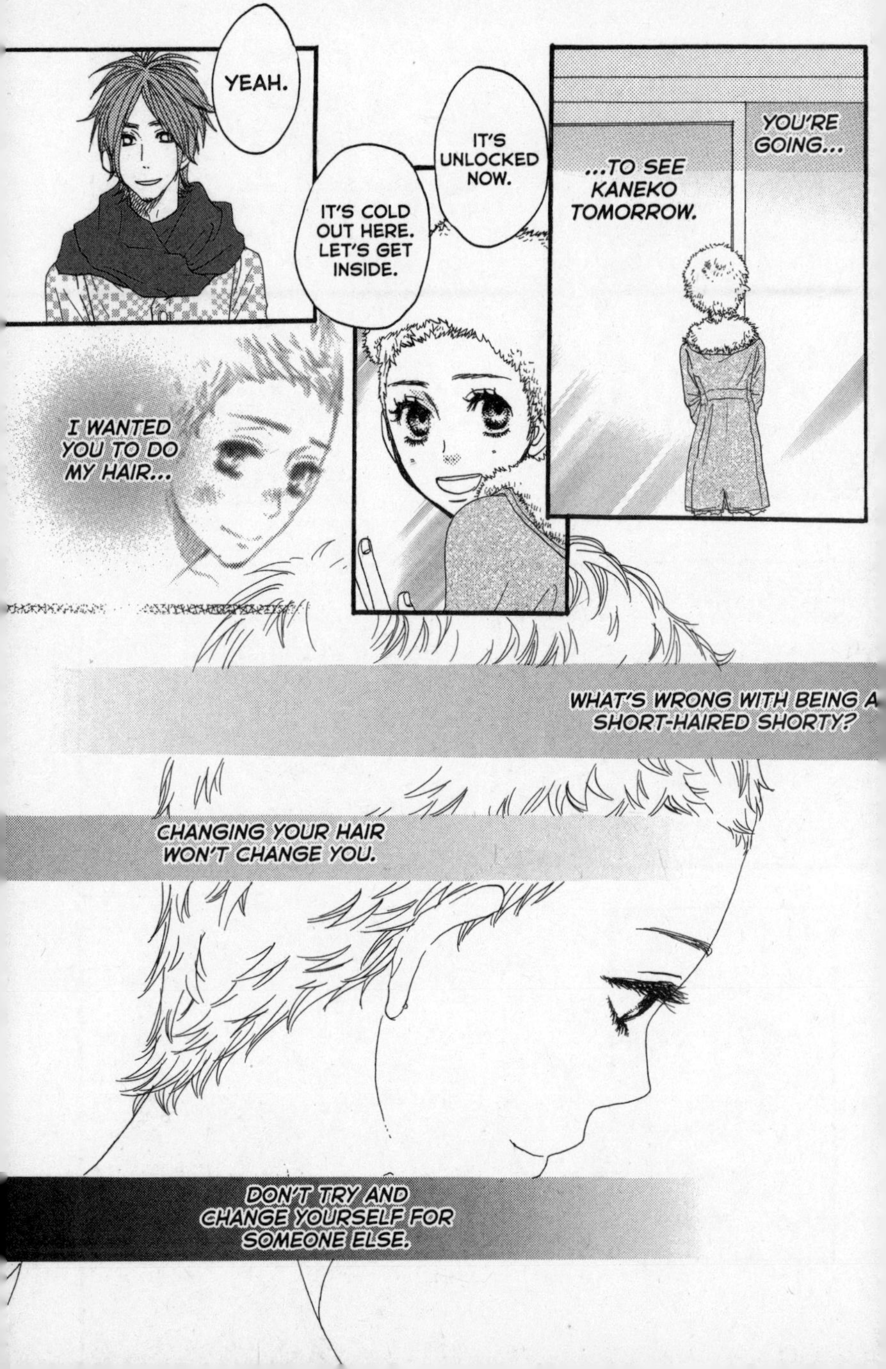
YOU'RE GOING...
...TO SEE KANEKO TOMORROW.
IT'S UNLOCKED NOW.
IT'S COLD OUT HERE. LET'S GET INSIDE.
YEAH.
I WANTED YOU TO DO MY HAIR...
WHAT'S WRONG WITH BEING A SHORT-HAIRED SHORTY?
CHANGING YOUR HAIR WON'T CHANGE YOU.
DON'T TRY AND CHANGE YOURSELF FOR SOMEONE ELSE.

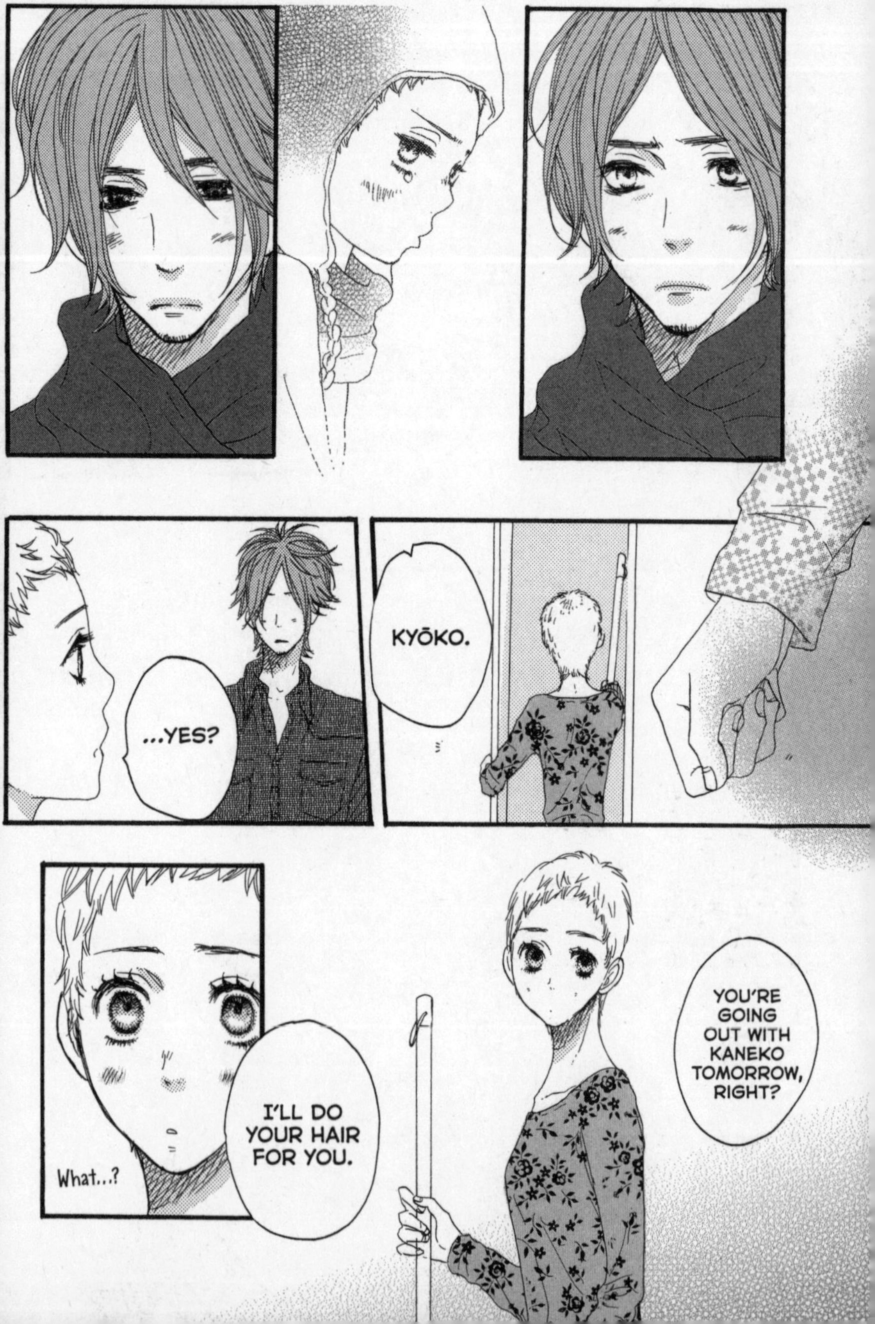
KYŌKO.
...YES?
YOU'RE GOING OUT WITH KANEKO TOMORROW, RIGHT?
I'LL DO YOUR HAIR FOR YOU.
What...?

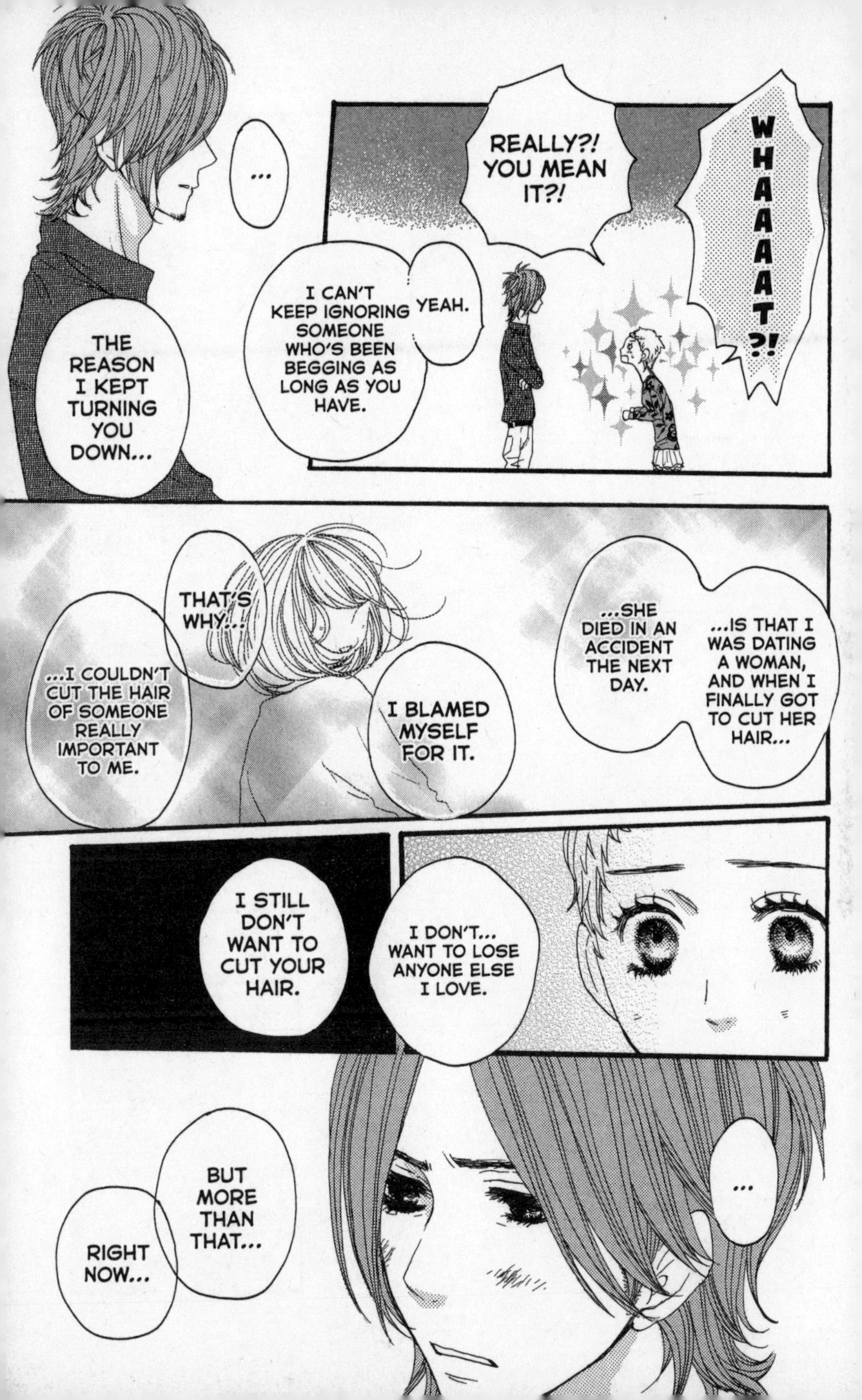
WHAAAAT?!
REALLY?! YOU MEAN IT?!
YEAH.
I CAN'T KEEP IGNORING SOMEONE WHO'S BEEN BEGGING AS LONG AS YOU HAVE.
...
THE REASON I KEPT TURNING YOU DOWN...
...IS THAT I WAS DATING A WOMAN, AND WHEN I FINALLY GOT TO CUT HER HAIR...
...SHE DIED IN AN ACCIDENT THE NEXT DAY.
I BLAMED MYSELF FOR IT.
THAT'S WHY...
...I COULDN'T CUT THE HAIR OF SOMEONE REALLY IMPORTANT TO ME.
I DON'T... WANT TO LOSE ANYONE ELSE I LOVE.
I STILL DON'T WANT TO CUT YOUR HAIR.
...
BUT MORE THAN THAT...
RIGHT NOW...

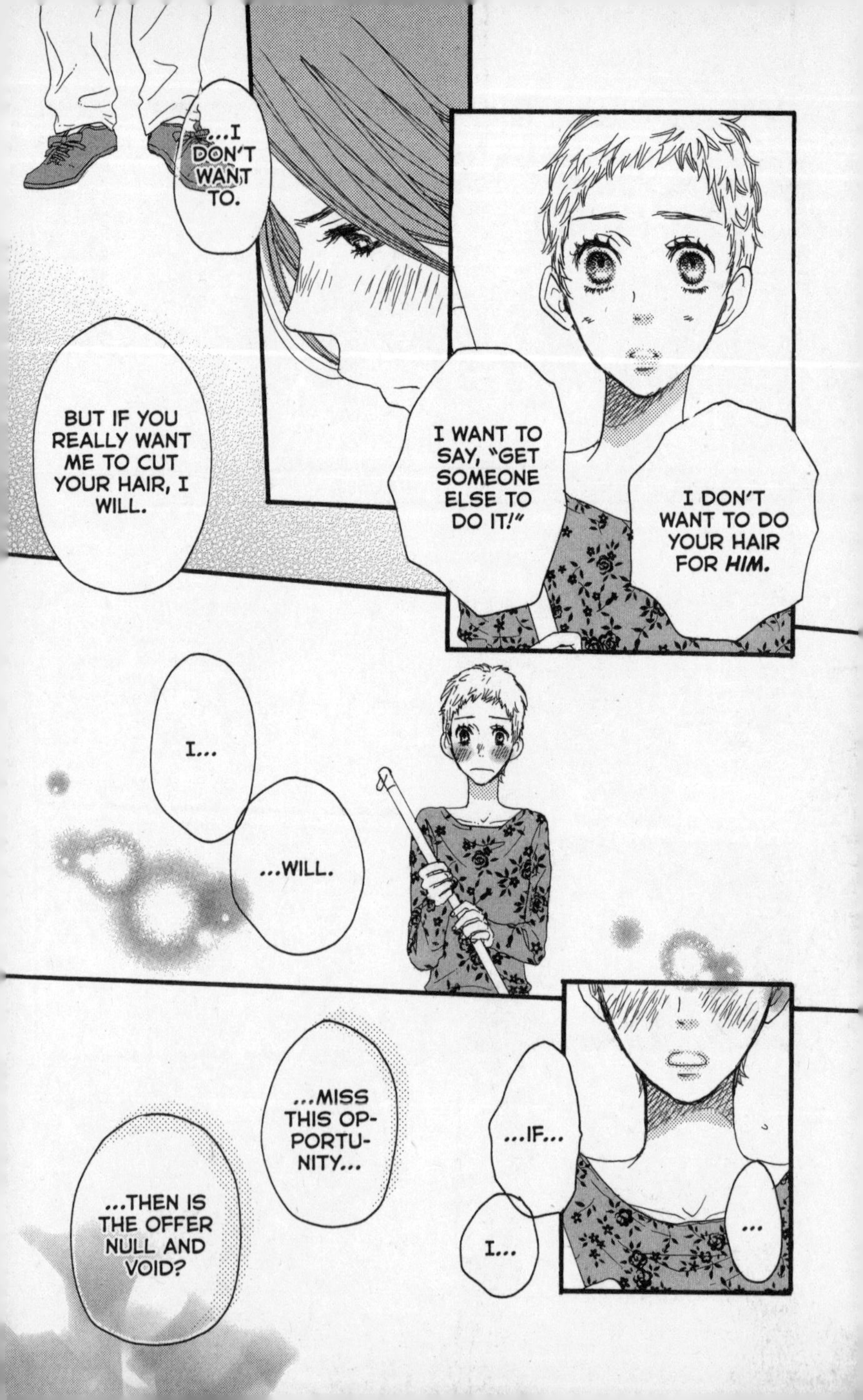
I DON'T WANT TO DO YOUR HAIR FOR *HIM*.
I WANT TO SAY, "GET SOMEONE ELSE TO DO IT!"
...I DON'T WANT TO.
BUT IF YOU REALLY WANT ME TO CUT YOUR HAIR, I WILL.
I...
...WILL.
...IF...
...
I...
...MISS THIS OP-PORTU-NITY...
...THEN IS THE OFFER NULL AND VOID?

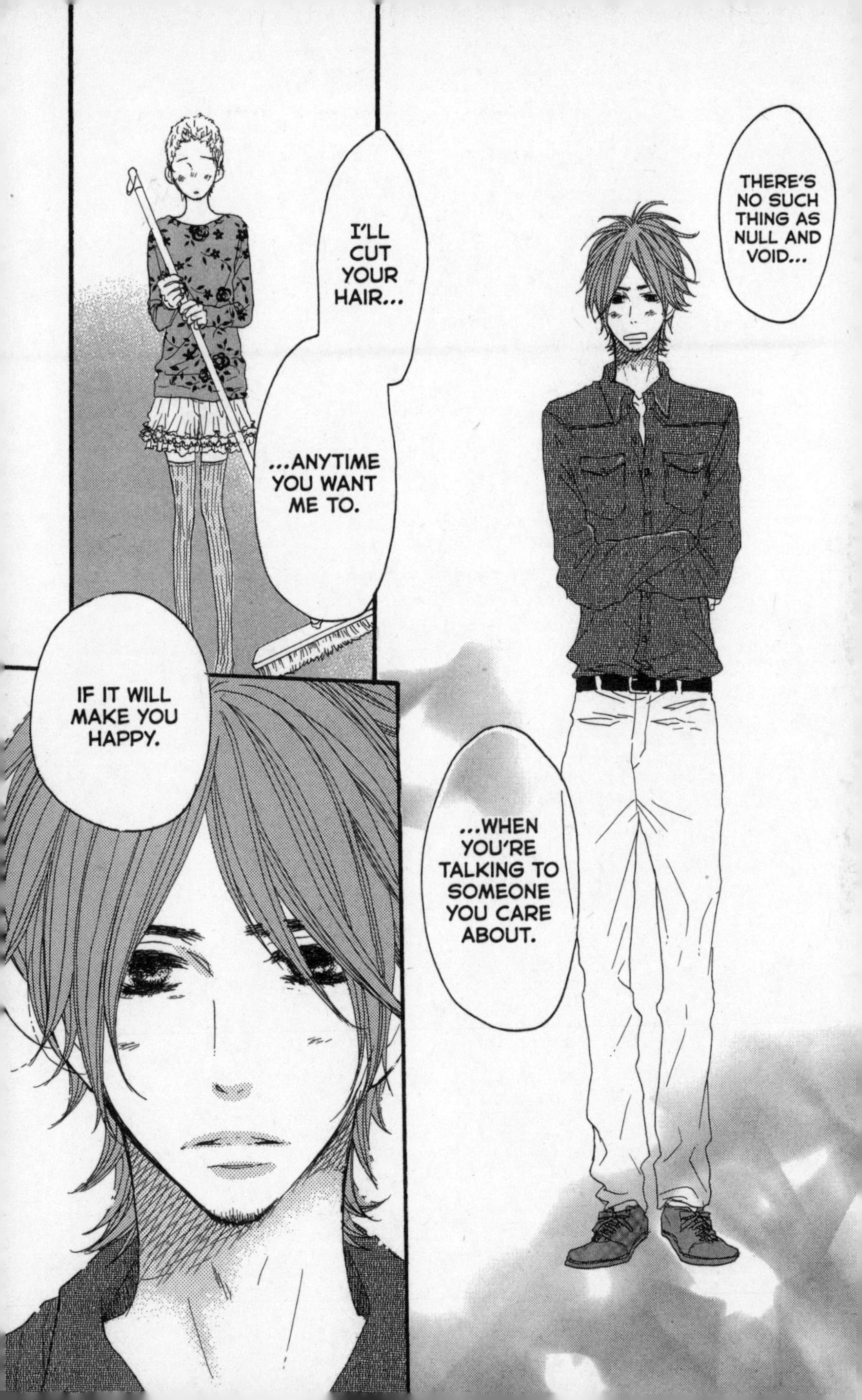
THERE'S NO SUCH THING AS NULL AND VOID...
...WHEN YOU'RE TALKING TO SOMEONE YOU CARE ABOUT.
I'LL CUT YOUR HAIR...
...ANYTIME YOU WANT ME TO.
IF IT WILL MAKE YOU HAPPY.

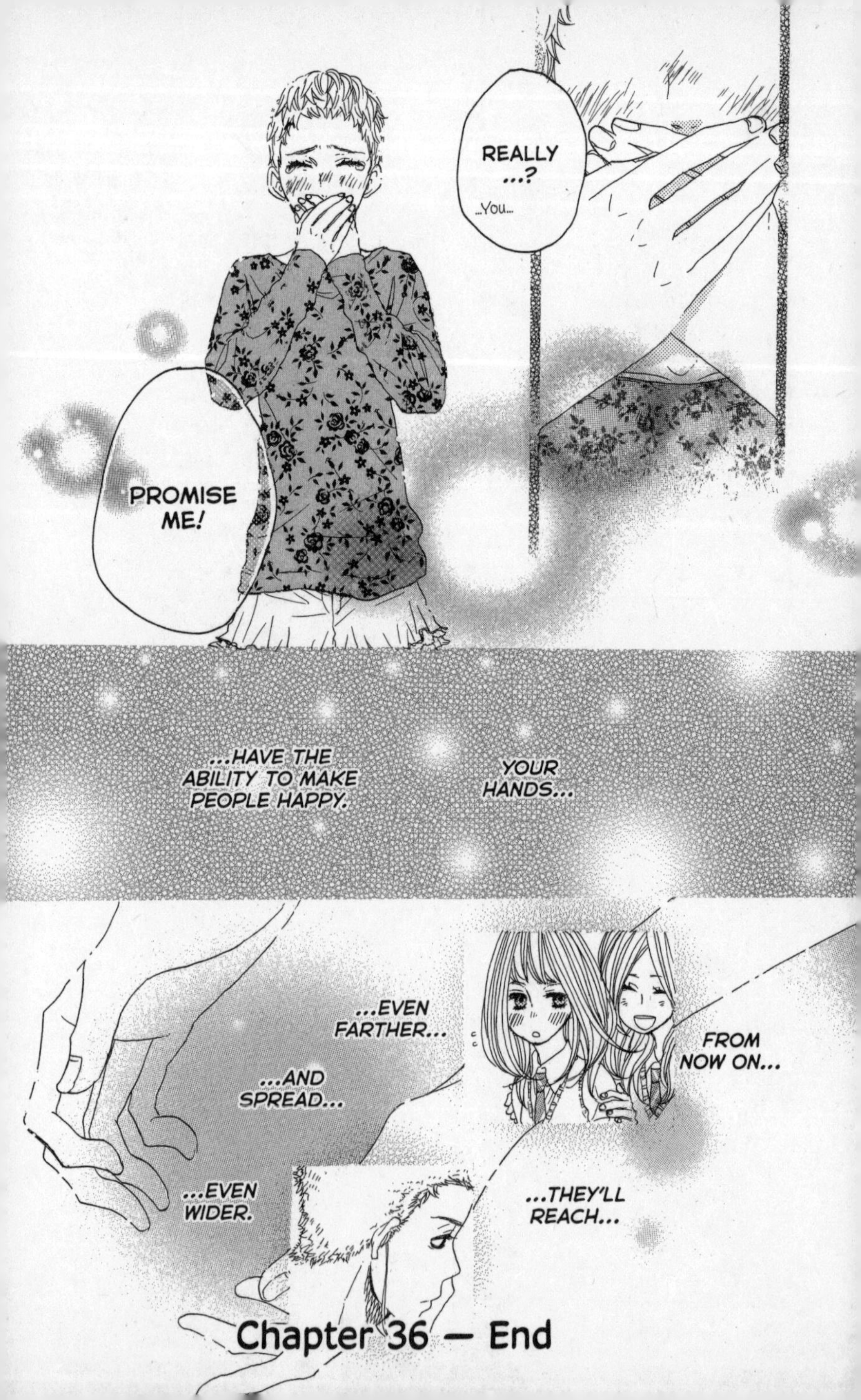
REALLY ...?
...You...
PROMISE ME!
YOUR HANDS...
...HAVE THE ABILITY TO MAKE PEOPLE HAPPY.
FROM NOW ON...
...THEY'LL REACH...
...EVEN FARTHER...
...AND SPREAD...
...EVEN WIDER.
Chapter 36 — End

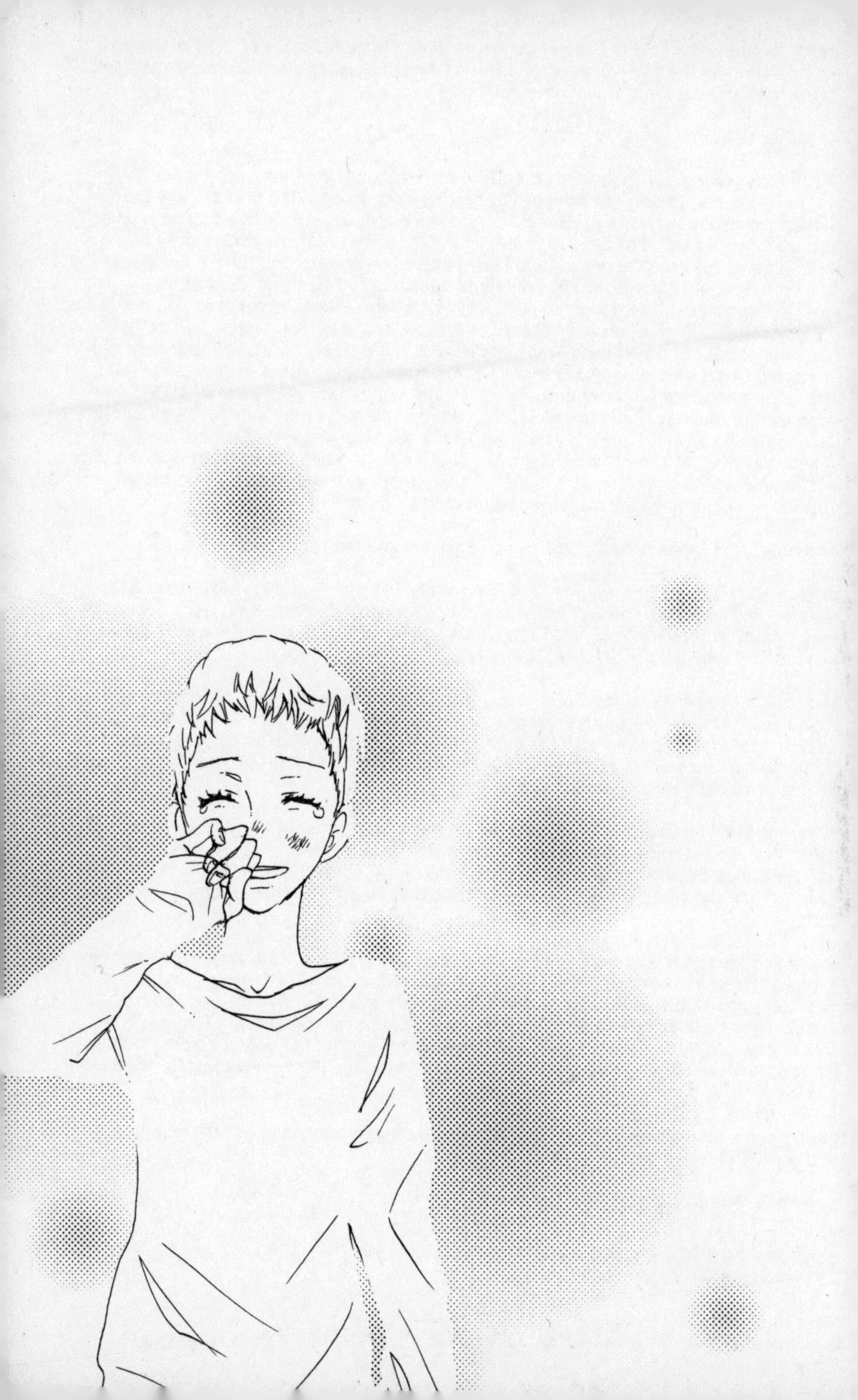

Hello, Kanae Hazuki here. Thank you for buying volume nine. I feel like I made it to nine volumes in the blink of an eye. But it's been four years since the series started. It doesn't feel that long at all. Time does fly.

As for what's going on with me...

If you're following me on Twitter, then I don't have anything new to say (;^ω^). Hmmm... If I had to say something, I'm getting back into baking bread. I say that, though my bread machine does most of the work. But it's still different. The aroma! The texture!! If I set it to bake in the morning, I get to savor the dream time of waking up to the smell of bread, lol. Also, I like to take tours of different bakeries, so I do that a lot. Right now, I'm really into sourdough. I don't know what it is, but you get the smell of the dough...or the smell of it fermenting...more than you get the buttery smell of fancier breads. The more I chew it, the better it gets. I secretly wish I could make it at home. And people are kind of talking about *shio koji* [a fermented mixture of a safe mold and salt] these days. I tried making some once last summer, but I didn't regulate the temperature very well, and I didn't really know what it was supposed to taste like, so it didn't work. So then I tasted some good *shio koji* and tried making it again this year, and it was a big success! ★ I can marinate meat and vegetables in it, or stew things in it... But best of all, is when I'm cooking rice, if I put a little *shio koji* in with it first, it is startlingly good!!! Just put in about one tablespoon for every two servings of rice. I want everyone to try it!

And here I am talking about food again. Shall we change the subject? (' ▽ `;)

Um, let's see, about this volume. The main focus is Daichi's story, which I had been keeping on the backburner for some time. I'm sorry to all of you who were hoping to read about Yamato and Mei, but I really really wanted to draw this for a long time, and now I finally got to! So there it is.

The title of the series is *Say I Love You.*, and Daichi wants to say it, but he can't—he feels like he shouldn't—and he's been running from his past trauma all this time, and I wanted to draw the story of him confronting that inner conflict and moving forward. It did have some fantasy elements, though. But that's okay. Life is full of fantasy, isn't it? ('^益^`) That's what makes it fun.

Everyone feels like they want to put a lid on the stuff in their life that doesn't smell so good. Not the temporary troubles, or things that they get from people around them, but the things about themselves. But when you want someone to move forward with you, the day will come when you have to take that lid off and show them. That's the truth.

And if you keep running, you'll never solve anything. You just stop time. The day will eventually come when you'll have to face it yourself. Instead of holding it in until it explodes, I think it's important to spit it out a little at a time, day by day. You are the one who decides how your life will go. No one else can decide that for you. It all comes down to how the other person will see the persona that you have created. Just be honest with yourself, and try as hard as you can not to let toxins build up inside you.

I still have a ton of toxic elements inside me. I want to hurry and get them out of me and feel better. Hee hee.

Now then. About the next volume.

Yamato and Mei will take a big step forward...!
I can say that with certainty!!

Mei's hard work will finally pay off...yes...! probably.
And now that I've gotten all your hopes up for the next volume (lol), I'm going to leave you here. ('•ω•')/

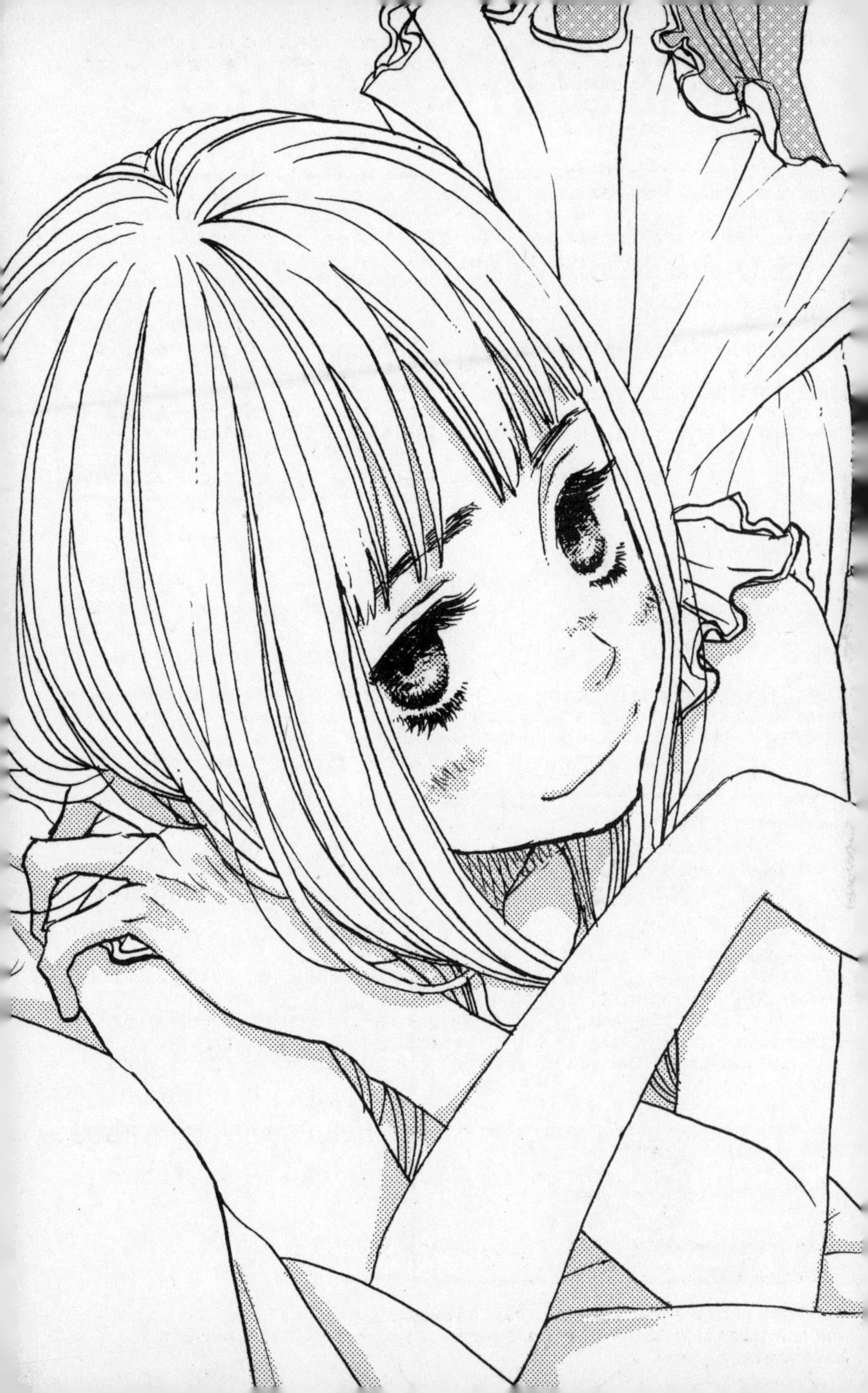

TRANSLATION NOTES

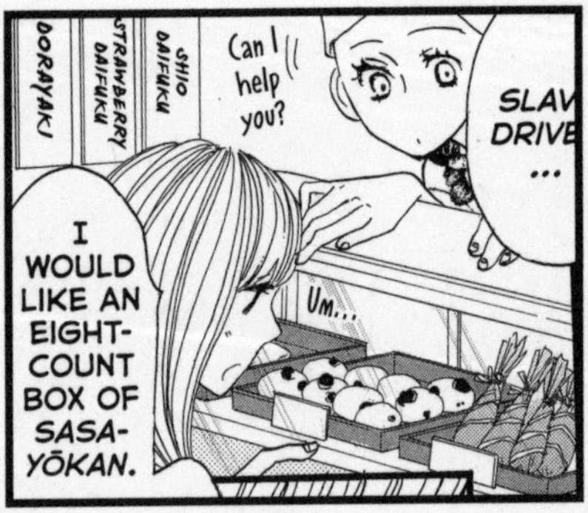
SLAV DRIVE ...
Can I help you?
SHIO DAIFUKU
STRAWBERRY DAIFUKU
DORAYAKI
UM...
I WOULD LIKE AN EIGHT-COUNT BOX OF SASA-YŌKAN.

age 24: Sasa-yōkan

ōkan is Japanese dessert onsisting of a thick jelly made rom bean paste. Sasa means bamboo grass", and in this case, efers to the fact that the *yōkan* s wrapped in, and likely also lavored with, bamboo leaves.

age 26: Tenchō

enchō means "head of the shop", and can refer to anyone in harge of any kind of shop—restaurants, clothing stores, and hair alons. Daichi owns and runs his salon, so that makes him the *enchō.* His assistant calls him by his title as a way of showing espect to her boss.

Page 38: Purikura

A "print club" (or *purikura* in Japanese) is something like a photo booth, only instead of just taking pictures, the people taking the picture can choose borders and write on the pictures, then print them out onto a sticker sheet.

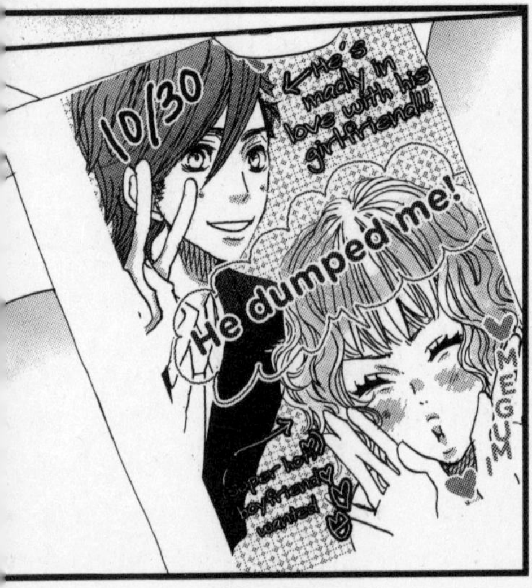
10/30
←He's madly in love with his girlfriend!!!
He dumped me!
MEGUMI
Super hot boyfriend wanted

Page 43: Natto pasta

Natto is a dish of fermented soy beans, known for its strong smell and slimy texture. Even in Japan, many people are grossed out by it, hence Yamato's surprise at Mei's reaction to his attempted joke.

Page 57: atm

Nau is the Japanese pronunciation of the English word "now" and is used as Internet slang to mean just that. It is often used at the end of sentences. So we translated it as "atm," Web slang for "at the moment."

Page 79: Yaki-imo

A *yaki-imo* is a roasted sweet potato. They are often sold from trucks like the one seen here, as the vendor sings out to advertise his presence. It's kind of like the autumn version of an ice cream truck.

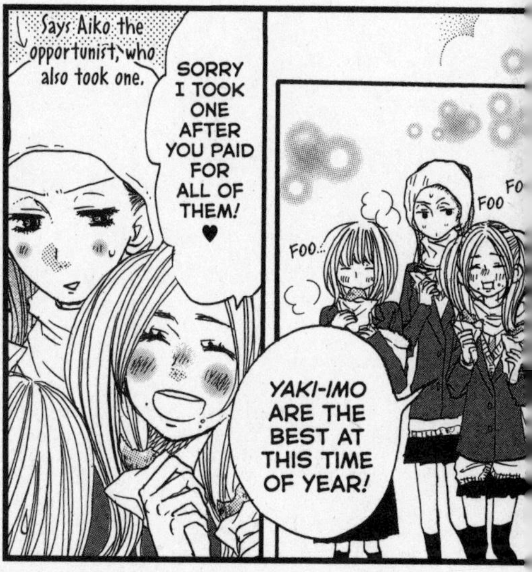
FOO
FOO
FO
FOO...
YAKI-IMO ARE THE BEST AT THIS TIME OF YEAR!
Says Aiko the opportunist, who also took one.
SORRY I TOOK ONE AFTER YOU PAID FOR ALL OF THEM! ♥

Page 121: Say something

Specifically, Daichi wants her to say *tadaima*, translated roughly as "I'm home." In Japan, when someone leaves their home, they say *ittekimasu*, which literally means "I will go and come back," or the more casual version, *ittekuru*, which is translated here as Suzu's last words to Daichi, "I'll see you soon." Then, when they get back, they say *tadaima*, to which the person who is waiting for them responds *okaeri*, or "welcome back."

Page 130: Mook
A combination of the words "book" and "magazine," a mook serves all the purposes of a magazine but is supposed to last as long as a book.

My Little Monster

OPPOSITES ATTRACT...MAYBE?

Haru Yoshida is feared as an unstable and violent "monster." Mizutani Shizuku is a grade-obsessed student with no friends. Fate brings these two together to form the most unlikely pair. Haru firmly believes he's in love with Mizutani and she firmly believes he's insane.

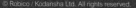
KC KODANSHA COMICS

SHERLOCK BONES

KC KODANSHA COMICS

DEDUCTIVE DOG DETECTIVE

When Takeru adopts a new pet, he's in for a surprise—the dog is none other than the reincarnation of Sherlock Holmes. With no one else able to communicate with Holmes, Takeru is roped into becoming Sherdog's assistant, John Watson. Using his sleuthing skills, Holmes uncovers clues to solve the trickiest crimes. 🐾

NO.6

A PERFECT LIFE IN A PERFECT CITY

For Shion, an elite student in the technologically sophisticated city No. 6, life is carefully choreographed. One fateful day, he takes a misstep, sheltering a fugitive his age from a typhoon. Helping this boy throws Shion's life down a path to discovering the appalling secrets behind the "perfection" of No. 6.

KC
KODANSHA
COMICS

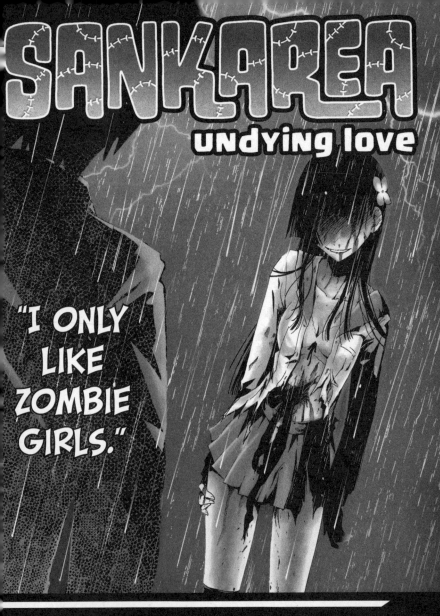

SANKAREA

undying love

"I ONLY LIKE ZOMBIE GIRLS."

...ihiro has an unusual connection to zombie movies. He doesn't feel bad for ...e survivors – he wants to comfort the undead girls they slaughter! When ...s pet passes away, he brews a resurrection potion. He's discovered by ...cal heiress Sanka Rea, and she serves as his first test subject!

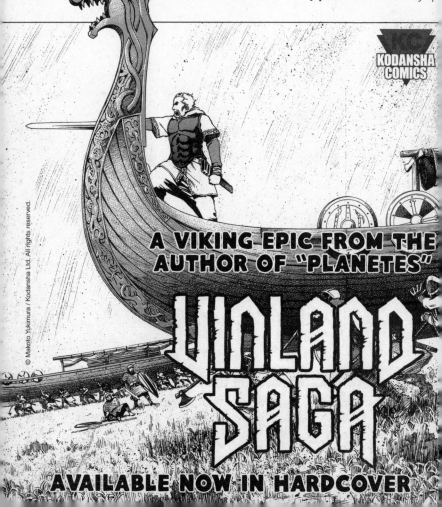

ATTACK ON TITAN

Humanity has been decimated!

A century ago, the bizarre creatures known as Titans devoured most of the world's population, driving the remainder into a walled stronghold. Now, the appearance of an immense new Titan threatens the few humans left, and one restless boy decides to seize the chance to fight for his freedom, and the survival of his species!

ANIMAL LAND

MAKOTO RAIKU

WELCOME TO THE JUNGLE

In a world of animals where the strong eat the weak, Monoko the tanuki stumbles across a strange creature the like of which has never been seen before - **a human baby!**

While the newborn has no claws or teeth to protect itself, it does have the rare ability to speak to and understand all the different animal.

ANIMAL LAND 1

MAKOTO RAIKU

Special extras in each volume! Read them all!

RATING OT AGES 10+

Say I Love You. volume 9 is a work of fiction. Names, characters, places, and incidents are the products of the author's imagination or are used fictitiously. Any resemblance to actual events, locales, or persons, living or dead, is entirely coincidental.

A Kodansha Comics Trade Paperback Original

Published in the United States by Kodansha Comics, an imprint of Kodansha USA Publishing, LLC, New York.

Publication rights for this English edition arranged through Kodansha Ltd, Tokyo.

First published in Japan in 2012 by Kodansha Ltd., Tokyo as *Sukitte iinayo.* volume 9.

ISBN 978-1-61262-674-1

Printed in the United States of America.

www.kodanshacomics.com

9 8 7 6 5 4 3 2 1
Translation: Alethea and Athena Nibley
Lettering: John Clark
Editing: Ben Applegate
Kodansha Comics edition cover design by Phil Balsman

TOMARE!

STOP

You're going the wrong way!

Manga is a completely different type of reading experience.

To start at the beginning, Go to the end!

That's right! Authentic manga is read the traditional Japanese way—from right to left, exactly the opposite of how American books are read. It's easy to follow: Just go to the other end of the book and read each page—and each panel—from right side to left side, starting at the top right. Now you're experiencing manga as it was meant to be!